A Student Grammar of French

A Student Grammar of French is a concise introduction to French grammar, designed specifically for English-speaking undergraduates. Keeping technical detail to a minimum, it explains the fundamentals of the grammar in accessible and simple terms, and helps students to put their learning into practice through a range of fun and engaging exercises. All the essential topics are covered, with chapters on verbs, nouns, adjectives, pronouns, determiners, prepositions, adverbs, negation, numerals, sentences and clauses. Every grammatical point is illustrated with a range of authentic examples drawn from magazines and newspapers, covering many areas of contemporary life such as fashion, health issues, relationships and sport. It is clearly organised into a user-friendly, numbered indexing system, allowing the learner to locate any grammatical topic quickly and easily.

Functioning as both an indispensable reference guide and a comprehensive workbook, this grammar will become the perfect accompaniment to any first- or second-year undergraduate course.

Malcolm Offord was formerly Lecturer and Reader in the Department of French, University of Nottingham. He is author of *Varieties of French* (1990), *French Sociolinguistics* (1996), *French Words, Past, Present and Future* (2001), *Francophone Literatures: A Literary and Linguistic Companion* (2001), *Using French: A Guide to Contemporary Usage* (with Ronald Batchelor, Cambridge University Press, 3rd edition 2000) and *Using French Synonyms* (with Ronald Batchelor, Cambridge University Press, 1993).

A Student Grammar of French

MALCOLM OFFORD

CAMBRIDGE
UNIVERSITY PRESS

CAMBRIDGE UNIVERSITY PRESS
Cambridge, New York, Melbourne, Madrid, Cape Town, Singapore, São Paulo

Cambridge University Press
The Edinburgh Building, Cambridge CB2 2RU, UK

Published in the United States of America by Cambridge University Press, New York

www.cambridge.org
Information on this title: www.cambridge.org/9780521547628

First published 2006

Printed in the United Kingdom at the University Press, Cambridge

A catalogue record for this publication is available from the British Library

ISBN-13   978-0-521-54762-8 paperback
ISBN-10   0-521-54762-8 paperback

Contents

Contents

Acknowledgements

The following newspapers and magazines have provided and inspired the illustrative examples used throughout this book: *Bien dans ma vie, Cosmopolitan, Elle, l'Équipe, Esprit femme, Femme actuelle, FHM, le Figaro, Glamour, Laura, Marianne, Marie Claire, Men's Health, Modes et travaux, le Monde, Monsieur, Optimum, Planète Foot, le Point, Solo, Sport et vie, Télérama, Top Santé, Triathlète, le Vif–Express, Vingt ans, Vital, Vivre.*

Her name should be Patience, but it's Judith and she has loyally and stalwartly supported me throughout the preparation of this book. Sincerest thanks to her and also to Helen Barton at Cambridge University Press, whose valuable advice, tendered in her gentle manner, ensured that the book didn't become, like its author, too eccentric.

Introduction

Grammar is a word that all too often strikes terror and a sense of panic into the breasts of modern language students. Grammar presents a cold, clinical, unemotional exterior – not exciting, straightforward and vibrant like vocabulary, especially when the latter tends towards the informal and slang. The mortar of language (grammar) is never so interesting as the bricks (vocabulary). Grammar is often seen as an obstacle to free expression – it makes you linger and dither over whether to use one preposition rather than another, whether an agreement is required or not – whereas you would rather press on, get your meaning across, communicate. Anything that impedes or slows down that expression is annoying and needs to be dealt with as soon as possible, or even ignored. But bricks without mortar are ugly and lack style, are in danger of collapsing and not fulfilling the purpose for which they were erected in the first place. What can we do about it?

First of all, there's no avoiding it – we need a grammar book. It's no good sticking your head in the sand – mortar is essential, the right consistency, the right thickness for maximum effect and to perform its job efficiently and discreetly. Secondly, we need a grammar book that is easy to use, that helps us identify our problems, that has a very clear and easily accessible index, that guides us to the right solution for us and explains what we need to know, expressed in language we can understand. Thirdly, when we get to the point where the explanation is, we need illustrations that are drawn from the world we live in – not taken from the nineteenth and twentieth centuries, not taken from the greatest authors, whose French we cannot ever hope to emulate; not boring examples that have been concocted to illustrate the point but don't connect with our world. We need examples that make us want to read on, that entertain us, that make us smile, that might even inform us on issues that are of interest to us, that make us look seriously at the way in which they are expressed – because they're cool. We don't want fuddy-duddy examples about the price of oranges (at least not too many), about who will bring the suitcases down, about (not) doing your homework, examples that suck. We want real, living examples – examples that are authentic, that express our reality – about relationships, sport, contemporary entertainment, fashion, social behaviour, weight-control and – another word that strikes terror into the breast of students, but not just the breast of students, it must be said – sex, and related matters: in short about daily living in the twenty-first century. Fourthly, we need a means of making sure that we have assimilated the grammatical points being illustrated.

This *Student Grammar of French* is aimed at meeting all those needs. It is conceived in such a way that no section is overwhelmingly long, that excessively technical language is avoided, that the index is straightforward and contains references to all the points contained in the book, and that the illustrative examples are worth a read in their own right and may inspire you to imitate their phraseology as well as take note of the grammatical point being illustrated. Since the vocabulary used in the examples is completely up-to-date, it's worth learning the contemporary words as well as noting how the examples work. It has to be admitted that some of the translations have been held back from being completely free, and thus more typically English, in order to allow the grammatical point under consideration to be seized more clearly – a more fluent translation might obscure the grammatical point.

A simple but effective way of helping to ensure that the grammatical point is understood and is becoming part of your personal grammatical apparatus is to test yourself with the exercises provided at the end of each chapter, exercises that use similar material to that contained in the examples in the text itself. These exercises are designed to consolidate your grammatical knowledge and perhaps increase your sociological and cultural awareness.

Mortar can be fun and the result of using it effectively and skilfully very satisfying – ask a bricklayer!

This grammar book has been designed according to the following plan. The first four chapters are devoted to verbs – verbs are absolutely essential to self-expression, they are the motors of speech; consequently it seems logical to place examination of them at the beginning of the book. The first chapter provides the forms that need to be acquired in order to be able to manipulate the verbs effectively. The second chapter shows how the verbs are used, especially the different tenses, and the third chapter introduces a large number of tables giving the full conjugations of the major verb groups, followed in the next chapter by a list of verbs that do not belong to the first, most common group of verbs (those ending in *-er*), and showing how these verbs relate to verbs illustrated previously. The fifth chapter deals with nouns and adjectives and concentrates upon the themes of gender and number (how to form plurals in particular). The sixth chapter examines the area of pronouns – personal pronouns, demonstrative pronouns, possessive pronouns and indefinite and quantifying pronouns. The next chapter examines the tricky area of determiners – the definite, indefinite, partitive and zero (what?!) articles, and demonstrative and possessive adjectives. Even more tricky is the topic of prepositions and these are fully treated in chapter 8 – though they are often extremely small words and you often glide over them without thinking about them, prepositions as linking words have a very important role to play in the unrolling of speech; this is a long chapter which attempts to cover all those environments where prepositions occur. The ninth chapter is devoted to adverbs and adverbial expressions – these lend more detail and precision to our speech and require skilful handling. Everything has been positive up to this stage – with the tenth chapter we enter the realm of negation, how to deny, refuse, cancel – very important in an age where science and technology are creating products which replace and supersede previously current products. The next chapter, the shortest, looks at numerals, which the speaker needs to be able to handle accurately – otherwise misunderstandings and more serious problems may ensue. The last chapter on sentences and clauses shows how all that has been learnt and hopefully assimilated in earlier chapters builds up into sophisticated language, making communication exciting, rewarding and challenging. The purpose of this chapter – and indeed of the book as a whole – is to allow us to express our thoughts, hopes and ideals in appropriate, well-formed, clear sentences, showing us to be intelligent and valuable members of society.

Just as there are many varieties of English, of which you are no doubt fully aware, so there are many varieties of French. Some are geographically based – the French of Paris differs in some ways from the French of the north-east of the country and from that of the south-west, and more so from the French of Belgium, Canada and francophone Africa. Others are based on age – youth-speak and wrinkly-speak differ considerably – still others on gender – males and females have different speech habits from time to time. However, the most important area of variety is that of formality – we speak formally, very formally, in certain circumstances, much less so in others. This grammar book takes as its basis the variety of French that oscillates between standard French – the French used for news broadcasts and in good-quality newspapers and magazines – and the upper end of informal French – that is to say French that is dynamic, fairly but not excessively relaxed, used amongst reasonably well-educated speakers, and at the cutting edge of linguistic development. The book avoids on the one hand the more starchy realms of literary, highly intellectual French, and on the other the cruder, often-grammar-disregarding depths of slang and vulgar French. The variety selected is one which is current among educated French-speakers, one with which it is hoped you will feel comfortable and which will serve your needs in an appropriate way.

Chapter 1 *Verbs: 1*

1 Introduction

In this first chapter, devoted to verbs, we examine the ways in which verbs are formed in French and the factors that have to be borne in mind when we are considering our choice of form.

The forms are chosen according to the role that the verbs play as they fit into sentences. We shall see that the form has to be adjusted according to who or what is the subject of the verb (known as the person), the time when the event or state indicated by the meaning of the verb occurs (the tense) and the syntactic circumstances in which the verb occurs.

To provide us with some technical terminology and a general framework in which to work, the following questions are answered – what is a **verb**? (see 2), what do the terms **infinitive** (see 4), **mood** (see 6), **person** (see 5), **tense** (see 7) mean?

2 Verbs

The verb is often the pivotal element of a sentence. Indeed mention of a verb is regularly included in the definition of a sentence or clause – but see 445, 449. The typical purpose of a verb is to indicate how a state, action or process takes place during time and to provide information about it.

3 Treatment of verbs

Verbs are so vital to communication – they provide information especially about the subject (whether it is a question of singular or plural, first, second or third person), about the time when the speech-event takes place (past, present, future) – that they need to be given extensive treatment.

The verbs are discussed from three perspectives –

1 a discursive treatment, showing how verbs may be grouped together and the relations that exist between them: see 4–165;
2 a tabular treatment showing how individual verbs and their derivatives (related verbs) are conjugated – that is how the verbs' endings are adjusted or how other modifications are made to the verbs in order to indicate their role in sentences: see 166–174;
3 a list of verbs, provided after the tabular treatment – this contains 1: the verbs discussed in the two preceding groupings; and 2: the most frequently encountered verbs not discussed in those sections – see 175–176; it does not include what are known as perfectly regular verbs ending in **-er** – see 15.

DISCURSIVE TREATMENT OF VERBS

Infinitives

4 Infinitives

When we learn a new verb, we usually learn it in the **infinitive** form. This form is the one dictionaries use to record verbs: the dictionary uses the infinitive as the headword for the verb.

An infinitive consists of two parts, the **stem**, which tells us the meaning of the verb, and the **ending** – see 11.

When a verb is conjugated, the stem remains more or less constant, but the ending varies according to how it is used in the sentence, depending upon the person it refers to, the time the event takes place and the syntactic circumstances involved. The expression 'syntactic circumstances' refers to whether the verb occurs in a main or a subordinate clause and what type of conjunction introduces the subordinate clause. These matters are discussed in 10, 11, 115–165.

Infinitives are discussed in more detail in 10 and 11.

Person

5 Person

Six persons are available for selection as subject of the verb –

je = *I*	first person singular
tu = *you*	second person singular
il = *he/it*	
elle = *she*	third person singular
on = *one*	
nous = *we*	first person plural
vous = *you*	second person plural (also used to indicate a single person in a polite manner)
ils = *they*	
elles = *they*	third person plural

The pronouns are discussed in more detail in 206–236.

Mood

6 Mood

Although there is controversy amongst grammar books as to what to include under the heading 'mood', it is generally agreed that **mood** indicates the degree of certainty with which something is said, and that there are at least three moods in French –

the **indicative**, which is the mood used in normal circumstances
the **imperative**, used to express a command

the **subjunctive**, often dependent upon particular syntactic circumstances and normally used to express something which is lacking in certainty.

The imperative mood is discussed in 115–123, 212.

As far as the other two moods are concerned, the choice as to which to use in a given circumstance is usually quite straightforward. However, as will be seen in 156–158, there are occasions where the choice is not so easy to make.

What is certain is that in the vast majority of cases, it is the indicative mood that is used; the indicative can be called the 'default' mood.

However, at times syntactic circumstances dictate that the subjunctive mood be used.

The simplest way of determining which mood to use is to list those circumstances in which the subjunctive mood is required, since they are much fewer in number than those requiring the indicative, and to assume that in all other circumstances the indicative is to be used.

These circumstances are listed in 144–158.

The situation in French is different from that in English, since in English the subjunctive is so rare as to be virtually non-existent in ordinary speech and writing; when used, it tends to sound somewhat pompous, eg

The judge insisted that the accused leave the courtroom.

The tenses associated with each mood are listed in 15–102.

Tense

7 Tense

It is the role of the **tense** of the verb to tell us the time when an event takes place in relation to the present moment. Some events take place in the past, others in the present; others are projected into the future.

The various uses of verb tenses are discussed in 125–147.

8 Tenses

To create some tenses the form of the verb itself is adjusted.

Using the verb ***donner*** = *to give* as a template, the following tenses fall under this heading –

the present tense – ***je donne*** = *I give*
the imperfect – ***je donnais*** = *I was giving*
the past historic – ***je donnai*** = *I gave*
the future – ***je donnerai*** = *I will give*
the conditional – ***je donnerais*** = *I would give*

To create other tenses, what is called an auxiliary verb – ***avoir*** = *to have* or ***être*** = *to be* – is added to the past participle –

the perfect – ***j'ai donné*** = *I have given*
the pluperfect – ***j'avais donné*** = *I had given*

the future perfect – *j'aurai donné* = *I will have given*
the conditional perfect – *j'aurais donné* = *I would have given*

All this will be explained in full detail below.

9 Presentation of tenses

A word of warning – although many French verbs are regular in their conjugations, we still have to learn them. Others are renowned for their irregularities, and we have to make even more of an effort to memorise them. Life is made somewhat easier if we remember that the verbs often belong to groups and subgroups; that is to say, verbs that are conjugated in similar ways may be grouped together for convenience of learning. So, if we can remember which verbs are in which groups and subgroups, there is slightly less learning to do!

A list of other verbs belonging to the various subgroups discussed here is provided in Chapter 4.

10 Infinitives and conjugations

Verbs are organised into four major groups or **conjugations** according to the ending of the infinitive. All verbs belong to one of these, and it is of vital importance that we are able to recognise which group or conjugation the verb concerned belongs to, and how to form correctly the various parts of its **paradigm** – the collection of forms which a particular verb can adopt in any circumstances.

11 Infinitive endings for the four groups

Group 1 verbs end in **–er –**
eg **aller** = *to go,* **danser** = *to dance,* **penser** = *to think,* **sembler** = *to seem*

Group 2 verbs end in **–ir –**
eg **courir** = *to run,* **finir** = *to finish,* **jouir** = *to enjoy,* **partir** = *to leave*

Group 3 verbs end in **–re –**
eg **faire** = *to do,* **mettre** = *to put,* **plaire** = *to please,* **vendre** = *to sell*

Group 4 verbs end in **–oir –**
eg **devoir** = *to have to,* **pouvoir** = *to be able to,* **recevoir** = *to receive,* **voir** = *to see*

12 Subgroups

For each group of verbs, there are subgroups (in other grammar books often called 'exceptions' or 'irregular verbs'). These will be recorded after the standard conjugations have been presented.

It should be noted that, as a general rule, in these subgroups, as far as the present tense is concerned, the first two persons of the plural tend to maintain the stem of the infinitive, whereas the three persons of the singular and the third person plural have distinctive but related forms. Taking **pouvoir** as an example –

pouvoir

nous pouvons, vous pouvez but **je peux, tu peux, il / elle peut, ils / elles peuvent**

13 Group 1 *-er* verbs, Group 2 *-ir* verbs, Group 3 *-re* verbs, Group 4 *-oir* verbs

Group 1 *-er verbs*

This is the most numerous conjugation, and all newly created verbs belong to this group. Most of the verbs belonging to this group form their tenses regularly. A few show minor irregularities and may be gathered together into subgroups. One verb – **aller** = *to go* – shows major departures from the norm.

Group 2 *-ir verbs*

The verbs belonging to this group may be divided into a number of subgroups. A major distinction is to be made between those verbs which add **–iss–** between the stem and the ending in certain tenses and persons – subgroup 1 – and those which do not – subgroup 2 –

subgroup 1

finir = *to finish* – **nous finissons**
jouir = *to enjoy* – **je jouissais**

subgroup 2 –

courir = *to run* – **je courais**
partir = *to leave* – **nous partons**

Group 3 *-re verbs* and Group 4 *-oir verbs*

The verbs in these groups often form small subgroups, but there are also a number of verbs which are complete one-offs, especially in Group 4.

14 The formation of tenses – simple and compound tenses

Normally, certain endings need to be added to the stem of the verb. Very occasionally the ending is subsumed into the stem, eg

il part – third person singular of **partir**

The stem is the element preceding the **–er/–ir/–re** ending of the infinitive of Groups 1 to 3 –

eg **port** – from **porter, fin** – from **finir, vend** – from **vendre**

Identifying the stem is more of a problem with Group 4 verbs.

Simple and compound tenses

Tenses are of two types – **simple** and **compound**.
Simple tenses – here it is the form of the verb itself that varies –

eg for **donner** present tense **je donne**, imperfect tense **je donnais**, future tense **je donnerai**

Compound tenses – here an auxiliary verb, either **avoir** or **être**, is combined with the past participle of the verb –

eg perfect tense **j'ai donné**, pluperfect tense **j'étais venu**

The tenses will be treated in the following order –

Simple tenses: present, imperfect, future, conditional;
Compound tenses: perfect, pluperfect, future perfect, conditional perfect. The past historic (simple) and past anterior (compound) are treated last as they are relatively rare.

It should be pointed out that, on a number of occasions, it is the spelling rather than the pronunciation that is affected. Precision and accuracy of spelling are very important in written French; spoken French does not need to reveal how certain forms are spelt! – so more latitude is permissible there. However, this grammar book is designed to promote orthographical accuracy.

INDICATIVE MOOD

Present tense

15 Group 1 –er Verbs

16 Present tense of Group 1 –er verbs
The endings for the typical Group 1 –*er* verb **porter** = *to carry* are added to the stem **port–**

	singular	plural
first person	*port–e*	*port–ons*
second person	*port–es*	*port–ez*
third person	*port–e*	*port–ent*

17 Subgroups
There are a few verbs that show slight changes in their stems in the three persons of the singular and the third person plural.

This also applies to the future and conditional tenses of those verbs in all persons, singular and plural.

Aller is an –*er* verb that shows major deviations from the norm.

For further details see the appropriate sections below.

18 –er verbs Subgroup 1
Verbs ending in –*eler* and –*eter*: there are two possibilities –

1 some verbs double the final consonant of the stem in the persons mentioned above;
2 others change the unstressed *e* of the stem to *è*.

Examples of Subgroup 1
1 doubling the final consonant of the stem in singular and third person plural –

appeler = *to call*

j'appelle, tu appelles, il/elle/on appelle, ils/elles appellent

but **nous appelons, vous appelez**

jeter = *to throw*

je jette, tu jettes, il/elle/on jette, ils/elles jettent
but **nous jetons, vous jetez**

2 changing **–e–** of stem to **–è–**

acheter = *to buy*

j'achète, tu achètes, il/elle/on achète, ils/elles achètent
but **nous achetons, vous achetez**

19 –*er* verbs Subgroup 2
Verbs, with **–e–** (apart from those in Subgroup 1) or **–é–** as the final vowel of the stem –

the **–e–** or **–é–** is changed to **–è–** in the persons mentioned above.

Examples of Subgroup 2

mener = *to lead*

je mène, tu mènes, il/elle/on mène, ils/elles mènent
but **nous menons, vous menez**

espérer = *to hope*

j'espère, tu espères, il/elle/on espère, ils/elles espèrent
but **nous espérons, vous espérez**

20 –*er* verbs Subgroup 3
Verbs with **–c–**, **–g–** occurring immediately before the ending – the /s/, /ʒ/ sounds are retained by changing **–c–** to **–ç–** or adding an **–e–** after the **–g–** respectively in the first person plural of the present tense (and also in other tenses before **a** (in imperfect and past historic) or **u** (in past historic) with certain subgroups); **–ç–** (= **s**-sound rather than a **k**-sound) is used in the spelling of these words to reflect the fact that the pronunciation of the **–c–** remains the same.
    For further details see 44, 76.
    Examples of Subgroup 3

commencer = *to begin*

je commence but **nous commençons** (also **je commençai, commençais**)

manger = *to eat*

je mange but **nous mangeons** (also **je mangeai, mangeais**)

21 –*er* verbs Subgroup 4
Aller = *to go* constitutes a major departure from the norms of the **–er** conjugation, not only in the present tense but also in the future and conditional. The same forms are affected as for subgroups 1 and 2.

aller

je vais, tu vas, il / elle / on va, ils / elles vont
but ***nous allons, vous allez***

s'en aller = *to go away* is conjugated in the same way.

22 Group 2 –*ir* Verbs

23 Present tense of Group 2 –*ir* verbs

We need to draw a distinction between those –*ir* verbs that insert –*iss*– between stem and ending with certain persons – Subgroup 1, by far the most numerous subgroup – and those that do not – the other subgroups.

24 –*ir* verbs Subgroup 1

The endings for the typical –*ir* verb ***finir*** = *to finish* are added to the stem ***fin*** for the three persons singular, and to the stem plus –*iss*– for the three persons plural –

	singular	plural
first person	*fin*–*is*	*fin*–*issons*
second person	*fin*–*is*	*fin*–*issez*
third person	*fin*–*it*	*fin*–*issent*

25 –*ir* verbs Subgroup 2

The endings for a typical –*ir* verb, without –*iss*– in the plural, are added to the stem. The treatment of the final consonant of the stem should be noted –

1 when the stem ends in –*r*–, the –*r*– is retained throughout the paradigm
2 when the stem ends in –*t*–, the –*t*– does not appear in the written form of the first two persons singular
3 when the stem ends in another consonant, the consonant does not appear in the singular but reappears in the plural.

Examples of Subgroup 2

1 ***courir*** = *to run*

	singular	plural
first person	*cour*–*s*	*cour*–*ons*
second person	*cour*–*s*	*cour*–*ez*
third person	*cour*–*t*	*cour*–*ent*

2 ***partir*** = *to leave*

je pars, tu pars, il / elle / on part
nous partons, vous partez, ils / elles partent

3 ***dormir*** = *to sleep*

je dors, tu dors, il / elle / on dort
nous dormons, vous dormez, ils / elles dorment

26 –*ir* verbs Subgroup 3

Certain verbs whose infinitive ends in **–*ir*** are in fact conjugated like Group 1 **–*er*** verbs.

Example of Subgroup 3

cueillir = *to gather*

je cueille, tu cueilles, il / elle / on cueille, nous cueillons, vous cueillez, ils / elles cueillent

27 –*ir* verbs Subgroup 4

Tenir = *to hold* and **venir** = *to come* and their derivatives form a subgroup with an irregular present tense.

The two persons of the plural are formed like Subgroup 2 **–*ir*** verbs, but it is the other persons that give this subgroup its particularity.

Example of Subgroup 4

venir

je viens, tu viens, il / elle / on vient, ils / elles viennent

but **nous venons, vous venez**

28 –*ir* verb *mourir* = *to die*

Mourir is the most irregular of the **–*ir*** verbs.

je meurs, tu meurs, il / elle / on meurt, nous mourons, vous mourez, ils / elles meurent

29 Group 3 –*re* Verbs

30 Present tense of Group 3 –*re* verbs

Group 3 **–*re*** verbs involve a number of subgroups, some of which differ only slightly from each other, others of which are much more radical in their deviations.

The endings for the present tense of most **–*re*** verbs follow a regular pattern for most persons except the third person singular, where either the stem only occurs or a final **-*t*** is added.

	singular	plural
first person	**–s**	**–ons**
second person	**–s**	**–ez**
third person	stem only or **–t**	**–ent**

31 –*re* verbs Subgroup 1

Subgroup 1 involves the use of the stem only in the third person singular. This subgroup includes verbs ending in **–andre, –endre** (except **prendre** = *to take* and derivatives), **–erdre, –ondre, –ordre**.

Examples of Subgroup 1

vendre = *to sell*

je vends, tu vends, il/elle/on vend, nous vendons, vous vendez, ils/elles vendent

perdre = *to lose*

je perds, tu perds, il/elle/on perd, nous perdons, vous perdez, ils/elles perdent

répondre = *to reply*

je réponds, tu réponds, il/elle/on répond, nous répondons, vous répondez, ils/elles répondent

32 –re verbs Subgroup 2

The only difference between this subgroup and Subgroup 1 is that **–t** is added to the stem of the verb for the third person singular.

This subgroup includes verbs ending in **–ompre**, and **conclure** = *to conclude*, **rire** = *to laugh* and derivatives.

Examples of Subgroup 2

rompre = *to break*

je romps, tu romps, il/elle/on rompt, nous rompons, vous rompez, ils/elles rompent

rire

je ris, tu ris, il/elle/on rit, nous rions, vous riez, ils/elles rient

conclure

je conclus, tu conclus, il/elle/on conclut, nous concluons, vous concluez, ils/elles concluent

33 –re verbs Subgroup 3

Battre = *to beat*, **mettre** = *to put* and derivatives subgroup: this subgroup is distinctive in that a single **–t–** (instead of the double **–tt–** that might be supposed) occurs in the singular.

Examples of Subgroup 3

battre

je bats, tu bats, il/elle/on bat, nous battons, vous battez, ils/elles battent

mettre

je mets, tu mets, il/elle/on met, nous mettons, vous mettez, ils/elles mettent

34 –*re* verbs Subgroup 4

Croire = *to believe* subgroup: this subgroup involves the addition of a –*t* for the third person singular, and –*i*– becomes –*y*– in the first and second persons plural.

Example of Subgroup 4

croire

je crois, tu crois, il/elle/on croit, nous croyons, vous croyez, ils croient

35 –*re* verbs Subgroup 5

Lire = *to read* and ***conduire*** = *to drive* subgroup: this subgroup involves the addition of a –*t* for the third person singular and of an –*s*– to the stem in all three persons of the plural.

Examples of Subgroup 5

lire

je lis, tu lis, il/elle/on lit, nous lisons, vous lisez, ils/elles lisent

conduire

je conduis, tu conduis, il/elle/on conduit, nous conduisons, vous conduisez, il/elles conduisent

36 –*re* verbs Subgroup 6

Écrire = *to write* subgroup: this subgroup involves the addition of a –*t* for the third person singular and of a –*v*– to the stem in all three persons of the plural.

Example of Subgroup 6

écrire

j'écris, tu écris, il/elle/on écrit, nous écrivons, vous écrivez, ils/elles écrivent

37 –*re* verbs Subgroup 7

This subgroup contains a series of common verbs which are very irregular in formation, and each of which has a distinctive conjugation for the present tense.

Examples of Subgroup 7

boire = *to drink*

je bois, tu bois, il/elle/on boit, nous buvons, vous buvez, ils/elles boivent

craindre = *to fear*

je crains, tu crains, il/elle/on craint, nous craignons, vous craignez, ils/elles craignent

dire = *to say*

je dis, tu dis, il/elle/on dit, nous disons, vous dites, ils/elles disent

faire = *to do*

je fais, tu fais, il/elle/on fait, nous faisons, vous faites, ils/elles font

prendre = *to take*

je prends, tu prends, il/elle/on prend, nous prenons, vous prenez, ils/elles prennent

vivre = *to live*

je vis, tu vis, il/elle/on vit, nous vivons, vous vivez, ils/elles vivent

and the supreme irregular **–re** verb
être = *to be*

je suis, tu es, il/elle/on est, nous sommes, vous êtes, ils/elles sont

38 Group 4 –*oir* Verbs

39 Present tense of Group 4 –*oir* verbs

Even more so than with Group 3 **–re** verbs, stem alterations and the existence of small subgroups are extremely common in this group.

Normally the first and second persons plural forms reflect the infinitive; the other forms are more distant from the original stem.

40 –*oir* verbs Subgroup 1

–cevoir subgroup: a number of stem alterations occur and **–c–** becomes **–ç–** before **–o–** (compare 20, 44, 75).

Example of Subgroup 1

recevoir = *to receive*

je reçois, tu reçois, il/elle/on reçoit, nous recevons, vous recevez, ils/elles reçoivent

41 –*oir* verbs Subgroup 2

Voir = *to see* and its derivatives subgroup: **–i–** becomes **–y–** in first and second persons plural. For other verbs in **–voir** see Subgroups 1 and 3.

Example of Subgroup 2

voir

je vois, tu vois, il/elle/on voit, nous voyons, vous voyez, ils/elles voient

42 –*oir* verbs Subgroup 3

As with Subgroup 7 of **–re** verbs, this subgroup contains a series of verbs that are very irregular in formation, and each of which has a distinctive conjugation for the present tense. The majority are very common.

Examples of Subgroup 3

asseoir = *to sit* – this verb (normally pronominal) has two conjugations for the present tense, the first of which is the more commonly used –

1 *je m'assieds, tu t'assieds, il/elle/on s'assied, nous nous asseyons, vous vous asseyez, ils/elles s'asseyent*
2 *je m'assois, tu t'assois, il/elle/on s'assoit, nous nous assoyons, vous vous assoyez, ils/elles s'assoient*

avoir = *to have*

j'ai, tu as, il/elle/on a, nous avons, vous avez, ils/elles ont

devoir = *to have to*

je dois, tu dois, il/elle/on doit, nous devons, vous devez, ils/elles doivent

falloir = *to be necessary* – an impersonal verb used only in the third person singular –

il faut

pleuvoir = *to rain* – an impersonal verb used only in the third person singular –

il pleut

pouvoir = *to be able to*

je peux (*puis-je* is used in the interrogative – see 161), *tu peux, il/elle/on peut, nous pouvons, vous pouvez, ils/elles peuvent*

savoir = *to know*

je sais, tu sais, il/elle/on sait, nous savons, vous savez, ils/elles savent

valoir = *to be worth*

je vaux, tu vaux, il/elle/on vaut, nous valons, vous valez, ils/elles valent

vouloir = *to want*

je veux, tu veux, il/elle/on veut, nous voulons, vous voulez, ils/elles veulent

Imperfect tense

43 Using and forming the imperfect tense
Usage
As will be explained in 129, the imperfect tense has a number of functions – mainly to indicate the passage of time or the repetition of an action or event in the past.

In all cases, except *être*, the imperfect tense is formed by taking the first person plural form of the verb, and replacing the *–ons* ending by the appropriate imperfect ending.

Endings
The endings for all verbs without exception are

singular	plural
–ais	*–ions*
–ais	*–iez*
–ait	*–aient*

44 Examples of the imperfect tense Groups 1–4

Group 1

porter

je portais, tu portais, il/elle/on portait, nous portions, vous portiez, ils/elles portaient

commencer

je commençais, tu commençais, il/elle/on commençait, nous commencions, vous commenciez, ils/elles commençaient

manger

je mangeais, tu mangeais, il/elle/on mangeait, nous mangions, vous mangiez, ils/elles mangeaient

aller

j'allais, tu allais, il/elle/on allait, nous allions, vous alliez, ils/elles allaient

Group 2

finir

je finissais, tu finissais, il/elle/on finissait, nous finissions, vous finissiez, ils/elles finissaient

partir

je partais, tu partais, il/elle/on partait, nous partions, vous partiez, ils/elles partaient

Group 3

vendre

je vendais, tu vendais, il/elle/on vendait, nous vendions, vous vendiez, ils/elles vendaient

être

j'étais, tu étais, il/elle/on était, nous étions, vous étiez, ils/elles étaient

Group 4

recevoir

je recevais, tu recevais, il/elle/on recevait, nous recevions, vous receviez, ils/elles recevaient voir

je voyais, tu voyais, il/elle/on voyait, nous voyions, vous voyiez, ils/elles voyaient

pouvoir

je pouvais, tu pouvais, il/elle/on pouvait, nous pouvions, vous pouviez, ils/elles pouvaient

avoir

j'avais, tu avais, il/elle/on avait, nous avions, vous aviez, ils/elles avaient

Future and conditional tenses

45 Using the future and conditional tenses

Because these two tenses are formed in a very similar way, it is convenient to treat them together.

Usage

As will be explained in 135, 138, the future tense refers to events that have yet to take place, the conditional to 'the future in the past' and to express doubt or probability.

46 Endings of future and conditional tenses

In the majority of cases, forming the future and conditional tenses is a relatively simple matter.

For all Group 1 **–er** verbs (except **aller** and **envoyer** – see 49), the following endings are added to the stem. However, the stem undergoes variation in a few cases – see 48.

Future tense		Conditional tense	
singular	plural	singular	plural
–erai	*–erons*	*–erais*	*–erions*
–eras	*–erez*	*–erais*	*–eriez*
–era	*–eront*	*–erait*	*–eraient*

For all Group 2 **–ir** verbs (except **cueillir** – see 51), the following endings are added to the stem –

Future tense		Conditional tense	
singular	plural	singular	plural
–irai	*–irons*	*–irais*	*–irions*
–iras	*–irez*	*–irais*	*–iriez*
–ira	*–iront*	*–irait*	*–iraient*

For Group 3 **–re** verbs, the following endings are added to the stem. All the subgroups form their future and conditional tenses in the same way, with the exception of **être** and **faire** – see 54.

Future tense

singular	plural
–rai	*–rons*
–ras	*–rez*
–ra	*–ront*

Conditional tense

singular	plural
–rais	*–rions*
–rais	*–riez*
–rait	*–raient*

For Group 4 *–oir* verbs, the situation is, inevitably, more complex. The endings are the same as for Group 3 *–re* verbs, but it is the stem that needs to be noted.

47 Examples of future and conditional tenses of Group 1 *–er* verbs

Future tense

singular	plural
je porterai	*nous porterons*
tu porteras	*vous porterez*
il/elle/on portera	*ils/elles porteront*

Conditional tense

singular	plural
je porterais	*nous porterions*
tu porterais	*vous porteriez*
il/elle/on porterait	*ils/elles porteraient*

48 Stem changes of Group 1 *–er* verbs

Subgroup 1

Verbs ending in *–eler* and *–eter*

1 some double the final consonant of the stem in all persons of the singular and the plural;
2 others change the unstressed *e* of the stem to *è*.

Examples

appeler

future

j'appellerai, tu appelleras, il/elle/on appellera, nous appellerons, vous appellerez, ils/elles appelleront

conditional

j'appellerais, tu appellerais, il/elle/on appellerait, nous appellerions, vous appelleriez, ils/elles appelleraient

jeter

future

je jetterai, tu jetteras, il/elle/on jettera, nous jetterons, vous jetterez, ils/elles jetteront

conditional

je jetterais, tu jetterais, il/elle/on jetterait, nous jetterions, vous jetteriez, ils/elles jetteraient

acheter

future
j'achèterai, tu achèteras, il/elle/on achètera, nous achèterons, vous achèterez, ils/elles achèteront

conditional
j'achèterais, tu achèterais, il/elle/on achèterait, nous achèterions, vous achèteriez, ils/elles achèteraient

Subgroup 2
Verbs with *–e–* as final vowel of stem – the *–e–* becomes *–è–* throughout both tenses.

Example

mener

future
je mènerai, tu mèneras, il/elle/on mènera, nous mènerons, vous mènerez, ils/elles mèneront

conditional
je mènerais, tu mènerais, il/elle/on mènerait, nous mènerions, vous mèneriez, ils/elles mèneraient

However, verbs with *–é–* as final vowel of stem retain *–é–*:
espérer

future
j'espérerai, tu espéreras, il/elle/on espérera, nous espérerons, vous espérerez, ils/elles espéreront

conditional
j'espérerais, tu espérerais, il/elle/on espérerait, nous espérerions, vous espéreriez, ils/elles espéreraient

49 Group 1 *–er* verbs with radical stem variation
Aller and *envoyer* both have highly irregular stems.
aller

future
j'irai, tu iras, il/elle/on ira, nous irons, vous irez, ils/elles iront

conditional
j'irais, tu irais, il/elle/on irait, nous irions, vous iriez, ils/elles iraient

envoyer

future
j'enverrai, tu enverras, il/elle/on enverra, nous enverrons, vous enverrez, ils/elles enverront

conditional

j'enverrais, tu enverrais, il/elle/on enverrait, nous enverrions, vous enverriez, ils/elles enverraient

50 Examples of future and conditional tenses of Group 2 –*ir* verbs

finir

future

je finirai, tu finiras, il/elle/on finira, nous finirons, vous finirez, ils/elles finiront

conditional

je finirais, tu finirais, il/elle/on finirait, nous finirions, vous finiriez, ils/elles finiraient

dormir

future

je dormirai, tu dormiras, il/elle/on dormira, nous dormirons, vous dormirez, ils/elles dormiront

conditional

je dormirais, tu dormirais, il/elle/on dormirait, nous dormirions, vous dormiriez, ils/elles dormiraient

51 –*ir* verbs Subgroup 3

Cueillir, etc

Just as the present tense of these verbs is formed differently from the norm, so are the future and conditional. Here and in the following sections the stems and endings for the first person singular and first person plural only for both tenses are given.

je cueillerai, nous cueillerons, je cueillerais, nous cueillerions

52 Group 2 –*ir* verbs with radical stem variation

A number of verbs have highly irregular stems.

tenir

je tiendrai, nous tiendrons, je tiendrais, nous tiendrions

venir

je viendrai, nous viendrons, je viendrais, nous viendrions

courir

je courrai, nous courrons, je courrais, nous courrions

mourir

je mourrai, nous mourrons, je mourrais, nous mourrions

53 Future and conditional tenses of Group 3 *–re* verbs

Future tense

singular	plural
je vendrai	*nous vendrons*
tu vendras	*vous vendrez*
il/elle/on vendra	*ils/elles vendront*

Conditional tense

singular	plural
je vendrais	*nous vendrions*
tu vendrais	*vous vendriez*
il/elle/on vendrait	*ils/elles vendraient*

54 The exceptions *être* and *faire*

être

future

je serai, tu seras, il/elle/on sera, nous serons, vous serez, ils/elles seront

conditional

je serais, tu serais, il/elle/on serait, nous serions, vous seriez, ils/elles seraient

faire

future

je ferai, tu feras, il/elle/on fera, nous ferons, vous ferez, ils/elles feront

conditional

je ferais, tu ferais, il/elle/on ferait, nous ferions, vous feriez, ils/elles feraient

55 Future and conditional tenses of Group 4 *–oir* verbs

Some of these verbs undergo radical stem alteration.

Subgroup 1 – verbs in *–cevoir*

Future tense

singular	plural
je recevrai	*nous recevrons*
tu recevras	*vous recevrez*
il/elle/on recevra	*ils/elles recevront*

Conditional tense

singular	plural
je recevrais	*nous recevrions*
tu recevrais	*vous recevriez*
il/elle/on recevrait	*ils/elles recevraient*

Subgroup 2 – *voir*

Future tense

singular	plural
je verrai	*nous verrons*
tu verras	*vous verrez*
il/elle/on verra	*ils/elles verront*

Conditional tense

singular	plural
je verrais	*nous verrions*
tu verrais	*vous verriez*
il/elle/on verrait	*ils/elles verraient*

Other Group 4 verbs

avoir

j'aurai, nous aurons, j'aurais, nous aurions

devoir

je devrai, nous devrons, je devrais, nous devrions

falloir

il faudra, il faudrait

pleuvoir

il pleuvra, il pleuvrait

pouvoir

je pourrai, nous pourrons, je pourrais, nous pourrions

savoir

je saurai, nous saurons, je saurais, nous saurions

valoir

je vaudrai, nous vaudrons, je vaudrais, nous vaudrions

vouloir

je voudrai, nous voudrons, je voudrais, nous voudrions

Participles

There are two participles: the present participle and the past participle.

56 Present participles

These are normally formed by adding the ending **–ant** to the stem of the first person plural of the verb.

Examples

Group 1 –er verbs
porter

portant

Subgroups
appeler – **appelant**; *acheter* – **achetant**; *mener* – **menant**; *espérer* – **espérant**; *commencer* – **commençant**; *manger* – **mangeant**; *aller* – **allant**

Group 2 –ir verbs
Subgroups

finir

finissant

partir

partant

cueillir – **cueillant**; *tenir* – **tenant**; *mourir* – **mourant**

Group 3 –re verbs
Subgroups
vendre - **vendant**; *rompre* - **rompant**; *battre* - **battant**; *croire* - **croyant**; *lire* - **lisant**; *écrire* - **écrivant**; *conduire* - **conduisant**; *craindre* - **craignant**; *boire* - **buvant**; *dire* - **disant**; *faire* - **faisant**; *prendre* - **prenant**; *vivre* - **vivant** *être* - **étant**

Group 4 –oir verbs
Subgroups
recevoir - **recevant**; *voir* - **voyant**; *asseoir* - **asseyant**; *devoir* - **devant**; *falloir* - no present participle; *mouvoir* - **mouvant**; *pleuvoir* - **pleuvant**; *pouvoir* – **pouvant**; *valoir* – **valant**; *vouloir* – **voulant**

57 Exceptions
There are a very few exceptions to this principle –

avoir - **ayant**
savoir - **sachant**

58 Past participles
The groups form their past participles in distinctive ways.

59 Formation of past participles Groups 1–3
Group 1 –er verbs
The **–er** of the infinitive is replaced by **–é**

Examples
porter – **porté**, *appeler* – **appelé**, *acheter* – **acheté**

Group 2 –ir verbs
The **–ir** of the infinitive is replaced by **–i**

Examples
finir - **fini**, *partir* - **parti**, *cueillir* - **cueilli**, *haïr* - **haï**
   However, there are certain exceptions.

Ending in **–u**

tenir - **tenu**, *venir* - **venu** and derivatives
courir - **couru**, *vêtir* - **vêtu**

Ending in **–ert**
ouvrir - **ouvert**, also **couvrir, découvrir, offrir, souffrir.**
Mourir has a distinctive past participle - **mort**

Group 3 –re verbs

Many Group 3 *–re* verbs form their past participle in *–u*

Examples

vendre – **vendu**, *rompre –* **rompu**, *battre –* **battu**, *croire –* **cru**, lire *–* **lu**, *taire –* **tu** = *fell silent,*
apparaître – **apparu** = *appeared* (note *croître –* **crû** = *grew*), *vaincre –* **vaincu** = *conquered,*
boire – **bu**.

However, many verbs in this group form their past participles in distinctive ways.

60 Group 3 –re verbs with distinctive past participles

absoudre – **absous** = *absolved, écrire –* **écrit**, *suivre –* **suivi** = *followed, conduire–* **conduit**,
craindre – **craint**, *dire –* **dit**, *faire –* **fait**, *prendre –* **pris**, *naître –* **né**, *être –* **été**

61 Past participles of Group 4 –oir verbs

All the verbs in this group (with the exception of **asseoir**, past participle – **assis**) form
their past participle in *–u*, but often with considerable modification of the stem.

Examples

recevoir – **reçu**, *voir –* **vu**, *devoir –* **dû**, but the form indicating feminine agreement is
due, *falloir –* **fallu**, *pleuvoir –* **plu**, *pouvoir –* **pu**, *savoir –* **su**, *valoir –* **valu**, *vouloir –* **voulu**,
avoir – **eu**

Compound tenses

62 General comments

The compound tenses of all verbs are formed by adding an auxiliary verb, either **avoir**
or **être**, to the past participle of the verb.

Certain verbs are always conjugated with **avoir**, others with **être**; a few may in certain
circumstances be conjugated with one or the other auxiliary verb.

63 *Avoir* or *être*?

Since the number of verbs conjugated with **être** is comparatively small, the focus here is
upon such verbs.

Verbs conjugated with être

The majority of these verbs are **intransitive**, in other words they are not followed by a
direct object. Most of them, but not all, indicate a movement.

The verbs are –

aller, arriver = *to arrive,* **demeurer** = *to stay,* **descendre** = *to go down,* **entrer** = *to*
enter and **rentrer** = *to go home,* **monter** = *to go up,* **mourir, naître, partir, passer** =
to pass, **rester** = *to stay,* **retourner** = *to return,* **sortir** = *to go out,* **tomber** = *to fall,* **venir**
and its derivatives **convenir** = *to suit,* **devenir** = *to become,* **intervenir** = *to intervene,*
parvenir = *to reach,* **revenir** = *to return,* **survenir** = *to happen.*

Verbs that are **pronominal** also always form their compound tenses with **être** –
see 104.

64 Verbs conjugated with *être* and agreement

In the case of these verbs, agreement between the past participle and the subject is compulsory –

if the subject is feminine, an **–e** is added to the participle;
if the subject is plural, an **–s** is added, if the subject is masculine or is used generically;
an **–es** is added if the subject is feminine plural.

Examples

Lorsqu'elle est entrée, je me suis dit que c'était ma chance = *when she came in, I said to myself, now's my chance*

Elle est devenue un objet de désir = *she became an object of desire*

Ses deux fils sont venus me demander du conseil = *his two sons came and asked me for advice*

Il y a des hommes qui ne sont pas sortis de l'enfance, même s'ils portent des costumes = *there are some men who have not left childhood, even if they wear suits*

J'ai rencontré beaucoup de filles qui sont tombées amoureuses au moins une fois par mois = *I've met lots of girls who fell in love at least once a month*

Comprenant qu'il y avait une lueur d'espoir, elles sont revenues au centre chaque jour = *realising that there was a glimmer of hope, they came back to the centre every day*

In the case of ***vous,*** an **–s** or **–es** is added only if the reference is to a plural subject; if ***vous*** refers to a singular subject, then no extra ending is added, unless a feminine subject is involved – thus

masculine singular

Après cette aventure, vous êtes sagement rentré auprès de votre femme et vous êtes enfin devenu raisonnable = *after this escapade, you returned quietly to your wife and at last became sensible*

masculine plural

Vous avez porté des pantalons à pattes d'éléphant – vous vous êtes moqués du bon goût = *you wore flares – you didn't care about good taste*

feminine singular

Peut-être avez-vous eu un parent exigeant – face à lui vous vous êtes sentie impuissante et vulnérable = *perhaps you had a demanding parent – confronted by him or her you felt powerless and vulnerable*

Vous êtes restée sans nouvelles de lui, et puis le beau garçon à qui vous aviez donné vos coordonnées vous contacte = *you hadn't had any news from him, and then the handsome guy you'd given your details to contacts you*

feminine plural

Mesdemoiselles, il faut faire attention au web caméra qui vous permet d'être filmées et vues sur l'écran de votre patron = *girls, you must beware of the web-cam which allows you to be filmed and seen on screen by your boss*

Si vous fumez ou êtes entourées de fumeurs, vous risquez de vous préparer une cinquantaine pénible = *if you smoke or are surrounded by smokers, you're in danger of preparing a very uncomfortable scenario for yourself at fifty*

65 Verbs which may be conjugated with either *avoir* or *être*

1 Some of the verbs listed in 63 may be used transitively as well as intransitively.

If they are used transitively, accompanied by a direct object, they are conjugated with *avoir* and not *être*, and no agreement with the subject takes place.

The verbs are

descendre, monter, passer, rentrer, retourner, sortir

Examples

Elle a descendu le coffre = *she brought down the trunk*

Nous avons monté leurs bagages = *we took their luggage up*

Ils ont passé le mois de janvier en Espagne = *they spent January in Spain*

Il a rentré son chien à cause du bruit = *he brought his dog into the house because of the noise*

Elle a retourné le vase pour évaluer sa qualité = *she turned the vase over to get an idea of its quality*

Ils ont sorti les déchets = *they brought the rubbish out*

2 Another group of verbs (not listed in 63) may be conjugated with either auxiliary without the matter of transitivity being involved. The normal procedure is – when an action is involved, *avoir* is used; when a state is implied, it is *être* which is used.

Examples

Ce magazine a paru le 29 janvier = *this magazine came out on 29 January*

Ce magazine est paru depuis longtemps = *this magazine came out a long time ago*

also *accourir, apparaître, disparaître*

Perfect tense

66 Formation
The perfect tense is formed by combining the present tense of *avoir* or *être* with the past participle of the verb.

67 Perfect tense of Group 1–4 verbs
Group 1 –er verbs
porter

j'ai porté, tu as porté, il / elle / on a porté, nous avons porté, vous avez porté, ils / elles ont porté

aller

je suis allé / allée, tu es allé / allée, il est allé, elle est allée, on est allé, nous sommes allés / allées, vous êtes allé / allée / allés / allées, ils sont allés, elles sont allées

Group 2 –ir verbs
finir

j'ai fini, tu as fini, il / elle / on a fini, nous avons fini, vous avez fini, ils / elles ont fini

partir

je suis parti / partie, tu es parti / partie, il / on est parti, elle est partie, nous sommes partis / parties, vous êtes parti / partie / partis / parties, ils sont partis, elles sont parties

ouvrir

j'ai ouvert, tu as ouvert, il / elle / on a ouvert, nous avons ouvert, vous avez ouvert, ils / elles ont ouvert

mourir

je suis mort / morte, tu es mort / morte, il / on est mort, elle est morte, nous sommes morts / mortes, vous êtes mort / morte / morts / mortes, ils sont morts, elles sont mortes

Group 3 –re verbs
vendre

j'ai vendu, tu as vendu, il / elle / on a vendu, nous avons vendu, vous avez vendu, ils / elles ont vendu

prendre

j'ai pris, tu as pris, il / elle / on a pris, nous avons pris, vous avez pris, ils / elles ont pris

descendre

je suis descendu / descendue, tu es descendu / descendue, il / on est descendu, elle est descendue, nous sommes descendus / descendues, vous êtes descendu / descendue / descendus / descendues, ils sont descendus, elles sont descendues

Group 4 –oir verbs
recevoir

j'ai reçu, tu as reçu, il / elle / on a reçu, nous avons reçu, vous avez reçu, ils / elles ont reçu

pouvoir

j'ai pu, tu as pu, il/elle/on a pu, nous avons pu, vous avez pu, ils/elles ont pu

Pluperfect tense

68 Formation
The pluperfect tense is formed by combining the imperfect tense of **avoir** or **être** with the past participle of the verb.

69 Pluperfect tense of Group 1–4 verbs
Group 1 –er verbs
porter

j'avais porté, tu avais porté, il/elle/on avait porté, nous avions porté, vous aviez porté, ils/elles avaient porté

aller

j'étais allé/allée, tu étais allé/allée, il/on était allé, elle était allée, nous étions allés/allées, vous étiez allé/allée/allés/allées, ils étaient allés, elles étaient allées

Group 2 –ir verbs
finir

j'avais fini, tu avais fini, il/elle/on avait fini, nous avions fini, vous aviez fini, ils/elles avaient fini

partir

j'étais parti/partie, tu étais parti/partie, il/on était parti, elle était partie, nous étions partis/parties, vous étiez parti/partie/partis/parties, ils étaient partis, elles étaient parties

mourir

j'étais mort/morte, tu étais mort/morte, il/on était mort, elle était morte, nous étions morts/mortes, vous étiez mort/morte/morts/mortes, ils étaient morts, elles étaient mortes

Group 3 –re verbs
vendre

j'avais vendu, tu avais vendu, il/elle/on avait vendu, nous avions vendu, vous aviez vendu, ils/elles avaient vendu

descendre

j'étais descendu/descendue, tu étais descendu/descendue, il/on était descendu, elle était descendue, nous étions descendus/descendues, vous étiez descendu/descendue/descendus/descendues, ils étaient descendus, elles étaient descendues

Group 4 –oir verbs
recevoir

j'avais reçu, tu avais reçu, il/elle/on avait reçu, nous avions reçu, vous aviez reçu, ils/elles avaient reçu

pouvoir

j'avais pu, tu avais pu, il/elle/on avait pu, nous avions pu, vous aviez pu, ils/elles avaient pu

Future perfect tense

70 Formation
The future perfect tense is formed by combining the future tense of **avoir** or **être** with the past participle of the verb.

71 Future perfect tense of Group 1–4 verbs
Group 1 –er verbs
porter

j'aurai porté, tu auras porté, il/elle/on aura porté, nous aurons porté, vous aurez porté, ils/elles auront porté

aller

je serai allé/allée, tu seras allé/allée, il/on sera allé, elle sera allée, nous serons allés/allées, vous serez allé/allée/allés/allées, ils seront allés, elles seront allées

Group 2 –ir verbs
finir

j'aurai fini, tu auras fini, il/elle/on aura fini, nous aurons fini, vous aurez fini, ils/elles auront fini

partir

je serai parti/partie, tu seras parti/partie, il/on sera parti, elle sera partie, nous serons partis/parties, vous serez parti/partie/partis/parties, ils seront partis, elles seront parties

ouvrir

j'aurai ouvert, tu auras ouvert, il/elle/on aura ouvert, nous aurons ouvert, vous aurez ouvert, ils/elles auront ouvert

mourir

je serai mort/morte, tu seras mort/morte, il/on sera mort, elle sera morte, nous serons morts/mortes, vous serez mort/morte/morts/mortes, ils seront morts, elles seront mortes

Group 3 –re verbs
vendre

j'aurai vendu, tu auras vendu, il / elle / on aura vendu, nous aurons vendu, vous aurez vendu, ils / elles auront vendu

prendre

j'aurai pris, tu auras pris, il / elle / on aura pris, nous aurons pris, vous aurez pris, ils / elles auront pris

descendre

je serai descendu / descendue, tu seras descendu / descendue, il / on sera descendu, elle sera descendue, nous serons descendus / descendues, vous serez descendu / descendue / descendus / descendues, ils seront descendus, elles seront descendues

Group 4 –oir verbs
recevoir

j'aurai reçu, tu auras reçu, il / elle / on aura reçu, nous aurons reçu, vous aurez reçu, ils / elles auront reçu

pouvoir

j'aurai pu, tu auras pu, il / elle / on aura pu, nous aurons pu, vous aurez pu, ils / elles auront pu

Conditional perfect tense

72 Formation
The conditional perfect tense is formed by combining the conditional tense of **avoir** or **être** with the past participle of the verb.

73 Conditional perfect tense of Group 1–4 verbs
Group 1 –er verbs
porter

j'aurais porté, tu aurais porté, il / elle / on aurait porté, nous aurions porté, vous auriez porté, ils / elles auraient porté

aller

je serais allé / allée, tu serais allé / allée, il / on serait allé, elle serait allée, nous serions allés / allées, vous seriez allé / allée / allés / allées, ils seraient allés, elles seraient allées

Group 2 –ir verbs
finir

j'aurais fini, tu aurais fini, il / elle / on aurait fini, nous aurions fini, vous auriez fini, ils / elles auraient fini partir

je serais parti/partie, tu serais parti/partie, il/on serait parti, elle serait partie, nous serions partis/parties, vous seriez parti/partie/partis/ parties, ils seraient partis, elles seraient parties

ouvrir

j'aurais ouvert, tu aurais ouvert, il/elle/on aurait ouvert, nous aurions ouvert, vous auriez ouvert, ils/elles auraient ouvert

mourir

je serais mort/morte, tu serais mort/morte, il/on serait mort, elle serait morte, nous serions morts/mortes, vous seriez mort/morte/morts/ mortes, ils seraient morts, elles seraient mortes

Group 3 –re verbs
vendre

j'aurais vendu, tu aurais vendu, il/elle/on aurait vendu, nous aurions vendu, vous auriez vendu, ils/elles auraient vendu

prendre

j'aurais pris, tu aurais pris, il/elle/on aurait pris, nous aurions pris, vous auriez pris, ils/elles auraient pris

descendre

je serais descendu/descendue, tu serais descendu/descendue, il/on serait descendu, elle serait descendue, nous serions descendus/descendues, vous seriez descendu/descendue/descendus/descendues, ils seraient descendus, elles seraient descendues

Group 4 –oir verbs
recevoir

j'aurais reçu, tu aurais reçu, il/elle/on aurait reçu, nous aurions reçu, vous auriez reçu, ils/elles auraient reçu

pouvoir

j'aurais pu, tu aurais pu, il/elle/on aurait pu, nous aurions pu, vous auriez pu, ils/elles auraient pu

Past historic tense

74 Past historic
A tense that is mainly restricted to the written medium (see 130) and which involves many irregularities of stem in Groups 3 and 4.

75 Past historic tense of Group 1 –er verbs

All **–er** verbs (even including **_aller_**) form their past historic tense regularly, by adding the endings listed below to their stem. The Subgroup 5 verbs, **_commencer_** and **_manger_**, etc, form their past historic tense according to the principles presented above – see 20.

The following endings are added to the stem.

singular	plural
–ai	**–âmes**
–as	**–âtes**
–a	**–èrent**

76 Examples of Group 1 –er verbs

porter

je portai, tu portas, il/elle/on porta, nous portâmes, vous portâtes, ils/elles portèrent

commencer

je commençai, tu commenças, il/elle/on commença, nous commençâmes, vous commençâtes, ils/elles commencèrent

manger

je mangeai, tu mangeas, il/elle/on mangea, nous mangeâmes, vous mangeâtes, ils/elles mangèrent

aller

j'allai, tu allas, il/elle alla, nous allâmes, vous allâtes, ils/elles allèrent

77 Past historic tense of Group 2 –ir verbs

All Subgroup 1 and Subgroup 3 (**_cueillir_**) verbs and many Subgroup 2 verbs form their past historic tense in the same way.

The following endings are added to the stem.

singular	plural
–is	**–îmes**
–is	**–îtes**
–it	**–irent**

78 Examples of Group 2 –ir verbs

finir

je finis, tu finis, il/elle/on finit, nous finîmes, vous finîtes, ils/elles finirent

partir

je partis, tu partis, il/elle/on partit, nous partîmes, vous partîtes, ils/elles partirent

cueillir

je cueillis, tu cueillis, il/elle/on cueillit, nous cueillîmes, vous cueillîtes, ils/elles cueillirent

79 *-ir* verbs Subgroup 4

venir and *tenir* have a distinctive form in the past historic –
venir

je vins, tu vins, il/elle/on vint, nous vînmes, vous vîntes, ils/elles vinrent

tenir

je tins, tu tins, il/elle/on tint, nous tînmes, vous tîntes, ils/elles tinrent

80 *-ir* verbs exceptions to Subgroup 2 and *mourir*

Certain *-ir* verbs form their past historic tense with the following endings.

singular	plural
-us	*-ûmes*
-us	*-ûtes*
-ut	*-urent*

Examples of *-ir* verbs forming their past historic in *-u-*
courir

je courus, tu courus, il/elle/on courut, nous courûmes, vous courûtes, ils/elles coururent

mourir

je mourus, tu mourus, il/elle/on mourut, nous mourûmes, vous mourûtes, ils/elles moururent

81 Past historic tense of Group 3 *-re* verbs

It will be remembered, from the presentation of the present tense of this group of verbs, that there are many subgroups. Since there are so many anomalies with this group of verbs in the past historic tense, the most straightforward way of presenting them is individually. Certain *-re* verbs form their past historic with endings in *-i-* and others in *-u-*.

Those verbs with endings in *-i-* will be dealt with first, then those whose endings are in *-u-*.

82 Group 3 *-re* verbs with past historic endings in *-i-*

singular	plural
-is	*-îmes*
-is	*-îtes*
-it	*-irent*

Example of *-re* verbs with endings in *-i-*
vendre

je vendis, tu vendis, il / elle / on vendit, nous vendîmes, vous vendîtes, ils / elles vendirent

Battre, perdre, répondre, rompre follow a similar pattern.

83 Group 3 *–re* verbs with stem variation

conduire: the stem acquires an *–s–*, as follows

je conduisis, tu conduisis, il / elle / on conduisit, nous conduisîmes, vous conduisîtes, ils / elles conduisirent

craindre, joindre and other verbs in *–aindre / –oindre*: the stem changes from *–aind / –oind* to *–aign / –oign.*

craindre

je craignis, tu craignis, il / elle / on craignit, nous craignîmes, vous craignîtes, ils / elles craignirent

joindre – je joignis, nous joignîmes

dire and *rire* – the *–i–* of the stem is absorbed into the ending; consequently at times the verb form is the same as the present tense. The past historic forms are

je dis, tu dis, il / elle / on dit, nous dîmes, vous dîtes, ils / elles dirent

écrire – the stem acquires a *–v–*, as follows –

j'écrivis, tu écrivis, il / elle / on écrivit, nous écrivîmes, vous écrivîtes, ils / elles écrivirent

faire

je fis, tu fis, il / elle / on fit, nous fîmes, vous fîtes, ils / elles firent

mettre – the stem is reduced to *m–*; the forms are

je mis, tu mis, il / elle / on mit, nous mîmes, vous mîtes, ils / elles mirent

prendre

je pris, tu pris, il / elle / on prit, nous prîmes, vous prîtes, ils / elles prirent

84 Group 3 *–re* verbs with past historic endings in *–u–*

The endings are

singular	plural
–us	*–ûmes*
–us	*–ûtes*
–ut	*–urent*

Quite often stem variation is also involved.

Examples of *–re* verbs with endings in *–u–*

boire

je bus, tu bus, il / elle / on but, nous bûmes, vous bûtes, ils / elles burent conclure

je conclus, tu conclus, il / elle / on conclut, nous conclûmes, vous conclûtes, ils / elles conclurent

croire

je crus, tu crus, il / elle / on crut, nous crûmes, vous crûtes, ils / elles crurent

être

je fus, tu fus, il / elle / on fut, nous fûmes, vous fûtes, ils / elles furent

lire

je lus, tu lus, il / elle / on lut, nous lûmes, vous lûtes, ils / elles lurent

vivre

je vécus, tu vécus, il / elle / on vécut, nous vécûmes, vous vécûtes, ils / elles vécurent

85 Past historic tense of Group 4 *–oir* verbs

It will be remembered, from the presentation of the present tense of this group of verbs, that many of them form that tense in highly irregular ways – see 39. The same applies to the past historic.

As with Group 3 *–re* verbs, some form their past historics in *–i–*, others – the majority – in *–u–*.

Group 4 *–oir* endings of past historic

singular	plural		singular	plural
–is	*–îmes*		*–us*	*–ûmes*
–is	*–îtes*		*–us*	*–ûtes*
–it	*–irent*		*–ut*	*–urent*

86 Group 4 *–oir* verbs with past historic endings in *–i–*

s'asseoir

je m'assis, tu t'assis, il / elle / on s'assit, nous nous assîmes, vous vous assîtes, il / elles s'assirent

voir

je vis, tu vis, il / elle / on vit, nous vîmes, vous vîtes, ils / elles virent

87 Group 4 *–oir* verbs with past historic endings in *–u–*

avoir

j'eus, tu eus, il / elle / on eut, nous eûmes, vous eûtes, ils / elles eurent

devoir

je dus, tu dus, il / elle / on dut, nous dûmes, vous dûtes, ils / elles durent

falloir

il fallut

pleuvoir

il plut

pouvoir

je pus, tu pus, il / elle / on put, nous pûmes, vous pûtes, ils / elles purent

recevoir

je reçus, tu reçus, il / elle / on reçut, nous reçûmes, vous reçûtes, ils / elles reçurent

savoir

je sus, tu sus, il / elle / on sut, nous sûmes, vous sûtes, ils / elles surent

valoir

je valus, tu valus, il / elle / on valut, nous valûmes, vous valûtes, ils / elles valurent

vouloir

je voulus, tu voulus, il / elle / on voulut, nous voulûmes, vous voulûtes, ils / elles voulurent

Past anterior tense

88 General comments
This is the least common of the indicative tenses and is only used in conjunction with the past historic, itself very uncommon in spoken French and in informal writing – see 133.

89 Formation
The past anterior tense is formed by combining the past historic tense of **avoir** or **être** with the past participle of the verb.

90 Examples of Group 1–4 verbs
Group 1
porter

j'eus porté, nous eûmes porté

aller

je fus allé(e), nous fûmes allé(e)s

Group 2
finir

j'eus fini, nous eûmes fini

partir

je fus parti(e), nous fûmes parti(e)s

Group 3
vendre

j'eus vendu, nous eûmes vendu

descendre

je fus descendu(e), nous fûmes descendu(e)s

Group 4
recevoir

j'eus reçu, nous eûmes reçu

pouvoir

j'eus pu, nous eûmes pu

SUBJUNCTIVE MOOD

Present subjunctive tense

91 Formation
The present subjunctive is normally formed by taking the third person plural form of the present indicative tense, deleting the ending **–ent** and adding the appropriate endings.
Obtaining the stem –

portent → port–, finissent → finiss–, courent → cour–, vendent → vend–, reçoivent → reçoiv–

The endings are

singular	plural
–e	*–ions*
–es	*–iez*
–e	*–ent*

Note that the usual stem variations apply according to the ending added.

92 Group 1 examples of the present subjunctive
porter

je porte, tu portes, il/elle/on porte, nous portions, vous portiez, ils/elles portent

appeler

j'appelle, nous appelions

jeter

je jette, nous jetions

acheter

j'achète, nous achetions

mener

je mène, nous menions

espérer

j'espère, nous espérions

commencer

je commence, nous commencions

manger

je mange, nous mangions

93 Group 1 verb which diverges from the normal pattern –
aller

j'aille, tu ailles, il / elle / on aille, nous allions, vous alliez, ils / elles aillent

94 Group 2 examples of the present subjunctive
finir

je finisse, tu finisses, il / elle / on finisse, nous finissions, vous finissiez, ils / elles finissent

courir

je coure, tu coures, il / elle / on coure, nous courions, vous couriez, ils / elles courent

cueillir

je cueille, nous cueillions

venir

je vienne, nous venions

95 Group 3 examples of the present subjunctive
vendre

je vende, tu vendes, il / elle / on vende, nous vendions, vous vendiez, ils / elles vendent

rompre

je rompe, nous rompions

battre

je batte, nous battions

croire

je croie, nous croyions

conduire

je conduise, nous conduisions

écrire

j'écris, nous écrivions

dire

je dise, nous disions

96 Group 3 verbs which diverge from the normal pattern
être

je sois, tu sois, il / elle / on soit, nous soyons, vous soyez, ils / elles soient

faire

je fasse, tu fasses, il / elle / on fasse, nous fassions, vous fassiez, ils / elles fassent

97 Group 4 examples of the present subjunctive
recevoir

je reçoive, tu reçoives, il / elle / on reçoive, nous recevions, vous receviez, ils / elles reçoivent

voir

je voie, tu voies, il / elle / on voie, nous voyions, vous voyiez, ils / elles voient

devoir

je doive, tu doives, il / elle / on doive, nous devions, vous deviez, ils / elles doivent

98 Group 4 verbs which diverge from the normal pattern
avoir

j'aie, tu aies, il / elle / on ait, nous ayons, vous ayez, ils / elles aient

pouvoir

je puisse, tu puisses, il / elle / on puisse, nous puissions, vous puissiez, ils / elles puissent

savoir

je sache, tu saches, il/elle/on sache, nous sachions, vous sachiez, ils/elles sachent

vouloir

je veuille, tu veuilles, il/elle/on veuille, nous voulions, vous vouliez, ils/elles veuillent

Imperfect subjunctive tense

99 Formation and usage

The imperfect subjunctive is extremely rare in everyday usage – see 145. When it occurs, it is normally the third person singular form that is found.

It is normally formed by taking the first person singular form of the past historic tense, deleting the last letter and adding the appropriate endings.

Obtaining the stem –

portai → porta–, finis → fini–, courus → couru–, vendis → vendi–, reçus → reçu–

The endings are

singular	plural
–sse	*–ssions*
–sses	*–ssiez*
–^t	*–ssent*

Note that for the third person singular a circumflex accent is added to the vowel of the stem.

100 Examples of the imperfect subjunctive
Group 1
porter

je portasse, tu portasses, il/elle portât, nous portassions, vous portassiez, ils/elles portassent

aller

j'allasse, tu allasses, il/elle/on allât, nous allassions, vous allassiez, ils/elles allassent

Group 2
finir

je finisse, tu finisses, il/elle/on finît, nous finissions, vous finissiez, ils/elles finissent

courir

je courusse, tu courusses, il/elle/on courût, nous courussions, vous courussiez, ils/elles courussent

Group 3
vendre

je vendisse, tu vendisses, il/elle/on vendît, nous vendissions, vous vendissiez, ils/elles vendissent

être

je fusse, tu fusses, il/elle/on fût, nous fussions, vous fussiez, ils/elles fussent

Group 4
recevoir

je reçusse, tu reçusses, il/elle/on reçût, nous reçussions, vous reçussiez, ils/elles reçussent

avoir

j'eusse, tu eusses, il/elle/on eût, nous eussions, vous eussiez, ils/elles eussent

pouvoir

je pusse, tu pusses, il/elle/on pût, nous pussions, vous pussiez, ils/elles pussent

Perfect and pluperfect subjunctive tenses

101 Formation
The perfect subjunctive is formed by combining the present subjunctive of the auxiliary verbs **avoir** or **être** with the past participle of the verb, and the pluperfect subjunctive similarly by combining the imperfect subjunctive of the auxiliary verbs **avoir** or **être** with the past participle of the verb.

102 Examples of Group 1–4 verbs
Group 1
j'aie porté, j'eusse porté

Group 2
j'aie fini, j'eusse fini

Group 3
j'aie vendu, j'eusse vendu

j'aie été, j'eusse été

Group 4
j'aie reçu, j'eusse reçu

j'aie eu, j'eusse eu

Pronominal verbs

103 Pronominal verbs

A **pronominal verb** is one which is accompanied by an unstressed object pronoun (see 208) in all its forms. The verbs are conjugated in exactly the same way as non-pronominal verbs – those ending in *–er* are conjugated like other verbs ending in *–er* with the same qualifications as apply to the latter (subgroups); and the same applies to the other groups of verbs. The pronouns are *me, te, se* (for third person singular and plural), *nous, vous*.

Present tense

Group 1
se lever = *to get up*

je me lève, tu te lèves, il / elle / on se lève, nous nous levons, vous vous levez, ils / elles se lèvent

Group 2
se souvenir = *to remember*

je me souviens, tu te souviens, il / elle / on se souvient, nous nous souvenons, vous vous souvenez, ils / elles se souviennent

Group 3
se plaindre = *to complain*

je me plains, tu te plains, il / elle / on se plaint, nous nous plaignons, vous vous plaignez, ils / elles se plaignent

Group 4
s'asseoir = *to sit down*

je m'assieds, tu t'assieds, il / elle / on s'assied, nous nous asseyons, vous vous asseyez, ils / elles s'asseyent

104 Compound tenses

The major difference between pronominal and non-pronominal verbs occurs in the area of compound tense formation. Whereas the majority of non-pronominal verbs use *avoir* as their auxiliary when they form their compound tenses (see 63, 64), and only a small minority do not, all pronominal verbs without exception use *être* for their compound tenses –

se lever – je me suis levé(e)
se souvenir – je me suis souvenu(e)
se plaindre – je me suis plaint(e)
s'asseoir – je me suis assis(e)

105 Agreement of past participles

The fact that the compound tenses of pronominal verbs are conjugated with *être* and not *avoir* has consequences for the agreement of the past participles – see 64. However, the situation is not quite so straightforward as with non-pronominal verbs conjugated with *être*. Agreement depends upon the syntactic status of the object pronoun – whether it is direct object or indirect object. In the former case, agreement occurs; in the latter it does not. It is important, therefore, to interpret the value of the pronouns correctly.

106 The variable values of reflexive pronouns – how to interpret the pronouns

The pronouns that are used in conjunction with pronominal verbs have a number of values.

1 They may be direct objects

The pronoun is directly affected by the action of the verb –

je me lave = *I get washed, I wash myself*

However, at times the action exerted by the verb is less obvious –

je me couche = *I go to bed*

je me suis assis = *I sat down*

elle s'est promenée = *she went for a walk*

In all these cases, in compound tenses, the past participle agrees with the subject of the verb.

2 They may be indirect objects

In this case the pronoun is not directly affected by the action of the verb, and no agreement occurs –

je me suis dit que . . . = *I said to myself that . . .*

je me lave les mains = *I am washing my hands*

– here **les mains** is the direct object, what is being washed; the indirect object indicates that the hands belong to the subject (see 257).

3 They may be used reflexively

In such circumstances the pronouns indicate that the subjects are doing something to themselves. This applies to all the previous examples given in *1* and *2*.

je me lave = *I wash myself*

je me couche = *I put myself to bed*

Elle se croyait enceinte = *she thought she was pregnant* (literally *she thought herself pregnant*)

4 They may be used without a reflexive value

The pronoun has no independence from the verb, and the verb and pronoun constitute a single semantic entity –

s'abstenir = *to abstain*, ***s'en aller*** = *to go away*, ***se douter*** = *to suspect*, ***s'endormir*** = *to go to sleep*, ***s'évanouir*** = *to faint*, ***se méfier*** = *to mistrust*, ***se repentir*** = *to repent*

In all these cases, in compound tenses, the past participle agrees with the subject of the verb.

5 They may have a reciprocal value

The pronoun is used to convey the fact that several subjects are doing the same thing to each other.

The pronoun may be direct or indirect object –
Direct object –

s'admirer = *to admire each other*, ***s'aimer*** = *to love each other*, ***se détester*** = *to hate each other*, ***se regarder*** = *to look at each other*

Indirect object –

se dire (la vérité) = *to tell each other (the truth)*, ***s'écrire*** = *to write to each other*, ***s'envoyer (un mail)*** = *to send each other (an e-mail)*, ***se raconter (des histoires)*** = *to tell each other (stories)*

A consequence of this is that certain verbs may be ambiguous in interpretation, sometimes being reflexive, sometimes reciprocal.

Examples
se connaître
in the singular a verb like ***se connaître*** is reflexive – ***je me connais*** = *I know (= understand) myself* –

but in the plural, it may be used

1 reciprocally – ***ils se connaissent*** = *they know each other* or
2 reflexively – ***ils se connaissent*** = *they know (= understand) themselves*.

se poser
The same would apply to ***se poser des questions*** – ***ils se posent des questions*** = *they ask each other questions* or *they ask themselves questions*.

En Afrique, la nourriture, c'est culturel. Les maris ne se posent pas la question de savoir si leur épouse cuisine bien = *in Africa food is a cultural matter. Husbands don't ask themselves whether their wife is a good cook*

se dire

1 ***Les analystes se sont dits déçus par le résultat net du troisième trimestre*** = *the analysts declared themselves disappointed by the net result of the third term*

2 ***Les analystes se sont dit des histoires pour égayer les résultats décevants*** = *the analysts told each other stories to enliven the disappointing results*

In 1 the analysts are describing themselves (direct object) as disappointed; in 2 they are telling stories (direct object) to themselves (indirect object).

A way of avoiding this potential ambiguity is to add the expression *l'un l'autre* in the appropriate form (for number and gender) in order to reinforce the reciprocal value –

Les hommes politiques se sont félicités d'avoir réussi leur campagne = *the politicians congratulated themselves on the success of their campaign*

Les hommes politiques se sont félicités les uns les autres d'avoir réussi leur campagne = *the politicians congratulated each other on the success of their campaign*

Sophie et Jessica se sont maquillées = *Sophie and Jessica made themselves up / put their make-up on*

Sophie et Jessica se sont maquillées l'une l'autre = *Sophie and Jessica made each other up / put each other's make-up on*

6 As an alternative to the passive voice

The pronominal form of many verbs may be used instead of or to avoid the passive voice – see 114.

Le français se parle au Québec = *French is spoken in Quebec*

Il est comptable – ça se voit bien = *he's an accountant, that can easily be seen (= that's obvious)*

Cette expression ne s'emploie plus = *that expression is no longer used*

Cette plante ne se trouve que dans très peu de jardins = *this plant is only found in a few gardens*

107 Occasional difficulty in deciding whether the pronoun is direct or indirect object

It is not always immediately clear, especially for an English speaker who tries to translate the French pronominal verb directly into English, whether the object pronoun is indirect or direct. Sometimes a moment's reflexion is necessary to establish which pronoun is involved; at other times, in order to grasp the relationship between the pronoun and the verb, mental gymnastics are required, as some of the examples quoted above illustrate.

The case of ***se souvenir*** = *to remember* and ***se rappeler*** = *to remember*

As far as ***se souvenir*** = *to remember* (see below) is concerned, the ***se*** is direct object, but, in the case of ***se rappeler*** = *to remember*, it is indirect object – the test here is that ***se souvenir*** is followed by ***de***, so that what is remembered depends upon a preposition, consequently making the ***se*** direct object (= *I remind myself*); whereas in the case of ***se rappeler*** what is remembered is the direct object and consequently the pronoun, as with ***se laver*** earlier, indicates who is being reminded (= *I recall to myself (?)*).

Elle s'est souvenue de mon anniversaire but ***elle s'est rappelé mon anniversaire*** = *she remembered my birthday*

If the pronominal verb is followed by ***de***, the pronoun is treated as a direct object.

108 The agreement in compound tenses of pronominal verbs with direct objects and those with indirect objects

1 Perfect tense of pronominal verbs with a direct object pronoun
se laver

je me suis lavé / lavée, tu t'es lavé / lavée, il s'est lavé, elle s'est lavée, nous nous sommes lavés / lavées, vous vous êtes lavé / lavée / lavés / lavées, ils se sont lavés, elles se sont lavées

Other examples –

s'asseoir, s'attaquer = *to attack,* *se baigner* = *to have a swim,* *se battre* = *to fight,* *se blesser* = *to hurt yourself,* *se cacher* = *to hide,* *se coucher* = *to go to bed,* *s'étendre* = *to stretch out,* *s'habiller* = *to get dressed,* *s'installer* = *to settle down,* *se lever,* *se mettre debout* = *to stand up,* *se mettre en route* = *to set out,* *se promener,* *se raser* = *to get shaved,* *se retrouver* = *to turn up,* *se rouler* = *to roll, to wrap yourself up*

2 Perfect tense of reflexive verbs with an indirect object pronoun
se rendre compte = *to realise*

je me suis rendu compte, tu t'es rendu compte, il / elle s'est rendu compte, nous nous sommes rendu compte, vous vous êtes rendu compte, ils / elles se sont rendu compte

Other examples –

s'admettre = *to admit,* *se demander* = *to wonder,* *se dire* = *to say to yourself,* *s'écrire* = *to write to yourself,* *se parler* = *to talk to yourself,* *se reprocher* = *to reproach yourself,* and all examples where an action is being undertaken on part of the body – *se brosser les dents* = *to brush your teeth,* *se casser la jambe* = *to break a leg,* *se frotter les mains* = *to rub your hands,* *se laver le visage* = *to wash your face*

For agreement of past participles with a direct preceding object, see 214.

109 Verbs that are always pronominal and those that are sometimes pronominal

It will have been clear from the above sections that certain verbs are always pronominal, whereas others sometimes are and sometimes are not. Most non-pronominal verbs may on occasions be used pronominally.

A small selection of verbs which are always pronominal in form –

s'abstenir = *to refrain,* *s'en aller* = *to go away,* *se blottir* = *to huddle up,* *s'évanouir* = *to faint,* *se réfugier* = *to take refuge,* *se souvenir* = *to remember*

A small selection of verbs which have pronominal and non-pronominal forms –

cacher = *to hide* (an object) – *se cacher* = *to hide (yourself)*
laver = *to wash* – *se laver* = *to get washed*
lever = *to raise up* – *se lever* = *to get up*
nourrir = *to feed* – *se nourrir* = *to feed yourself*
promener = *to take for a walk* – *se promener* = *to go for a walk*
raser = *to shave* – *se raser* = *to have a shave*

Voice

110 Active and Passive Voice

In simple terms, in the case of verbs in the **active voice**, the subject of the verb performs the action indicated by the verb.

In the case of verbs in the **passive voice**, the subject of the verb undergoes the action indicated by the verb – the object of an active verb becomes the subject of a passive verb –

Le ministre a manipulé l'opinion publique = *the minister manipulated public opinion* →

L'opinion publique a été manipulée par le ministre = *public opinion has been manipulated by the minister*

Sa femme le domine = *his wife dominates him* →

Il est dominé par sa femme = *he's dominated by his wife*

111 Restrictions on conversion from active to passive voice

Unlike English, where an indirect object may be transformed into the subject of a passive verb (eg *his girlfriend gave **him** the CD for his birthday* → ***he** was given the CD for his birthday by his girlfriend*), in French only direct objects can be so used. Indirect objects cannot become the subject of a verb in the passive voice.

112 Formation of the passive voice

The passive is formed by combining the past participle of the verb with the appropriate tense of the auxiliary verb ***être***. The past participle agrees with the subject of the verb.

The conjugation of ***porter*** in the passive voice –

porter
present tense passive –

je suis porté / e, tu es porté / e, il / on est porté, elle est portée, nous sommes portés / es, vous êtes porté / e / s / es, ils sont portés, elles sont portées

imperfect tense passive –

j'étais porté / e, tu étais porté / e, il / on était porté, elle était portée, nous étions portés / es, vous étiez porté / e / s / es, ils étaient portés, elles étaient portées

perfect tense passive –

j'ai été porté / e, tu as été porté / e, il / on a été porté, elle a été portée, nous avons été portés / es, vous avez été porté / e / s / es, ils ont été portés, elles ont été portées

future tense passive –

je serai porté / e, tu seras porté / e, il / on sera porté, elle sera portée, nous serons portés / es, vous serez porté / e / s / es, ils seront portés, elles seront portées

pluperfect tense passive –

j'avais été porté/e, tu avais été porté/e, il/on avait été porté, elle avait été portée, nous avions été portés/es, vous aviez été porté/e/s/es, ils avaient été portés, elles avaient été portées

The other tenses, subjunctive as well as indicative, are formed according to the same pattern.

113 Examples of the passive voice

Deux médecins de Palerme sont soupçonnés d'avoir soigné le parrain de Cosa Nostra = *two doctors from Palermo are suspected of having treated the godfather of Cosa Nostra*

Un sondage a été réalisé au mois de septembre = *a survey was carried out in September*

Ce mois-ci vous serez soulagée d'ajouter le mot « fin » à votre manuscrit = *this month you'll be relieved to add the word 'finished' to your manuscript*

La certitude d'étre trompé gagne du terrain = *the certainty of being cheated on gains ground*

Un accord a été passé entre la présidence du tribunal de Paris et le barreau = *an agreement has been signed between the president of the Paris court and the bar*

Les deux méthodes donnent d'excellents résultats, à condition qu'elles soient exécutées par de vrais pros = *the two methods give excellent results, provided that they are carried out by real professionals*

Un peu d'activité s'impose, car, même si votre capital beauté n'est pas encore entamé, il vaut mieux être prévoyante = *a little activity is called for, because even if your beauty capital hasn't yet been opened up, it's better to think ahead*

Votre patron n'est pas obligé d'embaucher, même si c'est l'esprit de la loi = *your boss isn't obliged to take on any extra staff, even if it's in the spirit of the law*

114 Avoiding and using the passive voice

In relative terms English uses more passive voice constructions than French. This is because French has a number of strategies that are regularly employed as alternatives to the passive voice. In other words, where a passive voice would be used in English, French sometimes uses a different construction. There are two strategies that are commonly used as alternatives to the passive voice in situations where, in English, a passive would be used.

1 The impersonal pronoun *on*

On is much more common as a pronoun in French than its equivalent *one* is in English – see 226 –

On dit que = *it is said that*

On croit que = *it is thought that*

On lui a réparé sa voiture = *his car has been repaired*

2 The pronominal form of the verb

L'ordinateur s'est inexorablement intégré dans le paysage professionnel = *computers have inexorably become an integral part of the professional scene*

Une prise de conscience qui s'accompagne d'une sacrée période de maturation = *a pang of conscience accompanied by a jolly good period of growing up*

Nous pensons que ce retard s'explique par une offre inacceptable = *we think that this delay may be explained by an unacceptable offer*

See also 106.

Using the passive voice

As the examples in 113 have shown, despite the comment that French avoids the passive voice, there are many instances where the passive voice is used. These tend to be in technical and semi-technical circumstances – in manuals, brochures, reports, official documents and so on.

Exercises

1 **Formation des verbes**
Pour chacun des verbes suivants, donnez la forme qu'on vous demande – indicatif

le présent

première personne du singulier –

courir, craindre, cueillir, devoir, écrire, être, lire, savoir, venir, vouloir

deuxième personne du pluriel –

aller, avoir, commencer, finir, manger, partir, pouvoir, prendre, voir, valoir

l'imparfait

deuxième personne du singulier –

avoir, être, faire, finir, manger, perdre, recevoir, rire, valoir, vendre

troisième personne du pluriel –

aller, commencer, conduire, courir, devoir, jeter, porter, recevoir, savoir, vouloir

le futur

troisième personne du singulier –

acheter, aller, boire, courir, être, pouvoir, savoir, venir, voir, vouloir

première personne du pluriel –

aller, commencer, devoir, envoyer, jeter, mener, mourir, partir, tenir, vendre

le passé simple

troisième personne du singulier –

aller, boire, croire, cueillir, être, porter, finir, pouvoir, savoir, vouloir

deuxième personne du pluriel –

avoir, conduire, courir, devoir, écrire, faire, lire, mener, mettre, vivre

subjonctif

le présent

troisième personne du singulier

avoir, dire, être, faire, finir, jeter, porter, savoir, valoir, vouloir

deuxième personne du pluriel

aller, boire, devoir, être, faire, manger, mettre, pouvoir, vendre, vouloir

l'imparfait

troisième personne du singulier

aller, avoir, boire, commencer, être, faire, finir, mener, savoir, vouloir

première personne du pluriel

acheter, courir, devoir, être, faire, partir, porter, pouvoir, vendre, vouloir

2 **Les auxiliaires**

Avec quel auxiliaire est-ce que les verbes suivants se conjuguent?

aller, arriver, s'asseoir, dire, falloir, mourir, naître, porter, pouvoir, recevoir, venir

3 **Les verbes pronominaux**

Donnez les formes des verbes pronominaux suivants qu'on vous demande; en plus donnez les pronoms sujets –

troisième personne masculine du singulier et deuxième personne du pluriel du présent de l'indicatif –

s'asseoir, se laver, se lever, se plaindre, se souvenir

troisième personne féminine du singulier et deuxième personne masculine du pluriel du passé composé de l'indicatif –

s'en aller, s'asseoir, se bercer, se laver, se lever, se méfier, se plaindre, se porter, se rappeler, se souvenir

4 **Réécrivez les passages suivants en transposant les verbes actifs en leur équivalent passif; le cas échéant, faites d'autres modifications pour garder le sens de la phrase –**

a. *On peut utiliser le tableau électronique interactif comme un tableau normal – le stylet remplace la craie. On peut également y projeter des infos prises directement sur internet où on peut trouver cartes, photos, graphiques; on peut illustrer les cours facilement.*

b. *Seule une solution associant robustesse et maîtrise totale de votre consommation peut vous satisfaire.*

c. *C'est aussi un conseiller qui vous accompagne à chaque étape de votre projet.*

d. *La clémentine confite, on la trouvera chez les confiseurs.*

Chapter 2 *Verbs: 2*

USING VERBS

Mood

The imperative mood

115 The imperative

The imperative is used to give commands and is, therefore, very common in everyday speech –

sit up, listen, don't do that, forget it

Certain sets of circumstances are very prone to generate large numbers of orders, which are then conveyed in the imperative mood – parents to children (and vice versa), teachers to students, in the military, in arguments, in making arrangements. The written medium makes less extensive use of the imperative mood – but it is common in manuals, recipes, instructions on products, etc.

116 The restricted forms of the imperative

The imperative is the verb reduced to its minimum proportions – no subject pronouns to use, used only with reference to the present time and with a very limited range of persons; in addition, sentences containing an imperative are often only one word long.

117 The forms of the imperative

The imperative derives mainly from the 'you'-forms of the present tense of the verb, second person singular and second person plural; less frequently an imperative based on the first person plural occurs.

118 Forming the imperative

For Group 1 –er verbs

The singular imperative is derived from the second person singular forms of the present tense, forms ending in **–es** or **–as** (***aller – vas***) (see 16), with the final **–s** deleted. This **–s** is reinstated in certain situations – see below.

The plural imperative is derived from the second person plural forms and the first person plural forms with no adjustment.

For Groups 2 –ir, 3 – re and 4 –oir verbs

The singular imperative is derived from the second person singular forms of the present tense without adjustment (see 23, 30, 40–42). The ***ouvrir*** subgroup forms its singular imperative like a Group 1 **–er** verb.

The plural imperative is derived from the second person plural forms and the first person plural forms without adjustment.

Examples
Group 1 *–er* verbs

porter – porte, portez, portons
jeter – jette, jetez, jetons
manger – mange, mangez, mangeons
aller – va, allez, allons

The *–s* that has been deleted to form the imperative is reinstated when the imperative is followed by the pronouns *en* and *y* –

Vas-y! = *off you go!*

Parles-en! = *talk about it!*

Group 2 *–ir* verbs

finir – finis, finissez, finissons
courir – cours, courez, courons
ouvrir – ouvre, ouvrez, ouvrons
venir – viens, venez, venons

Group 3 *–re* verbs

vendre – vends, vendez, vendons
dire – dis, dites, disons
écrire – écris, écrivez, écrivons
faire – fais, faites, faisons
mettre – mets, mettez, mettons

Group 4 *–oir* verbs

recevoir – reçois, recevez, recevons

119 Exceptions
There is a very small number of exceptions to the imperative-forming principle outlined above. However, the verbs involved are common ones –

avoir – aie, ayez, ayons
être – sois, soyez, soyons
savoir – sache, sachez, sachons
vouloir – veuille, veuillez, veuillons

120 Forming the imperative of pronominal verbs
The forms of the verb itself are created in exactly the same way as for non-pronominal verbs. The difference between the pronominal and non-pronominal imperative forms is that the former use the stressed form of the singular reflexive pronoun after the verb in positive situations, but unstressed forms of the pronoun before the verb in negative situations.

Positive

se cacher – cache-toi, cachez-vous, cachons-nous
s'asseoir – assieds-toi, asseyez-vous, asseyons-nous
se taire – tais-toi, taisez-vous, taisons-nous

Negative

ne pas se cacher – ne te cache pas, ne vous cachez pas, ne nous cachons pas
ne pas s'asseoir – ne t'assieds pas, ne vous asseyez pas, ne nous asseyons pas
ne pas se taire – ne te tais pas, ne vous taisez pas, ne nous taisons pas

121 Meaning of the imperative

The meaning of the second person forms is clear – a direct order –

cours, courez = *run*
mange, mangez = *eat up*
assieds-toi, asseyez-vous = *sit down*

The meaning of the first person plural form is less peremptory and is equivalent to English *let's* . . .

mangeons ensemble = *let's eat together*

asseyons-nous = *let's sit down*

122 Alternatives to the imperative

1 The infinitive used to give an order

In the written medium, particularly on notices, in manuals and instructions, it is common for the infinitive to be used to give an order. The impression given is of a more polite, moderated command –

Ne pas marcher sur l'herbe = *don't walk on the grass*

Tenir au frais = *keep in a cool place*

Battre les oeufs avec la crème = *whisk the eggs and cream together*

2 Using défense to express a negative command

In negative situations, usually associated with public notices, the word *défense* (= *prohibition*) is sometimes used –

Défense d'afficher = *stick no bills*

Défense de se pencher dehors = *do not lean out*

3 The future used to give an order

See 135.

4 Using voiloir to attenuate the imperative

See 163.

123 The imperative combined with object pronouns
See 212.

Indicative and subjunctive moods

124 The indicative and subjunctive moods and tenses

Indicative mood
Simple
Present
Imperfect
Past historic
Future
Conditional

Compound
Perfect
Pluperfect
Future perfect
Conditional perfect
Past anterior
Double compound

Subjunctive mood
Simple
Present
Imperfect
Compound
Perfect
Pluperfect

Present tense

125 Uses – 1: present moment; 2: habitual time; 3: universal time

Je mange is equivalent to English *I eat (my lunch at one o'clock)* and *I'm eating (my lunch as quickly as possible)*.

1 To describe events happening at the present moment
These fall into three main categories

Those relating to the present moment proper

L'anniversaire de Johnny Halliday est sans aucun doute l'événement musical de l'année = *Johnny Halliday's birthday is without doubt the musical event of the year*

La France dépense pour sa défense moins du dixième du budget militaire américain = *France's defence expenditure is less than a tenth of America's military budget*

Les récents feux de forêt montrent qu'il ne faut pas relâcher l'effort pour trouver une solution à ce problème majeur du sud de l'Europe = *the recent forest fires prove that it is vital not to relax efforts to find a solution to this very serious problem affecting southern Europe*

2 Those relating to habitual time

Voilà la clef du mystère – ce littoral exquis apparaît couvert deux jours sur trois par un brouillard à couper au couteau = *here's the key to the mystery – this exquisite coast-line is covered for two days out of three with a fog you could cut with a knife*

Elle rentre à dix-sept heures tous les jours = *she comes home every day at five o'clock*

Son menu-carte change toutes les trois semaines et les idées fusent ici et là = *he changes the menu every three weeks, and new ideas spurt out everywhere*

3 Those relating to universal time

Toute réussite est un travail d'équipe = *every success story is a matter of team effort*

Deux et deux font quatre = *two plus two makes four*

Une ville a besoin d'un système de transports auquel on peut faire confiance = *a town needs a transport system that inspires confidence*

Avec l'âge, on apprend que les autres ont peut-être raison, même si l'on est certain qu'ils ont tort = *with age, we learn that other people may perhaps be right, even if we're sure they're wrong*

126 4: Marking continuous time

In English it is possible to distinguish between a simple present tense (*I wonder if we should go*) and a continuous present tense (*I'm wondering if we should go*). French does not have this contrast.

Je me demande = *I wonder* and *I'm wondering*

However, if it is desirable for a French speaker to stress the length of time an action or event is taking, a special construction exists, involving *(être) en train de –*

A ce moment elle est en train de considérer toutes les possibilités pour sa carrière = *at the moment she's thinking about all her career possibilities*

Il est en train de dresser des plans pour l'avenir = *he's (in the process of) drawing up plans for the future*

127 Other uses of the present tense – 5: future; 6: past

5 To refer to the near and not-so-near future

Je viens te voir ce soir = *I'll come and see you this evening*

Nous arrivons dans un instant = *we'll be arriving in a moment*

On part pour le Vietnam la semaine prochaine = *we're leaving for Vietnam next week*

See also the use of **aller** 136.

6 To refer to past time

This use of the present tense is known as the historic present, and is very common in journalism and general literature, often to add a dramatic note or note of immediacy to the recounting of an incident.

Au 18e siècle les riches commencent à partir en vacances. Pour eux la plage est une sorte de salon avec vue sur mer. On vient pour l'air marin et la beauté des sites = in the eighteenth century, the rich began to go away on holiday. For them the beach was a sort of lounge with a sea-view. They went for the sea air and the beauty of the locations

Après son arrivée en France, elle trouve un poste de jeune fille au pair. Elle accepte pour le salaire, 700 euros par mois = after she arrived in France, she found a job as an au pair. She took it because of the pay – 700 euros a month

Past tenses

128 Past tenses

Three tenses may be used to express events taking place one step back in time from the perspective of the speaker/narrator:

the imperfect, the perfect, the past historic.

When it is a matter of two steps back from the perspective of the speaker/narrator, other tenses may be used:

the pluperfect, the past anterior, the conditional perfect, the double compound.

Imperfect tense

129 Uses –1: duration; 2: interrupted time; 3: description; 4: repeated action

Equivalent to English *I ate my lunch at college every Tuesday, I was eating my lunch when the doorbell rang, I used to eat my lunch with my friends.*

1 To express the duration of time
Son crime? – avoir botté les fesses de deux garnements qui chahutaient dans sa classe = what was his crime? – to have kicked the backside of a couple of tearaways who were making a nuisance of themselves in his class

L'épicier cherchait une plus importante part du marché en important des légumes du Maroc = the grocer was hoping to get a larger share of the market by importing vegetables from Morocco

Les représentants étaient reçus à l'Elysée le 3 décembre = the representatives were received by the President on 3 December

Il était conscient de ce qu'il faisait = he was aware of what he was doing

2 To express a period of time interrupted by an event
La jeune femme a obtenu le droit à un interview, pendant qu'elle dansait avec la vedette = the young woman obtained the right to an interview, while she was dancing with the celeb

Pendant qu'il parlait, les enfants ont ri avec impunité = while he was speaking, the kids laughed with impunity

Le chanteur qui roulait à 201 km/h sur l'autoroute A10, a été arrêté par la police = *the singer who was driving at 201 km an hour on the A10 motorway was arrested by the police*

3 To describe a set of circumstances

J'ai très vite senti que je n'étais pas un Européen, que je n'étais pas un Français, que j'étais un Nègre, c'est tout (Aimé Césaire) = *I soon realised that I wasn't a European, nor a Frenchman, but quite simply a Black*

En latin, il y avait trois genres, en français deux et en anglais seulement un = *Latin had three genders, French two and English only one*

Le document était sans valeur juridique = *the document was without legal value*

4 To express a repeated or habitual action

L'usine produisait une cinquantaine de voitures par jour = *the factory produced about fifty cars a day*

A l'époque, on estimait que beaucoup de conducteurs ignoraient les principes du code de la route = *at that time, it was thought that many drivers did not know the principles of the highway code*

Il naviguait avec aisance dans la société parisienne = *he circulated effortlessly in Parisian society*

Past historic tense

130 Uses

Il mangea is equivalent to English *he ate*, as in

Le Président mangea avec ses invités dans la salle à manger de l'Elysée = *the President had lunch with his visitors in the dining room of the Elysée Palace*

The past historic tense is used to refer to a point of time in the past with no link with or repercussion upon the present.

However, this role may also be played by the perfect tense (see 131). Consequently, it is important to understand the different values of these two competing tenses as far as this usage is concerned.

Usage of the past historic has tended to become restricted to certain situations.

Written French – it is the past tense most often used in fairly formal and formal written French – especially the French of novels, and in some but not all journalism.

Spoken French – its use in spoken (as opposed to written) French is very much confined to very formal situations – speeches, lectures, talks on the radio or television dealing particularly with historical matters.

Using the past historic automatically evokes a formal situation – it is completely inappropriate in normal spoken French.

From a novel –

Marthe haussa les épaules, prit un chandelier et courut au salon. Elle en revint, tenant un dictionnaire d'une main et se mit à lire une définition =

Martha shrugged her shoulders, took a candlestick and ran to the lounge. She came back with a dictionary in one hand and began to read out a definition

From a news magazine

Personne ne jugea bon d'approfondir la question – un comité international fut créé, présidé par Nicolas Nabokov qui usa de sa formidable énergie . . . = *no one thought it wise to go further into the matter – an international committee was formed, with Nicolas Nabokov as chairman who used his extraordinary energy . . .*

Née à Tunis en 1948, elle abandonna ses études de droit pour entrer à FR3 Marseille comme présentatrice = *born in Tunis in 1948, she gave up her law studies to enter FR3 Marseille [a radio station] as a presenter*

Perfect tense

131 Uses –1: past affecting present; 2: past divorced from present

J'ai mangé is equivalent to English *I have eaten (my lunch already), I ate (my lunch early today).*

1 The perfect tense is used to refer to a point of time in the past which has a link with or repercussion upon the present –
Qui a pris plus de 340 fois le Concorde? C'est un certain Pascal Leborgne = *who has flown Concorde more than 340 times? – A certain Pascal Leborgne*

Le défenseur de Nantes a été le symbole français. Très bon avant la mi-temps, il a complètement plongé par la suite = *the Nantes defender was a symbol of France's performance. He was very good in the first half, but faded completely subsequently*

Les ministres des Affaires sociales allemand, japonais et italien l'ont interrogé sur sa méthode = *the German, Japanese and Italian Social Affairs ministers have questioned him on his method*

2 To refer to a point of time in the past with no link with or repercussion upon the present
It is in this usage that the perfect competes with the past historic (see 130). Note that in spoken French, the perfect tense is the normal tense for conveying past time. It is also used in written French, particularly in journalism but also in novels, especially in those written in an informal register. Compare the situation with the past historic, described above.

À 76 ans, Fidel Castro ressort [historic present, see 127] **son légendaire treillis. Il a défilé en tête d'une manifestation contre les sanctions adoptées par l'Union européenne. Au cours d'un discours musclé, il a menacé les diplomates en poste de mesures de rétorsion** = *at 76 Fidel Castro got out his legendary combat fatigues and marched at the head of a demonstration against the sanctions adopted by the EU. In a vigorous speech, he threatened the diplomats in post with retaliatory measures*

Pluperfect tense

132 Uses
Equivalent to English *I had eaten my lunch when my friend joined me*

1 To refer to a point of time in the past that has taken place before another event in the past
(in other words which occurs two stages back in the past from the standpoint of the present)

Elle m'a dit qu'il l'avait suivie pendant deux semaines = *she told me that he had followed her for two weeks*

Le directeur avait décidé de punir les étudiants qui avaient interrompu les cours quand on l'avait appelé pour répondre aux questions d'un journaliste = *the head had decided to punish the students who had interrupted the classes when he was called to answer some questions from a reporter*

Il avait créé de nombreuses émissions de télévision = *he had produced a large number of television broadcasts*

Alessandra Mussolini avait affiché son sens de la famille en se mariant à Predappio, la ville où son père est enterré = *A M had signalled her sense of the family by getting married at P, the town where her father was buried*

Les supporters du président ivoirien ont repris leur harcèlement des troupes françaises qui avaient empêché les forces gouvernementales d'effectuer une percée vers le nord = *supporters of the President of the Ivory Coast have resumed their harassment of French troops, who had prevented the government forces from making a breakthrough towards the north*

2 To refer to a period of time in the past that has taken place before another event in the past
Les Romains avaient occupé la Gaule pendant quelques siècles avant l'invasion des Francs au 5ème siècle = *the Romans had occupied Gaul for several centuries before the invasion of the Franks in the 5th century*

Il est certain qu'avant d'écrire le livre, il avait passé beaucoup de temps à faire les recherches nécessaires = *it's certain that before writing the book he had spent a lot of time in research for it*

Après un bref passage sur TF1, elle était revenue dans le service public pour animer de nombreuses émissions = *after a short time on TF1 [a TV station], she returned to the public service and presented a large number of programmes*

Past anterior tense

133 Uses
Equivalent to English *She called me after I had finished eating*

The past anterior is used only in a very limited set of circumstances. Firstly, it is exclusively a written tense, and secondly it only occurs in subordinate clauses of time, when the tense of the verb of the main clause in the sentence is the past historic. (In other words, it is never found in combination with the perfect tense.)

The most common conjunctions with which it occurs are ***après que*** = *after*, ***aussitôt que*** = *as soon as*, ***avant que*** = *before*, ***dès que*** = *as soon as*, ***lorsque*** = *when*, ***quand*** = *when* (see 465) –

Dès qu'il eut signé le contrat, tout le monde le félicita = *as soon as he had signed the contract, everyone congratulated him*

Après qu'il eut créé sa compagnie en 2002, il commença ses expériences sur les livres électroniques = *after setting up his company in 2002, he began experimenting with electronic books*

Double compound past tense

134 Uses
This tense complements the past anterior – in other words it may be used when the circumstances that dictate the use of the past anterior occur in spoken rather than written French. However, the pluperfect may also be used in these circumstances –

Elle est sortie dès qu'elle a eu reçu (or ***avait reçu***) ***le message de son amie*** = *she went out as soon as she had got the message from her friend*

Quand son ami a eu fini (or ***avait fini***) ***son coke, ils ont quitté le bar ensemble*** = *when her boyfriend had finished his Coke, they left the bar together*

Future tense

135 Uses –1: future; 2: attenuation of imperative
1 To refer to events that will take place in the future
À partir du 29 janvier nous embaucherons une douzaine de nouveaux employés = *on 29 January we will take on a dozen new employees*

Si tu manges moins de frites, tu ne prendras pas tant de poids = *if you eat fewer chips, you won't put on so much weight*

Il ne fait pas de doute que les réformes des retraites finiront par être votées = *there's no doubt that the pension reforms will eventually be approved*

Les médailles leur seront remises par le ministre des affaires étrangères = *the medals will be presented to them by the Minister of Foreign Affairs*

Le Noël du personnel de Matignon n'aura pas lieu comme d'habitude à l'Opéra mais au Musée des Arts forains = *Christmas for the PM's staff will not take place as usual at the Opera but at the Musée des Arts forains*

2 As a means of attenuating the imperative – see 122
Vous ouvrirez la fenêtre, s'il vous plaît = *will you open the window, please?*

Je prendrai un kilo de bananes = *I'll have a kilo of bananas*

136 Other ways of referring to the future
1 By using the present tense – see 127

It should be noted that using the present tense instead of the future implies a less motivated intention –

Je passerai te voir ce soir suggests more determination than *je passe te voir ce soir*

2 By using aller + the infinitive

The use of *aller* + infinitive suggests a stronger likelihood that something will happen

Pour me maintenir en bonne santé, je vais aller à la piscine chaque samedi = *to keep healthy I'm going to go to the pool every Saturday*

Pour expliquer le système, il va utiliser les mots du professeur = *in order to explain the system, he's going to use the words of the professor*

Future perfect tense

137 Use
Equivalent to English *will have (eaten)*, the future perfect tense describes a future event from the standpoint of its completion –

J'espère que dans deux ans nous aurons achevé la rénovation de notre appartement = *I hope that in two years' time we will have completed the refurbishment of our flat*

Il est astucieux – son nouveau tube aura paru juste avant sa prochaine tournée = *he's a cunning so-and-so – his new hit will have been released just before his next tour*

Conditional tense

138 Uses –1: conveying future in reported speech; 2: as corollary of conditional clause; 3: conjecture
1 In reported speech to represent a future tense in direct speech –
Version in direct speech

Elle a dit: « Jamais personne ne viendra me voir maintenant » = *she said, 'No one will ever come and see me now'*

Version in indirect speech

Elle a dit que jamais personne ne viendrait la voir dès ce moment-là = *she said that no one would come and see her from that moment on*

Often there is no verb of speech introducing the reported item –

Ce ne serait point faire oeuvre de justice que de préférer les ténèbres à la lumière = *it wouldn't be acting justly if we preferred darkness to light*

2 In the main clause of a sentence containing a conditional clause
(ie one introduced by *si* – see 458)

Si tu mangeais moins, tu perdrais facilement un kilo = *if you ate less you'd easily lose a couple of pounds*

Leur légitimité serait bien plus forte s'ils s'appliquaient à eux-mêmes les réformes demandées aux autres = *their legitimacy would be much stronger if they applied to themselves the reforms they demand of others*

3 As a means of expressing uncertainty, an hypothesis or conjecture
– a use that does not have an equivalent in English; here a present or past tense is used with a suggestion that the event may not be entirely true –

Chez l'homme le désir serait avant tout visuel = *it is suggested that for men desire is above all visual*

Les trois principaux dirigeants réclameraient deux millions d'euros de dommages = *it's reported that / apparently the three principal directors have put in a claim for two million euros damages*

Cette machine neutraliserait les menaces qui pourraient nous nuire = *this machine, apparently, neutralises threats which might be harmful to us*

Le bégaiement serait trois fois plus fréquent chez les hommes que chez les femmes = *stammering is allegedly three times more common in men than in women*

Suivant certains experts de 7 à 30% des cancers seraient imputables à des facteurs environnementaux = *according to certain experts, from 7 to 30% of cancers are attributable to environmental factors*

Selon un récent rapport, la moitié des fruits, légumes et céréales consommés en France contiendrait des résidus de pesticides = *according to a recent report, half the fruit, vegetables and cereals consumed in France contain pesticide residues*

Conditional perfect tense

139 Uses –1: conveying future perfect in reported speech; 2: hypothesis; 3: conjecture
1 In reported speech to represent a future perfect tense in direct speech:
Version in direct speech

On le lit dans la presse – la compagnie aérienne aura vendu 150 exemplaires de l'Air Bus par 2006 = *it's in the papers – the aviation company will have sold 150 models of the Air Bus by 2006*

Version in indirect speech

On a lu dans la presse que la compagnie aérienne aurait vendu 150 exemplaires de l'Air Bus par 2006 = *we read in the papers that the aviation company would have sold 150 models of the Air Bus by 2006*

2 To refer to events that would have taken place if certain circumstances had been fulfilled

Les performances de l'athlète auraient été beaucoup mieux, s'il avait employé un autre entraîneur expérimenté = *the athlete's performance would have been much better if he had used an experienced trainer*

L'association n'aurait pas pu échapper à la saisie de ses biens sans les subventions des services du Premier ministre = *the organisation would not have been able to avoid having its assets seized if it had not been for the grants made by the Prime Minister's office*

Le porte-avions « Clémenceau » aurait dû se faire démembrer dans un pays éloigné = *the aircraft carrier 'Clémenceau' should have been dismantled in a far-away country*

3 As a means of expressing uncertainty, an hypothesis or conjecture
(see 138) –

Selon notre correspondant, la bombe aurait tué une vingtaine de personnes = *according to our correspondent, the bomb killed about twenty people*

Le maire aurait lâché une vérité qui tournait mal = *apparently the mayor blurted out a truth which caused problems*

En 2003, de 8 à 9% des Français auraient reçu au moins une fois dans l'année une eau dont la teneur en pesticides dépassait la norme = *in 2003, from 8 to 9% of the French population had reportedly been supplied at least once during the year with water that exceeded the norm in pesticide content*

140 Differences in tense usage in French and English
Tense usage is very much the same in the two languages. However, there are a few important differences, in addition to those outlined under the tenses discussed above. They involve

1 Sequence of tenses –
that is to say, in sentences consisting of more than one clause. Although generally, the French pattern is very much the same as in English, there is one notable exception – concerning the future and conditional tenses in time clauses.

2 The use of tenses with *depuis, il y a, voici, voilà*.
3 The use of tenses with *venir de = just*.

141 Differences between French and English use of tenses –1: sequence of tenses
1 Sequence of tenses involving the future and conditional tenses
The problem centres on usage with subordinate clauses of time to refer to future events. In English, the tense of the verb in the subordinate clause in such situations is either present or past, whereas in French a future or conditional tense is used

Future tense in subordinate clause in French where English has present tense –

Quand tu visiteras la galerie, tu seras sans aucun doute impressionné par les sculptures contemporaines = *when you come to the gallery, you will undoubtedly be impressed by the contemporary sculptures*

Vous seconderez le chef de projet aussitôt que vous serez embauché = *you will help the project leader as soon as you are taken on*

Future perfect in subordinate clause in French where English has past tense –

Lorsqu'il aura fait ses preuves comme président, on s'attendra à ce que la compagnie améliore ses performances boursières = *when he has proved himself as managing director, it is to be expected that the company's performance on the Stock Exchange will improve*

Vous serez en relation avec les différents établissements de soin de la région, dès que l'équipe aura été formée = *you will be in contact with the various care providers in the area as soon as the team has been set up*

Conditional tense in subordinate clause in French where English has past tense –

Il m'a demandé de trouver un traducteur de son roman, dès que les revues seraient positifs = *he asked me to find someone to translate his novel as soon as the reviews were positive*

Elle m'avait prié de lui donner un coup de téléphone, quand j'aurais fini ma mémoire = *she asked me to give her a ring when I'd finished my essay*

Conditional perfect tense in subordinate clause in French where English has pluperfect tense –

Elle lui a déclaré qu'elle le ferait quand il l'aurait payée = *she stated that she would do it as soon as he had paid her*

Aussitôt que la démocratie aurait été établie dans les pays de l'Europe de l'Est, on pourrait procéder à l'élargissement de l'Union européenne = *as soon as democracy was established in the countries of eastern Europe, the enlargement of the EU could proceed*

142 Differences between French and English use of tenses –2: *depuis, il y a*

2 The use of tenses with depuis, il y a, voici, voilà

When the present tense of a verb is used in French with ***depuis***, it is equivalent to an English past tense. ***Depuis*** may be translated by *for*, when the emphasis is upon the duration of the time, and by *since* when the emphasis is upon the starting point of the time (see 348) –

duration
Elle est comme ça depuis un an = *she's been like that for a year*

starting point
Elle est comme ça depuis la mort de son chien = *she's been like that since her dog died*

duration
Il est en prison depuis trois ans = *he's been in prison for three years*

starting point
Il est en prison depuis 2002 = *he's been in prison since 2002*

Other expressions can be used in the same way to achieve the same value –

Il y a / voilà / voici trois ans qu'il est en prison = *he's been in prison for three years*

When the imperfect tense of a verb is used with **depuis**, it is equivalent to the English pluperfect tense –

Je l'épiais depuis quelques minutes quand son petit ami est arrivé = *I had been spying on her for some minutes when her boyfriend turned up*

Il était en prison depuis trois ans = *he had been in prison for three years*

Il était en prison depuis 2002 = *he had been in prison since 2002*

The same expressions as mentioned above can again be used to achieve the same value –

Il y a / voilà / voici trois ans qu'il était en prison = *he had been in prison for three years*

143 Differences between French and English use of tenses–3: *venir de*
3 The case of venir de

Venir de is used to correspond to the English adverb *just* in such expressions as *she has just arrived, he had just begun.*

Where English uses a perfect tense, French uses the present tense of **venir de** –

Une note confidentielle vient d'être saisie par la justice = *a confidential note has just been seized by the police*

Il vient d'être nommé capitaine de l'équipe nationale = *he has just been appointed captain of the national team*

Where English uses a pluperfect tense, French uses the imperfect tense of **venir de** –

Elle venait de recevoir le prix de la meilleure actrice romantique, quand elle s'est évanouie = *she had just received the prize for best romantic actress when she fainted*

Début septembre, on a eu un peu de pluie, on venait de se dire que l'année ne serait pas merveilleuse – puis le soleil est apparu et tout a mûri = *it rained a little at the beginning of September, we had just said to ourselves that the year wasn't going to be that special – then the sun came out and everything ripened*

Subjunctive mood

144 When to use the subjunctive

The subjunctive mood of a verb is used only in certain grammatico-semantic situations. By 'grammatico-semantic' is meant

1 that a particular grammatical situation is required (the subjunctive is only used in subordinate clauses)
2 that certain types of meanings are expressed by the verb or expression governing the subordinate clause (eg joy, anger, doubt).

There are also some situations where a choice of indicative or subjunctive mood exists. These two types of situations will be reviewed and illustrated below.

145 Use of tenses in the subjunctive

In practice only two of the four tenses of the subjunctive are commonly used, the present and the perfect. The other two tenses, the imperfect and pluperfect, are restricted to very formal usage and almost exclusively in the written medium. This has implications for the sequence of tenses.

146 Sequence of tenses in the subjunctive

Because only two tenses are available for use in normal circumstances, the sequence of tenses involving the subjunctive mood is different from that involving the indicative.

Present tense – this may be used in a subordinate clause governed by **any** tense in the main clause.

Perfect tense – this is used to correspond to the perfect, pluperfect, future perfect and conditional perfect tenses of the indicative mood.

147 Illustration of the sequence of tenses in the subjunctive
Present tense

Il faut qu'elle parte lundi matin = *she must leave Monday morning*

Il fallait qu'elle parte lundi matin = *she had to leave Monday morning*

Il faudra qu'elle parte lundi matin = *she'll have to leave Monday morning*

Il faudrait qu'elle parte lundi matin = *she ought to leave Monday morning*

Il a fallu qu'elle parte lundi matin = *she had to leave Monday morning*

Il fallut qu'elle parte lundi matin = *she had to leave Monday morning*

Il avait fallu qu'elle parte lundi matin = *she had had to leave Monday morning*

Il aura fallu qu'elle parte lundi matin = *she'll have had to leave Monday morning*

Il aurait fallu qu'elle parte lundi mtin = *she would have had to leave Monday morning*

Perfect tense
Je ne crois pas qu'elle soit partie = *I don't believe she left*

Je ne croyais pas qu'elle soit partie = *I didn't believe she had left*

Il est arrivé avant qu'elle soit partie = *he arrived before she left*

Il était arrivé avant qu'elle soit partie = *he had arrived before she left*

À moins qu'elle ne soit partie, il ne serait pas venu = *unless she had left, he would not have come*

Grammatical circumstances requiring the subjunctive

148 In clauses introduced by a conjunctive expression
The expressions may be grouped in the following way according to their meanings –

although (see 457) –
bien que
Bien que j'aie 40 ans, je viens de rencontrer l'homme de mes rêves = *although I'm forty, I've just met the man of my dreams*

encore que
Encore que vous soyez mal à l'aise dans la compagnie des hommes, vous allez souvent vers eux = although you're uncomfortable in men's company, you often seek them out

malgré que
Malgré qu'elle sache que la nourriture est trop grasse, elle cède aux désirs de ses enfants de manger le fast-food = *although she knows that the food is too fatty, she gives in to her children's wish to eat fast-food*

Malgré que tu sois naturelle, vous gardez encore quelques mauvais réflexes = *despite the fact you're natural, you hang on to a few bad reactions*

quoique
Quoique nous préférions rester au lit le matin, il faut savoir que c'est vers 6 ou 7 heures que le taux de testostérone, qui favorise le développement des muscles, est le plus élevé = *although we prefer staying in bed in the morning, we need to realise that it's around 6 or 7 o'clock that the level of testosterone, which promotes muscle development, is at its highest*

When this group of conjunctive expressions refer to future time, the future tense is used –

Quoique l'agence bénéficiera de ce statut dans deux ans, pour le moment elle doit se contenter de la situation actuelle = *although the agency will benefit from this status in a couple of years' time, for the moment it will have to put up with the present situation*

before (see 465)
avant que
Retrempez-les une heure, avant que la sauce soit préparée = *soak them for another hour before the sauce is prepared*

Avant que Paul soit sorti de ma vie, je n'avais jamais l'occasion de rencontrer de nouvelles personnes = *before Paul walked out of my life, I never had the chance to meet new people*

The verb in the subjunctive may optionally be preceded by an 'expletive' **ne**, which adds nothing to the meaning – the presence of the **ne** suggests a higher register of language –

Quatre jours avant que l'invasion n'ait eu lieu, les pilotes préparaient leurs helicoptères pour une guerre acharnée = *four days before the invasion took place, the pilots were preparing their helicopters for a bitter war*

for fear that
de crainte que
Again the verb in the subjunctive may optionally be preceded by an 'expletive' **ne**, which adds nothing to the meaning – the presence of the **ne** suggests a higher register of language (see 417) –

Ceux qui sont hostiles à une telle loi, le sont de crainte qu'il n'y ait une éclosion d'écoles que l'Etat ne pourra pas contrôler = *those who are opposed to such a law are so for fear that there may be a proliferation of schools the State will not be able to control*

Vous regardez le plat de près, de crainte qu'il ne soit pas du tout à votre goût = *you look at the dish closely, for fear that it isn't to your taste*

de peur que
The same remarks apply here as to **de crainte que**

De peur que le régime artistique soit supprimé, je resterai directeur = *for fear that the artistic régime may be discontinued, I shall stay on as director*

however little
pour autant que
Pour autant qu'il vous ait trompée, vous avez raison de rompre avec lui = *however little he may have cheated on you, you're right to finish with him*

pour peu que
Pour peu que nous regardions la télévision, nous ne pouvons pas éviter son influence = *however little we watch television, we cannot escape its influence*

in order that, so that (see 460)
afin que
Afin que vous soyez épargné le stress, respirez profondément et . . . riez = *in order to be spared stress, breathe deeply and . . . laugh*

de façon que / de façon à ce que
Je crois qu'à ce moment-là j'avais besoin de me déculpabiliser, de façon que je me puisse me convaincre que je le faisais pour le bien-être de notre couple = *I think that at that moment I needed to set aside any guilt so that I could convince myself that I was doing it for the benefit of the two of us*

De façon que l'intérêt qu'il porte à ce sujet soit manifesté clairement, il a décidé de faire un discours télévisé = *so that his interest in this subject may be clearly shown, he decided to make a speech on television*

de manière que / de manière à ce que
Portez les lunettes à verres fumés, de manière qu'elles vous fassent un look d'enfer = *wear tinted glasses so that they give you a fabulous look*

de sorte que
De sorte que vous puissiez avoir une soirée entre amis dans une ambiance chaude, il n'y a qu'une seule adresse = *so that you can have an evening among friends in a warm atmosphere, there's just one address*

pour que
La Ministre de la Recherche redouble d'efforts pour que le site de Cadarache soit préféré à celui proposé par les Japonais = *the Minister of Research is redoubling her efforts so that the Cadarache site is preferred to the one proposed by the Japanese*

Bruxelles attendait ses rajustements pour qu'il se mette en conformité avec les prescriptions de la Commission = *Brussels waited for him to make some readjustments so that he would be in conformity with the Commission's prescriptions*

In the case of ***de façon que***, ***de manière que*** and ***de sorte que***, the subjunctive is used to express intention, not result. For examples of these expressions conveying result, when the indicative, not the subjunctive, is used, see 459.

De façon à ce que and ***de manière à ce que*** are replacing the shorter forms.

not that
non que / non pas que
Elle préfère rester chez elle, non qu'elle ait peur de sortir = *she prefers to stay at home, not that she's afraid of going out*

On dit que la femme française consomme 8, 2 paires de collants chaque année et l'homme 4, 1 slips – non que je sache si c'est vrai ou non! = *they say that a French woman gets through 8.2 pairs of tights a year and a man 4.1 pairs of underpants – not that I know if it's right or not!*

provided that
à condition que
Le syndicalisme fait partie du paysage social, à condition que l'Etat se fasse respecter = *trade unionism is part of the social fabric, provided that the State succeeds in making itself respected*

pourvu que
Pourvu que tu sois là à dix-neuf heures, je peux te conduire à la gare = *provided you're there at 7 o'clock, I'll give you a lift to the station*

sous réserve que
Il acceptait de le reconnaître sous réserve qu'il n'y ait pas de conséquences désagréables = *he was prepared to admit it provided there were no unpleasant consequences*

supposing that (see 458)
à supposé que
À supposé que vous vouliez consulter des bandes-annonces, des critiques ciné-dvd, faites un petit tour sur M6.fr = *supposing you want to consult banner announcements, film and dvd crits, take a stroll through M6.fr*

supposant que
Deux ex-fumeurs sur trois rechutent – supposant que vous vouliez tenir, suivez ce conseil = *two out of three ex-smokers relapse – supposing you want to persevere, take this advice*

supposé que
Supposé que tu aies raison, je n'ose lui écrire = *supposing you're right, I daren't write to her*

unless (see 458)
à moins que
In formal circumstances, **ne** is inserted before the verb; this **ne** has no real semantic value, but underlines the uncertain nature of the assertion (see 417).

Elles parlent d'une peau plus lisse, plus raffermie, à moins qu'elles ne soient victimes d'une campagne de publicité irrésistible = *they speak of a smoother, firmer skin – unless they're victims of an irresistible advertising campaign*

Il doit trouver un nouveau partenaire, à moins que les Américains ne raflent la mise = *he's got to find a new partner, unless the Americans snap up the bait*

until (see 465)
jusqu'à ce que
Jusqu'à ce qu'il y ait des tests antidopage plus probants, les athlètes continueront d'abuser du système = *until there are more conclusive antidrugs tests, athletes will continue to abuse the system*

Respirez doucement jusqu'à ce que votre respiration devienne plus régulière = *breathe gently until your breathing becomes more regular*

Sometimes **ne . . . que** is used as an equivalent to English *until* (see 425) –

Ils ne prendront la ville d'assaut que lorsqu'ils seront certains que les civils l'ont quittée = *they won't attack the town until they're sure the civilians have left*

whether . . . or (see 458)
soit que . . . ou / soit que or que . . . ou – see que below
Soit que tu viennes chez moi ou que je vienne te chercher chez toi, nous aurons assez de temps = *whether you come to my house or I come to yours, we'll have enough time*

Soit que vous perciez votre nombril vous-même, soit que vous demandiez à une amie de le faire, c'est toujours dangereux = *whether you pierce your navel yourself or ask a friend to do it, it's still dangerous*

Que ce soit vrai ou non, je vais continuer = *whether it's true or not, I'm going to carry on*

Qu'il s'agisse de votre vie amoureuse ou de vos liens amicaux, des tensions sont à craindre = *whether it's a matter of your love life or your friendships, tensions are inevitable*

Qu'il soit blanc ou noir n'a aucune importance = *whether he's white or black has no importance whatsoever*

while waiting for
en attendant que
En attendant que le docteur nous dise s'il y avait un problème, mon oncle a quitté son cabinet = *while waiting for the doctor to tell us if there was a problem, my uncle walked out of the surgery*

Vous devenez impatiente en attendant qu'il vous appelle = *you're becoming impatient waiting for him to give you a ring*

without
sans que
Il a continué de se droguer sans qu'on s'en soit remarqué = *he continued taking drugs without anyone noticing*

Les tics pompent beaucoup d'énergie, sans que l'on s'en rende compte = *tics demand a lot of energy, without us realising it*

La compagnie a posé des conditions démentes – une publication en aveugle, sans même que l'éditeur français puisse voir les photos = *the company set some crazy conditions – a blind publication, without the French publisher even being able to see the pictures*

149 In clauses depending upon a verb or expression conveying an emotion
Agreement / permission
after **consentir** = *to consent,* **permettre** = *to allow,* **refuser** = *to refuse*

L'arbitre a permis que le jeu soit différé à cause de la neige = *the referee allowed the game to be postponed because of the snow*

Elle a refusé qu'on vende ses peintures = *she refused to let anyone sell her paintings*

Anxiety / anticipation
after **attendre** = *to wait,* **s'attendre (à ce que)** = *to expect,* **veiller (à ce que)** = *to make sure*

On s'attend à ce que ce PDG hors norme devienne symbole d'une région industrielle qui réussit dans le secteur des technologies de pointe = *it is to be expected that this exceptional managing director will become the symbol of an industrial region successful in the advanced technology sector*

Veillez à ce que les enfants ne rentrent pas trop tard = *make sure the children don't come back too late*

Command / request

after **commander** = *to order,* **demander** = *to ask, to demand,* **exiger** = *to demand,* **insister (pour que)** = *to insist,* **ordonner** = *to order*

Ayant exigé que les recommandations soient votées, le président a passé au prochain point de l'ordre du jour = *having required that the recommendations be voted upon, the chairman passed on to the next item on the agenda*

Il a insisté pour que le transport alternatif ne soit utilisé qu'à titre exceptionnel = *he insisted that alternative transport should only be used in exceptional circumstances*

J'ai été si surprise que je ne demandais même pas qu'il le fasse encore une fois = *I was so surprised that I didn't even ask him to do it again*

Desire

after **aimer** = *to like,* **avoir envie** = *to want,* **désirer** = *to desire,* **préférer** = *to prefer,* **souhaiter** = *to wish,* **tenir (à ce que)** = *to want,* **vouloir** = *to want*

Il a préféré que le club renonce à cette rupture avec la tradition = *he preferred the club to abandon this break with tradition*

Je souhaite qu'elle lance une campagne en faveur des parents pauvres qui élèvent seuls leurs enfants = *my wish is that she will launch a campaign in favour of poor parents who bring up their children alone*

Il veut que ce soit elle qui fasse le premier pas = *he wants her to be the one who makes the first move*

Fear / anger

after **avoir peur** = *to be afraid,* **craindre** = *to fear,* **de crainte** = *for fear,* **de peur** = *for fear,* **être embêtant** = *to be annoying,* **être fâché** = *to be angry,* **être honteux** = *to be disgraceful,* **être mécontent** = *to be unhappy,* **s'indigner** = *to become indignant,* **redouter** = *to fear*

In the case of those verbs expressing fear, like the linked conjunctive expressions **de crainte que, de peur que,** the verb in the subjunctive may optionally be preceded by an 'expletive' **ne**, which adds nothing to the meaning – the presence of the **ne** suggests a higher register of language (see 417).

Il avait peur que son équipe ne soit éliminée de la compétition = *he was afraid that his team would be eliminated from the competition*

Il est embêtant que les technologies avancées aient de temps en temps mené à une perte d'élégance = *it's annoying that advances in technology have from time to time led to a loss in elegance*

J'avais un peu peur qu'elle fasse des comparaisons et qu'elle nous mette des notes = *I was afraid that she would make comparisons and give us marks*

Pleasure

after **être content** = *to be happy,* **être heureux** = *to be happy,* **être ravi** = *to be delighted,* **être satisfait** = *to be satisfied,* **se féliciter** = *to congratulate yourself,* **se réjouir** = *to be delighted*

Je suis contente que cet appareil te convienne = I'm pleased that this camera suits you

Elle s'est réjouie que les gendarmes l'aient arrêté sur présomption de viol = she was delighted that the police had arrested him on suspicion of rape

Nous sommes ravis qu'il ait passé son permis poids lourd afin d'emmener ses chevaux aux concours d'équitation = we're delighted he's taken his heavy vehicle licence test so as to be able to drive his horses to the horse trials

Sadness
after *être désolé* = to be sorry, *être triste* = to be sad, *se plaindre* = to complain, *regretter* = to be sorry

Je suis désolé que tu ne puisses pas venir ce soir = I'm sorry that you can't come this evening

Elle s'est plainte qu'une minorité de spectateurs ait toujours exigé plus de violence = she complained that a minority of viewers always demanded more violence

Je regrette profondément qu'elle ait refusé de me donner son adresse = I deeply regret that she refused to give me her address

Surprise
after *s'étonner* = to be astonished, *être choqué* = to be shocked, *être surpris* = to be surprised

Je m'étonne que tu n'aies pas réussi à ce test = I'm astonished you failed that test

Cela ne me surprend pas que ces innovations aient eu l'effet d'une bombe dans ce secteur conservateur = I'm not surprised that these innovations have had the effect of a bomb in that conservative area

J'étais choqué qu'elle ait mis son pied nu sur mon entrejambe = I was shocked that she put her bare foot on my inner thigh

150 In clauses depending upon a verb or expression conveying avoiding, chance, denial, evaluation, forbidding, (im)possibility, improbability, necessity, uncertainty
Avoiding
after *empêcher* = to prevent, *éviter* = to avoid

Beaucoup de choses vous intéressent, mais vous devez empêcher qu'elles veuillent vous maîtriser = lots of things interest you, but you have to avoid them wanting to dominate you

Pour éviter que la discussion devienne trop houleuse, il est parti furieux = in order to prevent the discussion from becoming too agitated, he stormed out

Chance
after *il arrive* = it happens, *il n'y a aucune chance* = there's no chance, *il y a de grandes chances* = there's every chance, *il y a le danger* = there's the danger, *risquer* = to take the risk

Il arrive de temps en temps que je me sente en faveur de l'euthanasie = *there are times when I feel in favour of euthanasia*

Il arrive parfois que ma copine soit de bonne humeur le matin – je suis euphorique pour toute la journée = *it sometimes happens that my girlfriend is in a good mood in the morning – I feel over the moon all day long*

Il y a de grandes chances que le rhinocéros disparaisse dans quelques décennies = *the chances are high that rhinoceroses will disappear in a few decades*

Denial
after *nier* = *to deny*

La police a nié que la victime n'ait porté qu'un pied de table et non un fusil = *the police denied that the victim was just carrying a table leg and not a rifle*

Elle a surpris tout le monde en niant qu'elle veuille rester vierge jusqu'au mariage = *she surprised everybody by denying that she wanted to remain a virgin till she was married*

Evaluation
after a large number of impersonal expressions – *il y a intérêt (à ce que)* = *it's a good idea*, *il/c'est dommage* = *it's a shame*, *peu importe* = *it scarcely matters*, *ce n'est pas la peine* = *it's not worth the effort*, *il est bon* = *it's worthwhile*, *il est curieux* = *it's strange*, *il est important* = *it's important*, *il est juste* = *it's fair*, *il est normal* = *it's normal*, *il est paradoxal* = *it's paradoxical*, *il est préférable* = *it's preferable*, *il est rare* = *it's rare*, *il semble* = *it seems*

Peu importe que le spectacle ait été annulé – cela ne m'intéressait pas du tout = *it didn't matter that the show was cancelled – I wasn't interested anyway*

Il est important que la compagnie trouve un second souffle = *it's important for the company to get a second wind*

Il est rare que quelqu'un puisse dire que personne ne l'a jamais aimé = *it's rare for anyone to be able to say that no one has ever loved them*

Note that when an indirect object is involved with *il semble* (= *it seems to . . .*), the indicative mood is used –

Il semble qu'on ait proposé trop d'activités extrascolaires aux enfants = *it seems that children have had too many extracurricular activities suggested to them*

Il me semble que certains sports sont susceptibles de mieux correspondre à son tempérament que d'autres = *it seems to me that certain sports are likely to correspond better to her temperament than others*

Forbidding
after *défendre* = *to forbid*, *interdire* = *to ban*

Il avait défendu que sa fille aille aux boîtes de nuit = *he had banned his daughter from going to nightclubs*

(Im)possibility and improbability

after a large number of impersonal expressions – *il y a opportunité* = *the opportunity exists*, *il est (im)possible* = *it's (im)possible*, *il est improbable* = *it's unlikely*, *il est inadmissible* = *it's unacceptable*, *il est invraisemblable* = *it's unlikely*, *il se peut* = *it's possible*, *il est peu probable* = *it's unlikely*

Dès qu'il a bu un coup de trop, il se peut qu'il soit méconnaissable, incontrôlable = *after he's drunk a bit too much, it's possible that he's unrecognisable, uncontrollable*

Il n'est pas impossible qu'il ait passé discrètement et ait échappé à notre surveillance = *it's not impossible that he passed by discreetly and avoided our surveillance*

Il est peu probable que nous gagnions le match samedi = *it's unlikely that we'll win the match on Saturday*

Although *il est peu probable* is followed by the subjunctive, *il est probable* = *it's probable / probably* is not –

Il est probable qu'on trouvera un médicament qui permettra de prolonger la durée de vie de patients atteints d'un cancer de la prostate = *they will probably find a cure which will allow patients suffering from prostate cancer to prolong their lives*

Necessity

after a large number of impersonal expressions – *il est essentiel* = *it's essential*, *il est impératif* = *it's imperative*, *il est inévitable* = *it's inevitable*, *il est naturel* = *it's natural*, *il est nécessaire* = *it's necessary*, *il est temps* = *it's time*, *il faut* = *it's necessary*, *il s'en faut de peu* = *within a little*

Il est essentiel que la coque du bateau soit modifiée après son retour de l'Australie = *it's essential for the boat's hull to be modified after its return from Australia*

Il faut que vous vous interrogiez sur les raisons de votre dépendance = *you must question yourself about the reasons for your dependency*

Il est temps que vous considériez la possibilité de vous remarier = *it's time you considered the possibility of remarriage*

Uncertainty

after a large number of impersonal expressions – *il n'est pas certain* = *it's not certain*, *il est douteux* = *it's doubtful*, *il semble* = *it seems* (but see *Evaluation* above), *il n'est pas sûr* = *it's not sure*, *il n'est pas vrai* = *it's not true*, *douter* = *to doubt* – and the following verbs when used negatively and/or interrogatively – *affirmer* = *to affirm*, *croire* = *to believe*, *dire* = *to say*, *penser* = *to think*, *trouver* = *to find*

Il n'avait jamais pensé qu'il aille falloir voter une loi contre le vagabondage = *he had never thought that it would be necessary to pass a law against vagrancy*

Quoique la fédération de foot ait poursuivi le dépistage sanguin, il n'est pas vrai qu'elle ait aussi réalisé des tests urinaires = *although the football federation undertook blood tests, it is not true that it undertook urine tests as well*

Je ne crois pas que ces rumeurs soient vraies = *I don't believe the rumours are true*

With expressions like ***il n'y a pas de doute que*** = *there's no doubt that*, which imply certainty, the indicative mood is used –

Il n'y a pas de doute que vous encouragerez son initiative en répondant à son sourire = *there's no doubt that you'll encourage her initiative if you respond to her smile*

151 In relative clauses depending upon a superlative formed with *plus* or *moins*

C'est le projet le plus ambitieux que l'université ait entrepris = *it's the most ambitious project the university has undertaken*

Les lettres qu'elle m'a écrites sont les plus tendres que j'aie jamais reçues = *the letters she wrote me are the most loving ones I've ever received*

C'est le moins qu'on puisse dire = *it's the least you can say*

The situation is less clear-cut with other types of superlative – see 155.

152 In noun clauses introduced by *le fait que* or *que* alone

Le fait que le Président ait dit non aux Américains donne à penser = *the fact that the President said no to the Americans gives food for thought*

Le fait qu'il n'y ait peu ou pas d'impôt sur les fortunes attire beaucoup de Français en Suisse = *the fact that there is little or no wealth tax attracts a good many French to Switzerland*

Que les célébrités veuillent rester anonymes autant que possible est bien connu = *it's well known that celebs want to stay anonymous as much as possible*

Que vous ayez gagné était une grande surprise pour tout le monde = *that you won was a great surprise for everyone*

153 In clauses depending upon a range of indefinite expressions, equivalent to English words ending in *–ever –* pronouns *whoever, whatever,* adjective *whatever,* adverbs *however, wherever*

(See 457.)

qui que = *whoever, anyone*
qui que is normally used in conjunction with ***être***; if a verb other than ***être*** is required, the expression ***qui que ce soit*** is used as subject or object or after a preposition, followed by ***qui*** + the required verb in the subjunctive mood, as appropriate –

Qui que vous soyez = *whoever you are*

Il défie qui que ce soit de descendre cette piste = *he challenges anyone to go down that piste*

Qui que ce soit qui téléphone, dis-lui que je suis sortie = *whoever phones, tell them I've gone out*

J'ai envoyé cette photo pour qui que ce soit qui l'apprécie = *I've sent this photo for whoever will appreciate it*

An alternative to **qui que** is **quiconque** which is used with the indicative and not the subjunctive mood –

Quiconque a dit cela est fou = *whoever said that is stupid*

Dis à quiconque veut écouter que les tarifs seront réduits ce soir = *tell anyone who wants to listen that prices are going to be reduced this evening*

Il sait cela mieux que quiconque = *he knows that better than anyone*

quoi qui / quoi que = *whatever*, pronoun
As with **qui que**, **quoi qui / quoi que** is normally used in conjunction with **être**; if a verb other than **être** is required, the expression **quoi que ce soit** is used as subject – but not object, when other verbs may be combined with it –

Quoi qu'il en soit = *be that as it may*

Quoi que ce soit qui vous énerve, essayez de rester calme = *whatever gets on your nerves, try to stay calm*

Quoi que tu fasses, prenez des vitamines = *whatever you do, take vitamins*

Quoi que tu dises, il n'en demeure pas moins que . . . = *whatever you say, the fact remains that . . .*

Sur quoi que ce soit que tu t'appuies = *whatever you rely on*

The following expressions are very common –

Quoi qu'il arrive / quoi qui se passe = *whatever happens*

If it occurs in a negative expression, **quoi que ce soit** = *anything*

Tu ne peux pas lui dire quoi que ce soit = *you can't tell her anything*

quelque que = *whatever*, adjective
There are two possible constructions –

Quelques vêtements que tu portes,	***tu me sembles toujours très***
Quels que soient les vêtements que tu portes,	***sexy*** =

whatever clothes you wear, you always look sexy to me
In the first instance **quelque** is written as a single word, precedes the noun and agrees with it in number (it is invariable for gender).

In the second instance, it is combined with **être** (as happens with **qui que** and **quoi que**), is written as two words, **quel + que**, and **quel** agrees in number and gender –

Quelles que soient les pièces que tu préfères,	***tu en trouveras dans notre théâtre*** =
Quelques pièces que tu préfères,	

whatever plays you prefer, you'll find some in our theatre

Les militaires doivent toujours être disponibles quelles que soient les circonstances = *soldiers must always be available whatever the circumstances*

quelque = *however*
quelque occurs as a single word before an adjective which it qualifies and, because it is an adverb, it is invariable in number and gender –

Quelque dur qu'il travaille, il ne semble jamais apprendre quoi que ce soit = *however hard he works, he never seems to learn anything*

Quelque riches qu'ils soient, ils ne veulent jamais donner de l'argent aux oeuvres caritatives = *however rich they are, they never want to make a donation to a charity*

There are a number of alternatives to this adverbial usage of *quelque* –

si, pour, aussi, tout
Si / pour / aussi séduisant que cela puisse paraître, il vaut mieux l'éviter = *however attractive it may appear, it's better to avoid it*

La passion, toute amoureuse qu'elle se prétende, ne naît pas de l'idylle pas plus qu'elle n'y conduit pas = *passion, however loving it may be, does not develop from an idyll any more than it leads to one*

It is worthwhile comparing the following examples which show the varying forms and usages of *quelque / quel que* –

Quelque difficulté que nous rencontrions
Quelle que soit la difficulté
Quelles que soient les difficultés
Quelque difficile que ce soit

nous avons l'intention de persévérer =

however difficult it is, we intend persevering

où que = *wherever, anywhere*
Où que tu ailles, je te suivrai dans mon coeur = *wherever you go I'll follow you in my heart*

Où que tu caches ce magazine, je le trouverai = *wherever you hide that magazine, I'll find it*

Instead of using *où que* in this way, *partout où* + indicative mood may be used –

Partout où tu vas, je te suivrai dans mon coeur = *anywhere you go, I'll follow you in my heart*

For usage with *n'importe qui / quoi / quel / où* – see 246, 457.

Grammatical circumstances where the subjunctive *may* be used

154 Optional subjunctive

In the previous sets of cases, the use of the subjunctive mood was obligatory. However, there are also a number of other sets of circumstances where its use is optional. Whether to use the subjunctive or not in these circumstances is largely a matter of style – the more

formal the style adopted by the speaker, the more likely it is that the subjunctive mood will be used; the more **informal** the style adopted, the more likely it is that the indicative mood rather than the subjunctive will be used.

155 In clauses depending upon a superlative not formed with *plus* or *moins* and upon such expressions as *dernier, premier, seul*

informal

C'est le meilleur / le pire magazine pour jeunes que je connais = *it's the best / worst young persons' magazine I know*

C'est la dernière fois que je te le dis = *it's the last time I tell you*

C'est le premier certificat qu'elle a reçu = *it's the first certificate she's received*

J'ai l'intention de vivre au maximum la seule vie que j'ai = *I intend living the only life I have to the full*

formal

C'est la meilleure pièce de théâtre que j'aie jamais vue = *it's the best play I've ever seen*

La réunion a été présidée par la dernière personne que j'eusse rêvée d'y trouver = *the meeting was chaired by the last person I imagined finding there*

C'est la seule chose qu'elle ait entendue parmi tous les bruits qui étaient criés autour d'elle = *it's the only thing she heard amongst all the noises shouted around her*

156 Other situations where the subjunctive is optional

There are a few verbs with which the use of the subjunctive is optional. This especially involves verbs that are used negatively or interrogatively (see 149, 150). The deciding factor is whether the proposition in the subordinate clause is seen as hypothetical or depending upon a subjective interpretation of the proposition, or whether it is seen as real or actual. In the former case, the subjunctive mood is used; in the latter, the indicative. Verbs coming under this heading are –

accepter = *to accept*, *admettre* = *to admit*, *comprendre* = *to understand*, *concevoir* = *to conceive*, *envisager* = *to envisage*, *expliquer* = *to explain*, *voir* = *to see*

J'admets qu'il est beaucoup plus intelligent que moi = *I admit he's a lot more intelligent than me*

Admettons qu'elle ait fini son travail, cela n'excuse pas son manque d'attention = *admitting she's finished her work, that's no excuse for not paying attention*

Elle comprenait que la possibilité de poursuivre sa carrière choisie dépendait de son application au travail = *she understood that the possibility of pursuing her chosen career depended on her application to work*

Je ne comprends pas que tu puisses parler à ta mère comme ça = *I don't understand how you can talk to your mother like that*

On voit que le décor politique ne s'éclaircit guère = *we can see that the political scene scarcely gets any clearer*

Où voyez-vous là-dedans que la République tienne son rang? = *where do you see in that action that the Republic preserves its reputation?*

The subjunctive mood is not usually used in a relative clause following the indefinite article. When, however, the sense of the proposition is less than fully certain, the subjunctive mood may be used to underline this –

Il a besoin d'un médecin qui comprend les allergies = *he needs a doctor who understands allergies* (and there is such a doctor)

Il a besoin d'un médecin qui comprenne les allergies = *he needs a doctor who understands allergies* (and such a doctor may not exist)

Coucher pour coucher – non! Je n'ai pas rencontré d'homme qui en vaille la peine! Je patiente = *to sleep with someone for the sake of it – no. I've not met a man who's worth the trouble. I'm waiting*

Elle m'a dit qu'elle a besoin d'un homme qui puisse satisfaire ses rêves – et ce ne sera pas moi = *she told me that she needs a man who can satisfy her dreams – and it's not me*

157 Use with *après que*

Après que is normally followed by a verb in the indicative mood in the subordinate clause. However, the subjunctive mood is also found (see 465) –

Après que le patient a été traité pour la dépression, il ne faut pas perdre de vue ses besoins à long terme = *after the patient has been treated for depression, it's important not to lose sight of his long-term needs*

Trois mois après qu'elle ait accouché de son premier bébé, son partenaire l'a quittée = *three months after she had given birth to her first child, her partner left her*

Je change la litière du chat immédiatement après qu'il y ait passé = *I change the cat's litter tray immediately after it's used it*

158 Pluperfect subjunctive equivalent to conditional perfect

Sometimes in formal circumstances, sometimes ironically, sometimes in semi-fixed constructions, the pluperfect subjunctive is used as an alternative to the conditional perfect – this occurs most frequently in the third person singular, only rarely elsewhere –

On a promené le vieux porte-avions d'un bout à l'autre de la Méditerranée comme on eût fait d'un pétrolier pourri = *they've dragged the old aircraft carrier from one end of the Med. to another as they would have done with a rusty tanker*

Qui l'eût dit, qui l'eût cru, que la question du voile nous bassinerait jusqu'à faire sortir quelques fantômes des placards de l'Histoire? = *who would have said, who would have thought that the issue of the [Islamic] veil would come to raise ghosts from the cupboards of History?*

Qui eût cru que le modeste thé est l'une des meilleures boissons pour la santé? = *who would have thought that unassuming tea is one of the best drinks from the health point of view?*

159 Definition of a modal verb

Modal verbs constitute a set of verbs that express a variety of attitudes concerning events and the participants in those events – obligation, permission, possibility, probability. In English such verbs as *can, may, must, should, ought* belong to this set of verbs.

In French, the verbs involved are – ***devoir*** = *to have to,* ***pouvoir*** = *to be able to,* ***savoir*** = *to know how to,* ***vouloir*** = *to want to.*

A major problem for English speakers is discovering the correlation between English modal verbs and their French equivalents. The principal reason for this is that English modal verbs are frequently anomalous in the formation of their tenses.

160 *devoir*

Equivalent to English *must, have to, ought, should,* ***devoir*** expresses moral certainty, probability, intention, obligation –

il doit = *he must, he has to*

Il peut arriver qu'après une fausse couche, les femmes aient plus de mal à concevoir car le corps comme le mental doivent être prêts = *it can happen that, after a miscarriage, women find it harder to conceive, because their body as well as their mental state has to be ready* = obligation

Vous devez penser qu'il est allé trop loin = *you must think he's gone too far* = probability

Je dois être en retard = *I must be late* = probability

Il doit être parti à dix-huit heures = *he must have / probably left at 6 o'clock* = obligation

Il doit partir à dix-huit heures = *he must / has to / has got to leave at 6 o'clock* = intention

Il doit être parti à dix-huit heures = *he must be gone by 6 o'clock* = obligation

il devait = *he used to, he had to, he was to, he must have*
Il devait partir à dix-huit heures chaque soir pour arriver chez lui à vingt heures = *he had to / used to leave at 6 o'clock every evening to get home by 8*

Il devait partir à dix-huit heures, mais hier il a changé de routine = *he was to leave [or = was in the habit of leaving] at 6 o'clock, but yesterday he changed his routine*

Il devait être fatigué quand il a eu l'accident = *he must have been tired when he had the accident*

il a dû = *he must have, he had to*
Il a dû partir à dix-huit heures, mais il n'est pas rentré = *he must have left at 6 o'clock, but he didn't come home*

Il a dû finir sa rédaction avant de partir = *he had to finish his essay before leaving*

Il n'a pas dû comprendre = *he must not have understood* (= *he probably did not understand*)

il devra = *he will have to*
Il devra finir sa rédaction avant de partir = *he'll have to finish his essay before leaving*

il devrait = *he should, he ought to*
Il devrait finir sa rédaction avant de partir = *he ought to / should finish his essay before leaving*

il avait dû = *he must have, he had had to*
Il avait dû finir sa rédaction avant de partir = *he had had / must have to finish his essay before leaving*

il aura dû = *he will have had to*
Il aura dû finir sa rédaction avant de partir = *he will have had to finish his essay before leaving*

il aurait dû = *he ought to have, he should have*
Il aurait dû finir sa rédaction avant de partir = *he should have / ought to have finished his essay before leaving* (see 139 for the use of the conditional perfect implying *it is alleged that*)

Note – the impersonal verb ***falloir*** = *to be necessary* may be used as an alternative to ***devoir*** in certain circumstances –

Il faut venir ce soir = *you* [or other appropriate subject] *must come this evening*

Il avait fallu demander conseil au pharmacien = *it had been necessary / we* [or other appropriate subject] *had had to ask the chemist for advice*

Pour gagner le prix, il fallait écrire un poème = *to win the prize, you had to write a poem*

Il faudrait une semaine d'hospitalisation pour se rétablir = *a week's hospitalisation would be necessary for recuperation*

Il aurait fallu choisir une couleur différente pour ses cheveux = *she* [or other appropriate subject] *should have / ought to have chosen a different colour for her hair*

Remember that as a transitive verb ***devoir*** = *to owe*

Il me doit cinq euros = *he owes me five euros*

161 *pouvoir*

Equivalent to English *to be able to* (physically), *can, could, may, might*, ***pouvoir*** expresses possibility, granting permission, capability, politeness

elle peut
= *possibility*
Elle peut arriver à tout moment = *she may arrive at any moment*

Elle peut le faire elle-même = *she can do it herself*

Note the expression ***il se peut que*** + subjunctive (see 150) –

Il se peut que nous oublions le nom du professeur = *it's possible that we'll / we may forget the teacher's name*

= *granting permission*
Elle peut sortir si elle a fini sa répétition = *she can go out if she's finished practising*

Tu ne peux pas sortir ce soir = *you can't go out this evening*

Puis-je ouvrir la fenêtre? = *may I open the window?*

Note that this special form of the first person singular of the present tense of ***pouvoir*** is used only in inverted questions (see 472).

= *capability*
Je peux nager sous l'eau = *I can swim underwater* (but see later)

= *politeness*
Puis-je vous aider? ⎤
Je peux vous aider? ⎦ = *may I help you?*

elle pouvait = *she could, she was able to*
Elle pouvait se souvenir de son nom = *she could / was able to remember his name*

Elle ne pouvait pas se souvenir de son nom = *she couldn't / wasn't able to remember his name*

The imperfect tense is used here because a mental state is being referred to (see 129).

elle a pu = *she could, she was able to, she managed to*
Elle a pu accomplir tout cela en deux heures = *she was able to / managed to finish all that in two hours*

Elle a pu courir plus vite que d'habitude parce qu'elle avait peur = *she could / was able to run faster than usual because she was afraid*

The perfect tense is used here because single events accomplished in a short space of time are being referred to.

elle pourra = *she can, she will be able to*
Elle pourra sortir quand elle aura fini sa répétition = *she can / will be able to go out when she's finished practising*

elle pourrait = *she could, she might (be able to)*
Elle pourrait accomplir beaucoup plus si elle le voulait = *she could do a lot more if she wanted*

Il se pourrait que nous ne le fassions pas = *we might not be able to do it*

Ça pourrait être le cas = *that might be the case*

On lui a dit qu'elle ne pourrait pas entrer en fac sans diplômes = *they told her*
she couldn't / wouldn't be able to go to university without qualifications

elle avait pu = *she had been able to*
Elle avait pu y aller parce que sa famille avait financé le projet = *she had been*
able to go, because her family had financed the project

elle aura pu = *she will have been able*
Avec de telles ressources, elle aura pu s'en occuper = *with such resources, she will*
have been able to deal with it

elle aurait pu = *she would have been able to, she might have, she could have*
Elle aurait pu préparer un clafoutis extraordinaire si elle avait eu des
framboises = *she could have made a fantastic clafoutis if she had had some raspberries*

Il aurait pu le perdre = *he might have lost it*

Est-ce que tu aurais pu le faire sans moi? = *could you have done it without me?*

Note 1 –
whereas ***pouvoir*** = *to be able*, to have the physical capability, ***savoir*** = *to be able*, to have
the intellectual capability (see 162) –

Elle sait parler français = *she can speak French*

Elle peut monter à cheval en dépit de son handicap physique = *she can ride a*
horse in spite of her physical handicap

Note 2 –
there are alternatives to using ***pouvoir*** – ***peut-être*** = *perhaps*, ***il est possible que*** =
it's possible that –

Elle viendra peut-être demain
Peut-être qu'elle viendra demain } = *she may come tomorrow*
Il est possible qu'elle vienne demain

Note 3 –
usage with ***peut-être*** – ***peut-être*** can occupy three positions in a clause, depending
upon the amount of prominence the user wishes to give it –

1 ***peut-être*** in initial position followed by ***que*** and normal word order;
2 ***peut-être*** in initial position with inversion of the subject and verb if the subject is a
 pronoun;
 or, if it is a noun, with the noun subject in initial position followed by ***peut-être***,
 followed by inversion of the verb and a subject pronoun echoing the noun
3 ***peut-être*** following the verb –

Peut-être que votre persévérance portera ses fruits } = *perhaps your*
Votre persévérance, peut-être portera-t-elle ses fruits } *perseverance will*
Votre persévérance portera peut-être ses fruits } *bear fruit*

Note 4 –

with verbs of perception, such as ***voir***, ***entendre***, ***sentir***, *can*, *could* etc, are not translated at all –

Je ne vois rien = *I can't see a thing*

Elle n'entendait pas ce que disait le prof = *she couldn't hear what the teacher said*

162 **savoir**

Equivalent to English *to know, to know how, to be able* (intellectually)

je sais

Je sais qu'elle est arrivée = *I know she's arrived*

Je sais jouer à la pétanque = *I can / know how to play bowls*

Je sais comment elle m'a trompé = *I know how she deceived me*

163 **vouloir**

Equivalent to English *to want to, to wish to, to like to*

il veut = *he wants to, he's willing to*
Il veut entreprendre une enquête sur le bruit = *he wants to undertake an investigation into noise*

il voulait = *he wanted to, he was willing to*
Il voulait devenir membre d'une association d'information pour les diabétiques = *he wanted to become a member of a support group for diabetics*

The imperfect tense is used here because a mental state is being referred to (see 129).

il a voulu = *he wanted to, he tried to*
Il a voulu trouver un poste, mais il n'y en avait pas = *he tried to find a job, but there weren't any*

The perfect tense is used here because a single event curtailed by lack of time is being referred to.

il voudra = *he'll want to, he'll be willing to*
Après avoir fait deux ou trois tractions en haut, on voudra passer à des exercices plus difficiles = *after doing two or three pull-ups, you'll want to move on to more difficult exercises*

il voudrait = *he'd like to, he'd want to*
Il voudrait voir le directeur = *he would like / wanted to see the principal*

Est-ce que tu viendras ce soir? – Je voudrais bien, mais je ne me sens pas bien = *are you coming this evening? – I'd like to, but I'm not feeling very well*

il avait voulu = *he had wanted to, he had been willing to, he had tried to*
***Il avait voulu croire que l'homme est brave et juste, mais l'expérience l'a
vite désillusionné*** = *he had wanted to believe that man is brave and just, but experience soon
disillusioned him*

il aurait voulu = *he would have liked to, he would have wanted to*
***Il aurait voulu être persuadé qu'elle avait plus de talent, mais hélas, ce
n'était pas vrai*** = *he would have liked to believe that she had more talent, but, alas, that wasn't
the case*

Note 1 –
English *would* referring to a future event that may or may not take place is normally
conveyed by the conditional tense of the verb (see 138) –

Elle viendrait si elle avait le temps = *she would come if she had the time*

Note 2 –
English *would* may also be used to indicate a habitual action in the past and is then
conveyed by the imperfect tense in French (see 129) –

Elle venait tous les vendredis = *she would come every Friday*

Note 3 –
the imperative of ***vouloir*** may be used to express a polite command (see 122) –

Veuille venir à 20 heures = *please come at 8 o'clock*

Veuillez fermer la fenêtre = *would you mind closing the window?*

Veuillez vous asseoir = *please sit down*

Note 4 –
the conditional and conditional perfect of ***aimer*** are sometimes used as alternatives to
the conditional and conditional perfect of ***vouloir*** –

J'aimerais tout recommencer = *I'd like to start all over again*

J'aurais aimé tout recommencer = *I'd have liked to start all over again*

Impersonal verbs

164 Impersonal verbs

Certain verbs are only used with the third person singular form ***il***, which in such circumstances is equivalent to English *it*. Although the pronoun is invariable, the verb changes
for tense. The verbs fall into the following categories –

1 Verbs relating to the weather
Il gèle = *it's freezing*
Il fait jour = *it's daylight*
Il neige = *it's snowing*
Il pleut = *it's raining*

Il tonne = *it's thundering*
Quel temps fait-il? = *what's the weather like?*
Il fait beau / mauvais / chaud / froid = *the weather is fine / awful / hot / cold*
Il fait un temps gris = *it's overcast*
Il fait du soleil / vent = *it's sunny / windy*

2 Impersonal expressions
il y a = *there is*
il faut que (+ subjunctive) = *it's necessary* (see 150)
il s'agit de = *it's a matter / question of*
il semble / paraît que (+ subjunctive) = *it seems that* (see 150)
il arrive = *it happens* (see 150)
Il m'arrive de temps en temps d'en dire trop = *it sometimes happens that I say too much*

3 Expressions involving être
Quelle heure est-il? – Il est dix-huit heures = *what's the time? – It's 6 o'clock* (see 440)
Il est temps de / que (+ subjunctive) = *it's time to / that* (see 150)
Il est question de / que (+ subjunctive) = *it's a matter of / that* (see 150)
Il était une fois = *once upon a time*
Il est possible / impossible / probable / peu probable / vrai / faux, etc = *it's possible / impossible / likely / unlikely / true / wrong* (see 150)

Defective verbs

165 Defective verbs

Certain verbs do not have a complete conjugation for each tense. These are known as **defective verbs**. They tend to be rather archaic, rare verbs.

absoudre = *to absolve*, *bruire* = *to rustle*, *choir / déchoir* = *to fall*, *clore* = *to close*, *dissoudre* = *to dissolve*, *frire* = *to fry*, *ouïr* = *to hear* (past participle only, *ouï*), *traire* = *to milk*

Most of these verbs mainly occur as infinitives and past participles, often acting as adjectives; their conjugated forms have by and large disappeared from common use.

Tous sont d'accord que ce dossier n'est jamais clos = *everyone agrees that this file is never closed*

Quand votre partenaire vous quitte pour une autre, on se sent déchu dans un univers terne et vide = *when your partner leaves you for someone else, you feel abandoned in an empty, drab world*

La fusion avec l'autre, c'est l'expérience inouïe = *to become united with your partner is an incredible experience*

However, one or two have lost only a few tenses – **absoudre** and **dissoudre** have retained all tenses except the past historic and imperfect subjunctive; **frire** no longer has the imperfect or past historic tenses or the simple subjunctive tenses. Even so, the tenses that are retained are very rarely used.

Exercises

1 **Les impératifs – réécrivez les passages suivants en donnant les formes de l'impératif qui conviennent.**

a *DON'T FORGET de fermer le récipient avant de mouliner son contenu.*

b *Le look gothique est à la page. BE AWARE toutefois qu'il faut en user avec modération.*

c *Avec un blouson en cuir, DARE les grosses ceintures cloutées ou à boucle en argent.*

d *Vous avez des problèmes de pellicules et pas de shampooing adéquat? TAKE deux aspirines effervescentes, DISSOLVE THEM dans un verre d'eau et RUB le cuir chevelu avec la préparation obtenue.*

e *Allongé sur le dos, la main droite derrière la tête, STRETCH votre jambe droite à la verticale et BEND celle de gauche, le pied au sol. En expirant, BRING votre main gauche TOWARDS de votre cheville droite. DO cinq séries de 15 répétitions.*

f *AVOID de poser la question brutalement.*

g *CONCENTRATE, CALM votre coeur: le stress se calme à son tour et disparaît.*

h *SEASON de sel, poivre et quatre-épices. MIX. INCORPORATE les morceaux de foie gras. COVER. COOK 1h 30 au bain-marie dans le four. ALLOW TO refroidir. KEEP 48h au réfrigérateur.*

2 **Réécrivez le texte suivant en style indirect, en changeant les temps du verbe, les pronoms, etc**

Commencez ainsi – *Planète Foot a demandé à Thierry quels sentiments . . .*

Planète Foot: *Thierry, quels sentiments t'ont traversé l'esprit lorsque l'arbitre a donné le coup de sifflet final de la dernière journée du championnat anglais?*

Thierry Henry: *Terminer un championnat invaincu, c'est vraiment formidable. Mais, sur le coup, je ne m'en rends pas compte. Tu sais que l'arbitre a sifflé, mais déjà, on était champions depuis presque un mois et, cinq jours après, on sait que l'on joue le Brésil au Stade de France. On n'a pas réellement le temps d'en profiter. Tu ne l'apprécies pas vraiment. Il faut passer à autre chose.*

3 **Subjonctif ou indicatif? Réécrivez les phrases suivantes en donnant la forme du verbe qui convient –**

a *Il faut bien que votre chéri SE DÉTENDRE de temps en temps.*

b *Je veux t'embrasser avant que on ÊTRE de retour à Calais.*

c *La première fois que je le VOIR, c'était en classe de seconde.*

d *Je veux qu'elle S'EN SORTIR vite.*

e *C'est le cinquième de ce type qu'elle CONNAÎTRE.*

f *Pour que le sommeil ÊTRE réellement réparateur, mettez votre esprit et votre corps en veille.*

g *Utilisez plusieurs cotons en vous démaquillant jusqu'à ce que vous LEVER toute trace de votre maquillage.*

h *Dans certaines séries les filles n'hésitent pas à se bagarrer, que ce ÊTRE les forces du mal ou les vampires.*

i *Il faut pondérer deux critères majeurs: la proportion de blessures enregistrées par sport en fonction du nombre des pratiquants et la gravité de celles-ci, quel que ÊTRE le niveau de pratique.*

   j ***En cas de surchauffe, un dispositif de coupure thermique évite que le robot (ne) PARTIR en fumée.***

   k ***Dommage que tu ne ÊTRE pas là.***

   l ***Si votre chapeau est vert clair avec des détails graphiques, la fille que vous draguez pensera que vous AVOIR de l'humour.***

  m ***La seule chose qu'il SAVOIR de son père c'est qu'il a probablement étudié ici.***

   n ***Garçons et filles ont des relations homosexuelles à cet âge sans que ce ÊTRE définitif.***

4 **Réécrivez les phrases suivantes en donnant la forme du verbe modal qui convient –**

   a ***Ils comprennent vite que pour réussir ils HAVE TO fabriquer leurs propres produits.***

   b ***La compagnie WOULD NOT HAVE BEEN ABLE TO réussir ses campagnes de publicité, sans ses produits phares.***

   c ***Quel MIGHT être l'objet d'une nouvelle loi?***

   d ***Il HAD TO éviter d'insulter ses collègues.***

   e ***Paris et Berlin DID NOT WANT TO édulcorer un projet qui donne à chaque État membre un nombre de voix plus en rapport avec son poids démographique.***

   f ***Le handball français CAN bien compter 220 000 licenciés dans tous les coins du territoire.***

   g ***Si ce traitement ne suffit pas, le dermatologue WILL BE ABLE TO vous prescrire des médicaments adaptés.***

   h ***Pour un soutien de poitrine optimal, deux mesures HAVE TO être prises en compte, celle du tour de buste (le chiffre) et celle des bonnets (la lettre).***

   i ***Des en-cas aux desserts les plus fins, le robot de cuisine CAN tout faire.***

   j ***Si l'insolation est grave, elle MAY nécessiter une hospitalisation, et la victime WILL HAVE TO être à jeun.***

   k ***Il est seul à TO BE ABLE TO atteindre sa cible de façon sélective.***

   l ***Si je l'avais rencontrée, je WOULD HAVE BEEN ABLE TO l'aimer, mais pas m'entendre avec elle.***

  m ***On se rassure comme on CAN.***

   n ***En Coupe d'Europe on ne MUST pas céder l'avantage à l'adversaire.***

   o ***On ne SHOULD pas accepter cet éloge funèbre de la presse – l'avenir appartient à la télévision digitale: la presse écrite est finie.***

Chapter 3 *Tabular treatment of verbs*

166 Order of presentation

The verbs are presented by major group, as set out in 1–114, indicative mood tenses first and then subjunctive mood tenses.

In the tables references are made to those sections where special mention is made of the particular tense of the verb.

175–176 provides an alphabetical list of verbs. The list does not include regular Group 1 *–er* verbs, but contains –

1 those verbs treated in the discursive section
2 those treated in the tabular section
3 other common verbs not mentioned in either of those sections. In this case an indication is given of which verb, dealt with in the two main sections, the verb is related to or conjugated like.

One or two verbs require separate treatment, as they do not relate to any other verbs.

For verbs conjugated with ***être*** in compound tenses, in order to economise on space and density of information, not every permutation of past participle endings has been indicated – third person singular and plural and second person plural have been shown as permitting variation in the form of the participle. However, it should be remembered that depending upon the gender of the subject of the other persons, an *–e* may have to be added (eg ***je suis allée, tu es allée, nous sommes allées, vous êtes allée, vous êtes allées***).

INDICATIVE MOOD

Group 1 –er Verbs

167 Group 1 –er verbs

All verbs ending in –er are conjugated like **porter**, unless they figure in the table below.

verb	present	imperfect	future	conditional	past historic	perfect	present participle
porter	**porte**	**portais**	**porterai**	**porterais**	**portai**	**ai porté**	**portant**
	portes	**portais**	**porteras**	**porterais**	**portas**	**as porté**	56
	porte	**portait**	**portera**	**porterait**	**porta**	**a porté**	
	portons	**portions**	**porterons**	**porterions**	**portâmes**	**avons porté**	
	portez	**portiez**	**porterez**	**porteriez**	**portâtes**	**avez porté**	
	portent	**portaient**	**porteront**	**porteraient**	**portèrent**	**ont porté**	
	16	44	47	47	76	67	
acheter	**achète**	**achetais**	**achèterai**	**achèterais**	**achetai**	**ai acheté**	**achetant**
	achètes	**achetais**	**achèteras**	**achèterais**	**achetas**	**as acheté**	56
	achète	**achetait**	**achètera**	**achèterait**	**acheta**	**a acheté**	
	achetons	**achetions**	**achèterons**	**achèterions**	**achetâmes**	**avons acheté**	
	achetez	**achetiez**	**achèterez**	**achèteriez**	**achetâtes**	**avez acheté**	
	achètent	**achetaient**	**achèteront**	**achèteraient**	**achetèrent**	**ont acheté**	
	18		48	48	76	67	
aller	**vais**	**allais**	**irai**	**irais**	**allai**	**suis allé**	**allant**
	vas	**allais**	**iras**	**irais**	**allas**	**es allé**	56
	va	**allait**	**ira**	**irait**	**alla**	**est allé(e)**	
	allons	**allions**	**irons**	**irions**	**allâmes**	**sommes allés**	
	allez	**alliez**	**irez**	**iriez**	**allâtes**	**êtes allé(es)**	
	vont	**allaient**	**iront**	**iraient**	**allèrent**	**sont allé(e)s**	
	21	44	49	49	76	67	

verb	present	imperfect	future	conditional	past historic	perfect	present participle
appeler	*appelle*	*appelais*	*appellerai*	*appellerais*	*appelai*	*ai appelé*	*appelant*
	appelles	*appelais*	*appelleras*	*appellerais*	*appelas*	*as appelé*	56
	appelle	*appelait*	*appellera*	*appellerait*	*appela*	*a appelé*	
	appelons	*appelions*	*appellerons*	*appellerions*	*appelâmes*	*avons appelé*	
	appelez	*appeliez*	*appellerez*	*appelleriez*	*appelâtes*	*avez appelé*	
	appellent	*appelaient*	*appelleront*	*appelleraient*	*appelèrent*	*ont appelé*	
	18		48	48			
commencer	*commence*	*commençais*	*commencerai*	*commencerais*	*commençai*	*ai commencé*	*commençant*
	commences	*commençais*	*commenceras*	*commencerais*	*commenças*	*as commencé*	56
	commence	*commençait*	*commencera*	*commencerait*	*commença*	*a commencé*	
	commençons	*commencions*	*commencerons*	*commencerions*	*commençâmes*	*avons commencé*	
	commencez	*commenciez*	*commencerez*	*commenceriez*	*commençâtes*	*avez commencé*	
	commencent	*commençaient*	*commenceront*	*commenceraient*	*commencèrent*	*ont commencé*	
	20	44			76		
envoyer	*envoie*	*envoyais*	*enverrai*	*enverrais*	*envoyai*	*ai envoyé*	*envoyant*
	envoies	*envoyais*	*enverras*	*enverrais*	*envoyas*	*as envoyé*	
	envoie	*envoyait*	*enverra*	*enverrait*	*envoya*	*a envoyé*	
	envoyons	*envoyions*	*enverrons*	*enverrions*	*envoyâmes*	*avons envoyé*	
	envoyez	*envoyiez*	*enverrez*	*enverriez*	*envoyâtes*	*avez envoyé*	
	envoient	*envoyaient*	*enverront*	*enverraient*	*envoyèrent*	*ont envoyé*	
			49	49			
espérer	*espère*	*espérais*	*espérerai*	*espérerais*	*espérai*	*ai espéré*	*espérant*
	espères	*espérais*	*espéreras*	*espérerais*	*espéras*	*as espéré*	56
	espère	*espérait*	*espérera*	*espérerait*	*espéra*	*a espéré*	
	espérons	*espérions*	*espérerons*	*espérerions*	*espérâmes*	*avons espéré*	
	espérez	*espériez*	*espérerez*	*espéreriez*	*espérâtes*	*avez espéré*	
	espèrent	*espéraient*	*espéreront*	*espéreraient*	*espérèrent*	*ont espéré*	
	19		48	48			

Infinitive	Present	Imperfect	Future	Conditional	Passé simple	Passé composé	Participle
jeter	jette	jetais	jetterai	jetterais	jetai	ai jeté	jetant
	jettes	jetais	jetteras	jetterais	jetas	as jeté	
	jette	jetait	jettera	jetterait	jeta	a jeté	
	jetons	jetions	jetterons	jetterions	jetâmes	avons jeté	
	jetez	jetiez	jetterez	jetteriez	jetâtes	avez jeté	
	jettent	jetaient	jetteront	jetteront	jetèrent	ont jeté	
	18		48	48			
manger	mange	mangeais	mangerai	mangerais	mangeai	ai mangé	mangeant
	manges	mangeais	mangeras	mangerais	mangeas	as mangé	56
	mange	mangeait	mangera	mangerait	mangea	a mangé	
	mangeons	mangions	mangerons	mangerions	mangeâmes	avons mangé	
	mangez	mangiez	mangerez	mangeriez	mangeâtes	avez mangé	
	mangent	mangeaient	mangeront	mangeraient	mangèrent	ont mangé	
	20	44	48	48	76		
mener	mène	menais	mènerai	mènerais	menai	ai mené	menant
	mènes	menais	mèneras	mènerais	menas	as mené	56
	mène	menait	mènera	mènerait	mena	a mené	
	menons	menions	mènerons	mènerions	menâmes	avons mené	
	menez	meniez	mènerez	mèneriez	menâtes	avez mené	
	mènent	menaient	mèneront	mèneront	menèrent	ont mené	
	19		48	48			

Group 2 –ir Verbs

168 Group 2 –ir verbs

Remember that Group 2 verbs are of two main types –

1 those like *finir* which form the three persons plural with *–iss–* between stem and ending;
2 those like *courir* which do not.

verb	present	imperfect	future	conditional	past historic	perfect	present participle
finir	*finis*	*finissais*	*finirai*	*finirais*	*finis*	*ai fini*	*finissant*
	finis	*finissais*	*finiras*	*finirais*	*finis*	*as fini*	56
	finit	*finissait*	*finira*	*finirait*	*finit*	*a fini*	
	finissons	*finissions*	*finirons*	*finirions*	*finîmes*	*avons fini*	
	finissez	*finissiez*	*finirez*	*finiriez*	*finîtes*	*avez fini*	
	finissent	*finissaient*	*finiront*	*finiraient*	*finirent*	*ont fini*	
	24	44	50	50	78	67	
courir	*cours*	*courais*	*courrai*	*courrais*	*courus*	*ai couru*	*courant*
	cours	*courais*	*courras*	*courrais*	*courus*	*as couru*	
	court	*courait*	*courra*	*courrait*	*courut*	*a couru*	
	courons	*courions*	*courrons*	*courrions*	*courûmes*	*avons couru*	
	courez	*couriez*	*courrez*	*courriez*	*courûtes*	*avez couru*	
	courent	*couraient*	*courront*	*courraient*	*coururent*	*ont couru*	
	25		52	52	80		
cueillir	*cueille*	*cueillais*	*cueillerai*	*cueillerais*	*cueillis*	*ai cueilli*	*cueillant*
	cueilles	*cueillais*	*cueilleras*	*cueillerais*	*cueillis*	*as cueilli*	
	cueille	*cueillait*	*cueillera*	*cueillerait*	*cueillit*	*a cueilli*	
	cueillons	*cueillions*	*cueillerons*	*cueillerions*	*cueillîmes*	*avons cueilli*	
	cueillez	*cueilliez*	*cueillerez*	*cueilleriez*	*cueillîtes*	*avez cueilli*	
	cueillent	*cueillaient*	*cueilleront*	*cueilleraient*	*cueillirent*	*ont cueilli*	
	26		51	51	78		
dormir	*dors*	*dormais*	*dormirai*	*dormirais*	*dormis*	*ai dormi*	*dormant*
	dors	*dormais*	*dormiras*	*dormirais*	*dormis*	*as dormi*	

	Present	Imperfect	Future	Conditional	Passé simple	Passé composé	Present participle
(dormir)	*dort* *dormons* *dormez* *dorment* 27	*dormait* *dormions* *dormiez* *dormaient* 44	*dormira* *dormirons* *dormirez* *dormiront* 50	*dormirait* *dormirions* *dormiriez* *dormiraient* 50	*dormit* *dormîmes* *dormîtes* *dormirent*	*a dormi* *avons dormi* *avez dormi* *ont dormi*	
mourir	*meurs* *meurs* *meurt* *mourons* *mourez* *meurent* 28	*mourais* *mourais* *mourait* *mourions* *mouriez* *mouraient*	*mourrai* *mourras* *mourra* *mourrons* *mourrez* *mourront* 52	*mourrais* *mourrais* *mourrait* *mourrions* *mourriez* *mourraient* 52	*mourus* *mourus* *mourut* *mourûmes* *mourûtes* *moururent* 80	*suis mort* *es mort* *est mort(e)* *sommes morts* *êtes mort(e/s)* *sont mort(e)s* 67	*mourant* 56
ouvrir	*ouvre* *ouvres* *ouvre* *ouvrons* *ouvrez* *ouvrent*	*ouvrais* *ouvrais* *ouvrait* *ouvrions* *ouvriez* *ouvraient*	*ouvrirai* *ouvriras* *ouvrira* *ouvrirons* *ouvrirez* *ouvriront* 52	*ouvrirais* *ouvrirais* *ouvrirait* *ouvririons* *ouvririez* *ouvriraient* 52	*ouvris* *ouvris* *ouvrit* *ouvrîmes* *ouvrîtes* *ouvrirent* 80	*ai ouvert* *as ouvert* *a ouvert* *avons ouvert* *avez ouvert* *ont ouvert* 67	*ouvrant*
partir	*pars* *pars* *part* *partons* *partez* *partent* 25	*partais* *partais* *partait* *partions* *partiez* *partaient* 44	*partirai* *partiras* *partira* *partirons* *partirez* *partiront* 52	*partirais* *partirais* *partirait* *partirions* *partiriez* *partiraient* 52	*partis* *partis* *partit* *partîmes* *partîtes* *partirent* 78	*suis parti* *es parti* *est parti(e)* *sommes partis* *êtes parti(e/s)* *sont parti(e)s* 67	*partant* 56
venir	*viens* *viens* *vient* *venons* *venez* *viennent* 27	*venais* *venais* *venait* *venions* *veniez* *venaient* 44	*viendrai* *viendras* *viendra* *viendrons* *viendrez* *viendront* 52	*viendrais* *viendrais* *viendrait* *viendrions* *viendriez* *viendraient* 52	*vins* *vins* *vint* *vînmes* *vîntes* *vinrent* 78	*suis venu* *es venu* *est venu(e)* *sommes venus* *êtes venu(e/s)* *sont venu(e)s* 67	*venant*

169 Group 3 –*re* verbs

Remember that Group 3 verbs belong to a number of subgroups.

verb	present	imperfect	future	conditional	past historic	perfect	present participle
battre	*bats*	*battais*	*battrai*	*battrais*	*battis*	*ai battu*	*battant*
	bats	*battais*	*battras*	*battrais*	*battis*	*as battu*	56
	bat	*battait*	*battra*	*battrait*	*battit*	*a battu*	
	battons	*battions*	*battrons*	*battrions*	*battîmes*	*avons battu*	
	battez	*battiez*	*battrez*	*battriez*	*battîtes*	*avez battu*	
	battent	*battaient*	*battront*	*battraient*	*battirent*	*ont battu*	
	33						
boire	*bois*	*buvais*	*boirai*	*boirais*	*bus*	*ai bu*	*buvant*
	bois	*buvais*	*boiras*	*boirais*	*bus*	*as bu*	56
	boit	*buvait*	*boira*	*boirait*	*but*	*a bu*	
	buvons	*buvions*	*boirons*	*boirions*	*bûmes*	*avons bu*	
	buvez	*buviez*	*boirez*	*boiriez*	*bûtes*	*avez bu*	
	boivent	*buvaient*	*boiront*	*boiraient*	*burent*	*ont bu*	
	37				84		
conclure	*conclus*	*concluais*	*conclurai*	*conclurais*	*conclus*	*ai conclu*	*concluant*
	conclus	*concluais*	*concluras*	*conclurais*	*conclus*	*as conclu*	
	conclut	*concluait*	*conclura*	*conclurait*	*conclut*	*a conclu*	
	concluons	*concluions*	*conclurons*	*conclurions*	*conclûmes*	*avons conclu*	
	concluez	*concluiez*	*conclurez*	*concluriez*	*conclûtes*	*avez conclu*	
	concluent	*concluaient*	*concluront*	*concluraient*	*conclurent*	*ont conclu*	
	38				84		
conduire	*conduis*	*conduisais*	*conduirai*	*conduirais*	*conduisis*	*ai conduit*	*conduisant*
	conduis	*conduisais*	*conduiras*	*conduirais*	*conduisis*	*as conduit*	56
	conduit	*conduisait*	*conduira*	*conduirait*	*conduisit*	*a conduit*	
	conduisons	*conduisions*	*conduirons*	*conduirions*	*conduisîmes*	*avons conduit*	

	présent	imparfait	futur	conditionnel	passé simple	passé composé	participe
	conduisez	conduisiez	conduirez	conduiriez	conduisîtes	avez conduit	
	conduisent	conduisaient	conduiront	conduiraient	conduisirent	ont conduit	
	35				83		
craindre	crains	craignais	craindrai	craindrais	craignis	ai craint	craignant
	crains	craignais	craindras	craindrais	craignis	as craint	57
	craint	craignait	craindra	craindrait	craignit	a craint	
	craignons	craignions	craindrons	craindrions	craignîmes	avons craint	
	craignez	craigniez	craindrez	craindriez	craignîtes	avez craint	
	craignent	craignaient	craindront	craindraient	craignirent	ont craint	
	37				83		
croire	crois	croyais	croirai	croirais	crus	ai cru	croyant
	crois	croyais	croiras	croirais	crus	as cru	
	croit	croyait	croira	croirait	crut	a cru	
	croyons	croyions	croirons	croirions	crûmes	avons cru	
	croyez	croyiez	croirez	croiriez	crûtes	avez cru	
	croient	croyaient	croiront	croiraient	crurent	ont cru	
	34				83		
dire	dis	disais	dirai	dirais	dis	ai dit	disant
	dis	disais	diras	dirais	dis	as dit	56
	dit	disait	dira	dirait	dit	a dit	
	disons	disions	dirons	dirions	dîmes	avons dit	
	dites	disiez	direz	diriez	dîtes	avez dit	
	disent	disaient	diront	diraient	dirent	ont dit	
	37				84		
écrire	écris	écrivais	écrirai	écrirais	écrivis	ai écrit	écrivant
	écris	écrivais	écriras	écrirais	écrivis	as écrit	56
	écrit	écrivait	écrira	écrirait	écrivit	a écrit	
	écrivons	écrivions	écrirons	écririons	écrivîmes	avons écrit	
	écrivez	écriviez	écrirez	écririez	écrivîtes	avez écrit	
	écrivent	écrivaient	écriront	écriraient	écrivirent	ont écrit	
	36				83		

verb	present	imperfect	future	conditional	past historic	perfect	present participle
être	*suis*	*étais*	*serai*	*serais*	*fus*	*ai été*	*étant*
	es	*étais*	*seras*	*serais*	*fus*	*as été*	56
	est	*était*	*sera*	*serait*	*fut*	*a été*	
	sommes	*étions*	*serons*	*serions*	*fûmes*	*avons été*	
	êtes	*étiez*	*serez*	*seriez*	*fûtes*	*avez été*	
	sont	*étaient*	*seront*	*seraient*	*furent*	*ont été*	
	37	44	54	54	84		
faire	*fais*	*faisais*	*ferai*	*ferais*	*fis*	*ai fait*	*faisant*
	fais	*faisais*	*feras*	*ferais*	*fis*	*as fait*	56
	fait	*faisait*	*fera*	*ferait*	*fit*	*a fait*	
	faisons	*faisions*	*ferons*	*ferions*	*fîmes*	*avons fait*	
	faites	*faisiez*	*ferez*	*feriez*	*fîtes*	*avez fait*	
	font	*faisaient*	*feront*	*feraient*	*firent*	*ont fait*	
	37		54	54	83		
lire	*lis*	*lisais*	*lirai*	*lirais*	*lus*	*a lu*	*lisant*
	lis	*lisais*	*liras*	*lirais*	*lus*	*as lu*	56
	lit	*lisait*	*lira*	*lirait*	*lut*	*a lu*	
	lisons	*lisions*	*lirons*	*lirions*	*lûmes*	*avons lu*	
	lisez	*lisiez*	*lirez*	*liriez*	*lûtes*	*avez lu*	
	lisent	*lisaient*	*liront*	*liraient*	*lurent*	*ont lu*	
	35		54	54	84		
mettre	*mets*	*mettais*	*mettrai*	*mettrais*	*mis*	*ai mis*	*mettant*
	mets	*mettais*	*mettras*	*mettrais*	*mis*	*as mis*	
	met	*mettait*	*mettra*	*mettrait*	*mit*	*a mis*	
	mettons	*mettions*	*mettrons*	*mettrions*	*mîmes*	*avons mis*	
	mettez	*mettiez*	*mettrez*	*mettriez*	*mîtes*	*avez mis*	
	mettent	*mettaient*	*mettront*	*mettraient*	*mirent*	*ont mis*	
	33				83		

	Présent	Imparfait	Futur	Conditionnel	Passé simple	Passé composé	Participe présent
perdre	perds	perdais	perdrai	perdrais	perdis	ai perdu	perdant
	perds	perdais	perdras	perdrais	perdis	as perdu	
	perd	perdait	perdra	perdrait	perdit	a perdu	
	perdons	perdions	perdrons	perdrions	perdîmes	avons perdu	
	perdez	perdiez	perdrez	perdriez	perdîtes	avez perdu	
	perdent	perdaient	perdront	perdraient	perdirent	ont perdu	
	31						
prendre	prends	prenais	prendrai	prendrais	pris	ai pris	prenant
	prends	prenais	prendras	prendrais	pris	as pris	56
	prend	prenait	prendra	prendrait	prit	a pris	
	prenons	prenions	prendrons	prendrions	prîmes	avons pris	
	prenez	preniez	prendrez	prendriez	prîtes	avez pris	
	prennent	prenaient	prendront	prendraient	prirent	ont pris	
	37				83	67	
répondre	réponds	répondais	répondrai	répondrais	répondis	ai répondu	répondant
	réponds	répondais	répondras	répondrais	répondis	as répondu	
	répond	répondait	répondra	répondrait	répondit	a répondu	
	répondons	répondions	répondrons	répondrions	répondîmes	avons répondu	
	répondez	répondiez	répondrez	répondriez	répondîtes	avez répondu	
	répondent	répondaient	répondront	répondraient	répondirent	ont répondu	
	31					67	
rire	ris	riais	rirai	rirais	ris	ai ri	riant
	ris	riais	riras	rirais	ris	as ri	
	rit	riait	rira	rirait	rit	a ri	
	rions	riions	rirons	ririons	rîmes	avons ri	
	riez	riiez	rirez	ririez	rîtes	avez ri	
	rient	riaient	riront	riraient	rirent	ont ri	
	32						
rompre	romps	rompais	romprai	romprais	rompis	ai rompu	rompant
	romps	rompais	rompras	romprais	rompis	as rompu	56
	rompt	rompait	rompra	romprait	rompit	a rompu	

verb	present	imperfect	future	conditional	past historic	perfect	present participle
	rompons	*rompions*	*romprons*	*romprions*	*rompîmes*	*avons rompu*	
	rompez	*rompiez*	*romprez*	*rompriez*	*rompîtes*	*avez rompu*	
	rompent	*rompaient*	*rompront*	*rompraient*	*rompirent*	*ont rompu*	
	32						
vendre	*vends*	*vendais*	*vendrai*	*vendrais*	*vendis*	*ai vendu*	*vendant*
	vends	*vendais*	*vendras*	*vendrais*	*vendis*	*as vendu*	56
	vend	*vendait*	*vendra*	*vendrait*	*vendit*	*a vendu*	
	vendons	*vendions*	*vendrons*	*vendrions*	*vendîmes*	*avons vendu*	
	vendez	*vendiez*	*vendrez*	*vendriez*	*vendîtes*	*avez vendu*	
	vendent	*vendaient*	*vendront*	*vendraient*	*vendirent*	*ont vendu*	
	31	44	53	53	83	67	
vivre	*vis*	*vivais*	*vivrai*	*vivrais*	*vécus*	*ai vécu*	*vivant*
	vis	*vivais*	*vivras*	*vivrais*	*vécus*	*as vécu*	
	vit	*vivait*	*vivra*	*vivrait*	*vécut*	*a vécu*	
	vivons	*vivions*	*vivrons*	*vivrions*	*vécûmes*	*avons vécu*	
	vivez	*viviez*	*vivrez*	*vivriez*	*vécûtes*	*avez vécu*	
	vivent	*vivaient*	*vivront*	*vivraient*	*vécurent*	*ont vécu*	
	37			53	84		

170 Group 4 –oir verbs

Remember that Group 4 verbs are very diverse in their tense formations.

verb	present	imperfect	future	conditional	past historic	perfect	present participle
(s')asseoir	assieds	asseyais	assiérai	assiérais	assis	suis assis	asseyant
	assieds	asseyais	assiéras	assiérais	assis	es assis	56
	assied	asseyait	assiéra	assiérait	assit	est assis(e)	
	asseyons	asseyions	assiérons	assiérions	assîmes	sommes assis	
	asseyez	asseyiez	assiérez	assiériez	assîtes	êtes assis(e/s)	
	asseyent	asseyaient	assiéront	assiéraient	assirent	sont assis(es)	
	42				86		
avoir	ai	avais	aurai	aurais	eus	ai eu	ayant
	as	avais	auras	aurais	eus	as eu	57
	a	avait	aura	aurait	eut	a eu	
	avons	avions	aurons	aurions	eûmes	avons eu	
	avez	aviez	aurez	auriez	eûtes	avez eu	
	ont	avaient	auront	auraient	eurent	ont eu	
	42	44	55	55	87		
devoir	dois	devais	devrai	devrais	dus	ai dû	devant
	dois	devais	devras	devrais	dus	as dû	56
	doit	devait	devra	devrait	dut	a dû	
	devons	devions	devrons	devrions	dûmes	avons dû	
	devez	deviez	devrez	devriez	dûtes	avez dû	
	doivent	devaient	devront	devraient	durent	ont dû	
	42		55	55	87		
falloir	faut	fallait	faudra	faudrait	fallut	a fallu	–
	42		55	55	87		
pleuvoir	pleut	pleuvait	pleuvra	pleuvrait	plut	a plu	pleuvant
	42		55	55	87		56

verb	present	imperfect	future	conditional	past historic	perfect	present participle
pouvoir	*peux*	*pouvais*	*pourrai*	*pourrais*	*pus*	*ai pu*	*pouvant*
	peux	*pouvais*	*pourras*	*pourrais*	*pus*	*as pu*	56
	peut	*pouvait*	*pourra*	*pourrait*	*put*	*a pu*	
	pouvons	*pouvions*	*pourrons*	*pourrions*	*pûmes*	*avons pu*	
	pouvez	*pouviez*	*pourrez*	*pourriez*	*pûtes*	*avez pu*	
	peuvent	*pouvaient*	*pourront*	*pourraient*	*purent*	*ont pu*	
	42	44	55	55	87	67	
recevoir	*reçois*	*recevais*	*recevrai*	*recevrais*	*reçus*	*ai reçu*	*recevant*
	reçois	*recevais*	*recevras*	*recevrais*	*reçus*	*as reçu*	56
	reçoit	*recevait*	*recevra*	*recevrait*	*reçut*	*a reçu*	
	recevons	*recevions*	*recevrons*	*recevrions*	*reçûmes*	*avons reçu*	
	recevez	*receviez*	*recevrez*	*receviez*	*reçûtes*	*avez reçu*	
	reçoivent	*recevaient*	*recevront*	*recevraient*	*reçurent*	*ont reçu*	
	40	44	55	55	87	67	
savoir	*sais*	*savais*	*saurai*	*saurais*	*sus*	*ai su*	*sachant*
	sais	*savais*	*sauras*	*saurais*	*sus*	*as su*	57
	sait	*savait*	*saura*	*saurait*	*sut*	*a su*	
	savons	*savions*	*saurons*	*saurions*	*sûmes*	*avons su*	
	savez	*saviez*	*saurez*	*sauriez*	*sûtes*	*avez su*	
	savent	*savaient*	*sauront*	*sauraient*	*surent*	*ont su*	
	42	44	55	55	87	67	

	Present	Imperfect	Future	Conditional	Past historic	Perfect	Participle
valoir	vaux	valais	vaudrai	vaudrais	valus	ai valu	valant
	vaux	valais	vaudras	vaudrais	valus	as valu	56
	vaut	valait	vaudra	vaudrait	valut	a valu	
	valons	valions	vaudrons	vaudrions	valûmes	avons valu	
	valez	valiez	vaudrez	vaudriez	valûtes	avez valu	
	valent	valaient	vaudront	vaudraient	valurent	ont valu	
	42	44	55	55	87		
voir	vois	voyais	verrai	verrais	vis	ai vu	voyant
	vois	voyais	verras	verrais	vis	as vu	56
	voit	voyait	verra	verrait	vit	a vu	
	voyons	voyions	verrons	verrions	vîmes	avons vu	
	voyez	voyiez	verrez	verriez	vîtes	avez vu	
	voient	voyaient	verront	verraient	virent	ont vu	
	41	44	55	55	87		
vouloir	veux	voulais	voudrai	voudrais	voulus	ai voulu	voulant
	veux	voulais	voudras	voudrais	voulus	as voulu	56
	veut	voulait	voudra	voudrait	voulut	a voulu	
	voulons	voulions	voudrons	voudrions	voulûmes	avons voulu	
	voulez	vouliez	voudrez	voudriez	voulûtes	avez voulu	
	veulent	voulaient	voudront	voudraient	voulurent	ont voulu	
	42		55	55	87		

SUBJUNCTIVE MOOD

Group 1 –er Verbs

171 Group 1 –er verbs

verb	present	imperfect	perfect	pluperfect
porter	*porte*	*portasse*	*aie porté*	*eusse porté*
	portes	*portasses*	*aies porté*	*eusses porté*
	porte	*portât*	*ait porté*	*eût porté*
	portions	*portassions*	*ayons porté*	*eussions porté*
	portiez	*portassiez*	*ayez porté*	*eussiez porté*
	portent	*portassent*	*aient porté*	*eussent porté*
	92	100		
acheter	*achète*	*achetasse*	*aie acheté*	*eusse acheté*
	achètes	*achetasses*	*aies acheté*	*eusses acheté*
	achète	*achetât*	*ait acheté*	*eût acheté*
	achetions	*achetassions*	*ayons acheté*	*eussions acheté*
	achetiez	*achetassiez*	*ayez acheté*	*eussiez acheté*
	achètent	*achetassent*	*aient acheté*	*eussent acheté*
	92			
aller	*aille*	*allasse*	*sois allé*	*fusse allé*
	ailles	*allasses*	*sois allé*	*fusses allé*
	aille	*allât*	*soit allé(e)*	*fût allé(e)*
	allions	*allassions*	*soyons allés*	*fussions allés*
	alliez	*allassiez*	*soyez allé(e/s)*	*fussiez allé(e/s)*
	aillent	*allassent*	*soient allé(e)s*	*fussent allé(e)s*
	93	100		

appeler

appelle	appelasse	aie appelé	eusse appelé
appelles	appelasses	aies appelé	eusses appelé
appelle	appelât	ait appelé	eût appelé
appelions	appelassions	ayons appelé	eussions appelé
appeliez	appelassiez	ayez appelé	eussiez appelé
appellent	appelassent	aient appelé	eussent appelé
92			

commencer

commence	commençasse	aie commencé	eusse commencé
commences	commençasses	aies commencé	eusses commencé
commence	commençât	ait commencé	eût commencé
commencions	commençassions	ayons commencé	eussions commencé
commenciez	commençassiez	ayez commencé	eussiez commencé
commencent	commençassent	aient commencé	eussent commencé
92			

envoyer

envoie	envoyasse	aie envoyé	eusse envoyé
envoies	envoyasses	aies envoyé	eusses envoyé
envoie	envoyât	ait envoyé	eût envoyé
envoyions	envoyassions	ayons envoyé	eussions envoyé
envoyiez	envoyassiez	ayez envoyé	eussiez envoyé
envoient	envoyassent	aient envoyé	eussent envoyé

espérer

espère	espérasse	aie espéré	eusse espéré
espères	espérasses	aies espéré	eusses espéré

verb	present	imperfect	perfect	pluperfect
	espère	espérât	ait espéré	eût espéré
	espérions	espérassions	ayons espéré	eussions espéré
	espériez	espérassiez	ayez espéré	eussiez espéré
	espèrent	espérassent	aient espéré	eussent espéré
	92			
manger	mange	mangeasse	aie mangé	eusse mangé
	manges	mangeasses	aies mangé	eusses mangé
	mange	mangeât	ait mangé	eût mangé
	mangions	mangeassions	ayons mangé	eussions mangé
	mangiez	mangeassiez	ayez mangé	eussiez mangé
	mangent	mangeassent	aient mangé	eussent mangé
	92			
mener	mène	menasse	aie mené	eusse mené
	mènes	menasses	aies mené	eusses mené
	mène	menât	ait mené	eût mené
	menions	menassions	ayons mené	eussions mené
	meniez	menassiez	ayez mené	eussiez mené
	mènent	menassent	aient mené	eussent mené
	92			

172 Group 2 *–ir* verbs

verb	present	imperfect	perfect	pluperfect
finir	*finisse*	*finisse*	*aie fini*	*eusse fini*
	finisses	*finisses*	*aies fini*	*eusses fini*
	finisse	*finît*	*ait fini*	*eût fini*
	finissions	*finissions*	*ayons fini*	*eussions fini*
	finissiez	*finissiez*	*ayez fini*	*eussiez fini*
	finissent	*finissent*	*aient fini*	*eussent fini*
	94	100		
courir	*coure*	*courusse*	*aie couru*	*eusse couru*
	coures	*courusses*	*aies couru*	*eusses couru*
	coure	*courût*	*ait couru*	*eût couru*
	courions	*courussions*	*ayons couru*	*eussions couru*
	couriez	*courussiez*	*ayez couru*	*eussiez couru*
	courent	*courussent*	*aient couru*	*eussent couru*
	94	100		
cueillir	*cueille*	*cueillisse*	*aie cueilli*	*eusse cueilli*
	cueilles	*cueillisses*	*aies cueilli*	*eusses cueilli*
	cueille	*cueillît*	*ait cueilli*	*eût cueilli*
	cueillions	*cueillissions*	*ayons cueilli*	*eussions cueilli*
	cueilliez	*cueillissiez*	*ayez cueilli*	*eussiez cueilli*
	cueillent	*cueillissent*	*aient cueilli*	*eussent cueilli*
	94			
dormir	*dorme*	*dormisse*	*aie dormi*	*eusse dormi*
	dormes	*dormisses*	*aies dormi*	*eusses dormi*
	dorme	*dormît*	*ait dormi*	*eût dormi*
	dormions	*dormissions*	*ayons dormi*	*eussions dormi*
	dormiez	*dormissiez*	*ayez dormi*	*eussiez dormi*
	dorment	*dormissent*	*aient dormi*	*eussent dormi*

verb	present	imperfect	perfect	pluperfect
mourir	*meure*	*mourusse*	*sois mort*	*fusse mort*
	meures	*mourusses*	*sois mort*	*fusses mort*
	meure	*mourût*	*soit mort(e)*	*fût mort(e)*
	mourions	*mourussions*	*soyons morts*	*fussions morts*
	mouriez	*mourussiez*	*soyez mort(e / s)*	*fussiez mort(e / s)*
	meurent	*mourussent*	*soient mort(e)s*	*fussent mort(e)s*
ouvrir	*ouvre*	*ouvrisse*	*aie ouvert*	*eusse ouvert*
	ouvres	*ouvrisses*	*aies ouvert*	*eusses ouvert*
	ouvre	*ouvrît*	*ait ouvert*	*eût ouvert*
	ouvrions	*ouvrissions*	*ayons ouvert*	*eussions ouvert*
	ouvriez	*ouvrissiez*	*ayez ouvert*	*eussiez ouvert*
	ouvrent	*ouvrissent*	*aient ouvert*	*eussent ouvert*
partir	*parte*	*partisse*	*sois parti*	*fusse parti*
	partes	*partisses*	*sois parti*	*fusses parti*
	parte	*partît*	*soit parti(e)*	*fût parti(e)*
	partions	*partissions*	*soyons partis*	*fussions partis*
	partiez	*partissiez*	*soyez parti(e / s)*	*fussiez parti(e / s)*
	partent	*partissent*	*soient parti(e)s*	*fussent parti(e)s*
venir	*vienne*	*vinsse*	*sois venu*	*fusse venu*
	viennes	*vinsses*	*sois venu*	*fusses venu*
	vienne	*vînt*	*soit venu(e)*	*fût venu(e)*
	venions	*vinssions*	*soyons venus*	*fussions venus*
	veniez	*vinssiez*	*soyez venu(e / s)*	*fussiez venu(e / s)*
	viennent	*vinssent*	*soient venu(e)s*	*fussent venu(e)s*

173 Group 3 –re verbs

verb	present	imperfect	perfect	pluperfect
battre	*batte*	*battisse*	*aie battu*	*eusse battu*
	battes	*battisses*	*aies battu*	*eusses battu*
	batte	*battît*	*ait battu*	*eût battu*
	battions	*battissions*	*ayons battu*	*eussions battu*
	battiez	*battissiez*	*ayez battu*	*eussiez battu*
	battent	*battissent*	*aient battu*	*eussent battu*
	95			
boire	*boive*	*busse*	*aie bu*	*eusse bu*
	boives	*busses*	*aies bu*	*eusses bu*
	boive	*bût*	*ait bu*	*eût bu*
	buvions	*bussions*	*ayons bu*	*eussions bu*
	buviez	*bussiez*	*ayez bu*	*eussiez bu*
	boivent	*bussent*	*aient bu*	*eussent bu*
conclure	*conclue*	*conclusse*	*aie conclu*	*eusse conclu*
	conclues	*conclusses*	*aies conclu*	*eusses conclu*
	conclue	*conclût*	*ait conclu*	*eût conclu*
	concluions	*conclussions*	*ayons conclu*	*eussions conclu*
	concluiez	*conclussiez*	*ayez conclu*	*eussiez conclu*
	concluent	*conclussent*	*aient conclu*	*eussent conclu*
conduire	*conduise*	*conduisisse*	*aie conduit*	*eusse conduit*
	conduises	*conduisisses*	*aies conduit*	*eusses conduit*
	conduise	*conduisît*	*ait conduit*	*eût conduit*
	conduisions	*conduisissions*	*ayons conduit*	*eussions conduit*
	conduisiez	*conduisissiez*	*ayez conduit*	*eussiez conduit*
	conduisent	*conduisissent*	*aient conduit*	*eussent conduit*
	95			

verb	present	imperfect	perfect	pluperfect
craindre	*craigne*	*craignisse*	*aie craint*	*eusse craint*
	craignes	*craignisses*	*aies craint*	*eusses craint*
	craigne	*craignît*	*ait craint*	*eût craint*
	craignions	*craignissions*	*ayons craint*	*eussions craint*
	craigniez	*craignissiez*	*ayez craint*	*eussiez craint*
	craignent	*craignissent*	*aient craint*	*eussent craint*
croire	*croie*	*crusse*	*aie cru*	*eusse cru*
	croies	*crusses*	*aies cru*	*eusses cru*
	croie	*crût*	*ait cru*	*eût cru*
	croyions	*crussions*	*ayons cru*	*eussions cru*
	croyiez	*crussiez*	*ayez cru*	*eussiez cru*
	croient	*crussent*	*aient cru*	*eussent cru*
	95			
dire	*dise*	*disse*	*aie dit*	*eusse dit*
	dises	*disses*	*aies dit*	*eusses dit*
	dise	*dît*	*ait dit*	*eût dit*
	disions	*dissions*	*ayons dit*	*eussions dit*
	disiez	*dissiez*	*ayez dit*	*eussiez dit*
	disent	*dissent*	*aient dit*	*eussent dit*
	95			
écrire	*écrive*	*écrivisse*	*aie écrit*	*eusse écrit*
	écrives	*écrivisses*	*aies écrit*	*eusses écrit*
	écrive	*écrivît*	*ait écrit*	*eût écrit*
	écrivions	*écrivissions*	*ayons écrit*	*eussions écrit*
	écriviez	*écrivissiez*	*ayez écrit*	*eussiez écrit*
	écrivent	*écrivissent*	*aient écrit*	*eussent écrit*
	95			
être	*sois*	*fusse*	*aie été*	*eusse été*
	sois	*fusses*	*aies été*	*eusses été*
	soit	*fût*	*ait été*	*eût été*
	soyons	*fussions*	*ayons été*	*eussions été*

	soyez	fussiez	ayez été	eussiez été
	soient	fussent	aient été	eussent été
	96	100		
faire	fasse	fisse	aie fait	eusse fait
	fasses	fisses	aies fait	eusses fait
	fasse	fît	ait fait	eût fait
	fassions	fissions	ayons fait	eussions fait
	fassiez	fissiez	ayez fait	eussiez fait
	fassent	fissent	aient fait	eussent fait
	96			
lire	lise	lusse	aie lu	eusse lu
	lises	lusses	aies lu	eusses lu
	lise	lût	ait lu	eût lu
	lisions	lussions	ayons lu	eussions lu
	lisiez	lussiez	ayez lu	eussiez lu
	lisent	lussent	aient lu	eussent lu
mettre	mette	misse	aie mis	eusse mis
	mettes	misses	aies mis	eusses mis
	mette	mît	ait mis	eût mis
	mettions	missions	ayons mis	eussions mis
	mettiez	missiez	ayez mis	eussiez mis
	mettent	missent	aient mis	eussent mis
perdre	perde	perdisse	aie perdu	eusse perdu
	perdes	perdisses	aies perdu	eusses perdu
	perde	perdît	ait perdu	eût perdu
	perdions	perdissions	ayons perdu	eussions perdu
	perdiez	perdissiez	ayez perdu	eussiez perdu
	perdent	perdissent	aient perdu	eussent perdu
prendre	prenne	prisse	aie pris	eusse pris
	prennes	prisses	aies pris	eusses pris
	prenne	prît	ait pris	eût pris
	prenions	prissions	ayons pris	eussions pris
	preniez	prissiez	ayez pris	eussiez pris
	prennent	prissent	aient pris	eussent pris

verb	present	imperfect	perfect	pluperfect
répondre	*réponde*	*répondisse*	*aie répondu*	*eusse répondu*
	répondes	*répondisses*	*aies répondu*	*eusses répondu*
	réponde	*répondît*	*ait répondu*	*eût répondu*
	répondions	*répondissions*	*ayons répondu*	*eussions répondu*
	répondiez	*répondissiez*	*ayez répondu*	*eussiez répondu*
	répondent	*répondissent*	*aient répondu*	*eussent répondu*
rire	*rie*	*risse*	*aie ri*	*eusse ri*
	ries	*risses*	*aies ri*	*eusses ri*
	rie	*rît*	*ait ri*	*eût ri*
	riions	*rissions*	*ayons ri*	*eussions ri*
	riiez	*rissiez*	*ayez ri*	*eussiez ri*
	rient	*rissent*	*aient ri*	*eussent ri*
rompre	*rompe*	*rompisse*	*aie rompu*	*eusse rompu*
	rompes	*rompisses*	*aies rompu*	*eusses rompu*
	rompe	*rompît*	*ait rompu*	*eût rompu*
	rompions	*rompissions*	*ayons rompu*	*eussions rompu*
	rompiez	*rompissiez*	*ayez rompu*	*eussiez rompu*
	rompent	*rompissent*	*aient rompu*	*eussent rompu*
	95			
vendre	*vende*	*vendisse*	*aie vendu*	*eusse vendu*
	vendes	*vendisses*	*aies vendu*	*eusses vendu*
	vende	*vendît*	*ait vendu*	*eût vendu*
	vendions	*vendissions*	*ayons vendu*	*eussions vendu*
	vendiez	*vendissiez*	*ayez vendu*	*eussiez vendu*
	vendent	*vendissent*	*aient vendu*	*eussent vendu*
	95	100		
vivre	*vive*	*vécusse*	*aie vécu*	*eusse vécu*
	vives	*vécusses*	*aies vécu*	*eusses vécu*
	vive	*vécût*	*ait vécu*	*eût vécu*
	vivions	*vécussions*	*ayons vécu*	*eussions vécu*
	viviez	*vécussiez*	*ayez vécu*	*eussiez vécu*
	vivent	*vécussent*	*aient vécu*	*eussent vécu*

Group 4 –oir Verbs

174 Group 4 –oir verbs

verb	present	imperfect	perfect	pluperfect
(s')asseoir	asseye	assisse	sois assis	fusse assis
	asseyes	assisses	sois assis	fusses assis
	asseye	assît	soit assis(e)	fût assis(e)
	asseyions	assissions	soyons assis	fussions assis
	asseyiez	assissiez	soyez assis (e / s)	fussiez assis (e / s)
	asseyent	assissent	soient assis(es)	fussent assis(es)
	98	100		
avoir	aie	eusse	aie eu	eusse eu
	aies	eusses	aies eu	eusses eu
	ait	eût	ait eu	eût eu
	ayons	eussions	ayons eu	eussions eu
	ayez	eussiez	ayez eu	eussiez eu
	aient	eussent	aient eu	eussent eu
		100		
devoir	doive	dusse	aie dû	eusse dû
	doives	dusses	aies dû	eusses dû
	doive	dût	ait dû	eût dû
	devions	dussions	ayons dû	eussions dû
	deviez	dussiez	ayez dû	eussiez dû
	doivent	dussent	aient dû	eussent dû
	97			
falloir	faille	fallût	ait fallu	eût fallu
pleuvoir	pleuve	plût	ait plu	eût plu
pouvoir	puisse	pusse	aie pu	eusse pu
	puisses	pusses	aies pu	eusses pu
	puisse	pût	ait pu	eût pu
	pouvions	pussions	ayons pu	eussions pu
	pouviez	pussiez	ayez pu	eussiez pu
	puissent	pussent	aient pu	eussent pu
	98	100		

verb	present	imperfect	perfect	pluperfect
recevoir	*reçoive*	*reçusse*	*aie reçu*	*eusse reçu*
	reçoives	*reçusses*	*aies reçu*	*eusses reçu*
	reçoive	*reçût*	*ait reçu*	*eût reçu*
	recevions	*reçussions*	*ayons reçu*	*eussions reçu*
	receviez	*reçussiez*	*ayez reçu*	*eussiez reçu*
	reçoivent	*reçussent*	*aient reçu*	*eussent reçu*
	97			
savoir	*sache*	*susse*	*aie su*	*eusse su*
	saches	*susses*	*aies su*	*eusses su*
	sache	*sût*	*ait su*	*eût su*
	sachions	*sussions*	*ayons su*	*eussions su*
	sachiez	*sussiez*	*ayez su*	*eussiez su*
	sachent	*sussent*	*aient su*	*eussent su*
	98			
valoir	*vaille*	*valusse*	*aie valu*	*eusse valu*
	vailles	*valusses*	*aies valu*	*eusses valu*
	vaille	*valût*	*ait valu*	*eût valu*
	valions	*valussions*	*ayons valu*	*eussions valu*
	valiez	*valussiez*	*ayez valu*	*eussiez valu*
	vaillent	*valussent*	*aient valu*	*eussent valu*
voir	*voie*	*visse*	*aie vu*	*eusse vu*
	voies	*visses*	*aies vu*	*eusses vu*
	voie	*vît*	*ait vu*	*eût vu*
	voyions	*vissions*	*ayons vu*	*eussions vu*
	voyiez	*vissiez*	*ayez vu*	*eussiez vu*
	voient	*vissent*	*aient vu*	*eussent vu*
	97			
vouloir	*veuille*	*voulusse*	*aie voulu*	*eusse voulu*
	veuilles	*voulusses*	*aies voulu*	*eusses voulu*
	veuille	*voulût*	*ait voulu*	*eût voulu*
	voulions	*voulussions*	*ayons voulu*	*eussions voulu*
	vouliez	*voulussiez*	*ayez voulu*	*eussiez voulu*
	veuillent	*voulussent*	*aient voulu*	*eussent voulu*
	98			

Exercises

Réécrivez les passage suivants en donnant les formes du verbe qui conviennent –

a **Naissance de la haine dans le couple**

« Je DÉPÉRIR en son absence. Je me VIDER de mon sens. Il SUPPORTER mal. En fait, je VOULOIR ÊTRE lui. Mais il CHANGER les règles du jeu; l'intranquillité me RENDRE haineuse. »

« Elle me ENTRAÎNER dans cette intensité et se LASSER. Je AVOIR la haine » RECONNAÎTRE Franck, « Je SE SENTIR MANIPULER et PERDRE. »

« Si je AVOIR 20 ans, je le QUITTER avec un plan de reconquête; mais à mon âge, je SAVOIR que le temps PASSER ÊTRE PERDRE pour son désir. Je POUVOIR SE FLINGUER parce que tout ÊTRE JOUER et que je ÊTRE lasse. »

b **Mon patron et moi**

Ce lundi-là, je CAUSER à Pénélope près de la machine à café. Mon patron PASSER devant nous et me LANCER, sans même nous REGARDER: « Je POUVOIR te VOIR, s'il te PLAIRE? », le « s'il te PLAIRE » qui FINIR un ton au-dessus du « Je POUVOIR te VOIR . . .», un « s'il te PLAIRE » qui VOULOIR DIRE: « Si ça te PLAIRE pas, ce ÊTRE pareil. » Je JETER mon gobelet et je OBÉIR docile comme un chien. Je SENTIR dans mon dos le regard de Pénélope PLANTER devant le distributeur d'expressos. Ce ÊTRE en SUIVRE le patron dans le couloir que je SAVOIR ce que je AVOIR à faire. Je DIRE: « Hervé! », avec le « vé » de Hervé un ton au-dessus. Il SE RETOURNER et je lui SAUTER à la gorge en PLANTER mes incisives dans son cou trop gras. Il MOURIR en GIGOTER comme un ver, dans le sang qu'il AVOIR toujours tiède.

c **Le Land Rover**

Si par essence toutes les automobiles CONCEVOIR pour le voyage, certaines en DEVENIR des icônes. Ce ÊTRE le cas du Land Rover dont la simple apparition ÉVOQUER la jungle la plus profonde, les sables du désert. Le « land » ÊTRE une légende vivante. Il CRÉER en 1947 et à l'origine CONSTRUIRE avec une carrosserie aluminium qui RÉCUPÉRER sur les carlingues des avions de chasse. Depuis ce temps-là, il POURSUIVRE sa carrière sans que rien ne SEMBLER POUVOIR le ARRÊTER. Quoi qu'en DIRE certains, cette automobile RESTER un extraordinaire moyen de transport.

d **J'aime le mec qu'il ne faut pas**

Tu ne CONVOITER point. « Les filles ÊTRE jalouses et envieuses même entre elles » PLAISANTER Victor Gérard. Elles VOULOIR toujours ce que AVOIR leurs copines. Même leur mec. Alors quand Anne, votre meilleure amie, vous ANNONCER toute fière qu'enfin elle METTRE ses mains sur Matthieu . . . Hier encore, vous ne le REMARQUER même pas, mais aujourd'hui il AVOIR tout de suite beaucoup plus d'intérêt. Avec le temps, les regards SE FAIRE de plus en plus APPUYER entre vous et lui. Il FALLOIR SE RENDRE à l'évidence: vous CRAQUER pour ce beau brun!

e **J'ai guéri de mon hépatite C**

Le virus DISPARAÎTRE, mais il FALLOIR toutefois CONTINUER les injections hebdomadaires d'interféron. Je SE RENSEIGNER via Internet. Je SAVOIR que l'interféron ÊTRE une substance naturelle PRODUIRE par les cellules CHARGER de DÉFENDRE l'organisme. Cela me RASSURER lors des injections, que je FAIRE moi-même. Je SE SENTIR de plus en plus FATIGUER mais je

S'ACCROCHER. L'enthousiasme de mon hépatologue me PORTER. Mais je
DÉCIDER de CHERCHER de l'aide ailleurs et je SE FAIRE PRESCRIRE des
séances de kinésithérapie, qui me RÉCONFORTER. Je aussi FAIRE appel à un
acupuncteur dans l'idée de mieux FAIRE CIRCULER les énergies – cela me
AIDER à SOULAGER mes douleurs musculaires.

Chapter 4 *Verb list*

175 Using the list

This list contains the most frequently used French verbs. However, it does not include verbs conjugated like ***porter***, ie those hundreds of verbs belonging to Group 1 *–er* verbs. Each verb occurs in the first column with its meaning, and in the second column has a reference to another verb with which its conjugation is identical or very closely linked, when the verb itself occurs in the tabular section. By referring to the verb mentioned in the second column, it will be possible to deduce the forms of the paradigm of the verb that is being looked up.

For example, to discover the paradigm of ***abattre***, it is simply a matter of consulting the ***battre*** entry in the Tables above, and making the appropriate adjustments to ***abattre*** in the light of the information contained there (169, 173), where reference is also made to the discursive section (33, 56).

176 The list

verb	conjugated like
abattre = to knock down	***battre***
abolir = to abolish	***finir***
aboutir = to finish up	***finir***
aboyer = to bark	***essayer***
abréger = to abridge	***espérer*** + ***manger***
absoudre = to absolve	present – ***absous / absous / absout / absolvons / absolvez / absolvent***; but no past historic tense or imperfect subjunctive; past participle – ***absous***
s'abstenir = to abstain	***venir***
accéder = to reach	***espérer***
accélérer = to speed up	***espérer***
accomplir = to accomplish	***finir***
accourir = to run up	***courir***
accueillir = to welcome	***cueillir***
acheter = to buy	***acheter***
achever = to complete	***mener***
acquérir = to acquire	present – ***acquiers / acquiers / acquiert / acquérons / acquérez / acquièrent***; future and conditional – ***acquerrai***, etc; ***acquerrais***, etc; past historic – ***acquis / acquis / acquit / acquîmes / acquîtes / acquirent***; past participle ***acquis***
adhérer = to stick	***espérer***
admettre = to admit	***mettre***

verb	conjugated like
adoucir = to soften	*finir*
affaiblir = to weaken	*finir*
affermir = to strengthen	*finir*
affliger = to afflict	*manger*
affranchir = to liberate	*finir*
agacer = to annoy	*commencer*
agir = to act	*finir*
agrandir = to enlarge	*finir*
aller = to go	*aller*
allonger = to lengthen	*manger*
alourdir = to weigh down	*finir*
altérer = to affect	*espérer*
amaigrir = to slim	*finir*
amener = to bring	*mener*
annoncer = to announce	*commencer*
apercevoir = to notice	*recevoir*
apparaître = to appear	*paraître*
appartenir = to belong	*venir*
appeler = to call	*appeler*
applaudir = to applaud	*finir*
apprendre = to learn	*prendre*
appuyer = to support	*essayer*
assaillir = to attack	*cueillir*
(s')asseoir = to sit (down)	*(s')asseoir*
atteindre = to reach	present – *atteins / atteins / atteint / atteignons / atteignez / atteignent*; past historic – *atteignis / atteignis / atteignit / atteignîmes / atteignîtes / atteignirent*; past participle – *atteint*
attendre = to wait	*vendre*
avancer = to advance	*commencer*
avertir = to warn	*finir*
avoir = to have	*avoir*
balancer = to sway	*commencer*
bannir = to banish	*finir*
battre = to beat	*battre*
bégayer = to stammer	*essayer*
bénir = to bless	*finir*
blanchir = to whiten	*finir*
blasphémer = to blaspheme	*espérer*
boire = to drink	*boire*
bondir = to leap	*finir*
bouger = to move	*manger*
broyer = to crush	*essayer*
brunir = to burnish	*finir*
cacheter = to seal	*jeter*
céder = to yield	*espérer*
célébrer = to celebrate	*espérer*
chanceler = to totter	*appeler*
changer = to change	*manger*
charger = to load	*manger*

verb	conjugated like
chérir = *to cherish*	**finir**
choisir = *to choose*	**finir**
combattre = *to fight*	**battre**
commencer = *to begin*	**commencer**
commercer = *to trade*	**commencer**
commettre = *to commit*	**mettre**
compléter = *to complete*	**espérer**
comprendre = *to understand*	**prendre**
compromettre = *to compromise*	**mettre**
concéder = *to concede*	**espérer**
concevoir = *to conceive*	**recevoir**
conclure = *to conclude*	**conclure**
conduire = *to drive*	**conduire**
confondre = *to confound*	**répondre**
connaître = *to know*	**paraître**
conquérir = *to conquer*	**venir** + **acquérir**
consentir = *to consent*	**courir**
considérer = *to consider*	**espérer**
construire = *to construct*	**conduire**
contraindre = *to constrain*	**craindre**
contredire = *to contradict*	**dire** but 2nd pers pl present – **contredisez**
contrefaire = *to counterfeit*	**faire**
convaincre = *to convince*	**vaincre**
convenir = *to admit, to agree*	**venir**
convertir = *to convert*	**finir**
corrompre = *to corrupt*	**rompre**
coudoyer = *to mix with*	**essayer**
courir = *to run*	**courir**
couvrir = *to cover*	**ouvrir**
craindre = *to fear*	**craindre**
crever = *to burst*	**mener**
croire = *to believe*	**croire**
cueillir = *to gather*	**cueillir**
cuire = *to cook*	**conduire**
débattre = *to discuss*	**battre**
décevoir = *to deceive*	**recevoir**
décharger = *to unload*	**manger**
décourager = *discourage*	**manger**
découvrir = *to discover*	**ouvrir**
décrire = *to describe*	**écrire**
dédicacer = *dedicate*	**commencer**
déduire = *to deduce*	**conduire**
défaillir = *to faint*	**faillir**
défaire = *to undo*	**faire**
défendre = *to defend*	**vendre**
définir = *to define*	**finir**
dégager = *to free*	**manger**

verb	conjugated like
dégeler = to defrost	**acheter**
délibérer = to discuss	**espérer**
déménager = to move	**manger**
démolir = to demolish	**finir**
dénoncer = to denounce	**commencer**
dépeindre = to depict	**atteindre**
dépendre = to depend	**prendre**
déplacer = to dislodge	**commencer**
déplaire = to displease	**plaire**
déranger = to disturb	**manger**
descendre = to descend	**vendre**
désespérer = to despair	**espérer**
désobéir = to disobey	**finir**
dessécher = to dry out	**espérer**
détendre = to release	**vendre**
détruire = to destroy	**conduire**
devancer = to outstrip	**commencer**
devenir = to become	**venir**
devoir = to owe	**devoir**
digérer = to digest	**espérer**
dire = to speak	**dire**
diriger = to direct	**manger**
disparaître = to disappear	**paraître**
dissoudre = to dissolve	**absoudre**; but no past historic or imperfect subjunctive
divertir = to entertain	**finir**
dormir = to sleep	**dormir**
éblouir = to dazzle	**finir**
échanger = to exchange	**manger**
éclaircir = to clarify	**finir**
écrire = to write	**écrire**
égayer = to enliven	**essayer**
élargir = to broaden	**finir**
élever = to raise	**mener**
élire = to elect	**lire**
embellir = to embellish	**finir**
émettre = to emit	**mettre**
emmener = to lead	**mener**
employer = to employ	**essayer**
encourager = to encourage	**manger**
endommager = to damage	**manger**
enfoncer = to push in	**commencer**
engager = to hire	**manger**
enlacer = to embrace	**commencer**
enlaidir = to make ugly	**finir**
enlever = to take off	**mener**
ennuyer = to bore	**essayer**
énoncer = to pronounce	**commencer**
enrichir = to enrich	**finir**
entendre = to hear	**vendre**

verb	conjugated like
entrelacer = *to intertwine*	**commencer**
entreprendre = *to undertake*	**prendre**
entretenir = *to maintain*	**venir**
entrevoir = *to glimpse*	**voir**
énumérer = *to enumerate*	**espérer**
envahir = *to invade*	**finir**
envisager = *to envisage*	**manger**
envoyer = *to send*	**envoyer**
épeler = *to spell*	**appeler**
éponger = *to mop*	**manger**
ériger = *to erect*	**manger**
espérer = *to hope*	**espérer**
essayer = *to try*	$y > i$ in sg + 3rd pers pl present tense; in future and conditional $-i-$ is used throughout – **essaierai**, etc; **essaierais**, etc
essuyer = *to wipe*	**essayer**
établir = *to establish*	**finir**
éteindre = *to extinguish*	**atteindre**
étendre = *to stretch*	**vendre**
étinceler = *to sparkle*	**appeler**
être = *to be*	**être**
étreindre = *to embrace*	**atteindre**
exagérer = *to exaggerate*	**espérer**
excéder = *to exceed*	**espérer**
exclure = *to exclude*	**conclure**
faiblir = *to weaken*	**finir**
faillir = *to almost*	present – **faux / faux / faut / faillons / faillez / faillent**
faire = *to do*	**faire**
falloir = *to be necessary*	**falloir**
feindre = *to feign*	**atteindre**
fendre = *to split*	**vendre**
feuilleter = *to leaf through*	**jeter**
finir = *to finish*	**finir**
fléchir = *to bend*	**finir**
foncer = *to tear along*	**commencer**
fondre = *to melt*	**répondre**
forcer = *to force*	**commencer**
franchir = *to cross*	**finir**
frémir = *to shudder*	**finir**
froncer = *to frown*	**commencer**
fuir = *to flee*	**courir** + **y** instead of *i* for 1st and 2nd pl in present
garantir = *to guarantee*	**finir**
garnir = *to garnish*	**finir**
geindre = *to whine*	**atteindre**
geler = *to freeze*	**acheter**
gémir = *to groan*	**finir**
grandir = *to get bigger*	**finir**
grimacer = *to grimace*	**commencer**
grincer = *to creak*	**commencer**

verb	conjugated like
grossir = *to get fatter*	**finir**
guérir = *to cure*	**finir**
haïr = *to hate*	**finir** + keeps diaeresis in pl, not sg, of present tense; retains diaeresis throughout past historic
haleter = *to pant*	**acheter**
harceler = *to harass*	**acheter**
immerger = *to immerse*	**manger**
incinérer = *to cremate*	**espérer**
inclure = *to include*	**conclure**
inférer = *to infer*	**espérer**
infliger = *to inflict*	**manger**
inquiéter = *to worry*	**espérer**
inscrire = *to enrol*	**écrire**
instruire = *to teach*	**conduire**
intercéder = *to intercede*	**espérer**
interdire = *to forbid*	**dire** but 2nd pers pl present – **interdisez**
interférer = *to interfere*	**espérer**
interpréter = *to interpret*	**espérer**
interrompre = *to interrupt*	**rompre**
intervenir = *to intervene*	**venir**
introduire = *to introduce*	**conduire**
jaillir = *to spurt*	**finir**
jaunir = *to turn yellow*	**finir**
jeter = *to throw*	**jeter**
joindre = *to join*	present – **joins / joins / joint / joignons / joignez / joignent; atteindre**
jouir = *to enjoy*	**finir**
juger = *to judge*	**manger**
lacer = *to lace up*	**commencer**
lancer = *to throw*	**commencer**
lécher = *to lick*	**espérer**
libérer = *to liberate*	**espérer**
lire = *to read*	**lire**
loger = *to lodge*	**manger**
luire = *to glow*	**conduire** but past historic **luis / luis / luit / luîmes / luîtes / luirent**
maigrir = *to slim*	**finir**
maintenir = *to maintain*	**venir**
malmener = *to manhandle*	**mener**
manger = *to eat*	**manger**
maudire = *to curse*	**dire** but pl present – **maudissez / maudissons / maudissent**
méconnaître = *to misunderstand*	**paraître**
médire = *to malign*	**dire** but 2nd pers pl present – **médisez**
mélanger = *to mix*	**manger**
menacer = *to threaten*	**commencer**
ménager = *to handle*	**manger**
mener = *to lead*	**mener**
mentir = *to lie*	**courir** – 1st pers present – **mens**
mettre = *to put*	**mettre**

verb	conjugated like
mordre = *to bite*	**perdre**
mourir = *to die*	**mourir**
munir = *to equip*	**finir**
nager = *to swim*	**manger**
naître = *to be born*	**paraître**; but past historic – **naquis/naquis/naquit/** **naquîmes/naquîtes/naquirent**
négliger = *to neglect*	**manger**
neiger = *to snow*	**manger**
nettoyer = *to clean*	**essayer**
noircir = *to blacken*	**finir**
noyer = *to drown*	**essayer**
nuire = *to harm*	**conduire**
obéir = *to obey*	**finir**
obtenir = *to obtain*	**venir**
offrir = *to offer*	**ouvrir**
omettre = *to omit*	**mettre**
opérer = *to operate*	**espérer**
outrager = *to outrage*	**manger**
ouvrir = *to open*	**ouvrir**
pâlir = *to turn pale*	**finir**
parachever = *to complete*	**mener**
paraître = *to appear*	present – **parais/parais/paraît/paraissons/paraissez/** **paraissent**; past historic – **parus/parus/parut/** **parûmes/parûtes/parurent**; past participle – **paru**
parcourir = *to peruse*	**courir**
partager = *to share*	**manger**
partir = *to leave*	**partir**
parvenir = *to reach*	**venir**
payer = *to pay*	**essayer**; has either –*i*– or –*y*– in future and conditional – **paierai/payerai**, etc; **paierais/payerais**, etc
pécher = *to sin*	**espérer**
peindre = *to paint*	**atteindre**
pendre = *to hang*	**vendre**
pénétrer = *to penetrate*	**espérer**
percer = *to pierce*	**commencer**
percevoir = *to notice*	**recevoir**
perdre = *to lose*	**perdre**
périr = *to perish*	**finir**
permettre = *to allow*	**mettre**
perpétrer = *to perpetrate*	**espérer**
peser = *to weigh*	**mener**
pincer = *to pinch*	**commencer**
placer = *to place*	**commencer**
plaindre = *to pity*	**craindre**
plaire = *to please*	present – **plais/plais/plaît/plaisons/plaisez, plaisent**; past historic **plus/plus/plut/plûmes/plûtes/plurent**
pleuvoir = *to rain*	**pleuvoir**
plonger = *to dive*	**manger**
ployer = *to fold*	**essayer**

verb	conjugated like
polir = *to polish*	**finir**
poursuivre = *to pursue*	**suivre**
pourvoir = *to provide*	**voir**, but future and conditional different – **pourvoirai**, etc; **pourvoirais**, etc
pouvoir = *to be able*	**pouvoir**
prédire = *to predict*	**dire** but 2nd pers pl present – **prédisez**
préférer = *to prefer*	**espérer**
prendre = *to take*	**prendre**
prescrire = *to prescribe*	**écrire**
prétendre = *to claim*	**vendre**
prévenir = *to warn*	**venir**
prévoir = *to foresee*	**voir**, but future and conditional different – **prévoirai**, etc; **prévoirais**, etc
produire = *to produce*	**conduire**
projeter = *to project*	**jeter**
prolonger = *to prolong*	**manger**
promener = *to walk*	**mener**
promettre = *to promise*	**mettre**
prononcer = *to pronounce*	**commencer**
proscrire = *to forbid*	**écrire**
protéger = *to protect*	**espérer** + **manger**
punir = *to punish*	**finir**
racheter = *to redeem*	**acheter**
rafraîchir = *to refresh*	**finir**
rager = *to rage*	**manger**
rajeunir = *to rejuvenate*	**finir**
rallonger = *to extend*	**manger**
ramener = *to bring back*	**mener**
ranger = *to put away*	**manger**
rappeler = *to recall*	**appeler**
ravir = *to delight*	**finir**
rayer = *to delete*	**essayer**
recevoir = *to receive*	**recevoir**
reconnaître = *to recognise*	**paraître**
recouvrir = *to recover*	**ouvrir**
recueillir = *to collect*	**cueillir**
rédiger = *to edit*	**manger**
réduire = *to reduce*	**conduire**
référer = *to refer*	**espérer**
réfléchir = *to reflect*	**finir**
refléter = *to reflect*	**espérer**
réitérer = *to reiterate*	**espérer**
rejeter = *to reject*	**jeter**
se réjouir = *to rejoice*	**finir**
reluire = *to glisten*	**conduire** but past historic – **reluis/reluis/reluit/reluîmes/ reluîtes/reluirent**
remplacer = *to replace*	**commencer**
remplir = *to fill*	**finir**
renoncer = *to renounce*	**commencer**

verb	conjugated like
renouveler = *to renew*	**appeler**
renvoyer = *to send away*	**essayer**
répandre = *to spread*	**vendre**
répartir = *to distribute*	**finir** (nb not **partir**)
se repentir = *to repent*	**courir** – present – **repens**
répéter = *to repeat*	**espérer**
répondre = *to reply*	**répondre**
reprendre = *to take back*	**prendre**
reproduire = *to reproduce*	**conduire**
requérir = *to require*	**venir** + **acquérir**
résoudre = *to resolve*	**absoudre**; but past historic – **résolus/résolus/resolut/résolûmes/résolûtes/résolurent**
ressentir = *to feel*	**courir** – present – **ressens**
retenir = *to retain*	**venir**
réunir = *to assemble*	**finir**
réussir = *to succeed*	**finir**
révéler = *to reveal*	**espérer**
revenir = *to come back*	**venir**
rire = *to laugh*	**rire**
rompre = *to break*	**rompre**
rougir = *to blush*	**finir**
saillir = *to jut out*	**cueillir**
saisir = *to seize*	**finir**
salir = *to soil*	**finir**
satisfaire = *to satisfy*	**faire**
savoir = *to know*	**savoir**
sécher = *to dry*	**espérer**
secourir = *to help*	**courir**
séduire = *to seduce*	**conduire**
semer = *to sow*	**mener**
sentir = *to feel*	**courir** – present – **sens**
servir = *to serve*	**courir** – present – **sers**
songer = *to daydream*	**manger**
sortir = *to go out*	**courir** – present – **sors**
souffrir = *to suffer*	**ouvrir**
soulager = *to relieve*	**manger**
soulever = *to lift*	**mener**
soumettre = *to submit*	**mettre**
soupeser = *to weigh up*	**mener**
sourire = *to smile*	**rire**
souscrire = *to subscribe*	**écrire**
soutenir = *to sustain*	**venir**
se souvenir = *to remember*	**venir**
subir = *to undergo*	**finir**
subvenir = *to meet*	**venir**
succéder = *to succeed*	**espérer**
suffire = *to suffice*	**lire**
suggérer = *to suggest*	**espérer**
suivre = *to follow*	present – **suis/suis/suit** otherwise **vendre**

verb	conjugated like
surgir = *to appear suddenly*	**finir**
surprendre = *to surprise*	**prendre**
suspendre = *to suspend*	**vendre**
taire = *to be quiet*	present – **tais / tais / tait / taisons / taisez / taisent**; past historic – **tus / tus / tut / tûmes / tûtes / turent**
tendre = *to hold out*	**vendre**
tenir = *to hold*	**venir**
tordre = *to twist*	**perdre**
tracer = *to draw*	**commencer**
traduire = *to translate*	**conduire**
trahir = *to betray*	**finir**
transcrire = *to transcribe*	**écrire**
transférer = *to transfer*	**espérer**
tressaillir = *to tremble*	**cueillir**
tutoyer = *to use 'tu'*	**essayer**
unir = *to unite*	**finir**
vaincre = *to vanquish*	present – **vaincs / vaincs / vainc / vainquons / vainquez / vainquent**; past historic – **vainquis / vainquis / vainquit / vainquîmes / vainquîtes / vainquirent**; past participle – **vaincu**
valoir = *to be worth*	**valoir**
vendre = *to sell*	**vendre**
venger = *to avenge*	**manger**
venir = *to come*	**venir**
vêtir = *to clothe*	**partir**; past participle – **vêtu**
vieillir = *to grow old*	**finir**
vivre = *to live*	**vivre**
voir = *to see*	**voir**
vomir = *to vomit*	**finir**
vouloir = *to want to*	**vouloir**
vouvoyer = *to use 'vous'*	**essayer**
voyager = *to travel*	**manger**

Chapter 5 *Nouns and adjectives*

Nouns

177 Nouns

As has been seen, the verb is the pivotal element of the sentence (see 2) – indeed a sentence may consist entirely of a verb (***viens!*** = *come on!*, ***écoute!*** = *listen!*) or a verb and subject pronoun (***je viens*** = *I'm coming*, ***j'écoute*** = *I'm listening*); see 453. But very often the verb is accompanied by one or more nouns, or a noun and an adjective or two, and this adds more information and detail to the sentence.

Nouns in French have very much the same characteristics as nouns in English and may be used in very much the same ways. What follows is a brief résumé of their major general characteristics and uses.

Nouns are words which are preceded by a determiner – such as the definite or indefinite article, demonstrative or possessive adjective – and/or an adjective, and may be followed by an adjective and/or an adjectival phrase or clause (see 178, 247–272) –

definite article – ***le succès*** = *success*, ***le secret de la coloration*** = *the secret of colouring*
indefinite article – ***une fois*** = *once*, ***un geste simple*** = *a simple gesture*
demonstrative adjective – ***ce cocktail que je viens de préparer*** = *this cocktail that I've just prepared*
possessive adjective – ***votre propriétaire*** = *your landlord*, ***ses réactions*** = *her reactions*

The noun may refer to concrete and abstract items – to people, objects, places, ideas.
As far as its function is concerned, it may be –
subject of the verb –

Des dents blanches sont un atout esthétique majeur = *white teeth are a major aesthetic asset*

complement of the subject or object –

Il est devenu un footballeur célèbre = *he became a famous football star*

Jacques Chirac l'a nommé président d'une commission de réflexion = *Jacques Chirac appointed him chairman of a think tank*

direct or indirect object –

Avant de prendre le volant = *before taking hold of the steering wheel*

Ce complément convient à tous les jeunes qui veulent contrôler leur poids = *this supplement is suitable for all those young people who want to control their weight*

in a prepositional expression –

N'oubliez pas de boire avant, pendant et après les efforts = *don't forget to drink before, during and after exertion*

Le temps des désillusions = *disillusionment time*

L'événement a été annoncé dans la revue interne de la compagnie = *the event was announced in the company's in-house journal*

Gender

178 Gender

Gender in English is based upon sexual characteristics – *girl, woman, actress, filly, cow, hen* are all female by virtue of their physical attributes, and *man, boy, lad, guy, bull, stallion* are all male by virtue of their physical attributes. Nouns that do not have sexual attributes, real or supposed (as a result of personification a boat may be called *her*), have no gender, are neutral.

In French the situation is different. French has a dual system for gender assignment.

1 Gender is dependent upon sexual identity in the same way as English – but this is only for a limited number of animate nouns.
2 For most nouns gender assignment is a grammatical matter, the result of syntactic tradition.

Consequently, as a result of the operation of system 1, male persons are indicated by the masculine gender, and female persons by the feminine gender. However, occasionally system 2, the grammatical principle, takes priority over sexual gender, and produces anomalies –

personne and ***victime*** are always feminine in gender even if they refer to male persons
and ***docteur*** and ***professeur*** are always masculine whether they refer to women or men.

The matter of sexual gender is discussed in 186.

Gender pervades a very large proportion of the French grammatical system. The gender of nouns affects the form of the **determiners** that modify them. The determiners involved are the definite, indefinite and partitive articles, possessive, demonstrative, relative and interrogative adjectives, and negative and indefinite adjectives. These are dealt with in 247–272. The gender of nouns also affects agreement of adjectives, pronouns, past participles. These are dealt with in 105, 108, 194, 207, 208, 225.

179 Assigning gender

Because grammatical gender permeates the French syntactic system, involving every noun and pronoun, together with the knock-on effect of agreement of adjectives and past participles with the nouns and pronouns, knowledge of the correct gender of a noun is of vital importance.

Fortunately, there are some patterns that help with assigning the correct gender to a noun, some connected with the meaning of the noun, others with its form. Unfortunately, there are exceptions to most patterns, and many nouns do not fall within these patterns. In such cases, the gender of the noun has to be learnt individually.

In the following lists, normally, two examples will be given for each case, plus all the most common exceptions. Although the exceptions may seem numerous, the nouns which 'observe the rule' are much more numerous – it's just that space does not allow them all to be mentioned.

180 Patterns for masculine gender
1 Patterns based on meaning
names of days of the week – ***le dimanche*** = *Sunday*, ***le mercredi*** = *Wednesday*
names of months – ***le janvier*** = *January*, ***le mars*** = *March*
names of seasons – ***le printemps*** = *spring*, ***l'été***(m) = *summer*
names of languages – ***le français*** = *French*, ***le roumain*** = *Romanian*
names of trees and shrubs – ***le chêne*** = *oak tree*, ***le poirier*** = *pear tree*

exceptions – ***une aubépine*** = *hawthorn*, ***la ronce*** = *bramble*, ***la vigne*** = *vine*

names of cheeses and wines – ***le brie, le camembert, le champagne, le bordeaux***
names of metals and minerals – ***le cuivre*** = *copper*, ***le mercure*** = *mercury*

exceptions – ***une émeraude*** = *emerald*, ***la perle*** = *pearl*, ***la roche*** = *rock*

names of colours – ***le jaune*** = *yellow*, ***le rose*** = *pink*
names of weights and measures, cardinal numbers – ***le litre*** = *litre*, ***le quart*** = *quarter*, ***le six*** = *(number) six*

exception – ***la moitié*** = *half*, and numerals ending in ***–aine*** (***la soixantaine*** = *about sixty*)

names of human agents, ending in ***–eur*** – ***le directeur*** = *the head teacher*, ***le docteur*** = *doctor*
names of human agents, ending in ***–ien*** – ***le Parisien*** = *Parisian*, ***le pharmacien*** = *pharmacist*
names of boats – ***le 'France', le 'Reine Elizabeth'***
names of aeroplanes – ***le Concorde, le Boeing***

exception – ***la Caravelle***

2 Patterns based on form
nouns formed from infinitives – ***le coucher*** = *bedtime*, ***le devoir*** = *duty*, ***le rire*** = *laughter*
nouns formed from adjectives – ***le possible*** = *what is possible*, ***le sérieux*** = *seriousness*
nouns ending in ***–acle*** – ***un obstacle*** = *obstacle*, ***le spectacle*** = *spectacle*
nouns with two or more syllables ending in ***–age*** – ***le clonage*** = *cloning*, ***le maquillage*** = *make-up*

exception – ***une image*** = *image*

nouns ending in ***–ai*** – ***le balai*** = *broom*, ***un essai*** = *try* (in rugby)
nouns ending in ***–ail*** – ***le détail*** = *detail*, ***le travail*** = *work*
nouns ending in ***–at*** – ***le certificat*** = *certificate*, ***le résultat*** = *result*

nouns ending in **–é** – **le café** = *coffee*, **le péché** = *sin*

    exceptions – **une acné** = *acne*, **la clé** (also spelt **clef**) = *key*

nouns ending in **–eau** – **le carreau** = *square*, **le plateau** = *tray*

    exceptions – **une eau** = *water*, **la peau** = *skin*

nouns ending in **–ède** – **un intermède** = *interlude*, **le remède** = *remedy*
nouns ending in **–ège** – **le collège** = *college*, **le manège** = *roundabout*
nouns ending in **–eil** – **le soleil** = *sun*, **le sommeil** = *sleep*
nouns ending in **–ème** – **le problème** = *problem*, **le système** = *system*

    exception – **la crème** = *cream*

nouns ending in **–er** when **–er** is sounded [e] – **le clocher** = *belfry*, **le petit déjeuner** = *breakfast* – and when **–er** is pronounced [ɛr] – **le cancer** = *cancer*, **le starter** = *choke* (of car)

    exceptions – **la cuiller** = *spoon*, **la mer** = *sea*

nouns ending in **–ès** – **le progrès** = *progress*, **le succès** = *success*
nouns ending in **–et** – **le projet** = *project*, **le secret** = *secret*
nouns ending in **–euil** – **le deuil** = *mourning*, **le seuil** = *threshold*
nouns ending in **–i** when sounded [i] – **un abri** = *shelter*, **le parti** (political) *party*

    exception – **la fourmi** = *ant*

nouns ending in **–ier** – **le calendrier** = *calendar*, **le papier** = *paper*
nouns ending in **–ing** – **le camping** = *campsite*, **le parking** = *car park*
nouns ending in **–isme** – **un organisme** = *organism*, **le scepticisme** = *scepticism*
nouns ending in **–ment** – **le divertissement** = *entertainment*, **le paiement** = *payment*

    exception – **la jument** = *mare*

nouns ending in **–o** – **le numéro** = *number*, **le zéro** = *zero*

    exception – **la dynamo** = *dynamo*

nouns ending in **–oi** – **un emploi** = *job*, **le tournoi** = *tournament*

    exceptions – **la foi** = *faith*, **la loi** = *law*

nouns ending in **–oir** – **le miroir** = *mirror*, **le peignoir** = *dressing gown*
nouns ending in **–ou** – **le chou** = *cabbage*, **le genou** = *knee*
nouns ending in **–our** – **le carrefour** = *crossroads*, **le retour** = *return*

    exceptions – **la cour** = *yard*, **la tour** = *tower* (not = *trick, turn* which is **le tour**)

nouns ending in **–ueil** – **un accueil** = *welcome*, **un orgueil** = *pride*
plus a few small sets of nouns, ending for example in **–gramme** (**le kilogramme** = *kilogramme*), **–mètre** (**le centimètre** = *centimetre*), **–scope** (**le magnétoscope** = *tape recorder*)
plus nouns ending in the following consonants –

    –c – **le lac** = *lake*, **le sac** = *bag*
    –d – **le bord** = *edge*, **le pied** = *foot*

and **–g**, **–l**, **–r**, **–t** as illustrated above.

181 Patterns for feminine gender
1 Patterns based on meaning
names of fruit and vegetables ending in **–e** – **la carotte** = *carrot*, **la fraise** = *strawberry*

> exceptions – **le concombre** = *cucumber*, **le pamplemousse** = *grapefruit*

names of academic subjects – **la linguistique** = *linguistics*, **la physique** = *physics*

> exception – **le droit** = *law*

names of cars – **une Renault, une deux-chevaux, une BMW**
names designating females ending in **–esse** – **une hôtesse** = *hostess*,
la princesse = *princess*
names of human agents ending in **–euse** – **la chanteuse** = *singer*,
la masseuse = *masseuse*
names of human agents ending in **–ienne** – **la pharmacienne** = *female pharmacist*,
la végétarienne = *vegetarian*
names of human agents ending in **–ière** – **la meurtrière** = *female murderer*,
une hôtellière = *hotelier*
names of human agents ending in **–trice** – **une actrice** = *actress*, **la directrice** =
head teacher

2 Patterns based on form
nouns ending in **–ace** – **la race** = *(ethnic) race*, **la surface** = *surface*

> exception – **un espace** = *space*

nouns ending in **–ade** – **une orangeade** = *orangeade*, **la promenade** = *walk*

> exceptions – **le grade** = *rank*, **le stade** = *stadium*

nouns ending in **–aie** – **la monnaie** = *currency*, **la plaie** = *wound*
nouns ending in **–aille** – **la bataille** = *battle*, **les fiançailles** = *engagement*
nouns ending in **–aine** – **la haine** = *hatred*, **la quinzaine** = *fortnight*
nouns ending in **–aison** – **la combinaison** = *combination*, **la raison** = *reason*
nouns ending in **–ance** – **une alliance** = *wedding ring, alliance*, **la distance** = *distance*
nouns ending in **–ée** – **une entrée** = *entry*, **la soirée** = *evening*

> exceptions – **le lycée** = *secondary school*, **le musée** = *museum*, **le trophée** = *trophy*

nouns ending in **–eine** – **la baleine** = *whale*, **la peine** = *punishment*
nouns ending in **–ence** – **la différence** = *difference*, **une influence** = *influence*

> exception – **le silence** = *silence*

nouns ending in **–euse** – **la perceuse** = *drill*, **la tondeuse** = *lawnmower*
nouns ending in **–ie** – **la partie** = *part*, **la vie** = *life*

> exceptions – **le génie** = *genius, engineering*, **un incendie** = *fire*, **le parapluie** =
> *umbrella*

nouns ending in **–ière** – **la bière** = *beer*, **la lumière** = *light*

> exceptions – **le cimetière** = *cemetery*, **le derrière** = *behind, bottom*

nouns ending in *–ine* – *la colline* = *hill*, *la piscine* = *swimming pool*

exception – *le magazine* = *magazine*

nouns ending in *–ise* – *la chemise* = *shirt*, *la marchandise* = *goods*

exception – *le pare-brise* = *windscreen* (see 187, 3)

nouns ending in *–sion* or *–tion* – *la télévision* = *television*, *la traduction* = *translation*
nouns ending in *–té* – *la bonté* = *goodness*, *la difficulté* = *difficulty*

exceptions – *un arrêté* = *decree*, *le comité* = *committee*, *l'été* = *summer*

nouns ending in *–tude* – *une attitude* = *attitude*, *la solitude* = *loneliness*
nouns ending in *–ure* – *la ceinture* = *belt*, *la figure* = *face*
nouns ending in a double consonant + *–e* – *une étoffe* = *material*, *la dentelle* = *lace*, *la poubelle* = *wastebin*, *la bouteille* = *bottle*, *la taille* = *waist, size*, *une antenne* = *aerial*, *la grippe* = *flu*, *la caisse* = *cashtill*, *la cuisse* = *thigh*, *la chaussette* = *sock*, *la serviette* = *towel, briefcase*

exceptions – *un intervalle* = *interval*, *le squelette* = *skeleton*, *le gorille* = *gorilla*, *le portefeuille* = *wallet*

plus a few small sets of nouns ending in *–èche* (*la brèche* = *breach*), *–èque* (*la discothèque* = *discotheque*), *–èse* (*une hypothèse* = *hypothesis*), *–ève* (*la grève* = *strike*)

182 Awkward cases of gender identity

Although in many, many cases it is possible to deduce the gender of a noun from its ending, we have seen that occasionally there are exceptions to the patterns outlined above. In addition to those examples that muddy the gender-assignment waters, there are other cases where it is difficult to guess the gender of a noun from its form, and there is no other recourse but to commit specific forms and genders to memory. What follows is a list of reasonably common nouns whose gender may not be immediately obvious.

1 These nouns are of **masculine gender** –
l'âge = *age*, *l'antidote* = *antidote*, *l'atome* = *atom*, *l'autoradio* = *car radio*, *le cadavre* = *corpse*, *le calme* = *calmness*, *le caractère* = *character*, *le charme* = *charm*, *le choix* = *choice*, *le crime* = *crime*, *le culte* = *worship*, *le dialecte* = *dialect*, *le dilemme* = *dilemma*, *l'échange* = *exchange*, *l'édifice* = *building*, *l'élastique* = *rubber band*, *l'emblème* = *emblem*, *l'épisode* = *episode*, *l'espace* = *space*, *l'exemple* = *example*, *le fleuve* = *river*, *le formulaire* = *form* (to fill in), *le générique* = *credits*, *l'hémisphère* = *hemisphere*, *l'incendie* = *fire*, *l'insecte* = *insect*, *l'intermède* = *interlude*, *l'intervalle* = *interval*, *le légume* = *vegetable*, *le liquide* = *liquid*, *le luxe* = *luxury*, *le manque* = *lack*, *le mascara* = *mascara*, *le masque* = *mask*, *les médias* = *media*, *le mérite* = *merit*, *le micro-ondes* = *microwave* (oven), *le mime* = *mime*, *le minuit* = *midnight*, *le molécule* = *molecule*, *le monopole* = *monopoly*, *le moustique* = *mosquito*, *le mythe* = *myth*, *l'ongle* = *nail*, *l'orchestre* = *orchestra*, *l'organe* = *organ*, *le panorama* = *panorama*, *le parachute* = *parachute*, *le parapluie* = *umbrella*, *le pétale* = *petal*, *quelque chose* = *something*, *le quota* = *quota*, *le reproche* = *reproach*, *le reste* = *remainder*, *le rêve* = *dream*, *le rire* = *laughter*, *le saxophone* = *saxophone*, *le service* = *service*, *le silence* = *silence*, *le sourire* = *smile*, *le squelette* = *skeleton*, *le suicide* = *suicide*, *le symptôme*

= *symptom,* **le tonnerre** = *thunder,* **le trombone** = *trombone, paper clip,* **le trophée** = *trophy,* **l'uniforme** = *uniform,* **l'ustensile** = *utensil,* **le vice** = *vice*

quelque chose –

Célébrer le nouvel an en famille, c'est créer un petit quelque chose d'inoubliable = *celebrating the New Year as a family is to create a little unforgettable something*

2 These nouns are of **feminine gender** –
l'ancre = *anchor,* **l'annexe** = *annex,* **l'artère** = *artery,* **l'atmosphère** = *atmosphere,* **la caractéristique** = *characteristic,* **la cendre** = *ash,* **la cible** = *target,* **la cime** = *summit,* **la circulaire** = *circular,* **la croix** = *cross,* **la dent** = *tooth,* **la dynamo** = *dynamo,* **l'énigme** = *enigma,* **l'espèce** = *species, sort,* **l'extase** = *ecstasy,* **la forêt** = *forest,* **la fourmi** = *ant,* **l'horreur** = *horror,* **l'idole** = *idol,* **la liqueur** = *liqueur,* **la noix** = *nut,* **l'oasis** = *oasis,* **l'ombre** = *shade,* **l'orbite** = *orbit,* **la pantomime** = *pantomime,* **la pédale** = *pedal,* **la pénicilline** = *penicillin,* **la recrue** = *recruit,* **la sentinelle** = *sentry,* **la sphère** = *sphere,* **la surface** = *surface,* **la toux** = *cough,* **la victime** = *victim,* **la vidéo** = *video,* **la vis** = *screw*

183 Names of countries, towns and rivers
The principle is that if the name of the country, town or river ends in **–e**, it is feminine; otherwise it is masculine. There are a few exceptions.

1 Countries
Feminine names
la Bolivie, la Chine, la France, la Grande-Bretagne, la Jamaïque, la Libye, la Russie, la Somalie, la Tanzanie

exceptions – **le Cambodge, le Mexique, le Mozambique, le Zimbabwe**

Masculine names
le Brésil, le Canada, le Danemark, les Etats-Unis, le Kenya, le Niger, le Pakistan, le Pérou, le Portugal, le Vietnam

Usage of prepositions with names of countries is discussed in 466.

2 Towns
L'été Paris s'est débarrassé d'une bonne partie de sa population = *in summer Paris divested itself of a large proportion of its population*

Besançon est entouré de montagnes = *Besançon is surrounded by mountains*

Marseille est située à l'est de la bouche du Rhône = *Marseilles is situated to the east of the mouth of the Rhône*

Valenciennes a été partiellement détruite pendant la deuxième guerre mondiale = *Valenciennes was partly destroyed during the Second World War*

3 Rivers
Feminine names
la Loire, la Marne, la Seine

exception – **le Rhône**

Masculine names
le Lot, le Rhin, le Tarn

4 French regions
le Languedoc, le Limousin, le Roussillon

l'Auvergne, la Bretagne, la Normandie

5 French departments
le Cantal, le Doubs, le Morbihan

la Corrèze, la Haute-Savoie, la Vaucluse

exception – **le Finistère**

6 American states
Sometimes there are distinctive French names for certain American States; these tend to be feminine.

la Californie, la Caroline du Nord, la Caroline du Sud, la Floride, la Géorgie, la Louisiane, la Pennsylvanie, la Virginie

exception – **le Nouveau-Mexique** – see 183

Those names which do not have a distinctive French form are masculine –

le Dakota du Nord, le Montana, le Texas

7 British counties
These are nearly always masculine.

le Nottinghamshire, le Suffolk, le Wiltshire

exception – **les Cornouailles** (fpl) = *Cornwall*

184 Homonyms
Nouns that are pronounced the same and/or are identical in form but have different meanings are known as **homonyms**.

The first list consists of orthographic homonyms – identical in spelling and pronunciation. In many cases, one of the meanings is more common than the other.

un aide = *assistant*	**le champagne** = *champagne*
l'aide (F) = *help, female assistant*	**la Champagne** = *Champagne region*
le chose = *thingummybob*	**le crêpe** = *crepe* (material)
la chose = *thing*	**une crêpe** = *pancake*
le critique = *critic*	**le finale** = *finale* (in music)
la critique = *criticism*	**la finale** = *final* (in sport)
le garde = *guard, warden*	**le greffe** = *record office*
la garde = *protection, nurse*	**la greffe** = *graft, transplant*

le livre = book
la livre = pound (weight, money)

le manoeuvre = labourer
la manoeuvre = manoeuvre

le merci = thank-you
la merci = mercy

le mort = dead person
la mort = death

le pendule = pendulum
la pendule = clock

le poêle = stove
la poêle = frying pan

le poste = job, station, set (radio, TV)
la poste = postal services

le somme = snooze
la somme = sum, amount

le vague = vagueness
la vague = wave

le vase = vase
la vase = mud, slime

le manche = handle
la manche = sleeve, leg (in sport);
la Manche = the English Channel

le mémoire = dissertation
la mémoire = memory

le mode = method
la mode = fashion

le page = page-boy
la page = page

le physique = physique
la physique = physics

le politique = politician
la politique = politics

le solde = balance, sale, bargain
la solde = pay

le tour = tour, trick
la tour = tower

le vapeur = steamer
la vapeur = steam

le voile = veil
la voile = sail

The second list is a small selection of homonyms that are pronounced the same but spelt differently and with different genders. Such homonyms are extremely common in French and underline the importance of correct spelling in written French.

l'air (M) = air
l'ère (F) = era

le bar = bar (in restaurant)
la barre = bar (of wood, metal)

le chêne = oak tree
la chaîne = chain

le cours = course, waterway
le court = court (in tennis)
la cour = courtyard

le foie = liver
la foi = faith
la fois = time, occasion

le père = father
la paire = pair, couple

le bal = ball (dance)
la balle = bullet, ball (spherical)

le capital = capital, assets
la capitale = capital city, letter

le col = collar, pass (in mountains)
la colle = glue, detention

le fait = fact
la fête = festival

le maire = mayor
la mer = sea
la mère = mother

le parti = (political) party
la partie = part

le poids = *weight*
le pois = *pea*
la poix = *pitch*

le pot = *pot*
la peau = *skin*

le sel = *salt*
la selle = *saddle*

le taon = *horsefly*
le ton = *tone*

185 Nouns requiring special attention

A very small number of nouns display unusual behaviour in terms of their gender assignment. Here are two of them.

les gens = *people* – adjectives preceding the noun are feminine in form but retain their masculine form when they follow it, either immediately or after a verb –

Certaines gens le disent = *certain people say that*

Les bonnes gens de Paris sont très gentils = *the good people of Paris are very kind*

J'ai horreur des gens bavards = *I can't bear people who talk too much*

Il y a des gens malheureux partout = *there are unhappy people everywhere*

un/une oeuvre = *work* (of literature, art) is feminine when it refers to an individual piece of work or a number of individual pieces of work, but masculine when the works are considered as a single entity –

Simenon acheva son dernier roman en 1972, encore une oeuvre fascinante
= *Simenon completed his last novel in 1972, yet another fascinating work*

L'oeuvre complet de Chopin = *Chopin's complete works*

186 Nouns designating people and animals

As mentioned above, usually grammatical gender and sexual gender coincide, so that a female person or animal is designated by feminine gender and a male person or animal by masculine gender –

un homme = *man*, *le fils* = *son*, *le garçon* = *boy*, *le neveu* = *nephew*, *un oncle* = *uncle*, *le père* = *father*, *le bélier* = *ram*, *le coq* = *cockerel*, *un étalon* = *stallion*, *le taureau* = *bull*

la femme = *woman*, *la fille* = *girl, daughter*, *la mère* = *mother*, *la nièce* = *niece*, *la tante* = *aunt*, *la brebis* = *ewe*, *la poule* = *hen*, *la jument* = *mare*, *la vache* = *cow*

In the case of animals, a generic term covering both sexes sometimes exists and is normally masculine – *le cheval* = *horse*, *le mouton* = *sheep*.

Sometimes the names for the two sexes of animals are closely connected, often the feminine being derived from the masculine – *le chat, la chatte, le chien, la chienne, le lion, la lionne* – and in such cases as these, it is the masculine form that serves as the generic. In the case of *le canard, la cane,* it is the masculine form that is derived from the feminine, but the masculine form remains the generic.

One form, two genders

Nouns such as the following may be masculine or feminine according to the sex of the person designated – *adulte* = *adult*, *camarade* = *friend*, *collègue* = *colleague*, *élève* = *pupil*, **enfant** = *child*, **esclave** = *slave*, **gosse** = *kid*, **ministre** = *minister*, **photographe** = *photographer*, **rebelle** = *rebel*, and nouns ending in **–aire** and **–iste**: **adversaire** = *enemy*, **bibliothécaire** = *librarian*, **fonctionnaire** = *civil servant*, **secrétaire** = *secretary*, **dentiste** = *dentist*, **journaliste** = *journalist*, **touriste** = *tourist*.

Related forms, two genders

Very often, an **–e** is added to the masculine form of a noun designating a person, to indicate the corresponding female –

un avocat, une avocate = *lawyer*, **un candidat, une candidate** = *candidate*, **un député, une députée** = *deputy, member of parliament*, **un employé, une employée** = *employee*, **un magistrat, une magistrate** = *magistrate*.

On other occasions, a masculine suffix is replaced by the corresponding feminine suffix to supply the feminine counterpart – **le berger, la bergère** = *shepherd, shepherdess*, **un hôte, une hôtesse** = *host, hostess*, **le prince, la princesse** = *prince, princess*, **un ambassadeur, une ambassadrice** = *ambassador*, **le directeur, la directrice** = *headteacher*, **le chanteur, la chanteuse** = *singer*, **le voleur, la voleuse** = *thief*, **le caissier, la caissière** = *checkout operator*, **le fermier, la fermière** = *farmer*.

Use of femme + masculine noun

On yet other occasions, in order to indicate a woman exercising a certain profession, the word **femme** is used with the masculine noun – **une femme auteur** = *female writer*, **une femme ingénieur** = *female engineer*, **une femme médecin** = *female doctor*. The consequence of this is that sometimes, when it is not appropriate or necessary to include the word **femme**, the masculine noun is used to refer to the female author, engineer, etc –

Sophie est devenue ingénieur = *Sophie became an engineer*

Use of feminine noun to designate male

The reverse situation also occurs, whereby a feminine noun is used to designate a male person – as stated above, **personne** = *person* and **victime** = *victim* are always feminine, whether they refer to a female or male, and the same applies to the following nouns – **la recrue** = *recruit*, **la sentinelle** = *sentry*, **la star** = *star, celebrity*, **la vedette** = *star, celebrity*.

187 Gender of compound nouns

Nouns that are formed by linking two or more words together by a hyphen or hyphens are known as compound nouns. On other occasions, no hyphen is used (use of the hyphen seems to depend upon historical acceptance and validation of the term), and the close relationship of the combined words justifies their also being considered compounds –

eg **une bande dessinée** = *comic strip* – **bande** and **dessinée** cannot be separated by another adjective; **une bande dessinée amusante** = *a funny comic strip* (not **une bande amusante dessinée**).

A number of different types of compound nouns exist. The gender of the compound noun depends upon the structure of the compound.

1 Noun + noun

The gender of this type of compound noun is assigned according to the gender of the head-word, usually the first noun –

un bateau-usine = *factory ship*
un chou-fleur = *cauliflower*
un roman-BD = *strip-cartoon novel*
un spectateur-auditeur = *viewer*
une cité-satellite = *satellite town*
une idée-choc = *startling idea*
une porte-fenêtre = *French window*
une ville-fantôme = *ghost town*

2 Adjective + noun or noun + adjective

The gender is assigned according to the gender of the noun.

le bas-ventre = *lower stomach*
un coffre-fort = *safe*
un grand-père = *grandfather*
les Pays-Bas = *Netherlands*
un rond-point = *roundabout*
une bande dessinée = *comic strip*
une chauve-souris = *bat*
une chaise roulante = *wheelchair*
une grand-mère = *grandmother*
la haute-fidélité = *hi-fi*
exception – **le rouge-gorge** = *robin*

3 Verb + noun or verb + verb

All such compounds are masculine in gender.

un chauffe-eau = *water-heater*
le laisser-aller = *sloppiness*
le pare-brise = *windscreen*
un porte-avions = *aircraft carrier*
le savoir-faire = *know-how*
un sèche-cheveux = *hair-drier*

4 Adverb or preposition + noun

The gender is assigned according to the gender of the noun, except when a plural is concerned, when masculine gender operates.

un demi-centre = *half-back*
un entre-deux-vols = *stopover*
les hors-travail (mpl) = *unemployed*
un sans-papier = *illegal immigrant*
une arrière-pensée = *ulterior motive*
l'avant-garde (f) = *avant-garde*
une contre-révolution = *counter-revolution*

la demi-finale = *semi-final*
une mini-jupe = *mini-skirt*
un deux-roues = *two-wheeler*
un mille-pattes = *centipede*
un quatre-heures = *afternoon snack*

5 Noun + prepositional phrase
The gender of the first noun determines the gender of the compound.

un arc-en-ciel = *rainbow*
un nid de poule = *pothole*
un pot-de-vin = *bribe*
une épingle à nourrice = *safety pin*
une lune de miel = *honeymoon*
la mise sous cloche = *putting on the back-burner*

6 Phrase
Such compounds are always masculine.

un je ne sais quoi = *certain something*
un pas-de-chance = *no-hoper*
le plus-que-parfait = *pluperfect tense*
le prêt-à-porter = *ready-to-wear clothes*
le va-et-vient = *coming and going*
le va-t'en-guerre = *warmonger*

Number

188 Count and mass nouns
Concrete nouns may be divided into two types according to whether they have a plural form or not.

Count nouns, as their name implies, are countable, that is to say they denote single items which can be counted; they therefore have both a singular and a plural form –

une boisson – des boissons = *drink – drinks*, **un guide – des guides** = *guide – guides*, **un pantalon – des pantalons** = *a pair of trousers – pairs of trousers*, **une voiture – des voitures** = *car – cars*

Mass nouns, on the other hand, are not countable; they denote nouns which refer to items not as individual entities but as a single unit, and they do not have a plural form –

le blé = *corn*, **la farine** = *flour*, **le lait** = *milk*, **le sable** = *sand*, **le sucre** = *sugar*

Some nouns cross the border between the two types and can be both count and mass nouns (see 192) –

le fromage = *cheese* (in general), **un fromage** = *type of cheese*, **les fromages de France** = *the cheeses of France*, **le pain** = *bread* (in general), **un pain** = *loaf of bread*, **un**

étalage de pains = *a display of loaves of bread*, *le vin* = *wine* (in general), *un vin* = *type of wine*, *les vins de France* = *French wines*

Abstract nouns tend not to be used in the plural –

l'amour = *love*, *la beauté* = *beauty*, *la haine* = *hatred*, *l'orgueil* = *pride*

189 Markers for forming the plural of nouns

1 By far the most common way of indicating a plural is to add an *–s* to the singular form of the noun.

This is perfectly clear in written French. However, in the majority of cases in spoken French, it is not possible to distinguish the plural form of a noun from the singular form in this way, since the *–s* is not sounded. Other markers are called upon to confirm whether a singular or plural form is intended, by the use, for example, of determiners, forms of the verb and so on –

un livre – des livres = *book – books*, *le modèle – des modèles* = *model – models*, *le visage – les visages* = *face – faces*

Les députés l'ont voté = *the MPs have voted for it*

Of course, if the singular form of the noun already ends in *–s*, the plural form is exactly the same –

une fois – des fois = *once – times*, *un Français – des Français* = *a Frenchman – Frenchmen*, *le mois – les mois* = *month – months*, *la souris – les souris* = *mouse – mice*

Similarly nouns ending in *–x, –z* do not have a separate form for the plural –

le choix – les choix = *choice – choices*, *un prix – des prix* = *prize – prizes*, *la toux – les toux* = *cough – coughs*

le gaz – des gaz = *gas – gases*, *le nez – les nez* = *nose – noses*

2 For words ending in *–al, –au, –eu, –eau, –oeu, –x* is added to form the plural –

–al
le carnaval – les carnavaux = *carnival – carnivals*, *le cheval – les chevaux* = *horse – horses*, *le festival – les festivaux* = *festival – festivals*, *le journal – les journaux* = *newspaper – newspapers*, *le signal – les signaux* = *signal – signals*

Les journaux sont d'accord que le ministre a fait un faux pas = *the papers are in agreement that the minister has put his foot in it*

exceptions – *le bal – les bals* = *ball – balls*

l'idéal = *ideal* has two plurals, *les idéals, les idéaux*

–au
le noyau – les noyaux = *stone* (of fruit) – *stones*, *le tuyau – les tuyaux* = *tube – tubes*

Le chirurgien a décidé qu'il faut débrancher tous les tuyaux = *the surgeon has decided that all the tubes should be switched off*

–eu

le cheveu – les cheveux = *hair*, **le jeu – les jeux** = *game – games*, **le neveu – les neveux** = *nephew – nephews*

N'oubliez pas de bien rincer les cheveux = *don't forget to rinse your hair thoroughly*

exceptions – **le bleu – les bleus** = *bruise – bruises*, **le pneu – les pneus** = *tyre – tyres*

–eau

le chapeau – les chapeaux = *hat – hats*, **l'eau – les eaux** = *water – waters*, **le manteau – les manteaux** = *coat – coats*, **le trousseau – les trousseaux** = *bunch–bunches*

Stupidement, j'avais laissé tous les trousseaux de clefs dans le bureau = *stupidly, I had left all the bunches of keys in the office*

–oeu

le voeu – les voeux = *wish – wishes*

Meilleurs voeux pour ton anniversaire = *best wishes for your birthday*

3 For nouns ending in **–ail, –ou, –s** is added to form the plural except in the following cases, when **–x** is used –

–ail

le bail – les baux = *lease – leases*, **le corail – les coraux** = *coral – corals*, **le travail – les travaux** = *work – works*

Les travaux vont commencer ce weekend = *work is due to begin this weekend*

–ou

le bijou – les bijoux = *jewel – jewels*, **le caillou – les cailloux** = *pebble – pebbles*, **le chou – les choux** = *cabbage – cabbages*, **le genou – les genoux** = *knee – knees*, **le hibou – les hiboux** = *owl – owls*, **le joujou – les joujoux** = *toy – toys*, **le pou – les poux** = *louse – lice*, **le ripou – les ripoux** = *conman – conmen*

Le musée a une bonne collection de bijoux datant de l'ère égyptienne = *the museum's got a good collection of jewels from Egyptian times*

4 Nouns with irregular plurals –

le ciel – les cieux = *sky – skies*, **l'oeil – les yeux** = *eye – eyes*

Some words, which were originally compound words, form their plurals in unorthodox ways –

monsieur – messieurs = *mister – gentlemen*, **madame – mesdames** = *Mrs – ladies*, **mademoiselle – mesdemoiselles** – *Miss – Misses*

In one or two cases, although the plural is formed normally, pronunciation of the plural form is affected –

le boeuf – les boeufs = *bullock – bullocks*, **l'oeuf – les oeufs** = *egg – eggs*, **–f–** not pronounced in plural; **l'os – les os** = *bone – bones*, **–s** sounded in singular but not in plural.

5 Plural of foreign words. This is a variable matter, usage depending upon the speaker's/writer's knowledge of the foreign language involved.

Treatment of English words – sometimes the plural is formed as if the word were an ordinary French word, sometimes it is given its authentic English form –

les sandwichs – les sandwiches, les matches – les matchs

However, words ending in **–man**, known as *false anglicisms*, because, although they resemble English words, they are in fact French creations, usually form their plural in **–men**

les rugbymen = *rugby players*, **les tennismen** = *tennis players*

On the other hand, the genuine English word *barman* has as its plural in French the form **barmans**.

Treatment of other foreign words – some words remain invariable, especially those of Latin origin –

les amen = *amens*, **les forum** = *forums*, **les veto** = *vetos*

Others tend to become aligned with French usage, especially those of Italian origin, although forms without **–s** are also found –

les confettis, les macaronis, les pizzas, les spaghettis

190 Plural of compound words

1 Noun + noun

If the nouns are both countable, they both take a plural form –

un bateau-citerne – des bateaux-citernes = *tanker(s)*, **un chou-fleur – des choux-fleurs** = *cauliflower(s)*, **un oiseau-mouche – des oiseaux-mouches** = *hummingbird(s)*

exception – **une auto-école – des auto-écoles** = *driving schools*

If only one noun is countable, then that noun only assumes a plural form –

une pause-café – des pauses-café = *coffee break(s)*, **un timbre-poste – des timbres-poste** = *stamp(s)*

2 Adjective + noun or noun + adjective

Plurals are formed in the normal way –

un beau-père – des beaux-pères = *father(s)-in-law*, **un rond-point – des ronds-points** = *roundabout(s)*, **un rouge-gorge – des rouges-gorges** = *robin(s)* **un cerf-volant – des cerfs-volants** = *kite(s)*, **un coffre-fort – des coffres-forts** = *strong boxe(s)*

exceptions – those feminine nouns with a masculine adjective preceding the noun: **une grand-mère – des grand-mères, une grand-route – des grand-routes** = *main road(s)*, **une grand-tante – des grand-tantes** = *great-aunt(s)*; but with the names of family members, a form with **grands** also occurs: **grands-mères, grands-tantes**.

3 Verb + noun

If the noun is countable, it takes a plural form; the verb, of course, remains invariable –

une garde-robe – des garde-robes = *wardrobe(s)*, **un ouvre-boîte – des ouvre-boîtes** = *tin-opener(s)*, **un tire-bouchon – des tire-bouchons** = *corkscrew(s)*

In some cases the singular form of the countable noun already involves the plural form –

un porte-avions – des porte-avions = *aircraft carrier(s)*, **un pèse-papiers – des pèse-papiers** = *paperweight(s)*, **un sèche-cheveux – des sèche-cheveux** = *hair-drier(s)*

exception – **un soutien-gorge – des soutiens-gorge** = *bra(s)*

If the noun is uncountable, it remains invariable in the plural –

un gratte-ciel – des gratte-ciel = *skyscraper(s)*, **un pare-brise – des pare-brise** = *windscreen(s)*, **un porte-monnaie – des porte-monnaie** = *purse(s)*

4 Adverb or preposition + noun

The form of the noun changes normally –

une arrière-pensée – des arrière-pensées = *ulterior motive(s)*, **un haut-parleur – des haut-parleurs** = *loudspeaker(s)*, **une mini-jupe – des mini-jupes** = *mini-skirt(s)*, **un sous-marin – des sous-marins** = *submarine(s)*

In some cases the singular form of the countable noun already involves the plural form –

des deux-roues = *two-wheeler(s)*, **des mille-pattes** = *centipede(s)*, **des quatre-heures** = *afternoon snack(s)*

5 Noun + prepositional phrase

In most cases the noun changes as appropriate –

un arc-en-ciel – des arcs-en-ciel = *rainbow(s)*, **un coup d'oeil – des coups d'oeil** = *glance(s)*, **une gueule de bois – des gueules de bois** = *hangover(s)*, **une pomme de terre – des pommes de terre** = *potato(es)*

Occasionally, the noun remains invariable –

un pied-à-terre – des pied-à-terre = *pied-à-terre(s)*, **une tête-à-tête – des tête-à-tête** = *private chat(s)*

6 Verb phrases

These remain invariable –

un laissez-passer – des laissez-passer = *passe(s)*, **un va-et-vient – des va-et-vient** = *coming(s) and going(s)*

191 Different usages of number in French and English

Sometimes a singular in French is conveyed by a plural in English –

un collant = *tights*, **un escalier** = *stairs*, **un générique** = *(film) credits*, **un jean** = *jeans*, **un pantalon** = *trousers*, **un pyjama** = *pyjamas*, **un short** = *shorts*, **un slip** = *underpants*

The converse also occurs – plural French for English singular –

les applaudissements = *applause*, ***les bagages*** = *luggage*, ***les funérailles*** = *funeral*, ***faire des progrès*** = *to make progress*, ***faire des recherches*** = *to do research*, ***avoir des remords*** = *to have remorse*, ***les ténèbres*** = *darkness*

Couvert is a special case – ***un couvert*** = *place setting*; ***les couverts*** = *cutlery*.

There are also a number of cases where a French singular is conveyed by an 'apparent' plural in English (ie they are usually followed by a singular verb) –

le diabète = *diabetes*, ***l'économie*** = *economics*, ***la linguistique*** = *linguistics*, ***la physique*** = *physics*, ***la politique*** = *politics*

However, it is the plural form ***les mathématiques*** = *mathematics* that is the norm; ***les maths*** is the more informal form.

192 Contrast between singular and plural usages in French

Certain French words have a singular–plural duality which the corresponding English words do not possess (see 191) –

un fruit = (a piece of) *fruit*, ***des fruits*** = *fruit*

un pain = *a loaf of bread*, ***des pains*** = *loaves*, ***du pain*** = *bread*

un raisin = (a type of) *grape*, ***des raisins*** = (different types of) *grapes*, ***du raisin*** = *grapes*, ***un grain de raisin*** = (single) *grape*

la recherche = (the practice of) *research*, ***les recherches*** = *detailed research*

une statistique = (single set of) *statistics*, ***la statistique*** = *statistics*, ***des statistiques*** = (series of) *statistics*

In the case of ***devoir***, in the singular it usually = *duty*, whereas in the plural it usually = *homework*.

Adjectives

193 Adjectives

Adjectives constitute a class of words that are used to qualify a noun – they may precede the noun (***une belle jupe***), or follow it (***un pantalon gris***), or occur at some distance from it (***cette voiture semble la meilleure***).

The adjective agrees in gender and number with the noun that it qualifies.

194 Adjectives and gender
1 The masculine and feminine forms are identical
This applies to adjectives which in the masculine form already end in **–e** –

difficile = *difficult*, ***impossible*** = *impossible*, ***jaune*** = *yellow*, ***sage*** = *wise*, ***unique*** = *unique*

See 6 below as well.

2 Feminine formed by adding –e to masculine

Normally, the feminine form of an adjective is created by adding an **–e** to the masculine form.

Sometimes this affects the pronunciation of the adjective –

exquis – exquise = *exquisite*, **fascinant – fascinante** = *fascinating*, **français – française** = *French*, **grand – grande** = *big*, **petit – petite** = *small*

But sometimes it does not –

âgé – âgée = *aged*, **bleu – bleue** = *blue*, **fermé – fermée** = *closed*, **trapu – trapue** = *stocky*

In the following cases, a dieresis is also added in writing, but the pronunciation is not affected –

aigu – aiguë = *high-pitched*, **ambigu – ambiguë** = *ambiguous*

3 Feminine formed as a result of more radical adjustment

–c to **–che**
blanc – blanche = *white*, **franc – franche** = *frank*, **sec – sèche** = *dry*

–c to **–(c)que**
grec – grecque = *Greek*, **public – publique** = *public*, **turc – turque** = *Turkish*

–eau to **–elle**
beau – belle = *beautiful*, **nouveau – nouvelle** = *new*

–eil to **–eille**
pareil – pareille = *similar*, **vermeil – vermeille** = *bright red*

–el to **–elle**
cruel – cruelle = *cruel*, **éventuel – éventuelle** = *possible*, **personnel – personnelle** = *personal*

–er to **–ère**
cher – chère = *dear*, **étranger – étrangère** = *foreign*, **fier – fière** = *proud*

–f to **–ve**
bref – brève = *brief*, **naïf – naïve** = *naïve*, **neuf – neuve** = *new*, **vif – vive** = *lively*

–g to **–gue**
long – longue = *long*

–ou to **–olle**
fou – folle = *foolish*, **mou – molle** = *soft*

vowel + **–n** to vowel + **–nne**
paysan – paysanne = *rural*, **ancien – ancienne** = *old*, **européen – européenne** = *European*, **bon – bonne** = *good*, **breton – bretonne** = *Breton*

4 Cases where there is variation in the formation of the feminine adjective

–et becomes either **–ète** or **–ette** –

complet – complète = *complete,* **inquiet – inquiète** = *worried,* **secret – secrète** = *secret*

muet – muette = *dumb,* **net – nette** = *clean*

–eur becomes either **–eure** or **–euse**; forms in **–teur** become **–trice** –

majeur – majeure = *major,* **meilleur – meilleure** = *best,* **supérieur – supérieure** = *superior*

flatteur – flatteuse = *flattering,* **trompeur – trompeuse** = *deceitful*

accusateur – accusatrice = *incriminating,* **destructeur – destructrice** = *destructive*

–s becomes either **–se** or **–sse** –

anglais – anglaise = *English,* **courtois – courtoise** = *polite,* **gris – grise** = *grey*

bas – basse = *low,* **épais – épaisse** = *thick,* **gros – grosse** = *fat*

There are a number of possibilities for adjectives ending in **–x** –

doux – douce = *soft*

heureux – heureuse = *happy,* **jaloux – jalouse** = *jealous*

faux – fausse = *false*

vieux – vieille = *old*

5 One-off cases

favori – favorite = *favourite,* **frais – fraîche** = *fresh,* **gentil – gentille** = *gentle,* **nul – nulle** = *useless*

6 Adjectives without specific feminine form

These adjectives are also usually invariable in the plural.

Certain names of colours (originally nouns that have been converted to adjectival use) –

une chemise lilas = *a lilac-coloured shirt,* **une chaussure marron** = *a brown shoe,* **une jupe saumon** = *a salmon-coloured skirt*

Names of colours when the colour is qualified –

des robes vert sombre = *dark green dresses,* **des briques gris clair** = *light grey bricks,* **des lèvres rouge foncé** = *dark red lips*

Certain adjectives of foreign origin –

une langue standard = *a standard language,* **de la musique pop** = *pop music,* **une jupe sexy** = *a sexy skirt,* **une femme snob** = *a snobbish woman,* **une livre sterling** = *one pound sterling*

chic – une fille chic = *a smart-looking girl* – varies in the plural only.

7 Usage with demi, nu *and* mi

When **demi** = *half* occurs before a noun, it remains invariable and is linked to the noun by a hyphen –

une demi-heure = *half an hour*, **une demi-bouteille de rouge** = *half a bottle of red wine*

If it follows the noun it agrees in gender –

un kilo et demi = *a kilo and a half*, **onze heures et demie** = *half past eleven*, **midi et demi** = *half past twelve*

When **nu** = *bare* precedes the noun, it is invariable –

nu-jambes = *with bare legs*, **nu-tête** = *bare-headed*

Il ne faut pas sortir nu-tête quand le soleil brille = *you shouldn't go out bare-headed when the sun shines*

However, if **nu** follows the noun, it agrees with it –

il ne faut pas sortir tête nue quand le soleil brille = *you shouldn't go out bare-headed when the sun shines*

As for **mi**, it always precedes the noun and is consequently invariable. Expressions created in this way are usually adverbial in function, but if they are nominal the expression becomes feminine whatever the gender of the noun –

à mi-chemin = *half-way*

la première mi-temps = *the first half* (of a match)

La boue nous arrivait à mi-corps = *the mud came half-way up our bodies*

Les informations de la mi-journée = *the lunchtime news*

195 Adjectives with a variable masculine form

A small set of adjectives have a distinctive masculine form when the adjective occurs before a noun beginning with a vowel or a 'silent' **h** –

beau – un bel homme = *a good-looking man*
fou – un fol enfant = *a wild child*
mou – un mol effort = *a feeble effort*
nouveau – un nouvel étudiant = *a new student*
vieux – un vieil ami = *an old friend*

196 Adjectives and number

The rules for forming the plural of adjectives are the same as those for forming the plural of nouns.

1 Normally an **–s** is added to the singular form, whether masculine or feminine, to indicate the plural of the adjective –

un personnage intéressant – des personnages intéressants = *interesting people*

une actrice célèbre – des actrices célèbres = *famous actresses*

2 **–x** is added to adjectives in **–eau** –

beau – beaux = *beautiful,* **nouveau – nouveaux** = *new*

3 Adjectives in **–al** sometimes form their plural by adding **–s**, or **–al** becomes **–aux** –

banal – banals = *ordinary,* **fatal – fatals** = *fatal,* **glacial – glacials** = *icy-cold,* **natal – natals** = *native,* **naval – navals** = *naval*

général – généraux = *general,* **marginal – marginaux** = *marginal,* **normal – normaux** = *normal,* **principal – principaux** = *principal*

idéal = *ideal* has as its plural both **idéals** and **idéaux**

4 Compound adjectives form their plurals in the usual way –

un sourd-muet – des sourds-muets = *deaf and dumb people*

un parti social-démocrate – des partis sociaux-démocrates = *social democrat parties*

197 Adjectives and agreement

1 The overarching rule is that adjectives agree in gender and number with the noun that they qualify –

des difficultés matrimoniales = *marriage problems*

une belle histoire ancienne = *a fine old tale*

2 When an adjective is qualifying a number of nouns in the singular, the adjective takes the plural form –

un mascara et un blush assortis = *matching mascara and blusher*

3 If one of the nouns in a group is masculine and the other(s) feminine, the adjective takes the masculine plural form –

une ombre à paupières et un mascara assortis = *matching mascara and eye shadow*

In such cases, it is better (in order to avoid what would otherwise look like an incorrect agreement) to place the masculine noun closest to the plural adjective.

4 If a plural noun is a collection of different individual items, the adjectives occur in the singular too –

les cultures française et britannique = *French and British cultures*

5 With a collective noun, the adjective agrees with the noun or the dependent nouns, depending upon the sense –

un tas de vêtements sales = *a pile of dirty clothes*

un tas de vêtements très haut = *a very high pile of clothes*

In the latter case, it is better (stylistically and logically) to place the adjective after the complete expression rather than after the noun it actually qualifies (**tas**).

6 In certain circumstances French can be more precise than English (at least in the written form), when it is a matter of knowing whether all the nouns in a group

of nouns are being qualified by an adjective or simply one (or more, as the case may be)

une jupe et un pull bleu = *a skirt and a blue jumper*, **_une jupe et un pull bleus_** = *a blue skirt and jumper* (both blue), **_une jupe bleue et un pull_** = *a blue skirt and jumper* (only skirt blue).

7 When a group of nouns are linked by **_ou_**, the adjective usually takes the plural form

Je ne sais pas si je vais mettre ma jupe ou mon pantalon bleus = *I don't know whether to wear my blue skirt or trousers*

8 Usage with **_on_** – as will be seen in 224, although **_on_** is usually treated as masculine singular (= *one*), it may also be considered as an equivalent of any personal pronoun. Consequently, adjectives qualifying **_on_** adopt the gender and number which are thought to be appropriate –

On est content de la voir = *it's great to see her* (singular reference)

On est contents que ces deux-là se sont trouvés = *we're pleased that those two have met* (masculine plural reference)

On est heureuses d'être ensemble encore une fois = *we're happy to be together again* (feminine plural reference)

La question qu'on se pose toutes, c'est – est-ce que ça cache quelque chose? = *the question we all ask ourselves is – is it hiding something?* (feminine plural reference)

On est tristes que ce soit ainsi = *we're sad it's come to that* (masculine or feminine plural reference)

198 Agreement of certain prepositional and adverbial expressions involving past participles

A small number of prepositional and adverbial expressions containing a past participle in their formation may occur either before or after the noun they qualify. When the expression precedes the noun it qualifies, the past participle remains invariable, but, when it follows, it agrees with it.

Expressions involved are –

excepté = *except* (see 366), **_y compris_** = *including* (see 331), **_ci-joint_** = *herewith*

On peut l'utiliser pour traiter toutes les conditions de peau y compris la dermatite = **_On peut l'utiliser pour traiter toutes les conditions de peau, la dermatite y comprise_** =	*you can use it to treat all skin conditions including dermatitis*
Veuillez trouver ci-joint les documents suivants = **_Veuillez trouver les documents suivants ci-joints_** =	*please find the following documents enclosed*

However, usage with **_étant donné_** is slightly more flexible – it remains invariable when it precedes the noun, but may or may not agree when it follows it –

Etant donné la situation actuelle = **_La situation actuelle étant donné / donnée_**	*given the present situation*

199 Comparison of adjectives – comparative and superlative forms – 1: Comparative and superlative of inequality; 2: Comparative of equality

1 Comparative and superlative of inequality

The French equivalents of the English 'comparative and superlative of inequality'– *bigger, biggest, more / less, most / least* – involve the use of ***plus / moins, le plus / le moins, la plus / la moins, les plus / les moins.***

The comparative and superlative adjectives are placed before or after the noun according to the position of the adjective when it occurs by itself, although, if an expression that would normally precede the noun is felt to be too awkward there, it may be placed after it.

The article of the superlative form agrees with the gender of the noun qualified.

Une jupe plus courte serait trop osée = *a shorter skirt would be too daring*

C'est la jupe la plus courte que j'aie jamais vue = *it's the shortest skirt I've ever seen*

Cette jupe est plus courte que celle-là = *this skirt is shorter than that one*

Le plus beau garçon de la fac = *the best-looking guy in the uni.*

La plus jeune enfant donnera le bouquet au maire = *the youngest child will present the bouquet to the mayor*

Le devoir le moins difficile c'est le français = *the least difficult homework is French*

Ce devoir est moins difficile que celui que nous devions faire hier soir = *this homework is less difficult than the one we had to do last night*

Le devoir que je trouve le moins difficile c'est le français = *the homework I find the least difficult is French*

There are special comparative and superlative forms for ***bon*** and ***mauvais*** –

***meilleur / meilleure, le meilleur / la meilleure, les meilleurs / meilleures
pire, le / la pire, les pires***

and a special superlative form for ***petit*** –

le moindre, la moindre, les moindres

La meilleure nourriture pour la santé, ce sont les légumes et les fruits frais = *the best food for your health is fresh fruit and vegetables*

C'est le meilleur / le pire prof que je connaisse = *he's the best / worst teacher I know*

Je n'en avais pas la moindre idée = *I hadn't got the least idea*

C'est le moindre de mes soucis = *it's the least of my worries*

However, ***plus mauvais*** for ***pire*** and ***plus petit*** for ***moindre*** are also used. ***Plus mauvais*** and, especially, ***plus petit*** tend to be used with concrete nouns and in more mundane situations –

Voici le plus petit portable sur le marché = *here's the smallest mobile on the market*

Cette plage est plus mauvaise que les autres = *this beach is worse than the others*

For comparison of adverbs, see 409.

2 Comparative of equality

'Comparison of equality' is expressed by **aussi** and, usually after a negative, **si** –

Ce devoir est aussi difficile que celui que nous devions faire hier soir = *this homework is as hard as the one we had to do last night*

Le film est aussi bon que le livre = *the film is as good as the book*

Ce devoir n'est pas si difficile que ça = *this homework is not as difficult as that*

Le film n'est pas aussi / si bon que le livre = *the film isn't as good as the book*

200 Use of *ne* / *le* in clauses following a comparative

In written French, **ne** and/or **le** may be placed before the verb in clauses following a comparative. Consequently, sometimes neither **ne** nor **le** will occur, at others one or the other, or both, will be used!

Il est plus facile de trouver une solution qu'on le pense = *it is easier to find a solution than you might think*

Est-ce que tu as jamais été plus surprise que tu l'es maintenant? = *have you ever been more surprised than you are now?*

Elle a trouvé qu'il est plus difficile de prouver son innocence qu'elle ne le croyait = *she found that it was more difficult to prove her innocence than she had thought*

Ils en savent plus qu'ils n'avouent = *they know more about it than they're prepared to admit*

201 *The more the merrier*

Whereas English uses a definite article in expressions of the above type, French does not.

Plus on est de fous, plus on rit = *the more the merrier*

Plus on fume, plus on risque d'endommager sa santé = *the more you smoke, the more you risk endangering your health*

Plus je passe de temps en France, moins je regrette l'Angleterre = *the more time I spend in France, the less I miss England*

Plus on pense à l'autre, plus on néglige ses propres sensations, moins on a de plaisir, moins l'autre a du plaisir = *the more you think about your partner, the more you neglect your own feelings, the less pleasure you have, the less your partner has too*

202 The position of adjectives

As far as the position of adjectives in relation to nouns is concerned, adjectives fall into three main groups –

those, few in number, that always precede the noun
those, most, that always follow the noun
those that may either precede or follow.

But it should be noted that the first two principles are not absolutely hard-and-fast, and adjectives occasionally occur in uncharacteristic positions. Generally speaking, however, it is wise to respect the traditional situation.

1 Adjectives that precede the noun –
These tend to be short, very common adjectives –

autre = *other*, ***beau*** = *beautiful, handsome*, ***bon*** = *good*, ***grand*** = *big, great*, ***gros*** = *big, fat*, ***haut*** = *high*, ***jeune*** = *young*, ***joli*** = *pretty*, ***mauvais*** = *bad*, ***meilleur*** = *better, best*, ***moindre*** = *less, least*, ***nouveau*** = *new*, ***petit*** = *small*, ***sot*** = *foolish*, ***vaste*** = *enormous*, ***vieux*** = *old*, ***vilain*** = *ugly, nasty*

or ordinal numbers and possessive, demonstrative, interrogative adjectives (see 265–271, 439, 478) –

C'est son premier roman = *it's her first novel*

Cette belle robe = *that beautiful dress*

When modified by a short adverb, such adjectives are still placed before the noun, but if the adverb or adverbial expression is relatively long, the adjective is placed after the noun –

Un très gros mec = *a very fat guy*

Un mec démesurément gros = *a disproportionately fat guy*

See the next section for other adjectives that precede the noun.

2 Adjectives that follow the noun –
An impossibly long list –
the vast majority of adjectives –

L'eau gazeuse = *sparkling mineral water*

L'ail râpé = *grated garlic*

Une influence artistique = *an artistic influence*

Une équipe néerlandaise a reconnu récemment un autre gène = *a Dutch team has recently identified another gene*

La source marine de votre nouvelle jeunesse = *the marine source of your new youthfulness*

3 Adjectives whose position may vary –
This may be for a number of reasons.
  Certain adjectives, like ***court*** = *short*, ***long*** = *long*, precede the noun in normal circumstances, but follow it when there is a contrast or an implied contrast with their opposite –

une longue soirée = *a long evening*, ***une longue rangée de chênes*** = *a long row of oak trees*

je préfère les cheveux courts = *I prefer short hair*, ***une robe longue*** = *a long skirt*

Dernier and ***prochain*** normally precede the noun –

Je descends au prochain arrêt = *I'm getting off at the next stop*

C'est mon dernier chewing-gum = *that's my last piece of chewing gum*

However, when they are used with expressions of time, their position may vary – when they precede the noun, they are the equivalent of English *the last, the next*, and when they follow, they are the equivalent of *last, next* –

C'est la dernière fois que tu feras ça = *that's the last time you'll do that*

Ça sera pour une prochaine fois = *that'll be for the next time*

À samedi prochain = *till next Saturday*

Vendredi dernier je ne pouvais pas venir = *last Friday I couldn't make it*

4 Adjectives whose meaning changes according to their position –
See next section.

5 Stylistic variation of position
For stylistic reasons an adjective that normally follows the noun may be used in front of it. This is particularly common in the media – in newspapers and magazines. Changing the position of an adjective from its traditional position after a noun to before it focuses attention on it and foregrounds the adjective. This is a subtle matter which space does not permit detailed discussion of here.

203 Adjectives which change their meaning according to their position

What follows is a list of common adjectives that change their meaning according to their position vis-à-vis the noun they qualify.

adjective	meaning before noun	meaning after noun
ancien	*former*	*old*
	une ancienne épouse = *a former wife*	***une épouse ancienne*** = *an old wife*
bon	*good, nice*	*thoughtful, kind*
	une bonne amie = *a good friend*	***une amie bonne*** = *a thoughtful friend*
brave	*obliging, honest*	*courageous*
	de braves gens = *decent people*	***des gens braves*** = *brave people*
certain	*certain, indefinite*	*certain, unquestionable*
	un certain fait = *some fact or other*	***un fait certain*** = *an indubitable fact*
cher	*dear, beloved*	*expensive*
	mon cher ami = *my dear friend*	***un tailleur cher*** = *an expensive suit*
différent	*various*	*different*
	différentes robes = *a variety of dresses*	***des robes différentes*** = *different sorts of dresses*

divers	*various*	*diverse, distinct*
	diverses opinions = *a variety of opinions*	**des opinions diverses** = *distinctly different opinions*
grand	*great*	*tall*
	un grand prêcheur = *a great preacher*	**un prêcheur grand** = *a tall preacher*
haut	*high, open* (of sea)	*high* (of tide)
	la haute mer = *the open sea*	**la mer haute** = *high tide*
jeune	*young*	*youthful*
	un jeune honme = *a young man*	**un homme jeune** = *a young-looking man*
léger	*slight* (figurative usage)	*light* (of weight)
	une légère reprise économique = *a slight economic upturn*	**une couche légère** = *a light covering*
méchant	*disagreeable*	*naughty, spiteful*
	être de méchante humeur = *to be in a foul mood*	**des propos méchants** = *spiteful talk*
même	*same*	*very, even*
	le même shampooing = *the same shampoo*	**j'arriverai ce soir même** = *I'll arrive this very evening*
pauvre	*poor, pitiful*	*impecunious*
	un pauvre effort = *a pathetic attempt*	**le quartier pauvre de la ville** = *the poor district of the town*
présent	*the one in question*	*present*
	la présente émission = *the programme on at the moment*	**les étudiants présents n'ont pas compris** = *the students present did not understand*
propre	*own, very*	*clean*
	mon propre travail = *my own work*	**des draps propres** = *clean sheets*
pur	*total, sheer*	*unadulterated*
	c'est une pure perte de temps = *it's an utter waste of time*	**l'air pur** = *pure air*
sale	*nasty*	*dirty*
	un sale tour = *a dirty trick*	**ton pantalon est très sale** = *your trousers are very dirty*
seul	*only, single, sole*	*lonely, alone*
	une seule objection = *a single objection*	**un enfant seul** = *a lonely child*
simple	*ordinary, only*	*simple, straightforward*
	pour la simple raison = *for the simple reason*	**des goûts très simples** = *very simple tastes*
triste	*dull, inauspicious*	*sad*
	c'est mon triste devoir = *it's my unfortunate duty*	**elle a les yeux tristes** = *she's got sad eyes*
vrai	*real, genuine*	*true*
	ce ne sont pas ses vraies dents = *they're not his own teeth*	**c'est une histoire vraie** = *it's a true story*

Another small group of adjectives also vary their position – an adjective that normally follows the noun may be placed before it, this time to achieve a figurative effect –

un ciel noir = *a black sky* – **de noirs desseins** = *dark intentions*

un lit mou = *a soft bed* – **une molle résistance** = *feeble resistance*

204 Adjectives that may occur before or after the noun without change of meaning

A small number of adjectives seem to be in free variation as far as position is concerned – in other words, their meaning remains constant whether they precede or follow the noun.

bas = *low*, **bref** = *brief*, **charmant** = *charming*, **court** = *short*, **double** = *double*, **énorme** = *enormous*, **excellent** = *excellent*, **fort** = *strong*, **futur** = *future*, **innombrable** = *innumerable*, **long** = *long*, **magnifique** = *magnificent*, **modeste** = *modest*, **principal** = *main*, **rapide** = *fast*, **terrible** = *terrible*

Un magnifique terrain de foot =
Un terrain de foot magnifique = } *a magnificent football ground*

Je prends mon principal repas à 19 heures =
Je prends mon repas principal à 19 heures = } *I have my main meal at 7 pm*

205 Multiple adjectives
1 Preceding the noun

Except when a cardinal number is involved, the order of groups of adjectives before the noun is the same in French as in English –

Une jolie petite fille = *a pretty little girl*

Un bon vieil ami = *a good old friend*

Un autre gros hamburger = *another big hamburger*

With cardinal numbers, the order in French is different from that in English – the cardinal number precedes the other adjective –

Les trois autres membres du groupe = *the other three members of the group*

Il a gagné les deux premières manches = *he won the first two sets*

2 Following the noun

The order of adjectives in French after the noun tends to be the mirror image of the English order – in both cases the adjective nearest the noun has the closer/closest relationship with it –

La guerre civile espagnole = *the Spanish Civil War*

Une crème anti-rides enrichissante = *an enriching anti-wrinkle cream*

Son conseiller fiscal personnel = *her personal tax consultant*

Exercises

1 **Réécrivez les passages suivants en remplissant les blancs avec l'article qui convient.**

  a *Nous offrons . . . opportunité unique de contribuer à . . . croissance de . . . société de renommée internationale active dans . . . monde artistique. . . . ambiance de travail jeune et informelle dans . . . petite équipe soudée.*

  b *. . . avènement . . . programmes d'échange interuniversitaires de type Erasmus ou . . . extension . . . stages professionnels à . . . étranger ont également motivé . . . secteur jusqu'ici assez traditionnel et relativement coûteux, . . . échanges internationaux . . . jeunes.*

  c *. . . billet d'avion de dernière minute à . . . prix défiant toute concurrence? Voilà qui est tentant, mais peut-être dangereux si . . . précipitation nous fait oublier . . . précautions à prendre. Chaque année . . . milliers de gens s'envolent pour . . . pays où sévit . . . paludisme, mais plus de . . . tiers entre eux ne sont pas correctement protégés contre cette maladie.*

  d *Compositeur phare de . . . musique vocale italienne baroque, Alessandro Scarlatti s'est illustré aussi bien dans . . . opéra que dans . . . genre religieux de . . . oratorio. . . . musique y explose à tout moment de . . . joie lumineuse, toujours originale, mêlant magnifiquement . . . voix à . . . écriture instrumentale scintillante.*

  e *. . . vigne rouge et . . . algue marine améliorent . . . fermeté et . . . élasticité de . . . peau, tandis que . . . huile essentielle de lavande accélère . . . pénétration . . . composants et active . . . micro-circulation. On a gardé . . . meilleur pour . . . fin: . . . texture est . . . régal. Parfaitement invisible, elle est moelleuse, fondante et onctueuse. Elle disparaît en . . . clin d'oeil dans . . . épiderme sans laisser de trace et file . . . coeur de . . . cellules.*

  f *Si quelqu'un, vous, moi ou n'importe qui, veut tester . . . sûreté de . . . aéroports, il le fera sans angoisse s'il sait qu'à tout moment il peut dire: « Stop, ceci est . . . jeu! » En revanche, . . . attitude de vrais terroristes réellement désireux de commettre . . . attentat les trahira et permettra à . . . personnels de sûreté de les identifier.*

  g *Pour faire parler . . . cadavre d'abeille dont . . . mort brutale, en compagnie de 22 millions de ses congénères, vient de plonger . . . campagnes françaises dans . . . polémique violente sur . . . utilisation de deux pesticides, il suffit de pratiquer . . . autopsie.*

  h *. . . bac en poche ou . . . examens de fac réussis, . . . nouvelle épreuve attend . . . étudiants: . . . chasse à . . . logement. C'est . . . marché qui fixe . . . règles et surtout . . . prix. Or, . . . petites surfaces, cibles naturelles de . . . étudiants, sont celles dont . . . renchérissement est . . . plus important.*

  i *Tout . . . monde peut avoir . . . maison, quatre murs, . . . toit. Mais . . . propriété, . . . demeure. – Bien entendu, . . . propriété, à . . . base, n'est rien d'autre que . . . maison. Mais c'est, dans . . .*

imaginaire immobilier, bien autre chose: . . . ancien, . . . grand, . . .
noble, . . . beau, . . . prestige. « Je vous invite à ma propriété » ça a
tout de même . . . toute autre allure que « on se fait . . . barbecue à . . .
maison ».

j *Je trouve que . . . maquillage me révèle plus qu'il ne me cache. C'est*
donc . . . façon de m'exhiber. Je me suis beaucoup inspiré de . . .
maître de cérémonies de . . . film Cabaret. C'est à . . . fois . . .
transformiste et . . . vampire, . . . monsieur Loyal, mais quelqu' . . .
de festif. J'aime bien ce balancement entre . . . bien, c'est-à-dire . . .
fête, et . . . mal. J'aime bien . . . ambiguïté, y compris sexuelle.

k *Votre point faible: . . . manque de persévérance. Vous ne prenez pas de*
décision, ou alors pas de façon durable: vous êtes incapable d'effort,
pas plus motivée par . . . succès que par . . . échec. Il n'y a que . . .
nouveauté, l'idée de . . . plaisir pour vous stimuler.

l *. . . beau jour, devant . . . miroir, on se prend à relever . . . coin de ses*
yeux, à tirer sur ses pommettes, et l'on se dit qu'on aurait . . . air
moins fatiguée, plus gaie comme ça. On oublie, et puis on apprend
que . . . telle a eu . . . lifting mais que « ça se voit », alors que pour
telle autre « on ne voit rien ». On lit . . . magazines, on examine . . .
« avant / après », on note . . . noms. On ne sait jamais.

2 **Réécrivez les passages suivants en donnant les formes des adjectifs et**
participes passés qui conviennent.

a *Il a beau jouer le super ministre, ANIMÉ par de GÉNIAL et NOUVEAU*
idées, ce sont les VIEUX recettes LIBÉRAL qu'il nous assène.

b *Ce printemps aussi INCERTAIN que VENTEUX n'aura pas facilité la*
tâche des jardiniers. Mais il faut maintenant sortir CERTAIN plantes
de là où elles ont été REMISÉ pendant la MAUVAIS saison. Si ces
plantes ont été LAISSÉ INTACT, juste DÉBARRASSÉ de leurs feuilles
GÂCHÉ, elles poussent déjà, elles aussi VILAIN comme TOUT,
BLANC comme des endives ou VERT PÂLE, plus PROCHE du tilleul
que de l'épinard.

c *Une DERNIER condition, à PREMIER vue SURPRENANT, est*
NÉCESSAIRE à la réussite d'une e-formation: l'accompagnement
d'un formateur bien RÉEL. Avec des taux d'abandon assez ÉLEVÉ
cette présence peut s'avérer ESSENTIEL. Même à l'heure de la
formation à distance, rien ne remplacera une présence HUMAIN.

d *On trouve dans la collection des sweaters REHAUSSÉ d'une lettre ou*
d'un chiffre, des pantalons MILITAIRE AMPLE ou des joggings
COMBINÉ à des tops ATHLÉTIQUE et des maillots de corps ou des
vestes ZIPPÉ, MARIÉ à une minijupe.

e *Les designers BELGE commencent à se tailler une SOLIDE réputation*
sur la scène INTERNATIONAL. ORIGINAL, bien PENSÉ, voire
carrément VISIONNAIRE, leurs créations séduisent un public de plus
en plus LARGE.

f *Ils sont trois sur leur île PARISIEN. La mère qui se bat contre un*
cancer. Cette lutte est la raison de vivre de sa fille. Puis il y a un
JEUNE homme AFFABLE, qui a su se rendre INDISPENSABLE en
rendant LÉGER les moments INSUPPORTABLE de la maladie.

g *Les cassis UTILISÉ pour cette crème de cassis sont les noirs de Bourgogne, CUEILLI dans la Côte-d'Or. Cette crème est d'une RARE authenticité. Ses parfums FRAIS, son fruité ONCTUEUX, sa bouche AMPLE et GÉNÉREUX et ses arômes PLEIN en font une liqueur d'exception.*

h *Vous souffrez des symptômes d'un état PROCHE de l'effondrement: la HORRIBLE sensation d'être LOURD et FLASQUE, ENGOURDI et TENDU à la fois, CONTRACTÉ au niveau des vertèbres, de la nuque jusqu'aux reins. Il est temps de remettre un peu d'huile dans les rouages!* (description d'une femme)

i *À l'occasion du NOUVEAU an, un de mes potes avait organisé une GROS fiesta chez lui. Il y avait de l'alcool à gogo, du foie GRAS à en veux-tu en voilà, et des filles SPLENDIDE aux quatre coins de la maison. Bref, tout était PARFAIT. Le SEUL problème: c'était moi! A minuit moins cinq, j'ai eu une crise d'angoisse et je suis allé m'enfermer dans les chiottes. Je ne voulais pas me plier à ce rituel RIDICULE d'embrassades.*

j *« Je suis DÉÇU, dit Sandrine Casar, car je me sentais bien en jambes, mais j'étais trop ISOLÉ face aux Brioches, qui avaient un comportement BIZARRE. Je n'ai pas compris leur façon de courir, leurs choix TACTIQUE, et je ne suis pas la SEUL. Elles-mêmes donnaient parfois l'impression de ne pas comprendre ce qu'elles faisaient. Dans de TEL circonstances, elles ont dû être très SATISFAIT du résultat. »*

k *On trouvera une GRAND baie, très BEAU, BORDÉ par une réserve NATUREL, BAPTISÉ le parc NATIONAL de Los Halises, que l'on visite en bateau, découvrant oiseaux MULTICOLORE, perroquets et tortues dans une végétation de mangroves TROPICAL.*

Chapter 6 *Pronouns*

206 Pronouns

The role of a pronoun is to help avoid repeating a noun phrase in its entirety and to act as a stand-in for it or abbreviation of it. The pronoun thus enhances the cohesion of what is said or written by providing a short-hand form for a longer expression and binding the text of what is said or written more tightly together.

There are a number of series of pronouns –

Personal pronouns –

> *Les profs reconnaissent qu'ILS ne peuvent rien sans les parents* = *the teachers admit that they can't do anything without parents' support*

avoiding repetition of ***les profs***.

Impersonal and neutral pronouns –

> *Comment peut-ON défendre le système des retraites en torpillant les réformes?* = *how can you defend the pensions system by torpedoing reforms?*

avoiding specifying who is being criticised.

> *Pour profiter pleinement de cet excellent petit instrument, IL est conseillé d'agir vite* = *in order to benefit fully from this marvellous little instrument, it's advisable to act quickly*

avoiding explaining who is doing the advising.

Demonstrative pronouns –

> *Faire grève et manifester sont des droits. Mais il ne faut pas que CEUX-CI empêchent la circulation sur la voie publique* = *going on strike and demonstrating are rights. But these must not prevent traffic from circulating on the public highway*

avoiding saying ***ces droits***.

Possessive pronouns –

> *Elle admire l'art de ses contemporains, mais LE SIEN est plus puissant, plus expressif* = *she admires her contemporaries' art, but hers is more powerful and more expressive*

avoiding saying ***son art***.

For relative pronouns, see 464.

Personal pronouns

207 Personal pronouns

These may be organised according to the role they play in a sentence – whether they are the subject, direct object or indirect object of the verb, whether they are used emphatically, whether they follow a preposition, whether they are singular or plural.

The neuter pronoun **il** = *it* only occurs as subject singular, and the reflexive/reciprocal pronoun **se** = *him/her/it/oneself, themselves* does not occur as subject.

208 The forms

It will be seen from the following table that there is much anomaly among the forms that the personal pronouns adopt in French. Although five different syntactic roles have been identified (singular and plural), there are never five distinct forms corresponding to them – a maximum of four and a minimum of one (in English there are never more than two different forms for the personal pronouns). Consequently, some forms have more than one function (eg **me, te**), some are confined to a particular person (eg **nous, vous**), others apply to more than one person (eg **lui, leur**).

The following table lists the five syntactic roles for each person and the forms that correspond to them.

person	syntactic role	singular		plural	
First person	subject	*je*	*I*	*nous*	*we*
	direct object	*me*	*me*	*nous*	*us*
	indirect object	*me*	*to me*	*nous*	*to us*
	after preposition	*moi*	*me*	*nous*	*us*
	stressed	*moi*	*I / me*	*nous*	*we/us*
Second person	subject	*tu*	*you*	*vous*	*you*
	direct object	*te*	*you*	*vous*	*you*
	indirect object	*te*	*to you*	*vous*	*to you*
	after preposition	*toi*	*you*	*vous*	*you*
	stressed	*toi*	*you*	*vous*	*you*
Third person masculine	subject	*il*	*he*	*ils*	*they*
	direct object	*le*	*him*	*les*	*them*
	indirect object	*lui*	*to him*	*leur*	*to them*
	after preposition	*lui*	*him*	*eux*	*them*
	stressed	*lui*	*he / him*	*eux*	*they / them*
Third person feminine	subject	*elle*	*she*	*elles*	*they*
	direct object	*la*	*her*	*les*	*them*
	indirect object	*lui*	*to her*	*leur*	*to them*
	after preposition	*elle*	*her*	*elles*	*them*
	stressed	*elle*	*she/her*	*elles*	*they/them*
Third person neuter	only occurs as subject	*il*	*it*		
		ce	*it*		
Third person **reflexive /** **reciprocal**	direct object	*se*	*him / her / it / oneself*	*se*	*themselves*
	indirect object	*se*	*to him / her / it/ oneself*	*se*	*to themselves*
	after preposition	*soi*	*him / her / it/ oneself*	*eux-mêmes* *elles-mêmes*	*themselves* *themselves*

person	syntactic role	singular		plural	
	stressed	**soi**	*him / her / it / oneself*	**eux-mêmes**	*themselves*
				elles-mêmes	*themselves*
Third person **indefinite**	subject	**on**	*oneself*	no plural forms	
	direct object	**se**	*oneself*		
	indirect object	**se**	*to oneself*		
	after preposition	**soi / nous / vous**	*oneself*		
	stressed	**soi / nous / vous**	*oneself*		

209 Elision of certain pronouns

Those pronouns consisting of a single consonant + **e** (**je, me, te, se, ce, le**) and **la**, lose their vowel before a verb beginning with a vowel or mute **h** or before **en** and **y**.

Je suis super complexée et cela m'empêche d'avancer = *I'm full of complexes and that stops me making any progress*

Il préfère s'acheter des jouets = *he prefers buying himself toys*

Tu t'égares en pensant cela = *you're mistaken if that's what you think*

Décrivez simplement votre mission, la façon dont vous l'avez menée et les résultats obtenus = *all you have to do is describe your aims, how you set about achieving them and the results obtained*

Son boulot consiste justement à s'en défaire = *his job is precisely to get rid of it*

210 Position of pronouns – 1: subject pronouns; 2: object pronouns

1 Subject pronouns

Normally the subject pronoun precedes the verb.

Il est champion de France = *he's the champion of France*

Ils affronteront la Grèce en demi-finale jeudi = *they'll play Greece in the semi-final on Thursday*

On s'attendait à ce qu'ils s'expriment sur le cas hier = *we were expecting them to pronounce on the case yesterday*

However, in certain circumstances it may follow it:

in questions (see 472) –

L'enfant, quand faut-il l'emmener aux urgences? = *when should you take your child to casualty?*

after certain adverbial expressions (see 403) –

> *Les Japonais passent pour avoir des pratiques cruelles – le découpage d'un poisson vivant. Du moins demandent-ils pardon au pauvre animal* = *the Japanese have the reputation of having some cruel practices – cutting up live fish. At least they ask the poor animal's forgiveness*

> *Toujours est-il qu'elle s'est présentée avec deux heures d'avance* = *the fact remains that she turned up two hours early*

2 Object pronouns

Except when an imperative is involved (see 212), the pronouns are placed immediately before the verb. This applies to simple tenses and to infinitives and present participles; in the case of compound tenses the pronoun precedes the auxiliary verb –

> *Dès le xvie siècle, le muguet était un parfum apprécié notamment des hommes. Aujourd'hui on l'utilise dans les parfums féminins* = *from the sixteenth century onwards, lily of the valley was a much appreciated perfume, especially by men. Nowadays it's used in perfumes for women*

> *Le mal de dos est remonté à la surface quand j'étais stressée, mais je l'ai évité en modifiant mon comportement* = *my backache returned when I was stressed out, but I avoided it by modifying my behaviour*

> *Collez les bandes sur les lanières des tongs en les croisant sur l'envers* = *stick the strips on the straps of the flip-flops, crossing them at the back*

> *Cinq légumes et fruits par jour – telles sont les recommandations de la santé publique. L'important est de les suivre sérieusement* = *five portions of fruit and veg per day – those are the recommendations of the public health authority. The important thing is to follow them seriously*

> *On parle contraception, sida, problèmes de coeur – elles ont si peu d'interlocuteurs, les tabous sont si lourds; j'ai vraiment l'impression de les aider* = *we speak about contraception, AIDS, relationships – they have so few people to speak to; taboos weigh heavy; I really feel I'm helping them*

If the verb is negative, the *ne* immediately precedes the pronoun –

> *On ne m'a pas interdit de chanter* = *I wasn't banned from singing*

> *Certaines tâches ménagères me sont impossibles – je ne les supporte pas* = *I find certain domestic tasks impossible – I can't stand them*

> *L'hépatite C, une maladie qui peut abîmer sérieusement le foie si on ne la soigne pas* = *hepatitis C, an illness that can seriously damage your liver if you don't treat it*

211 Order of object pronouns

When two or more object pronouns occur before the verb, finite or infinitive, they have to be used in a fixed order.

me				
te	le			
se	la	lui	y	en
nous	les	leur		
vous				

Faut-il le lui dire? = *should I tell him?*

Je me le dis souvent – il faut essayer d'y voir plus clair = *I often tell myself – you've got to try and see the situation more clearly*

On me l'a prescrite pour des problèmes d'acné et je n'ai plus aucun désir sexuel = *it's [the pill] been prescribed to me because of my acne and I don't feel any sexual desire any more*

Elle ne me le permet plus = *she doesn't let me do it any more*

Qu'on se le tienne pour dit. Qu'on se le tienne bien jalousement d'ailleurs = *let's keep it between ourselves. Let's guard it very jealously into the bargain*

S'il fait vraiment très chaud, on le brosse avec de l'eau fraîche avant de s'y allonger = *if it's really hot, brush it [a mattress] with fresh water before lying down on it*

La seule chose à se faire percer par quelqu'un d'autre, ce serait éventuellement l'oreille – je me la suis moi-même fait poinçonner par une amie = *the only thing you should have pierced by someone else is possibly your ear – I've had it done myself by a friend*

Oui, nous nous en souvenons = *yes, we remember*

Marcel est amoureux de Stéphanie, et pour le lui montrer, il est prêt à toutes les dépenses = *Marcel is in love with Stephanie, and to prove it to her he's prepared to pay what it costs*

On savait que Contrex était l'eau des femmes et de la minceur. Elle nous le prouve une fois encore avec une très jolie surprise – une collection de bijoux = *we knew that Contrex was the water for women and slimness. It proves it to us once again with a very pretty surprise – a collection of jewellery*

212 Order of pronouns with the imperative
The situation is different in the imperative mood.

1 With an **affirmative imperative**, the pronouns follow the verb in the same order as above. However, **me, te** become **moi, toi**, except when they are combined with **en, y**, in which case they remain as **me, te**. They are linked to the verb and each other by a hyphen, except when **me, te** are combined with **y, en**.

Prenez soin de votre peau, satinez-la de crème parfumée, pailletez-la = *take care of your skin; make it really smooth with perfumed cream, put glitter on it*

Faites tremper les haricots rouges une nuit. Puis mettez-les dans une casserole = *soak the red beans overnight. Then put them in a pan*

Les calories sont vos pires ennemies du mois et de votre ligne – réduisez-les = *calories are your worst enemies of the month and your waistline – cut them down*

Fous-toi donc de ce que les autres peuvent en penser = *don't give a damn about what others might think about it*

Maintenant remontez vos manches et prouvez-leur ce dont vous êtes capable = *now roll up your sleeves and show them what you're capable of*

Vénus vous fait les yeux doux. A vous d'aborder ce garçon et dites-le-lui = *Venus is smiling on you. It's up to you to approach that boy and tell him*

J'adore les pierres polies – achetez-m'en pour mon anniversaire s'il vous plaît = *I adore polished stones – get me some for my birthday please*

Contente-toi donc de ta joliesse = *be content with your own good looks*

Un affreux bouton à camoufler? – retenez-vous de presser le coupable = *a horrid pimple to cover up? – be careful not to squeeze the offending object*

2 With a **negative imperative**, the pronouns precede the verb and occur in the order outlined in 211 –

Pour les petites retouches en cours de journée, tamponnez légèrement votre visage avec un kleenex – mais ne le faites pas trop souvent = *for those minor touch-ups during the day, dab your face with a tissue – but don't do it too often*

Ne me posez pas de questions de ce type = *don't ask me that sort of question*

Si tu penses que ça peut être embêtant pour l'amitié, ne le fais pas = *if you think that might put a strain on your friendship, then don't do it*

Ne te laisse pas abattre = *don't allow yourself to be depressed*

213 Position of pronouns with an infinitive and the presentatives *voici* and *voilà*
Position of pronouns with an infinitive

When an infinitive is governed by a modal verb or verb with a similar function, the pronoun precedes the infinitive and not the modal verb –

L'été s'annonce chaud – si vous voulez le terminer bronzée et pas brûlée, prenez de bonnes résolutions = *it's going to be a hot summer – if you want to finish it tanned and not burnt, make some wise resolutions*

Mieux vaut ne pas y aller avec un homme = *better not to go with a man*

Personne ne semble pouvoir nous éclairer sur le rapport entre la coupe de cheveux et le nom d'un poisson (la morue) = *nobody seems able to enlighten us on the connection between the hairstyle and the name of a fish (mullet)*

Position of pronouns with voici, voilà

The unstressed pronoun forms are used before **voici** and **voilà** –

Me voici, prête à sortir = *here I am, ready to go out*

La voilà, dans le bar – *there she is, in the bar*

Nouns are placed after the presentatives –

Voici ma nouvelle veste en velours = *here's my new velvet jacket*

Voilà le type dont je te parlais hier = *there's the guy I was talking to you about yesterday*

214 Agreement of past participles with a preceding direct object

The agreement of past participles with the pronouns of pronominal verbs is discussed in 105–108.

Another scenario involves a preceding direct object and the agreement of a past participle. The gender and number of the preceding direct object are reflected in the form of the past participle.

If the preceding direct object is a noun, it will be repeated before the verb by an object pronoun –

Cette chemise, je l'ai achetée à Clermont = *I bought this shirt in Clermont*

Les filles, il les a draguées depuis l'âge de 15 ans = *he's chatted up girls since he was 15*

Les concombres, je ne les ai jamais aimés = *I've never liked cucumbers*

The preceding direct object may also be a relative pronoun, referring back to a noun in a previous clause –

J'aime bien cette chemise que j'ai achetée à Clermont = *I like this shirt that I bought in Clermont very much*

Cette histoire qu'il n'a jamais partagée avec qui que ce soit est digne d'être mieux connue = *this story which he's never shared with anyone is worthy of being better known*

Les sports qu'il a pratiqués sont tous traumatisants pour le corps = *the sports he's indulged in all take it out of the body big time*

215 First person personal pronouns

If the person using the first person pronoun is female, then any adjectives or past participles relating to it must be in the feminine form –

First person singular
J'ai toujours été prête à toutes les aventures = *I've always been up for any adventure*

Pauvre idiote que j'étais! = *What a fool I was!*

Le mec a voulu m'embrasser et je l'ai repoussé, choquée qu'il ait eu cette pensée! = *the guy tried to kiss me and I pushed him away, shocked that he could think like that*

J'ai perdu la trace de mes parents. Ou peut-être devrais-je dire que ce sont eux qui m'ont perdue = *I lost track of my parents. Or perhaps I should say they lost track of me*

First person plural

Nous étions vraiment d'une inconscience atroce et je ne sais pas comment nous nous en sommes sorties vivantes! = *We were unbelievably unaware of what we were doing and I don't know how we managed to get out of it in one piece!*

Nous sommes allés au meilleur restaurant de la ville = *we went to the best restaurant in town*

216 Second person personal pronouns

Whereas English uses *you* to address any interlocutor, whether known or unknown to the speaker, whether one or more than one person is involved and whatever the circumstances, French has a choice between *tu* and *vous* in the singular. Consequently, *vous* resembles *you* in that it is used as both a singular and plural pronoun, but is different in that it is not used in certain circumstances in the singular.

The general principle is that *tu* is used among friends and work colleagues of the same or similar status, within the family and when an older person talks to a younger one, ie a child – in other words in informal, relaxed, domestic situations. Otherwise *vous* is used.

Because deciding when to switch from *vous* to *tu* as one gets to know someone better is a difficult decision for a non-native French speaker, it is advisable to be led by the person you are talking to – don't switch until they do. To use *tu* too soon may be interpreted as being presumptuous and possibly offensive; to use it too late may make you seem priggish and distant!

The following examples are taken from a girls' magazine. Comments are made at the end of the section.

1 *Garçon de 13 ans qui se révolte contre la mère poule – « Tu m'empêches d'exister, j'suis pas une gonzesse »* = *13-year-old boy rebelling against his over-protective mother – 'You're suffocating me, I'm not a girl'*

2 *Vous êtes convaincue? Reste à trouver le rouge qui convient à vos babines* = *you're convinced? The next thing is to find a lipstick that suits your mouth*

3 *Ont-ils le droit de vous mettre à la porte? – Si vous êtes mariée, l'odieux ne peut décemment pas vous mettre à la porte* = *have they the right to ban you from the house? – If you're married the blighter can't decently do that*

4 *Chez des copains, vous vous sentez moins seule; pour les remercier de leur hospitalité vous vous sentez obligée de coucher avec le célibataire du lot* = *staying with mates, you feel less lonely; to thank them for their hospitality, you feel obliged to sleep with the one in the group who hasn't got a partner*

5 *Deux ou trois choses que je sais d'elle et qui m'énervent – Sophie s'est encore trouvé un beau mec, c'est louche, tu trouves pas?* = *two or three things*

that I know about her which drive me mad – Sophie's found another good-looking guy, it's the pits, don't you think?

6 ***Pas la même notion du temps, ni celle de l'argent – quand on la voit revenir des magasins, les bras chargés de douze paires de pompes tellement pas chères, regarde celles-ci, tu devineras jamais le prix*** = *you haven't got the same notion of time or money – when you see her coming back from the shops with her arms laden with a dozen pairs of shoes, so cheap, look at these, you'll never guess the price*

7 ***Je t'appelle car j'ai un problème et il est stipulé que tu répondes quand on t'appelle*** = *I'm calling you because I've got a problem and it's stipulated that you reply when you're called*

8 ***Je suis formelle, tu n'as aucune raison de culpabiliser ou de trouver ça honteux de ta part*** = *I am absolutely definite – you haven't got any reason to feel guilty or to find that shameful on your part*

9 ***Que tu aies des goûts bizarres, je ne vois pas tellement le problème*** = *that you've got some weird tastes, I can't see the difficulty*

In example 1 a young boy is talking (crossly) to his mother and uses ***tu***. In examples 2, 3 and 4, the reader is addressed as ***vous*** feminine singular – the writer does not know her audience personally but writes for a female reader. The alternation between ***vous*** and ***tu*** in these examples and examples 5 and 6 illustrates well the difference in tone and value of the two pronouns – ***vous*** is used by the writer to address the young female readership, whom she doesn't know and who are probably younger than her, whereas ***tu*** is used in those circumstances where two girls are imagined talking to or reacting to each other. In example 7, the reader is using ***tu*** to address the 'agony aunt', which is presumably done to achieve a sense of complicity, but seems impertinent. In examples 8 and 9, the 'agony aunt' uses the ***tu*** form to create a feeling of trust and intimacy between her and her correspondents. The contrast between examples 2, 3, 4 and examples 8 and 9 highlights well the delicacy and subtlety of the decision.

217 Third person personal pronouns

Not only do ***il*** = *he* and ***elle*** = *she*, both the pronouns also = *it* when they refer to or take the place of a masculine or feminine noun respectively. The same point applies to the plural forms too; ***ils, elles*** = *they* (the plural of *it*).

Le troisième type de vieillissement c'est le vieillissement hormonal – il démarre vers 35 ans par une baisse de taux d'oestrogène = *the third type of ageing is hormonal ageing – it's triggered at about 35 by a reduction in oestrogen levels*

Après une semaine, la transformation est radicale; visiblement fortifiée, la peau recouvre fraîcheur et luminosité; elle revit = *after a week, the transformation is radical; your skin, which is visibly strengthened, recovers its freshness and luminosity; it comes back to life.*

Les propositions de l'opposition feraient davantage avancer le pays. Mais elles ne diffèrent pas fondamentalement des projets gouvernementaux = *the opposition's proposals would benefit the country more. But they don't differ fundamentally from the government's projects*

Les projets européens les plus stratégiques, les entreprises françaises et européennes les plus sensibles ont un point commun – ils font appel aux crânes d'oeuf d'Altran = *the most strategic European projects and the most sensitive French and European businesses have a point in common – they appeal to Altran's eggheads*

In the last example, it should be noted that when a masculine noun (***projets***) and a feminine noun (***entreprises***) form a compound subject, the pronoun used to refer back to them is always masculine.

218 Different usages in French and English

Collective nouns referring to groups of people in British English – *team, government, political party, committee* – tend to be treated as plurals.

The government have decided to support a federalist stance

In French, the rule of grammar, rather than (perhaps) logic, prevails, and such nouns are treated as third person singulars and are followed by a singular verb –

En demi-finales, l'équipe a éliminé le Celtic Glasgow, finaliste la saison passée = *in the semi-final the team eliminated Glasgow Celtic, who were finalists last season*

L'opposition a vivement contesté le rapport de la mission d'évaluation sur les 35 heures = *the opposition have sharply contested the report of the committee which scrutinised the 35-hour week*

Mais si nous en sommes là, c'est parce que le gouvernement Jospin a fait voter en 2001 une loi prévoyant le transfert des impôts = *but if that's the predicament we're in, it's because the Jospin government put through a vote in 2001 on the transfer of taxes*

219 **Ce** and *il* with reference to persons

Although in the table of pronouns above, ***ce*** is classified as a neuter subject pronoun, there is one set of circumstances where it is used as the equivalent of the personal pronouns subject ***il / elle / ils / elles*** to mean *he / she / they*. This is with names of professions, nationality and social status.

The rule is

1 ***il / elle / ils / elles*** are used when the name is used without a determiner (***un / une / des, le / la / les***) –

Elle est française = *she's French*

Il est professeur = *he's a teacher*

Elle est actrice = *she's an actress*

Il est devenu président en 2004 = *he became president in 2004*

Elles sont couturières = *they're dress designers*

2 ***ce*** is used when a determiner is involved and when the noun is modified in some way –

C'est la fille d'une architecte = *she's the daughter of an architect*

Que pensez-vous des mannequins dans les magazines! – Ce sont des sacs d'os = *what do you think of the models in magazines? They're bags of bones*

Les stars se remettent à manger. Leur point commun: ce sont des femmes d'affaires bourrées d'ambition et de talent = *the stars are beginning to eat again. They have one point in common – they're business women full of ambition and talent*

Vous refusez obstinément de fréquenter nos bandes de potes, alors que ce sont des mecs sensibles, je te jure = *you stubbornly refuse to have anything to do with our mates, whereas, I assure you, they're a sensitive bunch*

Dominique? – c'est un garçon = *Dominique? – he's a boy*

220 Neuter subject pronouns

Apart from the situation described in the previous section, there are others where *ce* and *il* function as neuter subject pronouns in French. In practically all the situations where the two pronouns 'compete', it is the verb *être* that is involved.

In terms of agreement, *ce* is treated in exactly the same way as *il*; it is neuter – therefore, any adjective or past participle referring to it always occurs in the masculine, never the feminine. Unlike *il*, it is followed by a plural verb (for example *sont*) when it refers to a plural noun (in standard French – in informal French, the singular also appears) –

Ce sont mes CDs préférés = *they're my favourite CDs*

Ce sont les journalistes français qui ont été les premiers à dévoiler le scandale = *it was French journalists who were the first to uncover the scandal*

221 Ce or *il*? 1 – 1: when followed by an adjective; 2: followed by adjective + infinitive; 3: followed by adjective + clause

It is a perennial problem knowing when to use which pronoun. In general, *ce* has a wider application than *il*. However, since in English there is only one pronoun to fit all cases, it is important to know in French when to use one pronoun rather than the other. The situation in French is even more complicated because *il* = *he* and personal *it* (with reference to masculine items), as well as neuter *it*. Generally speaking, *ce* has a very vague, general value, referring to a context, an effect, an impression, rather than to a specific referent.

What follows is a series of categories that require one pronoun rather than the other or, in some cases, that admit both.

1 When it is / was *is followed by an adjective alone*

It is always *ce* that is used to = *it*, when the expression with the adjective forms a complete statement. If *il* is used, it = *he*. In translating *ce* different strategies may be used, as the examples below illustrate.

Ce sera dur, mais nous avons remporté des matches aussi durs = *it'll be tough, but we've already won equally tough matches* (= playing the game)

Si vous n'avez jamais goûté le chocolat à la tomate, tentez le coup – c'est délicieux = *if you've never tasted tomato-flavoured chocolate, give it a try – it's delicious*

Cela a donné des résultats. C'est clair = *that's produced results – that's for sure*

Des mélanges d'imprimés – c'est très british = *mixtures of print patterns – very British* (= these patterns evoke an impression associated with the UK)

La neige, le soleil, l'aventure, la culture – c'est incroyable = *snow, sun, adventure and culture – unbelievable*

Misez sur une minijupe. Avec vos jambes de gazelle, ce sera parfait = *go for a miniskirt. With gazelle-like legs like yours, it'll be perfect*

Sophie s'est encore trouvé un beau mec, c'est louche, tu trouves pas? = *Sophie's found another good-looking guy, it's the pits, don't you think?*

Il est dur / délicieux / clair / incroyable / parfait / louche would = *he is tough / delicious / clear / unbelievable / perfect / seedy*

2 When it is / was *is followed by an adjective + infinitive*

In this case, ***il*** is the required pronoun in standard French if the infinitive is followed by a complement, direct object or any further information.

Il est important de passer du temps ensemble = *it's important to spend time together*

Si vos vergetures sont rosacées, il est encore temps de demander à un dermatologue de vous prescrire une crème = *If your stretch marks are rosy-coloured, there's still time to ask a dermatologist to prescribe you a cream*

Il est difficile d'aller à la bataille électorale avec un tel résultat dans les sondages = *it's difficult to go into the elections with such a result in the polls*

Il était logique de faire appel aux propriétés de ce bijou des mers chaudes = *it was logical to appeal to the properties of this jewel from the warm seas*

Est-il utile de le répéter? = *is it useful to do it again?*

However, in less formal French, ***ce*** may also be used –

Ce serait dur d'aller vivre ailleurs = *it'd be hard to go and live somewhere else*

The following example shows how even this distinction of formality/informality is not always respected and the two constructions may occur even in the same sentence –

Maintenant il est impossible de doubler aux Jeux, mais c'est agréable d'avoir une alternative avec le marathon et le 10 000 m = *now it's not possible to enter for two events in the Games, but it's nice to have an alternative with the marathon and the 10 000 metres*

If the infinitive is not followed by a complement, direct object or any other information, ***ce*** is used, and the preposition before the infinitive is ***à*** rather than ***de*** –

En matière de drague, il s'agit avant tout de se faire remarquer. Ce n'est pas toujours facile à faire = *when you're on the pull, it's essential to get yourself noticed. It's not always easy to do*

On devrait faire confiance à ses amis. Malheureusement, c'est difficile à faire = *you should trust your friends. Unfortunately it's difficult to do*

3 When **it is** / **was** *is followed by an adjective* + *clause*

Again, it is *il* that is used in standard French, *ce* in less formal French –

Il est universellement reconnu qu'en cent ans le thermomètre mondial a déjà gagné 0,6 degré C = *it's widely accepted that in a hundred years the earth's thermometer has already risen by 0.6 degrees C*

Toujours est-il que je ne peux effectivement m'endormir sans passer par la salle de bains = *the fact remains that in effect I can't go to sleep without paying a visit to the bathroom*

Il est conseillé que si vous voulez vous exposez au soleil, vous le faites toujours avec modération = *it's advisable that, if you want to sunbathe, you always do it with moderation*

Ce n'est pas juste que tu aies eu la même note que moi – j'ai travaillé beaucoup plus dur que toi = *it's not fair that you got the same mark as me – I worked a lot harder than you*

The following example shows a change of construction –

C'est vrai que vous, il ne suffit pas d'appuyer sur un bouton pour vous faire réagir = *it's true that you, it isn't enough to press a button to make you react*

It should be noted that in a number of situations in informal French *ce* is encroaching upon the ground previously occupied by *il*. This is presumably due to the numerical supremacy of *ce* preceding *être* in these constructions and probably also due to the influence of *ça* – see 239.

222 Distinguishing *il* and *ce*: 2
When **it is** / **was** *is followed by another part of speech*

Here it is always *ce* that is used, and again the value of *ce* is difficult to define – it usually refers to a following scenario –

Ma mère me tape de plus en plus sur le système. Résultat – c'est disputes sur disputes = *my mother is getting on my nerves more and more. The result, argument after argument*

Sa stratégie, c'était de prendre à chaque coup une décision claire = *his strategy was to make a clear decision at each stroke* (in golf)

Vous êtes pourvue des qualités indispensables à qui veut se lancer à l'assaut des planches? Foncez, c'est pour vous! = *you've got the indispensable qualities for someone who is keen to tread the boards? Go for it – it's there for you*

C'est une attitude plutôt saine de vouloir s'isoler de temps en temps = *it's a fairly healthy attitude to want to spend time alone once in a while*

C'est bien simple: Julot sans sa troupe de copains, c'est comme un banana split sans la banane = *it's very simple – Fred without his troop of mates is like a banana split minus the banana*

223 The use of *c'est* to highlight a section of an utterance

The normal word order in French is Subject – Verb – Complement (adjective, object, etc). However, quite regularly in writing and even more so in speech, the speaker / writer wishes to emphasise a particular section of what he or she is sayng or writing. This can be done by taking the section in question and preceding it by *c'est*. *Il est* is never used in this way. The following examples illustrate the ways in which various sections can be highlighted. Note that *c'est* is almost invariable – and is used with reference to events in the past as well as in the present.

C'est à leur hotel que l'équipe a fêté sa qualification pour les demi-finales
= *it was in their hotel that the team celebrated qualifying for the semi-final*

Normal order – ***l'équipe a fêté sa qualification pour les demi-finales à leur hôtel***

Mais à la maison, c'est de l'ordre que vous exigez = *but in the house, it's tidiness that you demand*

Normal order – ***vous exigez de l'ordre à la maison***

Ce n'est qu'après avoir siroté une bonne douzaine de verres qu'il se décide enfin à vous suivre = *it's only after downing a good dozen glasses that he at last makes up his mind to follow you*

Normal order – ***il se décide enfin à vous suivre après avoir siroté une bonne douzaine de verres***

C'était qui au bout du fil? = *who was it on the phone?*

Normal order – ***qui était au bout du fil?***

Sur les tapis rouges de Hollywood, c'est à celle qui pèsera le moins lourd = *on the red carpets of Hollywood it's the one who'll weigh the least who wins*

C'est à l'acteur de relever ce défi = *it's up to the actor to meet the challenge*

C'est pas une petite nana comme vous qui allez lui faire perdre la face devant ses durs à cuire de potes = *it's not going to be a little tart like you who'll make him lose face in front of his hard mates*

See 463 for more discussion of highlighting.

224 Use of *on*

On is a widely used third person pronoun and covers a range of usages that would be served by a number of pronouns in English. Translating *on* into English, therefore, presents problems and choosing the most appropriate corresponding pronoun requires careful thought. A number of points will emerge from an examination of the following examples –

1. that *on* can be equivalent of almost any other pronoun,
2. that, just because it is used on a number of occasions in a single passage, that does not necessarily mean that it retains the same value throughout the passage; it is quite likely to change values from one occurrence to the next.

Aurions-nous oublié ces serpents sifflant sur la tête de Pompidou dans l'affaire Marcovic? Doit-on rappeler les fantasmagories sexuelles et délirantes dont les tricoteuses de la Révolution assaisonnaient Marie-Antoinette. On aura vu, convoqués sans vergogne et sur écran, des témoins douteux – mais rétribués – afin qu'ils débitent des insanités sans preuves = *could we possibly have forgotten those serpents hissing on Pompidou's head in the Marcovic affair? Must we remind ourselves of the sexual and outrageous fantasies with which the tricoteuses of the Revolution* [a group of staunchly revolutionary women] *spiced up Marie-Antoinette's reputation. We have undoubtedly seen dubious witnesses shamelessly assembled on television – but rewarded – to dish up loads of nonsense without any proof*

In this example, the alternation between **nous** and **on** shows how they can be used interchangeably in a context where the referent of the pronouns is not defined.

On me sollicite parfois pour que je donne un coup de main à l'occasion d'une affectation = *I'm sometimes asked to give a hand when an appointment is being made*

Here the best way to translate the **on** is by a passive construction – it is not at all clear who is asking for help.

On dit « c'est du Murat » comme on dit « c'est du Miossec / du Dominique A ». Des auteurs-compositeurs avec une vraie estampille, on n'en a pas tant que ça. On tombe sous le charme de ses yeux bleus d'amoureux. Ensuite, on remarque le mec, pas mal du tout = *they say 'that's pure Murat' just as they say 'that's pure Miossec or Dominique A'. We haven't got that many singer–songwriters with a genuine trademark. We fall under the charm of his blue love-smitten eyes. Then we notice the guy, not bad at all*

In this example, **on** seems to have a number of values – very vague in the first two instances; the third could refer to the French nation as a whole; the fourth and fifth, those attending his concerts.

Ce type était complètement dingue et s'est mis à me poser des questions d'un ton très pervers: « Alors on va à l'école? »; «Et on a des bonnes notes à l'école, on est une bonne fifille à sa maman? » Et dans ce genre de situation, l'emploi de la troisième personne du singulier augure quelque chose de terrifiant = *this guy was completely off his rocker and began to ask me questions in a very perverted way: 'So she goes to school?'; 'Does she get good marks at school, is she a good little girl for mummy?' In this type of situation, using the third person singular pronoun suggested something terrifying*

Here, as the girl indicates, **on** is being used in a disturbing way – an indefinite pronoun used in a highly personal situation, depersonalising the girl.

On veut que les gens nous aiment je suppose. Mais ça ne peut être la raison pour laquelle on écrit. On écrit un livre car on ressent l'absolue nécessité de le faire. Et non pas parce qu'on veut du fric, ou trouver une petite amie = *we/I want people to like us/me I suppose. But that can't be the reason for writing. We/I write a book because we/I feel absolutely constrained to do it – and not because we/I want some money, or to find a girlfriend*

In this example, as the translation implies, **on** becomes very close to being a substitute for **je** – it teeters between a personal reference and a more general one.

225 Agreement of adjectives and past participles with *on*

Because *on* bears so many values, this is brought out in the matter of agreement with adjectives and past participles (however, the verb never takes anything but the third person singular form) – see 197. Of course, this is more obvious in written French than in spoken French, where agreements are often not noticeable.

Ça devait être un plan d'une nuit, mais on est restés ensemble six mois = *it was meant to be a one-night stand, but we stayed together for six months*

Tu nous imagines comme ça – couchés, debout, assis? On est aussi vulgaires? = *can you see us like that – in bed, standing up, sitting down? Are we as common as that?*

Dans toutes les Caraïbes, les Cubains ont toujours été les plus bosseurs. Ma mère était institutrice, on n'était pas des privilégiés = *in all the Caribbean, the Cubans have always been the hardest working. My mother was an infant-school teacher; we didn't have any privileges*

C'est la femme qui a envie d'un enfant la première, surtout quand elle approche la quarantaine. Là, on devient même insistante = *it's the woman who's the first to want a baby, especially when she's getting close to forty. Then she even insists.*

Certains se lavent le nez sous la douche. Quand on est enrhumée, c'est différent = *some people wash their nose under the shower. When you've got a cold, that's different*

Quand on se croit seul(e) ou à l'abri des représailles, il arrive qu'on se lâche un peu ou carrément – *when you think you're alone or out of danger of reprisals, it happens that you let yourself go – a little bit or a lot*

In the first two examples, because *on* refers to a couple, the past participle and adjective have a masculine plural ending – but the verb remains in the third person singular. In the next example, *on* covers the whole family and not just the mother. In the fourth example, the person referred to is a woman, consequently *insistante*. In the second-last example, the use of the feminine past participle seems odd after the masculine pronoun *certains*, but is probably to be explained by reference to the fact that the example is taken from a women's magazine. In the last example, the author covers the possibility that the pronoun may refer to a girl or a guy by presenting the adjective in both genders.

226 *on* and its other forms

When it is necessary to refer to the subject pronoun *on* as a direct or indirect object or after a preposition, the reflexive forms are used –

Si on n'aime pas le cadeau, on peut le revendre et s'offrir un autre = *if you don't like the present, you can sell it and buy yourself another one*

Tu crois que c'est dangereux de se percer le nombril soi-même? = *do you think it's dangerous to pierce your navel yourself?*

On prend trois comprimés qui vont arrêter la grossesse en court-circuitant les sécrétions de progestérone. C'est indolore et on repart tranquillement chez soi = *you take three pills which will stop the pregnancy by short-circuiting the secretion of progesterone. It doesn't hurt and you can go home without a problem*

227 Personal pronouns – object

The following examples illustrate the use of the personal pronouns as direct and indirect objects –

First person singular

Je n'ai personne à qui me confier, j'espère que tu sauras m'écouter et peut-être m'aider = *I haven't got anyone to confide in. I hope you'll be able to listen to me and perhaps help me*

Je ne sais plus comment me coiffer – mes cheveux m'abandonnent peu à peu. Je ne peux plus rien faire des quelques cheveux me restant. Je devrai porter une perruque, ce qui ne m'enchante guère = *I don't know how to do my hair any more – my hair is gradually dropping out. I can't do anything with my few remaining hairs. I'll have to wear a wig, and that doesn't appeal to me at all*

Second person singular

Je t'ai reconnue, autant te dire qu'au milieu de mes lettres pas super-super tordantes du mois, la tienne m'a fait grand bien = *I picked you out – that's to say that in the middle of my not-so-very funny letters this month, yours has done me a lot of good*

Si tu veux te faire percer, va dans un lieu spécialisé = *if you want to have a piercing, go to a place that specialises in it*

J'ai hésité longtemps avant de t'écrire = *I kept hesitating before writing to you*

Je t'appelle car j'ai un problème = *I'm calling you because I've got a problem*

Third person singular

Je pense que c'est bien de le prendre dans les mains au début = *I think it's fine to take hold of it in your hands at the beginning*

Il me reproche de ne pas lui parler = *he accuses me of not talking to him*

Comment savoir si ça lui fait plaisir? = *how can I know if it gives her pleasure?*

J'ai un problème qui me tient énormément au coeur et je n'arrive pas à le résoudre = *I've got a problem that is very close to my heart and I can't sort it out*

Il n'arrive pas à le comprendre = *he can't manage to understand it / him*

Third person reflexive / reciprocal

Il faut se faire pousser les poils = *you'll need to grow hair*

C'est la deuxième fois qu'on se sépare = *it's the second time we've split up*

Entre êtres humains sentimentalement liés, il faut beaucoup se parler, se dire des choses = *Between human beings with a sentimental attachment, you have to talk a lot, tell each other things*

First person plural

Y a-t-il des risques que nous nous fassions arrêter par la police? = *is there a risk that we'll get ourselves arrested by the police?*

Faire fondre quelques rondeurs superflues sans nous priver = *How to get rid of a few excess bulges without depriving ourselves*

Second person plural
Oui, il y a des risques que vous vous fassiez arrêter par la police, mais ce n'est pas le pire qui puisse vous arriver = *yes, there is the risk that you'll get yourselves arrested by the police, but that's not the worst that might happen to you*

Pour tranformer vos petits kilos mous en muscles, nul besoin de vous imposer des kilomètres de footing ou des heures dans les salles de gym. Il vous suffit simplement d'opter pour la marche = *in order to transform your wee soft kilos into muscle, no need to impose kilometres of jogging on yourself or hours in the gym. All you need is simply to opt for walking*

Third person plural
Ça va bien les déboussoler, les autres, ça va bien les faire ruminer, médire, mais ça va leur faire clouer le bec = *that'll confuse them very nicely, it'll give them food for thought, make them curse, but it'll make them shut their gobs*

Je suis une fille bizarre, il ne m'arrive que des choses nulles, je les collectionne = *I'm a weird girl, only boring things happen to me, I collect them*

Le mieux serait de leur dire que pour moi c'est juste histoire de voir ce qu'ils valent au disco = *the best thing to do would be to tell them that for me it's just a matter of finding out how good they are at discoing*

A l'heure où tu liras ces lignes – grosso modo trois ou quatre semaines après que je les ai écrites = *when you read these lines – about three or four weeks after I've written them*

228 The various values of the reflexive pronouns *me, te, se, nous, vous*

1 to refer back to the subject

Belle et mince même sans se ruiner = *beautiful and slim even without ruining yourself*

Pas la peine de vous punir avec une diète complète de trois jours après une crise de chocolat = *not worth punishing yourself by not eating anything for three full days after a chocolate crisis*

2 to mark a reciprocal relationship

Nous nous aimons mais nos parents sont complètement contre = *we love each other but our parents are completely against it*

Soyez très clair avec votre petite amie – il faut surveiller vos paroles, vos actes pour vous protéger contre l'incompréhension = *be very honest with your girlfriend – you need to watch what you say and do to protect yourself from misunderstanding*

3 idiomatic usage with no corresponding value in English

Vous avez pris quelques kilos sans vous en rendre compte? = *you've put on a few kilos without realising it*

Sans me vanter je suis l'homme qui supporte le moins au monde « La Guerre des étoiles » = *without boasting I'm the bloke who likes 'Star Wars' the least of anybody*

229 *le* referring to a previously expressed concept

Quite often *le* is used to refer not to a previously expressed or understood noun but to a concept expressed in a preceding (or subsequent) statement or question. English tends not to pick up the concept in this way.

J'ai décidé de vous proposer quelques sujets de rédac que je corrigerai dans ces pages, si le temps le permet = *I've decided to suggest a few essay questions which I'll mark in these pages, if time allows*

Personne ne vous reprochera d'avoir tenté médecine avant de vous orienter sur la gestion. Le tout est de le justifier sans fausse honte = *no one will criticise you for having attempted medicine before having a go at business. What counts is to justify it without false modesty*

Il évoque l'affaire comme « l'accident qui a mis fin » à sa carrière au journal « de la même manière imprévisible que l'aurait fait une attaque cardiaque ou un accident d'avion » = *he describes the affair as 'the accident which put an end' to his career in the paper 'in the same unforeseeable way as a heart attack or plane accident would have done'*

Le message est clair: comme le montre l'histoire européenne, l'antisémitisme ne touche pas que les juifs, mais concerne les libertés de tous = *the message is clear: as the history of Europe demonstrates, anti-Semitism doesn't affect just the Jews, but concerns everyone's liberties*

In the first three examples, the *le* refers back to a previous concept – in the first example = *to mark the essays*; in the second = *the change of career ambitions*; in the third = *the end to his career*. In the last example, it anticipates the idea that follows. Note that only in example 2 does the English translation use an *it*.

230 Dealing with the anticipatory *it* of English

Whereas English uses an anticipatory *it* to introduce a following idea, French does not: therefore, it should not be rendered into French.

Les médecins considèrent essentiel de suivre un programme d'exercices = *doctors consider it essential to follow a programme of exercises*

Je trouve difficile de ne pas être paresseux = *I find it difficult not to be lazy*

Elle estime important que les parents ne voient pas dans la garde alternée des enfants une façon de régler leur comptes entre eux = *she thinks it important for parents not to see in alternating looking after their children a way of settling scores between them*

Je trouve choquant qu'il s'est servi de propos tellement obscènes = *I find it shocking that he used such obscene language*

231 Stressed personal pronouns: 1

The stressed forms may occur alone or combined with **même**. They are used for emphasis, when the pronoun is separated from the verb or follows a preposition, and in sentences without a verb.

First person singular

Moi qui suis une fille et qui aimerais être un garçon = *me a girl who'd love to be a boy*

Je suis un traitement, mais il reste inefficace sur moi = *I've been following a course of treatment but it hasn't had any effect on me*

Je comprends bien évidemment ton désarroi, ayant été fasciné moi-même par la joliesse de Sinéad O'Connor = *I can certainly understand your confusion, because I myself have been fascinated by Sinéad O'Connor's good looks*

Qui c'est? – Moi = *who is it? – Me*

Il ne sait pas comment le faire – Ni moi non plus = *he doesn't know how to do it – Nor do I*

Second person singular

Quoi que tu puisses répondre, je pense à toi = *whatever you may say in reply, I keep thinking of you*

Dans la série « toi aussi joue avec Kylie », voici la poupée Kylie Minogue = *in the series 'you too can play with Kylie', here's the KM doll*

De qui est-ce qu'il parlait? – Toi = *who was he talking about? – You*

Third person singular

Il ne cesse de faire parler de lui = *he's always making himself talked about*

J'avais un perroquet, mais mon premier mari m'a dit: « C'est lui ou moi » = *I had a parrot, but my first husband said to me: 'It's either him or me'*

Cet animal m'évoque mon père. Je ne sais pas trop pourquoi, mais c'est tout à fait lui = *this animal makes me think of my dad. I don't know why, but it's him to a tee.*

Merci à Dido, qui, elle, nous a offert un vrai spectacle = *thanks to Dido who gave us a real show*

Elle explique qu'elle n'avait jamais dit du mal d'elle = *she explains that she had never spoken ill of her*

Cette période houleuse s'arrange généralement d'elle-même vers 18–20 ans = *this stormy period normally sorts itself out when you're between 18 and 20 years old*

Third person reflexive

Soi is used with reference to an indefinite or unexpressed antecedent and in the expression **estime de soi** = *self-esteem.*

Il faut se sentir très à l'aise avec soi-même et son partenaire = *you have to feel completely relaxed with yourself and your partner*

J'aide les femmes à se sentir belles, à entretenir leur estime de soi = *I help women to feel beautiful, to maintain their self-esteem*

First person plural
Il y a un risque qu'entre nous ce ne soit plus pareil = *there's the danger that between ourselves it may not work out like that*

Aujourd'hui, nous, on a la guerre d'Irak, la mondialisation et l'alimentation bio = *today we've got the war in Iraq, globalisation and bio foods*

Second person plural
Apprenez à vous imposer. Ne comptez que sur vous = *learn to impose yourself. Don't rely on anyone except yourself*

Il y en aura pour tous les goûts et toutes les formes près de chez vous = *there'll be one for all tastes and shapes near you*

Third person plural
Tous mes amis me disent de garder le moral, mais c'est facile pour eux = *all my mates tell me to keep a stiff upper lip, but that's easy for them*

Je sais que pour eux c'est juste histoire de se défouler = *I know that for them it's just a matter of letting off steam*

J'ai peur d'éprouver quelque chose pour l'un d'eux = *I'm afraid of having a feeling for one of them*

Au fil des mois, ces fines rayures vont blanchir et donc s'estomper d'elles-mêmes = *as the months go by, these fine lines will turn pale and therefore blend in by themselves*

Un marathon du baiser a eu lieu à Manille aux Philippines. Il était réservé aux amoureux mariés ou fiancés, mais selon les participants, beaucoup d'entre eux ne l'étaient pas = *a kissing marathon was held in Manila in the Philippines. It was restricted to lovers who were married or engaged, but according to the participants not everyone was*

232 Stressed personal pronouns: 2
The third person pronoun, singular and plural, can be used as the direct subject of the verb, whereas for the other persons the unstressed pronouns need to be used as well –

Il voudrait faire l'amour deux ou trois fois par jour. Si je le repousse, il est abattu. Lui prétend que je ne suis pas normale, donc c'est l'impasse = *he'd like to make love two or three times a day. If I reject him, he gets depressed. He claims I'm not normal, so we've reached an impasse*

Mon copain critique mon anatomie et cela me blesse. Lui dit que mes seins sont trop petits, mais moi, j'en suis contente = *my boyfriend keeps criticising my body. He says that my breasts are too small, but I'm happy with them*

Un homme âgé, lui, trouve au contraire valorisant de conquérir une partenaire moins âgée que lui = *a older man on the other hand finds it enhances his prestige if he conquers a partner younger than himself*

Il arrive à mon père de m'accompagner jusqu'aux cabinets d'essayage. Est-ce choquant? Moi, j'y suis habituée et ça ne me gêne pas = *it happens that my dad goes with me to the fitting rooms. Is that shocking? I'm used to it and it doesn't worry me*

La question est de savoir si toi tu as les qualités pour réveiller ce groupe = *the question is to know if you've got the qualities needed to shake this group up*

Devenue rédactrice en chef, le Guide, c'était elle, les billets pleins d'humour et de rosserie parfois, elle encore = *having become editor in chief, she was the guide, notes full of humour, sometimes of nastiness too, that was her again*

La mauvaise humeur du matin, le match du foot, vous, vous y échappez = *the bad mood in the morning, the football match, you can escape all that*

It is also possible for the third person pronoun to be repeated as with the other persons

Il faut dire qu'elle, elle ne pose pas de questions = *it has to be said that she doesn't ask questions*

233 Stressed personal pronouns: 3

With certain verbs stressed pronouns are used to express *to me, you, him, her*, etc, rather than the regular pronouns (*me, lui, en*, etc):

With *faire attention à* = *to pay attention to*, *s'habituer à* = *to get used to*, *penser à* = *to think of*, *avoir recours à* = *to have recourse to*, *rêver à* = *to dream of*, *songer à* = *to think of*, *tenir à* = *to be fond of*

Je suis folle amoureuse d'un mec, je rêve à lui tout le temps = *I'm madly in love with a guy; I dream about him all the time*

Ménager sa colonne vertébrale contribue à prévenir les maux – pense à elle avant de faire des mouvements trop brusques = *managing your spinal column will help avoid problems – think about it before making too sudden movements*

With verbs of movement

Elle a couru à moi les larmes aux yeux = *she ran to me with tears in her eyes*

Mon petit ami m'a quittée – je ne sais pas comment m'y prendre pour qu'il revienne à moi = *my boyfriend has left me – I don't what to do to make him come back*

However, if the 'movement' is intellectual, the unstressed pronouns are used –

Il me vient à l'esprit que l'important n'est pas le commentaire mais l'acte = *it occurs to me that the important thing is not so much talk as action*

234 *en* and *y*

En and *y* are like the personal pronouns dealt with earlier in that –

1 they are placed between the subject and the verb when there is a subject, and 2 they are used in exactly same way with the imperative.

235 *en*

En is a pronoun which

1 is the equivalent of **de** + a noun or the idea contained in a phrase and = *of, about, from* + *it / they*; very often it is a matter of a verb with a prepositional object, eg

   se servir de, se moquer de, se débarrasser de

2 is used in partitive constructions = *some / any of it / them*;
3 is the equivalent of the possessive determiner in English in certain circumstances;
4 is part of certain verbal expressions.

1 the equivalent of de + noun

J'adore ce t-shirt avec ces longues manches fendues aux coudes. Qu'est-ce que tu en penses? = *I adore this t-shirt with its long sleeves, split at the elbows. What do you think of it?*

Les lentilles les plus connues sont vertes ou rouges, mais il en existe d'autres variétés = *the best known lentils are green or red, but other varieties exist*

Son épouse reprochait à l'entourage du président d'avoir accaparé les voitures de son mari et au président d'en avoir eu connaissance = *his wife accused the president's entourage of having seized her husband's cars and the president of being aware of it*

Si la rose est la reine des fleurs, le jasmin en est le roi = *if the rose is the queen of the flowers, jasmine is the king*

J'avais l'air d'un nain travesti entouré de gazelles. Tout le monde s'en marrait = *I looked like a dressed-up gnome surrounded by gazelles. Everybody took the mickey*

Le diagnostic d'un médecin reste indispensable. N'hésitez pas à vous en servir = *a doctor's diagnosis is indispensable. Don't hesitate to use it*

Ces photos, personne n'en conteste l'authenticité = *no one disputes the authenticity of these photos*

Quand il y a des informations sur la torture des prisonniers, des sanctions doivent être prises très vite; cela responsabilise les personnes qui en ont la charge = *when there's information about the torture of prisoners, sanctions must be taken very quickly; that makes the people who are in charge of them responsible*

2 = some / any of it / them

Vous êtes exigeantes avec vous-même – voilà pourquoi vous conseillez à celles qui n'ont pas de tenue ASICS d'en avoir une = *you're demanding with yourself, that's why you advise those who haven't got an ASICS outfit to get one*

Je lis des textes sur l'économie d'Afrique. J'en ai un tas = *I read texts on the economy of Africa. I've got stacks of them*

Pour ne garder que l'essentiel du café, la compagnie retire le marc au moment de l'élaboration. Mais si vous y tenez, on peut vous en envoyer = *in order to preserve nothing but the essentials of the coffee, the company removes the grounds when it is being produced. But if you want, they can send you some*

Coupez les oranges en lamelles; sucrez-en la moitié = *slice the oranges thinly; sprinkle sugar on half of them*

Le succès des légumes secs s'explique en partie par leur richesse en protéines. Crus, ils en contiennent jusqu'à 25%, et environ 10% après cuisson = *the success of dried vegetables may in part be explained by their richness in proteins. Uncooked they contain up to 25%, and about 10% after cooking*

3 = English possessive determiner

Seul un interrogatoire détaillé de l'enfant et de ses parents permettra d'en dépister la cause [de sa maladie] = *only a detailed interrogation of the child and its parents will allow its cause to be traced*

« Les photos sont choquantes mais nos rapports sont pires » dit Mme Notari mais qui refuse d'en préciser le contenu = *'the photos are shocking but our reports are worse', said Mme Notari, who, however, refused to give details of their contents*

4 There are also a number of verbal expressions involving en, where the en seems to have little particular value –

Il en va de même avec les soutiens-gorges en matière élastique = *it's the same with elasticated bras*

Je lui en veux de m'avoir légué son nez en patate = *I hold it against him for having bequeathed me his nose like a potato*

J'ai vu Fabien, plié en deux, se tenant le ventre, mort de rire – il n'en pouvait plus = *I saw Fabien, doubled up, holding his stomach, laughing as if he was about to give up the ghost – he couldn't help it*

Le clown revient. Mais il n'en peut plus, le clown = *the clown has come back. But he can't help it, the clown*

Je suis seule. Je fais rire tout le monde, et je suis seule. J'en ai marre = *I'm all alone. I make everybody laugh, and I'm all alone. I'm fed up with it*

J'en ai assez qu'on me telephone pour m'inviter à les faire rigoler = *it gets on my nerves when they ring me up to invite me to make them laugh*

Personne n'en veut de mes soucis = *no one wants to hear about my problems*

236 y

Y is a pronoun which

1 is the equivalent of ***à*** + a noun or the idea contained in a phrase and = *at, about* + *it / they*; very often it is a matter of a verb with a prepositional object

   eg *faire attention à, penser à, renoncer à*

2 = *there*

1 Equivalent of à + noun

Que l'on ait arrêté de fumer au début d'année ou depuis quelques années, le spectre de la rechute rode. On n'ose pas ne pas y faire attention = *whether you stopped smoking at the beginning of the year or some years ago, the spectre of starting again is ever present. You dare not not pay attention to it*

J'y ai renoncé il y a trois mois = *I gave up three months ago*

Si vous n'y tenez pas, vous pouvez les supprimer = *if you don't like them, you can get rid of them*

Une fois que vous y aurez pris goût = *once you've got a taste for them*

2 = there

J'y ai rencontré celui qui allait devenir mon mari = *I met the man there who was to become my husband*

Sous un chapiteau bleu magique on rit de bon coeur – clowns, contortionnistes, trapézistes, acrobates – tout y est = *in a magic blue big top everyone has a good laugh – clowns, contortionists, trapeze artists, acrobats – everything is there*

Nous n'avons pas besoin de photos pour savoir ce qui s'y est passé et c'est inacceptable = *we don't need photos to know what happened there – it's unacceptable*

Demonstrative pronouns

237 Demonstrative pronouns

These are equivalent to English *the one, this one, that one, those*.

The forms

masculine singular	***celui***	*the one*
masculine plural	***ceux***	*the ones*
feminine singular	***celle***	*the one*
feminine plural	***celles***	*the ones*

The pronouns are very often combined with a relative pronoun.

On many other occasions the pronouns are combined with ***–ci, –là*** to indicate proximity or remoteness.

masculine singular	***celui-ci***	*this one, the latter*
	celui-là	*that one, the former*
masculine plural	***ceux-ci***	*these ones, the latter*
	ceux-là	*those ones, the former*
feminine singular	***celle-ci***	*this one, the latter*
	celle-là	*that one, the former*
feminine plural	***celles-ci***	*these ones, the latter*
	celles-là	*those ones, the former*

The former, the latter sound rather pompous and formal in English – note the way forms with ***-ci /-là*** are translated in the following examples.

For demonstrative adjectives, see 265–266.

238 Examples of demonstrative pronouns

+ *relative pronoun*

Voici celui qui a gagné le jackpot = *here's the one who's won the jackpot*

Ceux qui la connaissaient savaient qu'elle était aussi pleine de larmes = *those who knew her knew that she was also full of tears*

Quand on commence à conduire on n'est jamais très à l'aise et la vitesse à laquelle roulent certains peut effrayer. Celles qui ont déjà conduit comprennent ce que je veux dire = *when you begin to drive, you are never completely comfortable and the speed at which some drivers drive can be frightening. Those (women) who already know how to drive understand what I mean*

Vous ne voulez causer problème à ceux qui vous ont invitée = *you don't want to be a nuisance to those who have invited you*

Surtout tous ceux qui murmurent que « la vie, c'est bien compliqué », il les déteste = *he especially detests those who murmur that 'life's jolly complicated'*

Comment être celle que l'on raccompagne . . . et pas celle qui raccompagne = *how to be the one taken home . . . and not the one who takes home*

Il y a celles et ceux qui en parlent beaucoup mais qui ne font pas grand-chose, et ceux qui restent plus discrets sur le sujet = *there are those of both sexes who talk a lot about it but don't do anything, and those who remain more discreet on the subject*

In the following case the relative clause is reduced to a past participle –

Des distributeurs automatiques de pommes verront bientôt le jour. Ce système est déjà en place en Belgique – mais le sien diffère de celui prévu pour la France = *automatic apple dispensers will soon be on the market. This system is already in operation in Belgium, but it differs from the one envisaged for France*

+ *de* + *infinitive / noun*

L'incapacité à dire non renvoie à une peur infantile. Celle de ne pas être aimé si l'on dit non à ses parents = *the inability to say no evokes a childhood fear – that of not being loved if you say no to your parents*

C'est le même message – celui de vous diriger vers le but de l'harmonie du couple = *it's the same message – that of aiming towards achieving harmony for your twosome*

+ *-ci / -là*

Le rôle parental, c'est de protéger les enfants contre les trop grandes souffrances et les trop grands excès. Celui-ci s'exerce naturellement = *a parent's role is to protect their children against too much suffering and too much excess. It [the latter] comes into play naturally*

Kylie aurait présenté son fiancé Olivier Martinez à ses parents lors des vacances de Noël. Ceux-ci seraient tombés sous le charme du beau frenchy

= *it's reported that Kylie introduced her fiancé O M to her parents during the Christmas vacation. The latter are said to have fallen under the charm of the good-looking Frenchman*

Ce spectacle de confusion ne va pas précipiter l'adhésion de Londres à l'euro. Celle-ci est remise à des calendes grecques = *this confused spectacle isn't going to precipitate London joining the euro. This has been postponed indefinitely*

Mais la grosse actualité du moment, c'est la margarine anticholestérol, commercialisée par Johnson & Johnson. Celle-ci fait un veritable tabac en Finlande = *but the hot news of the moment is anticholesterol margarine, put on the market by J&J. This [the latter] is making a big hit in Finland*

Les regards qui se détournent, Toulouse qui ne parle « que de ça », les couloirs où l'on chuchote. Ceux-là, tous ceux-là le mettent en rage = *the looks that don't meet your eye, Toulouse which speaks about nothing but 'that', the corridors where everyone is whispering. These people, all such people, infuriate him*

Il y a des parents qui n'ont pas su nous protéger. Ceux-ci n'ont pas su nous aimer non plus = *there are some parents who didn't know how to protect us. They [the latter] didn't know how to love us either*

Il faut apprendre à l'enfant à se méfier du « trop », des gens trop méchants tout comme des gens trop gentils. Il faut savoir comment mettre ceux-ci comme ceux-là à l'écart = *you must teach your child to be on their guard against 'too much', people who are too nasty as well as people who are too nice. They need to know how to avoid both types [the former as well as the latter]*

239 The neuter demonstrative pronouns *ceci, cela*, ça

The function of these pronouns is to refer to the general content of a statement – **ceci** to what has yet to be stated, and **cela** to what has already been stated – or to some unspecified object. **Ceci** normally = *this*, **cela** normally = *that*. **Ça** takes the place of both **ceci** and **cela** in informal French and is very common indeed.

Prenez / écoutez ceci = *take / listen to this* [something about to be explained]

Ces règles automatiques prévoient ceci – que si l'on anticipe sa succession, cela permet d'aider de son vivant ses enfants = *these automatic rules foresee this – that if you anticipate your succession, that allows you to help your children during your lifetime*

Ne fais pas cela = *don't do that* [something already mentioned]

L'association europhile souligne que le référendum sur la monnaie unique est une belle victoire. Cela ne trompe personne = *the europhile association keeps stressing that the referendum on the single currency is a splendid victory. That deceives no one*

Quand ça empoisonne la vie à chaque cycle, il ne faut pas hésiter à en parler à un gynécologue = *when that messes up your life every month, you mustn't hesitate to speak about it to a gynaecologist*

En amour, ça ne bouge pas assez, et vous aimeriez secouez votre coeur = *in love things are not moving enough and you'd like to give your heart a good shake*

Comme ça, au moins, c'est équitable = *at least, like that it's fair*

Possessive pronouns

240 Possessive pronouns

These are the equivalent of English *mine, yours, his, hers, its, ours, theirs.*

The forms

first person	masculine singular	*le mien*	*mine*	*le nôtre*	*ours*
	masculine plural	*les miens*	*mine*	*les nôtres*	*ours*
	feminine singular	*la mienne*	*mine*	*la nôtre*	*ours*
	feminine plural	*les miennes*	*mine*	*les nôtres*	*ours*
second person	masculine singular	*le tien*	*yours*	*le vôtre*	*yours*
	masculine plural	*les tiens*	*yours*	*les vôtres*	*yours*
	feminine singular	*la tienne*	*yours*	*la vôtre*	*yours*
	feminine plural	*les tiennes*	*yours*	*les vôtres*	*yours*
third person	masculine singular	*le sien*	*his, hers, its*	*le leur*	*theirs*
	masculine plural	*les siens*	*his, hers, its*	*les leurs*	*theirs*
	feminine singular	*la sienne*	*his, hers, its*	*la leur*	*theirs*
	feminine plural	*les siennes*	*his, hers, its*	*les leurs*	*theirs*

A reminder that, as with the personal pronouns, the gender of the possessive pronoun depends upon the gender of the noun it refers to, not the gender/sex of the person who 'possesses' it. See 267–271 for possessive adjectives.

241 Examples of possessive pronouns

Sa famille habite en Italie, la mienne en Roumanie = *his family lives in Italy, mine in Romania*

Je t'ai reconnue, autant te dire qu'au milieu de mes lettres pas super-super tordantes du mois, la tienne m'a fait grand bien = *I picked you out – that's to say that in the middle of my not-so-very funny letters this month, yours has done me a lot of good*

Ma mère est institutrice – la sienne l'était aussi = *my mum's a primary school teacher, hers was too*

Des distributeurs automatiques de pommes verront bientôt le jour. Ce système est déjà en place en Belgique – mais le sien diffère de celui prévu pour la France = *automatic apple dispensers will soon be on the market. This system is already in operation in Belgium, but it differs from the one envisaged for France*

Changez vos habitudes et les siennes par la même occasion car les concessions réciproques seront le ciment de votre couple = *change your habits and his on the same occasion because concessions you make to each other will cement your twosome*

Il est possible qu'il ne comprenne pas votre malaise – le sien est beaucoup moins aigu = *it's possible that he won't understand your misgivings – his are a lot less serious*

Un groupe d'étudiants américains est envoyé au Moyen-Age en France et n'a que six heures pour trouver le moyen de revenir à leur époque (qui est aussi la nôtre) = *a group of American students has been sent back to the Middle Ages in France and has only got six hours to find a way of getting back to their time (which is also ours)*

Les vergetures vont de pair avec la puberté. Si les vôtres sont rosacées, il est encore temps de demander à un dermatologue de vous prescrire une crème = *stretch marks go hand in hand with puberty. If yours are rosy-coloured, there's still time to ask a dermatologist to prescribe you a cream*

Nous étions très ambitieux et les équipes que j'ai vues n'étaient pas forcément meilleures que la nôtre = *we were very ambitious and the teams I saw weren't necessarily better than ours*

J'aime les vêtements créés par les Japonais – les leurs ont un look très exotique = *I like clothes designed by the Japanese – theirs have a very exotic look*

Je dois avouer que nous avons tous les deux des secrets – le mien, je n'oserai jamais le lui dire, le sien je le connais, mais il ne le sait pas = *I must confess that we've both got secrets – I'll never dare tell him mine; I know his, but he doesn't know I know*

Quantifying and indefinite pronouns

242 Quantifying pronouns

The main quantifying pronouns are – ***beaucoup de*** = *many*, ***certains*** = *a certain number*, ***la plupart de*** = *most*, ***un (grand / petit) nombre de*** = *a (large / small) number of*, ***quantité de*** = *lots of*, ***la majorité de*** = *the majority of*, ***la minorité de*** = *the minority of*, ***plus de*** = *more than*, ***moins de*** = *less / fewer than*, ***peu de*** = *few*. In these cases the linking ***de*** remains ***de***, unless it is combined with the definite article – as in the examples below.

However, in the case of ***bien des*** = *many*, ***des*** links the pronoun to its complement – see below.

Closely connected to quantifying pronouns are the numeral nouns, ***une douzaine*** = *dozen*, ***une vingtaine*** = *score*, ***une centaine*** = *about a hundred* – see 437.

The issue at stake with quantifying pronouns is whether, when the pronoun is subject of a verb, the verb should agree with the pronoun (which is usually singular in form) or the complement (which is usually plural).

Practice is to make the verb agree with the complement – a plural complement attracts a plural verb, a singular complement a singular verb.

This sometimes leads to seeming anomalies, when the complement is not specified or is understood, since, in such cases, a singular pronoun will be accompanied by a plural verb.

243 Examples of quantifying pronouns
Pronouns with plural complements
Beaucoup des photos contenues dans cette collection sont étonnantes = *many of the photos in this collection are stunning*

Plus de la moitié des femmes ont moins de pêche en automne–hiver = *more than 50% of women feel low in autumn–winter*

Un grand nombre de jeunes veulent faire des prouesses = *a large number of youngsters want to do something outstanding*

La majorité de nos solutions sont adaptées pour protéger vos proches en cas d'accidents = the majority of our solutions are designed to protect those close to you in case of an accident

J'ai vu quantité de gens feuilleter les livres de grammaire dans les librairies = I've seen lots of people leafing through grammar books in the bookshops

Peu de gens ont voulu croire que le danger est écarté = very few people accepted that the danger was over

La tête d'une petite fille décapitée dans un accident roule sur la chaussée – certains vomissent, d'autres détournent leur regard = the head of a little girl, decapitated in an accident, rolls onto the road – some throw up, others look away

Moins de femmes sourdes que de femmes entendantes sont mariées = fewer deaf women than those with hearing are married

Si un proche meurt d'une crise cardiaque en faisant l'amour, on oublie facilement de préciser qu'il n'était pas avec sa légitime – c'est le cas de la moitié de Allemands trépassés dans ces conditions = if a relative dies from a heart attack while making love, specifying that he wasn't with his legitimate partner is easily overlooked – such is the case with half the Germans who pass away in such circumstances

On a pris plus de la moitié de leurs ballons = we picked up more than half their balls

Pronouns with singular complements
Beaucoup du maquillage qu'on achète ici est fabriqué en Espagne = a lot of the make-up you buy here is made in Spain

La majeure partie de la population est contre une nouvelle expansion de l'UE = most of the population is against a further expansion of the EU

Il voulait remettre un peu d'ordre à son appartement = he wanted to tidy up his flat

244 *La plupart*
La plupart is only used with plural nouns – except in the combination *la plupart du temps* = most of the time

La plupart du temps je préfère être seul = most of the time I prefer to be alone

La plupart des journaux ont reproduit cette histoire = most of the papers printed that story

La plupart pensent qu'ils tiennent le destin entre leurs mains = most believe that they hold their destiny in their hands

La plupart [des billets] ont été loués quinze jours auparavant = most were sold a fortnight ago

La plus grande / majeure partie de replaces *la plupart de* before a singular complement – see 243.

245 Indefinite pronouns and related expressions
The majority of these involve the phrase *n'importe* followed by a relative pronoun or adjective.

chacun / chacune = *everyone,* ***n'importe qui*** = *anyone,* ***n'importe où*** = *anywhere,*
n'importe comment = *anyhow,* ***n'importe lequel*** = *any one*

These expressions cannot be followed by a relative clause. For example, if it is necessary to translate English *anyone who thinks that* into French, ***n'importe qui*** cannot be used; instead ***qui que ce soit qui pense ça*** has to be used – see 153.

Neither can ***quiconque*** = *whoever, anyone* be followed by a relative pronoun or adjective, but it can be used to translate *anyone who thinks that* – ***quiconque pense ça***

For ***chaque,*** see 272.

246 Examples of indefinite expressions

Chacun pour soi = *everyone for himself*

Chacun devrait savoir que la baisse des fumeurs en France est moins importante chez les hommes que chez les femmes = *everyone should know that the decrease in smokers in France is less for men than for women*

Je lui dis de ne pas me lire. Il y a le choix, n'importe qui – n'importe qui sauf son fils = *I told her not to read me. There's a choice, anyone – anyone but her son*

Il y a un moment de la vie quand on se sent vraiment seul – n'importe quel premier jour d'année scolaire = *there are times in your life when you feel really lonely – for example, the first day back in any new school year*

A partir du moment où ça n'a pas marché, elle a fait un peu n'importe quoi, comme une junior sans expérience = *from the moment that didn't work, she behaved a bit anyhow, like a junior without experience*

Tu peux venir me chercher à n'importe quelle heure du soir = *you can come and fetch me at any time this evening*

Mettez-les n'importe où = *put them anywhere*

Tout est calculé en fonction de l'image qu'elles veulent donner à on ne sait qui = *everything is calculated in terms of the image they want to present to goodness knows who*

Il a demandé à je ne sais qui de l'aider = *he asked somebody or other to help him*

Le vol a été reporté à je ne sais quand = *the flight's been postponed till goodness knows when*

Exercises

1 **Réécrivez les passages suivants en changeant tout ce qui a rapport aux pronoms personnels comme il vous est indiqué –**

tu > vous
 a *Ce qui s'est passé pour ton amie aurait pu arriver n'importe quand. Tu n'as pas contraint ton amie, tu l'as simplement encouragée. Tu peux être fière d'être à ses côtés et de la soutenir.*
 b *Cette année, tu organises le réveillon du jour de l'an chez toi et tu as envie de profiter de la fête sans passer ton temps à faire des*

aller-retours entre la table et la cuisine. Alors, adopte la formule buffet. Tu pourras ainsi préparer tes plats à l'avance et la soirée sera détendue pour toi.

vous > *tu*

c *Vous voici à présent dans un climat de grande sensibilité, et votre vie relationnelle et intime sera la plus touchée. Votre rythme de vie risque d'être bouleversé après une rencontre, et certains contacts pourraient jouer un rôle important dans l'aboutissement de vos projets. D'heureuses perspectives s'offrent à vous.*

d *Vous allez vous dépenser sans compter, en relevant de nombreux défis. Vos démarches sont menées avec une détermination qu'on ne vous connaît pas, et vous prenez des décisions importantes en ce qui concerne vos parents ou vos amis. Vous orientez ainsi votre vie sociale et affective conformément à vos aspirations.*

je > *elle* et puis *je* > *il*

e *J'ai l'impression que mon identité a été remise en question. Je n'arrive plus à faire de projets, ma vie est comme suspendue. C'est terrible car je ne suis pas de nature dépressive, j'aime la vie, j'ai un compagnon formidable, je suis très attachée à mes animaux. Je me sens terriblement seule face à ce problème.*

vous > *elle*

f *Vous avez eu la main un peu lourde sur la pince à épiler. Résultat, vos sourcils sont beaucoup trop fins, votre regard n'est plus aussi envoûtant et votre visage a perdu en caractère. En attendant que les poils repoussent, vous devez vous mettre à vos pinceaux. Pour redessiner et étoffer tout ça, utilisez un crayon. Choisissez toujours une teinte proche de la couleur de vos cheveux, pas trop sombre, pour ne pas durcir votre regard.*

je > *il*

g *Je gagne très bien ma vie, alors c'est normal que je paye des impôts et que ça profite aux autres. Et plus tard à mes enfants. J'aurais pu partir à l'étranger comme beaucoup de sportifs, mais j'ai toujours dit que si j'avais décidé de payer des impôts en France, c'est parce que ma famille et moi avons une qualité de vie que je ne trouverais pas ailleurs.*

elles > *nous*

h *Il ne voulait pas savoir ce qu'elles ont fait, où elles étaient ni de quoi elles ont parlé.*

2 **Réécrivez les passages suivants en remplaçant** *on* **par d'autres pronoms ou en utilisant d'autres stratégies de remplacement –**

a *Un teint qui atteint la perfection? On en rêve toutes.*

b *Pourquoi ne pas faire les corvées avec une copine: on se sent moins seule et on s'en amuse. Tout de suite on est moins tendue.*

  c *À peine est-on de retour des vacances que l'on a déjà l'impression d'avoir perdu le bénéfice qu'elles avaient apporté ou pire de n'être jamais parties.*

  d *Pour cet examen, on voit apparaître l'image du squelette sur l'écran. Sur le tableau de l'écran on repère différentes courbes de couleur. Ainsi on peut analyser différentes parties du squelette que l'on sait plus fragiles que d'autres.*

  e *Se sentir belle et séduisante lorsque l'on est ronde, c'est la mission de Taillisime qui vous propose des modèles jusqu'au 58. Adieu la lingerie tristoune et vieillotte quand on a la chance d'avoir un décolleté généreux!*

3 **Réécrivez les passages suivants en remplissant les blancs du pronom qui convient – pronom démonstratif, possessif, personnel ou relatif. Notez que quelquefois il y a plus d'un blanc à remplir –**

  a *Il faut connaître ses emotions, pour mieux . . . tenir compte.*

  b *Le bon cadeau est un autre langage que l'inconscient perçoit comme positif, et . . . peut amener . . . . . . reçoit à tomber amoureuse.*

  c *Elle porte un gros carton sur . . . est collée une longue plume rose.*

  d *Dans le film, il s'agit de deux jeunes filles, comme le titre . . . indique.*

  e *Quelquefois . . . . . . se trompent sur nos goûts . . . trouvent un intérêt.*

  f *La fatigue est la manifestation d'un blocage qui empêche l'énergie de circuler. Bonne nouvelle, . . . ne demande qu'à être débloquée.*

  g *Listez une dizaine de petites joies. Chaque jour piochez dans la liste pour . . . . . . offrir trois.*

  h *Mes désirs évoluent avec le temps, je . . . laisse venir. Je . . . crois à fond et j'imagine des plans pour . . . réaliser.*

  i *Tu connais Amélie – quand on a des fesses comme . . . . . . , on évite le cuir rouge!*

  j *On attendait avec une infinie curiosité le livre . . . il allait raconter une autre de ses passions: l'Afrique.*

  k *Même sans les muscles, tu peux . . . arriver.*

  l *Rien ne vous empêche de prendre une vraie collation quelques heures après le réveil: . . . vous évitera le coup de barre de fin de matinée.*

  m *Il . . . dit « Inutile de . . . faire un cadeau, . . . avoir à mes côtés est déjà le plus beau des présents imaginables. » Je ne sais jamais quoi . . . offrir.*

  n *Les gentils font partie de cette catégorie-là, ... n'utilisera jamais vos faiblesses pour . . . tirer profit, ... ne . . . enviera jamais votre magnifique petit copain ou vos succès.*

  o *Il faut choisir une tonalité qui se superpose le plus exactement possible à . . . .*

  p *Il est issu d'une famille de petits entrepreneurs de bâtiments. . . . . a exercé toutes sortes de petits boulots.*

  q *J'ai commencé à travailler sur des églises et des discothèques gonflables, . . . on m'a demandés de créer.*

r *2,92 milliards d'euros, c'est la somme dépensée en un an par les Britanniques pour l'achat de cocaïne, . . . la consommation a augmenté de plus de 200% ces trois dernières années.*

s *Le président a été consulté sur la réforme du Sénat . . . souhaitent bon nombre des sénateurs.*

t *La victoire de la jeune Belge n'a rien à voir avec le style des Américaines. Là où . . . affichent des parents envahissants et peu sympathiques, Justine évoque la figure émouvante d'une mère disparue alors qu'elle avait 13 ans.*

u *C'est un accessoire que les femmes achètent pour le plaisir – . . . . . . mais aussi . . . de leur partenaire.*

v *Pensez à . . . lancer dans un programme d'activités physiques. Préférez . . . de plein air.*

w *On va . . . offrir des cadeaux. Ça, je . . . avais déjà pensé, mais c'est bon de . . . . . . répéter.*

x *Ce sont des personnes avec . . . j'avais sympathisées dans mon ancien travail . . . . . . ont signalé un poste à prendre.*

y *Toute perte est irréparable. Et le monde dans . . . l'enfant aurait dû vivre n'est plus le même monde.*

z *J'ai vu Béatrice au « Bon Marché »: une vendeuse . . . a dit qu'elle . . . a vendu un string.*

aa *Son père se heurte à . . . . . . aurait pu être, à . . . . . . aurait dû être, à . . . . . . n'est pas et ne sera jamais.*

bb *Cette situation peut témoigner d'un problème au niveau des relations personnelles. . . . peuvent être difficiles ou inexistantes.*

cc *Elle a dû démonter la douche en bois construite sur son toit, . . . la présence gênait le voisinage.*

dd *Quant aux cadeaux, ... – je . . . . . . donnerai plus tard, quand on sera en tête à tête.*

ee *25 raisons d'aimer Noël . . . vous n'auriez pas pensé.*

Chapter 7 *Determiners*

247 Determiners

Determiners are those syntactic items which precede and qualify a noun.

They comprise the definite (*le, la, les*), indefinite (*un, une, des*) and partitive (*du, de la, des*) articles, the demonstrative adjectives (*ce, cet, cette, ces*), the possessive adjectives (*mon, ma, mes, ton, son, notre, votre, leur*, etc).

The articles

248 The three articles

The **definite article** corresponds, mostly, to English *the* and basically refers to something or somebody that has already been or is implicitly identified and specified.

Elle donne à LA tournée électorale un air de psychothérapie = *she brings an atmosphere of psychotherapy to the electoral trail*

Tunisie – LE rêve méditerranéen = *Tunisia – the Mediterranean dream*

Longtemps proposés comme une panacée AUX troubles de LA ménopause, LES traitements hormonaux sont mis sous surveillance = *for a long time seen as a panacea for the problems of the menopause, hormonal treatment is being investigated*

Cent ans en bleu – tous LES matches, tous LES joueurs, LES stars, LES épopées, LES capitaines, LES sélectionneurs DU foot français = *a hundred years in blue – all the matches, all the players, the stars, the legends, the captains, the selectors of French football*

The **indefinite article** corresponds, mostly, to English *a, an, some*, and basically refers to something or someone that has not yet been identified or specified; it introduces a new, countable noun into a conversation or piece of writing –

UN corps sans vie a été trouvé = *a lifeless body has been discovered*

UNE vaste enquête a été entamée sur le dopage = *a wide-ranging investigation has been undertaken into drug taking*

Ce fut UNE parodie de justice, UNE mascarade de procès = *it was a parody of justice, a masquerade of a trial*

Définition d'UN oiseau – UN animal au corps recouvert de plumes, dont les membres antérieurs sont des ailes, dont la tête est munie d'UN bec = *the definition of a bird – an animal with a body covered with feathers, the front limbs of which are wings, the head of which is supplied with a beak*

UNE omelette est faite d'oeufs battus et cuits à la poêle = *an omelette is made from beaten eggs cooked on a stove*

In the plural, it refers to an unspecified number of countable items –

DES soldats américains ont été envoyés au point chaud = *American soldiers have been sent to the hot spot*

Il vend DES fromages de toutes les régions de France = *he sells cheeses from all over France*

La télé accomplit parfois DES miracles . . . cinématographiques = *from time to time the telly performs miracles . . . cinematographic miracles*

The **partitive article** also corresponds to English *some* and is used with mass nouns; basically it refers to objects or people envisaged as part of a whole; quite often no article is used in English in such cases.

Votre journée type est – on boit DES verres, on fait DU shopping – *a typical day for you – having a few drinks, shopping*

Pour éviter les soucis de la constipation, il suffit, la veille au soir, de mettre DES pruneaux dans DE L'eau et de la boire le lendemain = *to avoid constipation problems, all you have to do is to put some prunes into some water overnight and drink it the next day*

N'oubliez pas de manger DU fruit chaque jour = *don't forget to eat some fruit every day*

Comment peut-on faire un dessert aussi délicieux et aussi pratique avec juste DU lait, DES oeufs frais, DU sucre, DU caramel et un peu DE vanille! = *how can you make such a delicious and practical dessert with just milk, fresh eggs, sugar, caramel and a little vanilla!*

Later we discuss instances where no article is used – in such cases the term **zero article** seems appropriate; see 258.

The similarities and differences between the French and English systems will be dealt with in 251–257.

249 Forms of the three articles

The articles vary in form for gender and number (singular and plural). The gender distinction applies only in the singular; in the plural, the forms may be masculine or feminine. The plural of the indefinite article and the partitive article are the same – ***des***.

	msg	fsg	plural
definite article	***le***	***la***	***les***
indefinite article	***un***	***une***	***des***
partitive article	***du***	***de la***	***des***

When the forms ***le, la*** would occur before a word beginning with a vowel or mute ***h***, the vowel in the article is deleted. If ***du*** would occur in a similar situation, it becomes ***de l'*** –

le garçon but ***l'adolescent, l'homme***
la fille but ***l'adolescente, l'héroïne***

du lait but *de l'alcool, de l'humour*
de la bière but *de l'eau, de l'huile*

When an aspirate *h* is involved, the forms do not change –

le hibou, la haie, du houx

When the preposition *à* precedes the definite article, it merges with it to form *au* in the masculine singular and *aux* in the plural –

le lit → *au lit*
les lits → *aux lits*
les chaises → *aux chaises*

The same applies when the preposition *de* precedes the definite article – the same forms are produced as for the partitive article –

le lit → *du lit*
les lits → *des lits*
les chaises → *des chaises*

250 Position of the articles

The article is usually the first element in the expression of which it is part –

Pelez LE poireau et LA carotte = *peel the leek and the carrot*

UN produit qui donne UNE sensation de légèreté = *a product that gives a feeling of lightness*

Vous pouvez aussi constituer DES petites haies ravissantes = *you can also plant charming little hedges*

Je ferai DU potage pour le déjeuner = *I'll make some soup for lunch*

En lâchant DU lest sur le deuxième point = *by making concessions on the second point*

LA chair à saucisse, coupée AU couteau, avec de L'huile d'olive de Sicile = *sausage meat, cut with a knife, with olive oil from Sicily*

However, if in an expression involving the definite or, less commonly, the indefinite article, the adjective *tout / tous / toute / toutes* = *all, every* is also included, this precedes the article –

Peut-on se laver les cheveux tous LES jours = *is it all right to wash your hair every day?*

Tout LE monde est d'accord = *everyone is in agreement*

Tous LES murs sont couverts de peintures = *all the walls are covered in paintings*

C'est toute UNE histoire = *it's quite a story*

But if the *tout* qualifies an adjective, it follows the article and precedes the adjective –

C'est UNE toute autre histoire = *it's quite another story*

For *tout*, see 272.

251 Differences between French and English usages of the articles – article in French where none is used in English: 1

As stated above, in the majority of cases, English and French use the articles in the same circumstances.

However, there are a few differences that need to be noted – however (again!), it is all too clear that usage fluctuates, as will be illustrated in the following sections.

Consequently 'No article' means *normally* no article, and 'Article' means *normally* an article!

Article in French

where none is used in English 1 –

with nouns denoting classes of items –

LE tabac est mauvais pour la santé = *tobacco / smoking is bad for your health*

LE vin peut améliorer votre bien-être = *wine can improve your sense of well-being*

LES légumes sont bons pour vous = *vegetables are good for you*

LES passagers sont priés de se présenter à la porte numéro 4 = *passengers are requested to proceed to gate number 4*

La Chypre, là où LES mirages ont une autre consistence = *Cyprus, where mirages assume a very different texture*

Pour LES porcs, il y a très peu de subventions = *for pigs, there are very few grants*

with abstract nouns –

Elle cherche LA beauté, LE bonheur, LE succès = *she's searching for beauty, happiness, success*

Il aime LA linguistique, LA musique, LE jardinage = *he likes linguistics, music, gardening*

Elle cherche LE bonheur qu'apporte LE succès = *she's searching for the happiness that success brings*

However, an indefinite article is used when reference is made to a particular, but un-defined, instance of the concept denoted by the abstract noun –

UN silence lourd est tombé sur la foule = *a heavy silence fell on the crowd*

Je préfère UNE beauté formée par la maturité = *I prefer beauty formed by maturity*

and a definite article when the reference is to a specific, defined instance –

Pour supprimer les rides, il faut provoquer LA décontraction de la peau = *in order to eliminate wrinkles, it is necessary to make your skin decontract* [cause the decontraction of your skin]

Jadis dispensateurs du sésame républicain de L'ascension sociale = *in days gone by dispensers of the French Republic's 'open sesame' to social advancement*

and the partitive article when abstract qualities are attributed to people or things –

Il faut montrer DE LA tolérance envers ceux de religions différentes = *you have to demonstrate tolerance towards people with a different religion*

Avoir DU courage quand le danger menace est très difficile = *having courage when danger threatens is very difficult*

252 Article in French where none is used in English: 2
With names of countries and regions
Most names of continents, countries, islands, regions and rivers are accompanied by the definite article –

continents (all feminine)
l'Afrique = *Africa*, *l'Amérique du Nord* = *North America*, *l'Asie* = *Asia*, *l'Europe* = *Europe*

countries
masculine

le Brésil = *Brazil*, *le Canada* = *Canada*, *le Chili* = *Chile*, *le Danemark* = *Denmark*, *le Japon* = *Japan*, *le Niger* = *Niger*, *le Portugal* = *Portugal*, *le Zimbabwe* = *Zimbabwe*

feminine

l'Afrique du Sud = *South Africa*, *l'Angleterre* = *England*, *la Chine* = *China*, *la France* = *France*, *la Grande-Bretagne* = *Great Britain*, *la Libye* = *Libya*, *la Russie* = *Russia*, *la Tunisie* = *Tunisia*

A l'extrême partie orientale de LA Sibérie, cette péninsule de la taille de LA France = *at the eastern extremity of Siberia, that peninsula the size of France*

L'Islande a bondi du Moyen Age au 21e siècle = *Iceland has leapt from the Middle Ages to the twenty-first century*

Note – no article is used with *Israël* = *Israel* –

Il a été accuse par Israël de négationnisme = *he has been accused by Israel of negative thinking*

islands
Usage varies with the names of islands.

with article

la Barbade = *Barbados*, *la Corse* = *Corsica*, *la Guadeloupe* = *Guadeloupe*, *le Haïti* = *Haiti*, *la Jamaïque* = *Jamaica*, *la Sardaigne* = *Sardinia*, *la Sicile* = *Sicily*

without article

Chypre = *Cyprus*, *Corfou* = *Corfu*, *Cuba, Ibiza, Java, Madagascar*, *Majorque* = *Majorca*, *Malte* = *Malta*, *Taïwan*

For a more detailed discussion of the usage of the definite article and prepositions with regions, rivers, French departments, American states and British counties, see 393.

253 Article in French where none is used in English: 3
With names of languages –
Nous apprenons LE roumain = *we're learning Romanian*

LE français, L'espagnol, LE portugais et L'italien sont tous des langues romanes = *French, Spanish, Portuguese and Italian are all Romance languages*

Le Canada a deux langues officielles – L'anglais et LE français = *Canada has two official languages – English and French*

Note – with *parler* the article is normally not used –

On parle anglais ici = *English is spoken here*

However, as soon as there is some qualification of the noun, an article is usually used

Elle parle bien LE maltais = *she speaks Maltese well*

Il parle UN français impeccable = *he speaks an impeccable French*

With various sets of nouns –
names of seasons –
Je préfère LE printemps à L'automne = *I prefer spring to autumn*

L'été tout le monde se précipite à la côte = *in summer everyone rushes to the coast*

names of substances, products –
L'héroïne est une drogue très dangereuse = *heroin is a very dangerous drug*

LE jus de pamplemousse prend particulièrement soin de votre corps et même de votre esprit = *grapefruit juice takes special care of your body and even your mind*

names of illnesses –
Mon traitement contre LA migraine m'a fait grossir – *the treatment I've had for migraine has made me put on weight*

LE psoriasis peut se confondre avec LA dermatite = *psoriasis may be confused with dermatitis*

Special cases
to translate last, next *in expressions of time –*
L'année dernière = *last year* (*LA dernière année* = *the last year*)

LA semaine prochaine = *next week* (*LA prochaine semaine* = *the next week*)

with names of the days of the week to indicate a habitual action; the name of the day is retained in the singular –
Les permanents de nos agences reçoivent une formation LE mercredi = *the permanent members of staff from our agencies are given training every Wednesday*

LE jeudi on visite le restaurant Tivoli avec sa belle terrasse = *every Thursday we go to the Tivoli with its beautiful outside seating*

See also 438 for usage with fractions.

254 Differences between French and English usages of the articles – no article in French where there is one in English
No article in French – zero article – where there is one in English in appositions
where one noun is used to supply more information about a preceding one –

Alain, fils cadet de Jean-Luc = *Alain, the younger son of Jean-Luc*

Alphonse Daudet, auteur d'un nombre de livres remarquables = *Alphonse Daudet, the author of a number of remarkable books*

Leclerc, supermarché numéro un de France = *Leclerc, the number one supermarket in France*

Le dernier miracle en date vient de l'Italie, pays fertile en apparitions = *the latest miracle comes from Italy, a country much given to apparitions*

But, it should be noted that the article may also be used in these situations.

Thierry Defforey, actionnaire de Carrefour, François Dalle, L'ancien patron de l'Oréal, Roger Zannier, LE roi du vêtement pour enfants = *Thierry Defforey, a share-holder in Carrefour, François Dalle, (the) ex-boss of l'Oréal, Roger Zannier, the king of kids' clothes*

Summary – usage is mixed, with the article being more commonly used when a more specific reference is being made.

To indicate a person's profession or status with such verbs as être, devenir, rester, nommer –
Elle est restée célibataire toute sa vie = *she remained a spinster all her life*

Il est devenu journaliste = *he became a journalist*

Note – if the noun is qualified in any way, the article is used, ie when the noun ceases being general and becomes particular –

Il est devenu UN journaliste célèbre = *he became a famous journalist*

Elle est LA meilleure mère du monde – *she's the best mother in the world*

With the exclamative quel, etc = *what a*
Quelle surprise! = *what a surprise!*

Quel dommage! = *what a shame!*

Quel début pour la jeune actrice! = *what a start for the young actress!*

With par = *per*
Ils le font deux fois par semaine = *they do it twice a week*

Ça fait dix euros par personne = *that comes to ten euros a person / per person*

255 Differences between French and English usages of the articles – a different article in French from English
Definite article in French vs indefinite in English
to indicate quantities, prices, ratios –
Les oranges sont à 6 euros LE kilo = *oranges are 6 euros a kilo*

Combien? – 7 euros LE tube = *how much? – 7 euros a tube*

Au prix de 0,34 euros LA minute = *at a cost of 0.34 euros a minute*

Definite article in French vs possessive adjective in English
with parts of the body –
Debout, LES bras le long DU corps, montez LA jambe vers LE buste, en plaquant LE genou sur LA poitrine = *standing upright, with your arms by your side, bring your leg up towards your chest, pulling your knee into your torso*

Ces maillots de bain soutiennent LES seins, gomment LES rondeurs, font LE ventre plat et LA cuisse longue = *these swimsuits support your breasts, smooth out your bulges, flatten your stomach and make your legs look longer*

Allongez-vous sur LE dos, LES bras en croix, LES paumes au sol, LES jambes à 90 degrés = *lie on your back, with your arms crossed, your palms facing downwards, your legs at a right angle*

Note – when an action is performed upon your own or someone else's body, an indication of whose body it is is provided by using an indirect object pronoun –

Elle s'est fait masser LE dos tout doucement = *she had her back massaged very gently*

Quand faut-il se faire opérer AU genou? = *when should you have a knee operation / an operation on your knee?*

Petits conseils pour bien se laver de LA tête AU pied = *advice on washing yourself thoroughly from head to toe / your head to your toe*

However, the possessive adjective may also be used in these situations –

Croisez vos bras = *fold your arms*

Si votre genou est arthrosique = *if your knee is arthritic*

Dérouiller ses articulations, tonifier ses muscles – pour avoir la forme, rien ne vaut une bonne séance de gymnastique douce = *loosen up your joints, tone up your muscles – to keep in good shape, there's nothing like a good session of gentle exercise*

The possessive adjective is normally used when the body part is subject of the verb –

En trente ans nous avons grandi – nos jambes se sont allongées = *in thirty years we've got bigger – our legs have grown longer*

Mes cheveux ne sont plus aussi bruns qu'il y a cinq ans = *my hair is no longer as brown as it was five years ago*

À la fin d'un été passé sous le soleil, vos cheveux ont besoin de se ressourcer = *after a summer spent in the sun, your hair needs to be restored*

When reference to a body part is general rather than specific, the definite article is used –

Les cheveux blancs ne sont pas uniquement l'apanage de l'âge = *white hair is not just the prerogative of age*

Summary of usage – when the reference is to a body part in general, the definite article is normally used; when the reference is more individual, the possessive adjective is more commonly used, especially when the body part is subject of the verb.

256 Differences between French and English usages of the articles – usage with titles

Monsieur and ***Madame*** plus a title or 'job description' are frequently used in French as a form of address. In such cases the definite article is inserted after ***Monsieur*** or ***Madame***. There is no equivalent in English.

Monsieur le Maire = *Mr Mayor*

Madame la directrice = *the principal / the head*

Monsieur le directeur des finances = *the finance director*

Madame la ministre de l'intérieur = *the Home Office minister*

With names of kings, queens and popes, French and English usages differ, English using an article whereas French does not –

Elizabeth II (Elizabeth deux) = *Elizabeth II (Elizabeth the second)*

Benoît XVI (Benoît seize) = *Benedict XVI (Benedict the sixteenth)*

Titles followed by a proper name require an article in French –

Le Président Chirac = *President Chirac*

Le professeur Collard = *Professor Collard*

Le docteur Decaux = *Dr Decaux*

But not for the names of saints or barristers –

Saint Paul, Sainte Agnès

Maître Vergès

257 Differences between French and English usages of the articles – lists of nouns

In English, in lists of nouns, the definite article is usually used before the first noun, but is not repeated thereafter, unless the noun is qualified or is specific in denotation. In French, the article is regularly repeated before each noun – although in journalism quite often no articles are used at all.

Articles
Il suit le surgissement des nouvelles hérésies: LE Flower Power du mouvement hippie, ***LA fièvre anti-société de consommation des jeunes Français, LE printemps de Prague et LA brutale réplique soviétique*** = *he traces the emergence of the new heresies – the Flower Power of the hippy movement, the anti-consumer-society fever of the French youth, the Prague spring and the brutal response of the Soviet government*

Cela n'aidera pas ces pays pauvres à lutter contre L'empoisonnement des gros carnivores, LE braconnage et LE pâturage sauvage = *this won't help these poor countries to fight against the poisoning of large carnivores, poaching and illegal grazing*

No articles

Absence de fiches de paie, contrat de travail bidon et recours à des intérimaires non déclarés sont les principales infractions enregistrées = *lack of pay slips, bogus contracts and use of undeclared temporary staff are the main offences recorded*

Les femmes ont ce mérite de « cibler » des pratiques connues qui répugnent à nos moeurs et nos lois: mariages forcés, contraintes et dévoiements de l' « honneur » machiste des pères et des frères = *the women have the merit of targeting those known practices which offend our traditions and laws – forced marriages, constraint and corruption of the macho honour of fathers and brothers*

258 Zero article

In many cases, nouns are not preceded by a determiner. We have already seen this with nouns in apposition, names of profession following ***être***, etc; see 254. This state of affairs may be described as involving the zero article. Apart from those already mentioned, the most common circumstances are the following –

noun + preposition + noun

The prepositions most frequently used in this way are –

à

une carte à mémoire = *memory card*

une cuillère à café = *tea spoon*

une imprimante à jet d'encre = *ink-jet printer*

une planche à voile = *wind-surfer*

une robe à volants = *flounced dress*

de

la gestion de patrimoine = *personal portfolio management*

un placement d'attente = *short-term investment*

une robe d'été = *summer dress*

une salle de bains = *bathroom*

une tasse de café = *cup of coffee*

en

une chemise en coton = *a cotton shirt*

un escalier en colimaçon = *spiral staircase*

un mouchoir en papier = *paper handkerchief*

une occasion en or = *golden opportunity*

un toit en ardoise = *slate roof*

sous

la mise sous cloche = *putting on the back-burner*

past participle + noun

Une table décorée de fleurs = *a table decorated with flowers*

Une action dépourvue de sens = *an action without any meaning*

Un champ entouré de barbelés = *a field surrounded with barbed wire*

Habillé de jeans = *wearing jeans*

Une cave remplie de bons vins = *a cellar full of good wine*

adverbial expressions consisting of preposition + noun

à gauche / à droite = *on the left / on the right*

à portée de main = *within reach*

avec difficulté = *with difficulty*

avec plaisir = *with pleasure*

en été = *in summer*

en route = *on the way*

par insouciance = *out of carelessness*

par minute = *per minute*

sans effort = *effortlessly*

sans hésitation = *without hesitation*

sans pitié = *without pity*

When the noun is qualified in some way, the indefinite article is used –

par une insouciance incroyable = *with unbelievable carelessness*

avec un plaisir considérable = *with considerable pleasure*

However, with **grand**, the zero article is often retained –

avec grande difficulté = *with great difficulty*

set phrases

avoir besoin = *to need*

avoir faim = *to be hungry*

avoir honte = *to be ashamed*

avoir sommeil = *to be tired*

demander pardon = *to ask for forgiveness*

faire défaut = *to be lacking*

faire plaisir = *to give pleasure*

rendre service = *to help*

tenir tête = *to defy*

259 When *des* becomes *de*
1 When a plural adjective precedes the noun
DE belles opportunités peuvent faire naître DE beaux projets = *good opportunities can produce good projects*

Il y a DE simples règles pour éviter ces malaises = *there are some simple rules to avoid such discomfort*

DE jolis pulls en coton = *pretty cotton jumpers*

Les Belges fabriquent D'excellents chocolats = *the Belgians make excellent chocolates*

Les bactéries bénéfiques que contient le yaourt chassent D'éventuelles bactéries néfastes = *the beneficial bacteria in yoghurt eliminate possible harmful bacteria*

However, when the adjective and noun are regularly used together and form a sort of unit in themselves, this rule does not apply –

Il y avait DES jeunes filles qui attendaient que le groupe de rock quitte le bâtiment = *there were some girls waiting for the rock group to leave the building*

Apporte-moi DES petits pois = *get me some peas*

Il fait DES petits pains aux grains de pavot = *he makes bread rolls with poppy seeds*

But if an evaluative adjective precedes the noun as well, the rule is reapplied –

Il fait DE magnifiques petits pains aux grains de pavot = *he makes fantastic bread rolls with poppy seeds*

In ordinary speech the rule is less and less often observed.

2 Preposition de + *indefinite or partitive article* des
Quite often grammatical logic would require a combination of the preposition ***de*** and the indefinite or partitive article ***des***. In such circumstances, the article and the preposition coalesce to form a single ***de*** –

Décorez DE framboises, DE feuilles de menthe = *decorate with strawberries and mint leaves*

La combinaison d'un régime alimentaire et DE soins hebdomadaires la séduisent = *she is delighted by the combination of a diet and weekly care*

Cette répétition annuelle D'inondations désastreuses amène à s'interroger sur leur origine = *this annual event of disastrous floods prompts us to think about what causes them*

Pour avoir autant DE bénéfices que dans un yaourt nature, il faudrait que vous consommiez deux flacons DE lait = *to have the same amount of calcium as in a natural yogurt, you would have to consume two cartons of milk*

This only applies to the preposition **de**; with others, the indefinite article appears in its full form –

L'utilisation de ce bon pour un autre achat que celui mentionné donnera lieu à DES poursuites = *the use of this coupon for a purchase other than that stated will lead to legal proceedings being taken*

Grâce à DES propriétés remarquables, il agit là où est le problème = *thanks to remarkable properties, it acts where the problem lies*

Je travaille sur DES nouvelles que j'espère bien publier = *I'm working on some stories which I'm very hopeful of being able to publish*

3 After quantifiers and similar expressions

Expressions of quantity involved are – **assez** = *enough*, **autant** = *as much, as many*, **beaucoup** = *many, much, a lot of*, **combien** = *how much, how many*, **moins** = *less*, **peu** = *little, few*, **un peu** = *a little*, **plus** = *more*, **tant** = *as much, so much, as many, so many*, **trop** = *too much, too many*.

Other expressions denote the idea of grouping objects or people together, of describing quantities of anything.

Beaucoup D'étudiants aimeraient leur propre voiture = *lots of students would like their own car*

Une trentaine DE potiers, D'artisans, D'artistes de renom et de talent = *about thirty well-known and talented potters, craftsmen and artists*

J'ai pris deux mois DE vacances = *I took two months' holiday*

Bon nombre DE soldats libyens seront formés par des instructeurs italiens = *a large number of Libyan soldiers will be trained by Italian instructors*

Des tonnes DE déchets s'accumulent tous les jours = *tons of rubbish pile up every day*

Vous pouvez emporter de jolies boîtes DE galettes bretonnes = *you can take away pretty boxes of Breton galettes*

Certaines associations D'aveugles se focalisent sur un seul métier = *certain organisations for blind people concentrate on a single profession*

Exceptions – **bien des** = *many*, **encore des** = *still more*

It should be pointed out that when any of the quantifiers mentioned above are combined with the definite articles, the **de** contracts with the article to becomes **des** –

Beaucoup DES investissements promis n'ont pas vu le jour = *many of the promised investments did not see the light of day*

La fourmi électrique est tellement agressive qu'elle menace beaucoup DES écosystèmes fragiles du pays = *the electric ant is so aggressive that it threatens many of the country's fragile ecosystems*

260 More *de* – use of indefinite and partitive articles with a negative expression

In such cases, the article, whether singular or plural, becomes *de* (see 416, 427) –

Je n'ai pas DE carottes, ni DE poireaux = *I haven't got any carrots or leeks*

Il n'y a pas DE centre équivalent en Belgique = *there isn't an equivalent centre in Belgium*

Ces minidoses sont calculées de façon de ne pas laisser DE traces d'EPO synthétique dans les urines des athlètes = *these minidoses are calculated in such a way that no trace of synthetic EPO is left in the athletes' urine*

Le caleçon – il n'a plus rien DE vulgaire et se retrouve sous une mini-jupe = *there's no longer anything vulgar about pants – wear them under a mini-skirt*

Je renouvelle cette séance deux fois par an, quand le produit n'a plus D'effet = *I repeat this session twice a year when the product no longer has any effect*

This does not apply when *être* is used in a defining sense; in such cases the full form of the indefinite or partitive article is preserved –

En revanche, ce ne sont pas DES concentrés de lait comme les yaourts = *on the other hand, they're not milk concentrates like yoghurt*

Ce ne sont pas DES endives mais DES poireaux = *they're not endives but leeks*

261 Repetition of article

The articles are repeated before each noun in a series unless it is considered that the nouns form a single unit.

Ajoutez LES poireaux, LA menthe, DU sel, DU poivre et UN peu d'eau = *add the leeks, the mint, salt, pepper and a little water*

Pour LES lampes et veilleuses [= the lighting as a whole], *évitez les ampoules à forts ampérages qui risquent de provoquer DE graves brûlures et DES incendies* [= separate dangers] = *for lamps and nightlights, avoid those with a high ampage which might cause serious burns and fires*

D'autres saveurs ont pris le relais, comme LA lavande, LA rose ou L'oeillet = *other scents have taken over such as lavender, rose or carnation*

In lists, even of only two items, which do not seem to form a single unit, this principle is not always observed –

Jusqu'alors sous la forme de pâtes, crèmes ou poudres exclusivement, c'est en 1879 que le premier savon rond apparaît dans l'histoire = *until then only in the form of pastes, creams or powders, it was in 1879 that the first round soap made its appearance in history*

262 Which article?

Although the definite and indefinite articles in English and French have many similarities in terms of their use, there are still many occasions when knowing which article to use in French is a major difficulty. The best way to overcome this difficulty is to observe the articles you hear and see in spoken and written French respectively and decide for yourself whether you would have used them in the same way, and attempt to discern and deduce the principles behind their use.

In the following example of written French, all cases where an article is used and also those where no article precedes a noun are denoted by a number or asterisk. In the next section the reasons for the use or non-use of the article are explained.

263 *La[1] nouvelle Athènes*

Du[2, 5] 13 au[3,5] 29 août, la[4] Grèce accueille les[1] 28e olympiades d'[10]été. Pour l'[1]événement, la[1] capitale s'est embellie et remodelée

«*Ce que les[1] Athéniens ont entrepris dans leur ville est digne des travaux d'Hercule*», s'exclame Anna Iliokratidou,[8] directrice de l'[1]*Office* national du[2] tourisme hellénique. Depuis sa désignation officielle, le[5] 5 septembre 1997, comme[8] cité hôte des[2] Jeux de l'[2]été 2004[a], Athènes vit au[3] rythme des[2] pelleteuses, dans un[6] décor surréaliste d'[9]échafaudages, de[9] tranchées, de[9] gravats et de[9] palissades. Mais le[1] résultat est là. Enfin, presque.

« *Il y a eu du[7] cafouillage au[3] début des[2] travaux, mais, à quatre mois et demi de la[1] cérémonie d'[10]ouverture, les[1] Athéniens mettent les[11] bouchées doubles. Tout ce qui est nécessaire au[3] bon déroulement des[2] épreuves sera vraisemblablement opérationnel. Ce qui a été fait est colossal*», souligne Xavier de Neuville,[8] président-directeur général d'Héliades,[8] voyagiste officiel des[2] Jeux[b]. Ce n'est pas rien.

Outre les[1] installations sportives (six nouveaux stades ont été construits), Athènes a entrepris une[6] restructuration radicale de son espace urbain: [12] création d'un[6] périphérique de 73 km,[12] construction de 8 km de[9] lignes de[10] métro et de 24 km de[10] tramway, entre le[1] centre et Glyfada,[12] construction d'un[6] nouvel aéroport international à la[1] périphérie de la[1] ville et mise en[11] place d'une[6] voie ferrée pour le raccorder au[3] centre ville, une[6] autoroute, des[2] routes[c], la[1] modernisation du[2] réseau téléphonique, un[6] village olympique . . . Le[1] tout, pour un[6] budget total avoisinant 4,5 milliards d'[9]euros.

Ce qui est déjà opérationnel (l'[1]aéroport international Elefterios Venizelos ouvert en 2001, l'un[d] des[2] plus performants d'[10]Europe, alors que l'[1]ancien détenait le record des[2] retards, deux nouvelles lignes de[10] métro, la[1] voie Attique qui, depuis six mois, contourne le[1] nord de la[1] ville . . .) améliore déjà notablement le[1] quotidien. Tant celui des[2] habitants que celui des[2] touristes.

Des[6] quartiers branchés à la[1] manière occidentale surgissent. Gazi, tout proche de l'[1]agora, où la[1] municipalité vient de reconvertir un[6] hangar de l'[1]ancienne usine à[10] gaz en[10] centre culturel (Metropolis) où se succèdent expositions d'[10]art contemporain,[12] conférences,[12] spectacles.[12]

Technopolis, un[6] parc culturel dédié à la[1] musique[e] (c'est ici qu'aura lieu le[1] traditionnel Festival de[10] jazz en[10] mai) qui avait déjà investi cette friche industrielle depuis trois ans, envisage de doubler son espace.[12] Restaurants branchés,[12] bars à la[1] mode,[12] discothèques,[12] terrasses de[10] café ont aussitôt fleuri dans les[1] environs, ouvrant et fermant au[3] rythme des[2] tocades. Dans le[1] quartier de Psiri, à côté du[2] cimetière du[2] Céramique (la[1] plus ancienne nécropole de l'[1]Attique), des[6] galeries d'[10]art investissent les[1] anciens entrepôts de[10] grossistes. Des[6] restaurants et des[6] tavernes d'où s'échappent des[6] odeurs de[10] brochettes s'installent dans des[6] maisons à moitié en[10] ruine, un[6] cinéma de[10] plein air occupe une[6] friche.   *Le Figaro 13 mai 2004*

264 Key

[1]definite article with specified noun
[2]*de* combined with **le, les** with specified noun
[3]*à* combined with **le, les** with specified noun
[4]definite article with name of country

[5]definite article with date
[6]indefinite article with previously unspecified noun
[7]partitive article with unspecified amount of mass noun
[8]noun in apposition
[9]*de* + quantity
[10]preposition + noun with adjectival value
[11]idiom
[12]noun in list

Cases requiring particular comment
[a]*Jeux de l'été 2004* – the definite article is used here, in contrast to *les 28e olympiades d'été* earlier, because in the current case *été* is qualified by *2004*, whereas in the earlier case it is not; it is used generically.

[b]*voyagiste officiel des Jeux* – although *voyagiste* is qualified by *officiel*, in which case one might expect an article to be used (*le voyagiste officiel*), it seems as if the whole expression *voyagiste officiel* is being considered as the name of a profession.

[c]*une autoroute, des routes* – in this long sentence, there is ellipsis of *construction d'* before these two nouns.

[d]*l'un* – the definite article has been inserted before *un* for reasons of euphony, specifically, to separate the *un* of *2001* from the following indefinite article and thus avoiding an awkward repetition of the same syllable.

[e]*un parc culturel dédié à la musique* – normally a noun in apposition is not preceded by an article – see examples with [8]; however, because *parc* is qualified by *dédié à la musique*, an article becomes necessary.

Demonstrative determiners

265 Demonstrative determiners – demonstrative adjectives – the forms
These are equivalent to English *this, that, these, those.*

The forms

masculine singular	*ce, cet*	*this, that*
masculine plural	*ces*	*these, those*
feminine singular	*cette*	*this, that*
feminine plural	*ces*	*these, those*

The form *cet* for masculine singular is used before a word, noun or adjective beginning with a vowel (it is triggered into operation like the adjectives *bel, fol, mol, vieil* for *beau, fou, mou, vieux* – see 195).

Occasionally, the adjectives are combined with *-ci, -là* to indicate and emphasise proximity or remoteness; the *-ci, -là* is added to the noun modified by the adjective.

masculine singular	*ce, cet . . . -ci*	*this*
	ce, cet . . . -là	*that*
masculine plural	*ces . . . -ci*	*these*
	ces . . . -là	*those*
feminine singular	*cette . . . -ci*	*this*
	cette . . . -là	*that*
feminine plural	*ces . . . -ci*	*these*
	ces . . . -là	*those*

This does not occur so often as with the demonstrative pronouns. For demonstrative pronouns, see 237–239.

266 Examples of demonstrative adjectives

ce

Pour soulager un peu votre peine, nous vous envoyons 24 cannettes de ce breuvage = *in order to relieve your distress, we're sending you 24 cans of that brew*

Un site consacré aux sandales portées avec des chaussettes. Ce site dispose d'une collection photographique énorme = *a website devoted to sandals worn with socks. This website disposes of an enormous collection of photographs*

Vous trouverez tous les renseignements dans ce numéro ou sur notre site = *you'll find all the details in this number or on our website*

cet

Si vous voulez faire un peu d'argent cet été = *if you want to make a bit of money this summer*

Toute boisson au cola contient E338 – pour les chimistes cet élément a plusieurs noms = *any cola drink contains E338 – chemists know this element by several names*

ces

Ces tacticiens hors pair ont des convictions solidement ancrées, et la passion chevillée au corps = *these master tacticians have solidly anchored convictions and boundless passion*

Je peux vous dire que ces jeunes gens, surdoués intellectuellement, sont fragiles et complètement désarmés face à des situations difficiles = *I can tell you that these youngsters, super-smart intellectually, are fragile and completely at sea when faced with tricky situations*

ce . . . ci

S'il réussit ce nouveau challenge-ci, il y gagnera une grande confiance en lui = *if he succeeds in this new challenge, he'll gain a great deal of self-confidence*

ce . . . là

Tout a commencé un vendredi 13 – ce jour-là la fille de ses rêves cède à ses avances = *everything began one Friday 13th – that day the girl of his dreams yielded to his advances*

ces . . . -là
Ces clients-là supportent si mal certains de leurs membres qu'ils se font amputer par pur mal-être = *those patients have so little tolerance of certain of their limbs that they have themselves amputated by pure despair*

cette
Grâce à cette machine vous allez pouvoir faire votre propre barbe à papa = *thanks to this machine you'll be able to make your own candy floss*

Cette année ça peut être vous = *this year it could be you*

Cette tache originelle, le scrutin de 2004 n'aura pas réussi à l'effacer = *that original flaw will not have been removed by the 2004 election*

Cette femme ne veut pas tant attraper que s'arranger (astucieusement) pour se faire attraper = *that [such a] woman doesn't so much want to catch [a man] as organise herself (cunningly) to have herself caught*

cette . . . ci
Cette ligne-ci vous propose des solutions astucieuses = *this line proposes some amusing solutions*

Cette photo-ci rappelle celles que j'avais vues dans l'autre collection = *this photo reminds me of those I had seen in the other collection*

cette . . . là
Un monde parfait, avec des gens jeunes et beaux éternellement, cette image-là je ne la reconnais pas – *a perfect world full of the eternally young and beautiful, I don't recognise that picture*

Je ne peux pas supporter cette émission-là – c'est trop débile = *I can't stomach that programme – it's too pathetic*

ces . . . ci
Les chercheurs émettent l'hypothèse que ces personnes-ci dépourvues de toute oreille attentive réagissent au stress de manière plus prononcée = *researchers propose the hypothesis that these people who do not have someone to listen to them react to stress in a more obvious way*

ces . . . là
Si vous trouvez que ce régime-ci vous convient, n'hésitez pas à abandonner toutes ces méthodes-là = *if you find that this diet suits you, don't hesitate to abandon all those other methods*

Possessive determiners

267 Possessive determiners – possessive adjectives
These consist of the set of **possessive adjectives**. The adjectives are the equivalent of English *my, your, his, her, its, our, their*.

		singular		plural	
first person	masculine	**mon**	*my*		
				notre	*our*
	feminine	**ma**	*my*		
	plural	**mes**	*my*	**nos**	*our*
second person	masculine	**ton**	*your*		
				votre	*your*
	feminine	**ta**	*your*		
	plural	**tes**	*your*	**vos**	*your*
third person	masculine	**son**	*his, her, its*		
				leur	*their*
	feminine	**sa**	*his, her, its*		
	plural	**ses**	*his, her, its*	**leurs**	*their*

The masculine singular form **mon, ton, son** is used before a feminine word beginning with a vowel or mute **h** –

Ma réussite extraordinaire = *my extraordinary success*

Mon extraordinaire réussite = *my extraordinary success*

Mon amie = *my girlfriend*

Ton odeur puissante = *your strong smell*

Son équipe de diététiciens = *his / her team of dieticians*

It is vital to remember that the form of the possessive adjective is determined by the gender of the noun it precedes, not the sex of the person involved – hence **mon, ton, son** are used before masculine nouns regardless of whether they refer to a male or female; similarly **ma, ta, sa** are used before feminine nouns regardless of the sex of the person involved.

The distinction between the two sets of forms for the second person singular, **ton, ta, tes** and **votre, vos** corresponds to that between **tu** and **vous** discussed in 216.

The use of a possessive adjective and its 'rivalry' with the definite article with parts of the body is discussed in 255.

For discussion of the possessive pronouns, see 240–241.

268 The **son** series

The matter of agreement is particularly acute with the **son** series of possessive adjectives because each form has a number of potential meanings. For example, **son** does not necessarily always = *his*; it may, but it also = *her, its*; likewise, **sa** does not necessarily always = *her*; it may, but it also = *his, its*. Remember that the form used is determined by the number and gender of the noun qualified not by the gender of the possessor. The third person adjective is also used as the possessive adjective corresponding to the indefinite pronoun **on** – see 224 for the values of **on** – this complicates the situation still further. The following examples illustrate the different values that the **son** series may have –

= her

Je suis consciente qu'une jeune femme musulmane n'est pas censée concrétiser toutes ses pulsions = *I'm aware that a young Muslim girl is not supposed to fulfil all her impulses*

Quand on lui demande où elle puise son imagination, elle évoque son enfance et le peu de plaisir que lui procurait le mobilier de sa chambre = *when she's asked where her imagination came from, she mentions her childhood and the small amount of pleasure that she got from her bedroom furniture*

Son nouvel album n'est peut-être pas son meilleur = *her latest album is perhaps not her best*

Elle pourra profiter de son talent exceptionnel = *she'll be able to benefit from her exceptional talent*

Elle mène une vie d'enfer à ses parents = *she leads her parents a terrible dance*

= his

Un Italien a été assassiné d'une balle dans la nuque – ses ravisseurs menacent de tuer trois de ses compatriots = *an Italian has been put to death by a shot in the neck – his kidnappers are threatening to kill three of his compatriots*

Après 48 jours de mer dans sa tentative de record du tour du monde à la voile, Olivier Kersauson et son équipage progressaient à un peu plus de 10 noeuds = *after 48 days at sea in his attempt to break the round-the-world record, Olivier Kersauson and his crew made progress at just over ten knots*

= its

On aime aussi la version hyper-puissante – son secret? = *its hyper-powerful version is also popular – its secret?*

France Loisirs vous fait découvrir des plumes originales – ses auteurs vous transportent dans des univers décalés = *France Loisirs helps you discover some original writers – its authors transport you to unfamiliar worlds*

= one's / your / their

Deux mois pour sculpter son corps = *two months to shape your (one's) body*

pour ressusciter sa peau = *to give new life to your (one's) skin*

Freud appelle « transfert » le mouvement par lequel le patient revit, dans sa relation avec son psychanalyste, un fragment de son passé affectif = *Freud uses the term 'transfer' to describe the process whereby the patient relives, in his relationship with his psychoanalyst, a fragment of his affective past history*

269 Possible ambiguity of meaning of *son* series

Because, as mentioned above, the ***son*** series = *his, her, its, one's*, it sometimes happens that it is not clear who the possessor referred to by the adjective actually is. In order to disambiguate any problems, it is necessary to add a prepositional phrase to the noun – ***à*** + personal pronoun –

Je préfère les couleurs de sa chambre à elle que celles de sa chambre à lui = *I prefer the colours in her bedroom to those in his*

Son parfum à elle est délicieusement sophistiqué = *her perfume is delightfully sophisticated*

Elle portait son pull à lui = *she was wearing his jumper*

270 *votre / vos*

Whereas the series **ton, ta, tes** always refers to a single person, the series **votre, vos** can refer to either a single person or a group of people. The context is likely to be more formal when it refers to a single person – for more details see discussion of **vous / tu**, 216.

singular

Je regrette de dire que votre progrès n'est pas satisfaisant, jeune homme = *I'm sorry to say that your progress is not satisfactory, young man*

Mademoiselle, voulez-vous laisser votre manteau dans le vestiaire? = *do you want to leave your coat in the cloakroom, Miss?*

Votre nouvel album est plus rock et moins funk = *your latest album is more rock and less funk*

singular or plural

Écrivez votre nom en majuscules = *write your name in capital letters*

Mettez vos affaires dans la chambre à coucher = *put your things in the bedroom*

Comment réagirez-vous quand un mec vient chercher votre fille pour une soirée? = *how will you react when a guy comes round to take your daughter out for the evening?*

Vos cheveux sont désormais raides = *now your hair is straight*

Impossible de boutonner votre jean fétiche, alors que samedi dernier il vous allait encore comme un gant? Si vous attendez vos règles, ça n'a rien de surprenant = *impossible to do up your lucky jeans, whereas last Saturday they still fitted you like a glove? If your period's due, it's not at all surprising*

plural

Vous avez été nombreux à écrire – n'oubliez pas de préciser vos coordonnées = *many of you have written – don't forget to supply your details*

Tout le monde est arrivé – il est temps de faire le point sur vos projets = *everyone's arrived – it's time to give an up-date on your plans*

271 Examples of the other persons of the possessive adjectives
mon, ma, mes
J'ai fait croire à mes proches que j'étais mort = *I made my nearest and dearest believe I was dead*

Quand la chambre de ma fille vire à la porcherie, je suis aussi gonflant que l'étaient mes parents = when my daughter's bedroom turns into a pigsty, I'm as annoying as ever my parents were

Je voudrais changer mon nez, mes cheveux, mes ongles, mes épaules et mes orteils = I'd like to change my nose, my hair, my nails, my shoulders and my toes

ton, ta, tes
Même si tu connais ta taille, rien ne vaut un bon essayage en boutique = even if you know your size, there's nothing better than trying it on in the shop

Ta femme y voit probablement une forme de soumission = your wife probably sees it as a form of submission

Je me serais fâchée tout rouge à ta place = in your place I would have become absolutely incandescent

notre, nos
Un truc pour aider nos lecteurs à séduire un top modèle = a wheeze to help our readers seduce a top model

Au bout d'une semaine nos discussions se sont orientées vers le sexe = after a week our discussions turned to sex

On ne doit pas brader ce que nos ancêtres nous ont laissé = we must not undervalue what our ancestors left us

Depuis toujours leurs odeurs ont imprégné nos corps = their perfumes have always impregnated our bodies

leur, leurs
Leurs joueurs ont si souvent échoué lors des grands rendez-vous à cause de leurs querelles intestines interminables = their players have so often collapsed during major events because of their interminable internal feuds

De très nombreux supporters anglais sont restés dans le pays en dépit de l'élimination de leur équipe en quart de finale = a good many English supporters have stayed on in the country despite the fact that their team was eliminated in the quarter finals

Les lecteurs voteront pour leurs candidates préférées = readers will vote for their favourite candidates

Leur objectif porte sur la défense d'intérêts corporatistes = their aim focuses on the defence of corporatist interests

Les relations à distance, ça n'a pas que des inconvénients – leur mauvaise humeur, leur match de foot, leurs copains qui s'incrustent, vous, vous y échappez = relationships at a distance don't only have disadvantages – their bad moods, their football match, their mates always hanging around, you avoid all that

The following instances in French illustrate a difference between French and English usage. In English the equivalent of **maillot** = trunks, **peau** = skin would be in the plural – belonging to the group – but it is in the singular in French – belonging to each individual –

***Quoiqu'il ait essayé de nous faire nous quitter notre maillot, nous avons
décidé de le garder*** = *although he tried to make us take our trunks off, we decided to keep
them on*

Trois potes mal dans leur peau = *three mates uneasy within themselves*

Indefinite determiners

272 Indefinite determiners – *chaque, tout*
The most frequently encountered indefinite determiners are ***chaque, tout***.

chaque = *each, every*
***Chaque fille aime donner l'impression qu'elle est réservée et que c'est à
vous de lui révéler sa féminité*** = *every girl likes to give the impression she's reserved and
that it's up to you to bring out her feminine side*

Votre frustration va monter chaque jour d'un cran = *every day your frustration goes
up a notch*

Chaque lecteur permet de stocker de 20 à 100 heures de vidéo = *each reader
allows you to store between 20 ands 100 hours of videos*

For ***chacun*** see 242–243.

tout
Tout acts as a determiner in two ways –

1 ***tout*** in the singular and directly preceding the noun it determines = *any*;
2 ***tout*** in singular or plural and preceding the definite article or another determiner =
all, every.

The forms of ***tout*** are –

masculine singular ***tout***   masculine plural ***tous***
feminine singular ***toute***   feminine plural ***toutes***

examples of 1
Toute personne qui prendrait cette hormone risque d'encourir un cancer =
any person taking this hormone risks getting cancer

Où mettre le parfum? – toute zone qui n'est pas exposée à l'air = *the best place
to put perfume? – any spot not exposed to the air*

Tout homme devrait faire aussi attention à leur odeur qu'à leur look = *any*
man should pay as much attention to their smell as to their appearance

examples of 2
***Toutes les femmes aiment vous raconter ce qu'elles ont vécu, comment
elles ont perçu les autres*** = *all women love to tell you how they've been, how they view others*

Tous les Français consomment plus de 20 kilos de fromage par an = *all*
French people consume more than 20 kilos of cheese a year

Maintenant tous les salariés sentent qu'ils ont été entendus = *now all those on the payroll feel that they've had a hearing*

Toute l'équipe a bien joué = *the whole team played well*

On y a cru malgré tous ces petits signes du destin = *we believed it in spite of all those little signs of destiny*

Tous mes amis ont échangé un clin d'oeil = *all my friends winked at each other*

See 250.

Exercises

1 **Réécrivez les passages suivants en ajoutant les articles qui conviennent – défini, indéfini, partitif ou zéro –**
  a *Pour savoir si on a . . . jambes de . . . rêve, repérez dans . . . glace . . . creux entre . . . cuisses, . . . autre au-dessus de . . . genou et . . . dernier à . . . niveau de . . . chevilles. S'il en manque un ou deux, il faut déclencher . . . plan Orsec!* (equivalent of AA/RAC)
  b *Chez . . . homme . . . cerveau est responsable de toutes . . . facultés cognitives et de . . . contrôle de . . . émotions et de . . . instincts. Toutes . . . informations provenant de . . . monde extérieur y sont reçues et traitées, . . . comportements organisés, . . . raisonnements élaborés et . . . actions décidées. Sa fonction essentielle est de nous permettre d'apporter . . . réponses originales à . . . problèmes posés par notre environnement. C'est avec lui que nous sommes capables de faire . . . choix, bons ou mauvais.*
  c *Après . . . vêtements jetables, maintenant . . . frasques mangeables. . . . idée arrive de . . . royaume de . . . pommes chips. . . . styliste anglaise a préparé . . . première robe à . . . frites, avec . . . chapeau assorti. C'est de . . . goût exquis!*
  d *. . . mirabelles – elles doivent être dorées avec . . . taches de rousseur, et exhaler . . . parfum léger. Leur peau, souple sous . . . doigt, est recouverte de . . . fine pellicule qui les protège de . . . dessèchement.*
  e *Lorsque . . . crise se produit ou . . . scandale est dévoilé, . . . première réaction de nombreux personnages publics de nos jours est de jaillir en . . . torrent . . . remords.*
  f *. . . nouvelle Peugeot 407 intègre . . . produits innovants qui répondent à . . . exigences de . . . sécurité, . . . confort et . . . environnement. En particulier . . . nouveau système de . . . essuie-glace qui permet d'optimiser . . . surface et . . . qualité de . . . essuyage.*
  g *Quatorze patients hospitalisés à . . . CHU ont trouvé . . . mort à . . . terme de . . . pratiques de . . . euthanasie directe ou indirecte. Telle est . . . conclusion de . . . expertise médicale citée dans . . . presse régionale.*
  h *. . . gouvernement espagnol a décidé de rapporter d'au moins un an . . . entrée en vigueur, prévue pour . . . 25 mai, de . . . loi visant à*

ouvrir . . . transport ferroviaire à . . . concurrence. Cette loi avait été condamnée par plusieurs régions autonomes de . . . pays et par . . . cheminots de . . . chemins de . . . fer espagnols.

i . . . nuit, pendant que . . . bonne partie de . . . population ronfle tranquillement, un demi-million de . . . auditeurs, de tous . . . âges et tous . . . milieux sociaux, restent collés à leur poste de . . . radio.

j . . . rosiers sont de plus en plus souvent proposés en . . . pot. Tentant, mais est-ce bien raisonnable? Non, s'il s'agit de . . . rosiers malingres mis en . . . pot à . . . dernier moment ou encore de . . . rosiers produits industriellement dans . . . tourbe pure. Mais s'il s'agit de . . . rosiers mis en . . . pot depuis . . . hiver, dans . . . conteneurs profonds remplis de . . . terreau contenant . . . argile, pas . . . hésitation.

k Votre point faible: . . . manque de . . . persévérance. Vous ne prenez pas . . . décision, ou alors pas de . . . façon durable; vous êtes incapable de . . . effort, pas plus motivée par . . . succès que par . . . échec. Il n'y a que . . . nouveauté, . . . idée de . . . plaisir pour vous stimuler.

l . . . bonne alimentation – . . . sucres lents (. . . pâtes, . . . pommes de . . . terre) qui apportent . . . énergie tout à . . . long de . . . dure journée, et non . . . sucres rapides – . . . pâtisseries, . . . bonbons – qui donnent . . . coup de . . . fouet immédiat, mais induisent . . . coup de . . . pompe dans . . . heures qui suivent.

m Yacco propose . . . nouvelle gamme de 14 lubrifiants moteurs. . . . conduite urbaine, . . . trajet autoroutier, . . . compétition: tous . . . besoins sont pris en compte par ces huiles qui répondent à . . . nouvelles exigences – . . . réduction des émissions polluantes, . . . réduction de . . . consommation de . . . carburant, . . . espacement de . . . vidanges, . . . lutte contre . . . usure, etc.

n Si l'on se réfère à . . . langage de . . . couleurs, . . . jaune stimule . . . mémoire et . . . attention, . . . bleu calme . . . esprits, . . . vert apporte . . . équilibre et . . . rouge stimule . . . sens.

2 **Réécrivez les passages suivants en ajoutant le déterminant possessif ou l'article qui convient –**

a *Pompe* (= press-up) *avec levé de . . . jambe. En position de pompe classique, . . . mains sont dans l'alignement de . . . épaules, mais un peu plus espacées que la largeur de ces dernières. Descendez . . . corps en fléchissant . . . bras et en levant . . . jambe aussi haut que possible sans plier . . . genou. Quand . . . torse est près du sol, gardez la pose quelques secondes, puis tendez . . . bras pour revenir à la position de départ. Changez de . . . jambe.*

b *. . . corps est couvert de taches blanches – j'ai des taches blanches sur . . . corps, . . . visage, . . . cheveux, et . . . poils sont également affectés. Je suis obsédée par . . . corps et surtout . . . visage.*

c *Pour utiliser le flexi-ball, un gros ballon en plastique souple, posez . . . ventre sur le flexi-ball, . . . mains au sol, . . . bras tendus. . . . jambes sont jointes et tendues. En faisant pression avec . . . hanches, levez . . . jambes le plus haut possible. Gardez la position 5 secondes.*

3 **Réécrivez les passages suivants en ajoutant le déterminant démonstratif qui convient –**

a *. . . mois, on examine la machine à laver le linge.*

b *Il s'agit de faire plaisir à toute la famille. Celui-ci se nourrirait exclusivement de pâtes et de riz, . . . autre rechigne face à une assiette de courgettes, et . . . dernier ne tolère pas les légumes.*

c *Une circulaire ministérielle précisait que le poids d'un cartable d'écolier ne devrait pas excéder de 10% celui de l'enfant. . . . norme n'est toujours pas respectée.*

d *Disposez de l'herbe tondue en l'éparpillant autour des légumes. En 15 jours, . . . paillis (= mulch) disparaît.*

e *Sans l'aide de . . . crème, j'aurais certainement mis plus de temps à me débarrasser de tous . . . kilos.*

f *Seul point commun entre . . . enfants psychiquement atteints: . . . cocktails hormonaux pris par les mères! D'où l'idée d'un lien possible entre . . . psychoses et l'empreinte hormonale au stade foetal.*

4 **Réécrivez les passages suivants en ajoutant le déterminant possessif qui convient –**

a *Les huiles diffèrent par . . . teneur en vitamine E, . . . résistance à la chaleur et, bien sûr, . . . goût.*

b *Il est urgent que nous redonnions à . . . enfants le goût de l'eau.*

c *Dire que Golovin joua à . . . meilleur niveau serait exagéré.*

d *Entre ces deux compétitions, j'aurai le temps de changer . . . patins et de corriger . . . programmes.*

e *Comment qualifieriez-vous . . . sexualité actuelle?*

f *L'apparence est fondamentale pour une femme qui veut réussir dans . . . société. Je suis donc très attentive à maintenir . . . image sur . . . lieu de travail.*

g *On tient à te féliciter de . . . bon sens et . . . réponses toujours percutantes.*

h *Ce qui peut être intéressant pour nous, c'est qu'il apporte plus de profondeur à . . . jeu.*

Chapter 8 *Prepositions*

273 Prepositions
Small but highly significant, prepositions enable sentences to be expanded and more and more complex ideas to be expressed.

Prepositions perform two major syntactic functions –

1 linking verbs to adjectives, nouns and other verbs
2 preceding nouns to form prepositional expressions

274 French prepositions
The following is a list of French prepositions. Some consist of a single word, others consist of more than one word.

1 Single-word prepositions
à, après, avant, avec, chez, compris, contre, dans, de, depuis, derrière, dès, devant, durant, en, entre, envers, environ, excepté, malgré, par, parmi, pendant, pour, sans, sauf, selon, sous, suivant, sur, vers

2 Multi-word prepositions
à cause de, à condition de, à côté de, afin de, à force de, à moins de, à partir de, à travers de, au bout de, au cours de, au-delà de, au-dessous de, au-dessus de, au lieu de, auprès de, autour de, au travers de, d'après, de crainte / peur de, de façon / manière à, de la part de, du côté de, du haut de, en dehors de, en dépit de, en face de, face à, grâce à, hors de, jusqu'à, le long de, lors de, par-dessous, par-dessus, par suite de, près de, quant à

Prepositions which link

275 Prepositions which link
Prepositions are like hooks which link together elements of language, specifically adjectives, nouns and verbs to verbs.

The number of linking prepositions is small. The prepositions in question are *à, de, par*.

It should be noted that sometimes the French preposition is an exact equivalent of the one used in English, sometimes it is different, and on yet other occasions no preposition is used in French where one is used in English and vice versa.

This last possibility is known as a **zero preposition** and describes those cases where a preposition might be used but is in fact not. We will deal with the zero preposition first.

276 Zero preposition

The zero preposition is used to link certain verbs with a following infinitive. The most common verbs involved are –

adorer = to adore, **aimer** = to like, to love, **aimer mieux** = to prefer, **aller** = to go, **amener** = to bring, **arriver** = to arrive, **avoir beau** = to do in vain, **compter** = to count on, **confirmer** = to confirm, **courir** = to run, **croire** = to believe, to think, **daigner** = to deign, **déclarer** = to declare, **descendre** = to go down, **désirer** = to desire, **devoir** = to have to, **dire** = to say, **écouter** = to listen, **emmener** = to take away, **entrer** = to go in, **espérer** = to hope, **estimer** = to reckon, **faillir** = to fail, **falloir** = to be necessary **(il faut** = it is necessary), **(s')imaginer** = to imagine, **manquer** = to miss, **mener** = to lead, **monter** = to go up, **nier** = to deny, **oser** = to dare, **paraître** = to appear, **partir** = to leave, **penser** = to think, **pouvoir** = to be able, **préférer** = to prefer, **prétendre** = to claim, **se rappeler** = to remember, **reconnaître** = to recognise, **rentrer** = to return home, **retourner** = to return, **se révéler** = to turn out, **revenir** = to come back, **savoir** = to know, **sembler** = to seem, **sortir** = to go out, **souhaiter** = to wish, **valoir mieux** = to be better, **vouloir** = to wish, to want

It is perhaps worth pointing out that all the modal verbs act in this way; see 159–163.

277 Examples of verb + zero preposition

J'adorerais créer des parfums en labo = I'd adore creating perfumes in a lab

J'aime entreprendre des choses et je sais ce que je veux = I love doing things and I know what I want

Il a su que j'allais être la femme de sa vie = he knew I was going to be the woman in his life

Tout va bien se passer = everything's going to work out well

Vous avez la sensation d'être mieux rasé quand vous n'utilisez pas de produit avant-rasage – ça ne devrait pas arriver! = you feel as if you've had a better shave when you don't use a pre-shaving product – that shouldn't happen!

Il faut marcher au moins 3 à 5 km par jour – ça augmente de sept ans l'espérance de vie = you should walk 3 to 5 km a day – that increases your life expectancy by seven years

Pourquoi cours-tu? – A quel autre moment un homme peut-il porter du lycra moulant rose? = why do you go running? – When else can a man wear pink, tight-fitting lycra?

De là à choisir une femme dépressive en croyant pouvoir lui redonner le goût de vivre, il y a un pas que même un psychologue ne sait pas franchir = from there to choosing a depressive woman believing that you can give her back a taste for living, there's a step that not even a psychoanalyst knows how to take

En classe, je préfère porter des pantalons baggy et des baskets pour ne pas me faire remarquer = at school I prefer wearing baggy trousers and trainers so as not to make myself noticed

Le document se révèle être d'un intérêt primordial = the document turns out to be of the greatest interest

Ne sachant pas cuisiner, je me demande si une femme apprécierait une pizza surgelée pour dîner = *since I don't know how to cook, I wonder if a woman would appreciate a frozen pizza for dinner*

Les itinéraires des jeunes filles ont été étudiés par les enquêteurs, ce qui a semblé rassurer leur père = *the routes the young girls took have been studied by the investigators, which seemed to reassure their father*

Bon moment pour sortir s'entraîner à marcher, grimper, sauter = *it's a good moment to go outside to practise walking, climbing, jumping*

Pour bien démarrer, mieux vaut prévoir un temps d'apprentissage = *in order to make a good start, it's better to allow time to learn the ropes*

J'aurais voulu ressembler à Marilyn Monroe, mais c'est raté! = *I'd have liked to look like Marilyn Monroe, but no luck!*

278 *faire, entendre, envoyer, laisser, regarder, sentir, voir*

These verbs are also linked to a following infinitive by a zero preposition –

faire
La drogue a fait naître une narcoculture = *drugs have produced a drug culture*

Faites durer le plaisir = *make the pleasure last*

Le tabac fait chuter le taux de vitamine C = *tobacco reduces the level of vitamin C*

Faites monter la température en lui donnant des frissons = *make her temperature rise by giving her the shivers*

Les risques de se faire attraper vont être de plus en plus grands = *the risks of getting caught are going to get bigger and bigger*

laisser
Opter pour un masque réparateur – laisse poser dix minutes puis rincer ou faire pénétrer en massant = *opt for a rejuvenating face pack – leave it on for ten minutes, then rinse it off or massage it in to make it penetrate*

Laisser la peau se reposer en oubliant le maquillage pour un jour = *allow your skin to rest by not putting on any make-up for one day*

voir
Rien ne destinait Elisabeth et Claire à voir leurs destins se croiser et encore moins s'unir = *nothing destined Elisabeth and Claire to see their destinies cross let alone unite*

However, if two objects are involved, one of the finite verb and the other of the infinitive, different constructions occur.

1 If the finite verb is ***faire,*** the former appears as an indirect object –

C'est ce qui lui faisait sélectionner des symptômes sinon les inventer = *that's what made him select symptoms if not invent them*

Il a fait dessiner sa nouvelle maison à un architecte = *he had his new house designed by an architect*

Si ton mec n'est pas trop grand, fais-lui porter une veste de la couleur de son pantalon, afin d'allonger la silhouette = *if your guy isn't very tall, make him wear a jacket the colour of his trousers in order to lengthen his silhouette*

2 If the finite verb is one of the others, a choice of constructions is available, if pronouns are involved –

Elle les lui laisse raconter sans interruption⎫ = *she let her rabbit on without*
Elle la laisse les raconter sans interruption ⎭   *interrupting her*

If a noun or nouns is involved, the construction is as follows –

Restez au moins une heure dans l'eau pour laisser aux muscles le temps de se dénouer = *stay in the water for at least one hour to allow your muscles time to relax*

Restez au moins une heure dans l'eau pour les laisser le temps de se dénouer = *stay in the water for at least one hour to allow them time to relax*

Elle a entendu son amie dire des imbécillités = *she heard her friend talk nonsense*

Elle l'a entendue dire des imbécillités = *she heard her talk nonsense*

à

279 *à* linking an adjective to a following infinitive
Amongst the most common adjectives are –
apte = *capable*, *assis* = *sitting*, *bon* = *good*, *couché* = *lying*, *debout* = *standing*, *décidé* = *determined* , *déterminé* = *determined*, *disposé* = *disposed*, *dû* = *due*, *enclin* = *inclined*, *facile* = *easy*, *fermé* = *closed*, *fondé* = *justifiable*, *habile* = *skilful, good*, *lent* = *slow*, *long* = *long*, *ouvert* = *open*, *préparé* = *prepared*, *prêt* = *ready*, *prompt* = *prompt*, *propre* = *appropriate*, *résolu* = *determined*, *sensible* = *sensitive*, *unanime* = *unanimous*, *utile* = *useful*

C'est . . . à is dealt with in 221.

280 Examples of *à* linking an adjective to a following infinitive
Vous allez toujours au bout de vos projets, déterminé à supporter ou encaisser beaucoup = *you always carry through your projects determined to put up with or take on a lot*

Il faut être disposé à prendre le temps d'observer les courants et les habitudes locales = *you have to be willing to take time to observe the trends and local habits*

Le manque de tonus peut s'expliquer par des erreurs faciles à corriger = *lack of energy can be explained by mistakes that are easy to correct*

Elle n'est pas très ouverte à accepter les opinions des autres = *she's not very open to accepting other people's opinions*

Les compagnies aériennes sont prêtes à tout faire pour éviter d'encombrer les tapis des aéroports = *airlines are prepared to do anything to avoid clogging up the airport departure lounges*

Vous êtes toujours prête à dramatiser les situations réelles ou à imaginer d'hypothèques pour ne rien faire = *you're always ready to dramatise real situations or imagine hypothetical ones so as not to do anything*

Je suis résolu à ouvrir une boîte de nuit – que faut-il faire pour réussir? = *I'm determined to open a night club – what must I do to succeed?*

Dilué, cet élément est utile à fabriquer les engrais = *in its dilute state, it's useful for making fertilisers*

281 à linking a noun to a following infinitive

Common nouns involved are –

acharnement (m) = *tenacity*, **aisance** (f) = *ease*, **aptitude** (f) = *competence*, **ardeur** (f) = *enthusiasm*, **avidité** (f) = *eagerness*, **détermination** (f) = *determination*, **difficulté** (f) = *difficulty*, **facilité** (f) = *ease*, **habileté** (f) = *skill*, **hésitation** (f) = *hesitation*, **impuissance** (f) = *powerlessness*, **insistance** (f) = *insistence*, **intérêt** (m) = *interest*, **persistance** (f) = *persistence*, **regret** (m) = *regret*, **répugnance** (f) = *repugnance*, **retard** (m) = *delay*, **tendance** (f) = *tendency*

282 Examples of à linking a noun to a following infinitive

Elle a montré son acharnement à défendre les réfugiés = *she showed her determination to defend refugees*

Ton aisance à t'accommoder de la solitude te rend peu vulnérable aux événements extérieurs = *the ease with which you adapt yourself to solitude stops you being vulnerable to outside events*

Il a montré sa détermination à tenir ses promesses = *he showed his determination to keep his promises*

Vous ne faites pas preuve d'hésitation à prendre des risques, parce que vous ne savez pas être prudente = *you don't show any hesitation about taking risks, because you don't know how to be cautious*

Son insistance à disputer le match malgré ses blessures lui a valu un éloge général = *his insistence on playing the match in spite of his injuries won him universal praise*

Le retard du club à le nommer comme membre permanent de l'équipe lui a coûté cher – il est parti pour Toulouse = *the club's delay in appointing him as a permanent team member cost it dear – he's left for Toulouse*

Vous avez tendance à faire un blocage quand vous devez improviser = *you tend to have a block when you should improvise*

283 à linking a verb to a following infinitive

The following are the main verbs involved –

s'abaisser = *to stoop*, **s'abêtir** = *to act stupidly*, **s'abrutir** = *to become stupefied*, **s'accoutumer** = *to get used*, **s'acharner** = *to be very keen*, **s'adonner** = *to devote oneself*, **s'affoler** = *to panic*, **aider** = *to help*, **amener** = *to bring*, **s'amuser** = *to amuse oneself*, **appeler** = *to call*, **s'appliquer** = *to apply oneself*, **apprendre** = *to learn*, **s'apprêter** = *to get ready*, **arriver** = *to manage*, **aspirer** = *to aspire*, **s'attacher** = *to attach oneself*, **s'attarder** = *to take one's time*, **s'attendre** = *to expect*, **autoriser** = *to authorise*, *avoir* = to have, *se borner* = to limit oneself, *chercher* = to search, *commencer* = to begin, *condamner* = to condemn, *conduire* = to lead, *se consacrer* = to devote oneself, *consentir* = to consent, *consister* = to consist, *conspirer* = to conspire, *se consumer* = to waste away, *continuer* = to continue, *contraindre* = to constrain, *contribuer* = to contribute, *convier* = to invite, *se décider* = to decide, *demander* = to ask, *dépenser de l'argent* = to spend, *(se) déterminer* = to determine, *se dévouer* = to be devoted, *se disposer* = to be disposed, *se divertir* = to amuse oneself, *s'employer* = to be used, *encourager* = to encourage, *s'énerver* = to get worked up, *(s')engager* = to get involved, *s'enhardir* = to become bold, *s'ennuyer* = to be bored, *enseigner* = to teach, *s'entêter* = to be stubborn, *(s')entraîner* = to train (oneself), *s'épuiser* = to get exhausted, *équivaloir* = to be equal, *s'essayer* = to try, *s'essouffler* = to run out of breath, *exhorter* = to exhort, *se fatiguer* = to get tired, *(s')habituer* = to get used, *se hasarder* = to risk, *hésiter* = to hesitate, *inciter* = to incite, *incliner* = to be inclined, *insister* = to insist, *(s')intéresser* = to be interested, *inviter* = to invite, *s'irriter* = to get angry, *se limiter* = to limit oneself, *(se) mettre* = to put (oneself), *s'obstiner* = to be obstinate, *(s')occuper* = to be busy, *s'offrir* = to offer oneself, *s'oublier* = to forget oneself, *parvenir* = to succeed, *passer son temps* = to spend time, *perdre son temps* = to waste time, *persévérer* = to persevere, *persister* = to persist, *se plaire* = to please oneself, enjoy, *se plier* = to submit, *pousser* = to push, *(se) prendre* = to set about, *prendre plaisir* = to take pleasure, *(se) préparer* = to prepare (oneself), *se refuser* = to refuse, *se réjouir* = to rejoice, *renoncer* = to renounce, *répugner* = to be reluctant, *se résigner* = to resign oneself, *se résoudre* = to decide, *réussir* = to succeed, *se risquer* = to take a risk, *servir* = to serve, *songer* = to dream, *surprendre* = to surprise, *tarder* = to delay, *tendre* = to tend, *tenir* = to hold, *s'en tenir* = to keep, *travailler* = to work, *s'user* = to wear oneself out, *utiliser* = to use, *veiller* = to take care, *viser* = to aim

284 Examples of *à* linking a verb to a following infinitive

Le nouveau produit aide à stimuler la formation osseuse et à ralentir l'ostéoporose = the new product helps stimulate bone growth and slow down osteoporosis

Je m'apprête à lui donner des explications mais il refuse d'écouter = I'm prepared to explain things to him, but he refuses to listen

Il y a des filles qui savent jouer les sceptiques, pour qu'on cherche à les convaincre, à les séduire = there are some girls who know how to play the sceptic to make you try to persuade them and seduce them

On se lave trop, avec trop de produits trop souvent agressifs, n'hésite pas à dire le Pr Lorette = we wash ourselves too much with too many products that are too harsh, Professor Lorette does not hesitate to say [is quick to say]

Surmontant l'aversion qu'il avait envers lui, il l'a invité à dîner à la maison une semaine plus tard = overcoming the aversion he felt for him, he invited him home to dinner a week later

Il faut se limiter à prendre une douche par jour, et de préférence le matin = you should limit yourself to having one shower a day, preferably in the morning

Je me suis mise à fumer, à boire, mais je ne l'ai pas trompé = I began to smoke and drink, but I didn't cheat on him

Sur certains matchs, sans être bien, on parvenait à gagner ou du moins à ne pas perdre = *for certain matches, without being good, we managed to win or at least not lose*

Si vous persistez à vous rendre en cours nu(e) ou à porter des accessoires susceptibles de heurter les sensibilités, vous avez peu de chances de terminer l'année = *if you persist in coming to class naked or wearing accessories that might well offend other people's sensitivities, there's little hope that you'll complete the year*

On n'a qu'à s'en prendre à nous-mêmes pour ne pas s'être montrés suffisamment malins = *all we can do is blame ourselves for not having shown ourselves to be sufficiently crafty*

Monaco a réussi à atteindre les quarts de finale = *Monaco succeeded in reaching the quarter finals*

Il faut veiller à ne pas trop utiliser les soins dégraissants = *you need to be careful not to use too many skin cleansing products*

285 *contraindre, forcer, obliger*

For this group of verbs, practice varies according to whether the verb occurs in the active or passive voice.

1 If the active voice is concerned, the preposition *à* is used –

Qu'est-ce qui nous contraint à fumer une cigarette ou à boire un café? – Le stress et l'envie de prolonger un moment de détente = *what induces us to smoke a cigarette or have a coffee? – Stress and the desire to prolong a relaxing moment*

En vacances il faut forcer le corps à faire quelques entorses au régime habituel pour éviter les frustrations = *on holiday you have to force your body to vary your usual regime in order to avoid becoming frustrated*

2 On the other hand, if the passive voice is concerned, it is the preposition *de* which is used –

Pour certains, en cas de forte chaleur, on se sent forcé de réduire son alimentation = *for some of us, when it's particularly hot, we feel forced to reduce our food intake*

Mieux vaut être obligé de faire l'amour tous les jours plutôt que de traîner au lit à longueur de grasses matinées = *it's better to be forced to make love every day rather than laze in bed for hours on end*

286 *à* linking a verb to a noun

The major verbs involved are –

assister = to attend, *s'attaquer* = to attack, *s'attendre* = to expect, *se confier* = to confide, *consentir* = to consent, *croire* = to believe, *déplaire* = to displease, *désobéir* = to disobey, *échapper* = to escape, *faillir* = to almost, *se fier* = to trust, *manquer* = to fail, *se mêler* = to mix, *nuire* = to harm, *obéir* = to obey, *pardonner* = to forgive, *parer* = to ward off, *participer* = to participate, *penser* = to think, *plaire* = to please, *prendre part* = to take part, *remédier* = to cure, *renoncer* = to renounce, *répondre* = to reply, *répugner* = to be averse, *résister* = to resist, *ressembler* = to resemble, *réussir* = to succeed, *servir* = to serve, *songer* = to think, *subvenir* = to meet,

succéder = *to succeed* (inheritance), ***suffire*** = *to suffice*, ***survivre*** = *to survive*, ***téléphoner*** = *to telephone*

287 Examples of *à* linking a verb to a noun

Une fois par semaine un musicien donne un concert – tous y assistent = *once a week a musician gives a concert – everyone attends*

Les héros s'attaquent aux jeux vidéo – les héros de BD font le grand saut – les voilà désormais en jeux vidéo = *the heroes are attacking video games – comic strip heroes are making a great leap – and here they are now in video games*

Mon copain a des furoncles – est-ce qu'ils sont dûs à la crasse? = *my mate's got boils – are they due to the fact he's a dirty slob?*

On n'est pas là pour leur faire plaisir – parfois on leur dit des choses qu'ils n'ont pas envie d'entendre = *we're not there for their pleasure – sometimes we tell them things they don't want to hear*

Au travail, vous répondez favorablement à une offre, certaine de ne pas commettre d'erreur = *at work you reply favourably to an offer, convinced you're not making a mistake*

Pensez à toutes les astuces qui permettent de varier les goûters, surtout s'ils sont pris à l'extérieur = *think of all the tricks that allow you to vary their snacks, especially if they're eaten outdoors*

Le fromage blanc, doux et frais, répond à toutes nos envies de simplicité et se prête à des recettes variés = *soft and fresh white cheese is the answer to all our desires for simplicity and lends itself to a variety of recipes*

Avec une protection anti-UVA et UVB, voici le duo idéal pour résister aux effets nocifs d'un soleil trop brutal = *with its anti-UVA and UVB protection, here's the ideal two-piece to resist the harmful effects of an over-cruel sun*

Songez à votre partenaire pour qui vos demandes peuvent parfois sonner comme des ordres = *spare a thought for your partner for whom your requests may sometimes sound like orders*

La rémunération annuelle doit suffire à vos besoins de dépenses normales = *your annual income must be sufficient for the needs of your normal expenditure*

de

288 *de* linking an adjective to a following infinitive

The most common adjectives involved are –
avide = *greedy*, ***capable*** = *capable*, ***certain*** = *certain*, ***confus*** = *embarrassed*, ***content*** = *happy*, ***curieux*** = *curious*, ***désireux*** = *desirous*, ***désolé*** = *sad*, ***étonné*** = *astonished*, ***fier*** = *proud*, ***heureux*** = *happy*, ***impatient*** = *impatient*, ***incapable*** = *incapable*, ***libre*** = *free*, ***mécontent*** = *discontent*, ***ravi*** = *delighted*, ***reconnaissant*** = *grateful*, ***responsable*** = *responsible*, ***satisfait*** = *satisfied*, ***sûr*** = *sure*

Usage with impersonal ***il est*** is dealt with in 164.

289 Examples of *de* linking an adjective to a following infinitive

Rien ne sert d'essayer de se retenir d'éternuer, même si cela vous paraît bruyant et peu élégant – nous ne sommes pas capables d'y résister – *there's no point trying to stop yourself sneezing, even if it seems noisy and inelegant – we're incapable of resisting*

Vous pouvez être certaine d'avoir des jambes impeccables – en une minute sous la douche avec ce rasoir à tête pivotale = *you can be sure of having perfect legs – in a minute under the shower with this razor with a revolving head*

Je suis sûr que vous serez content de savoir que les rêves érotiques sont un signe de bonne santé psychique = *you'll be pleased to know that erotic dreams are a sign of good mental health*

Si vous êtes curieux de découvrir plus sur les postes commerciaux que nous offrons, contactez-nous au plus vite = *if you're curious to discover more about the commercial posts we're offering, contact us as soon as possible*

Si vous êtes désireux de savoir vos droits de salarié et les bonnes attitudes à adopter pour discuter efficacement avec votre patron, ce guide pratique vous aidera = *if you're keen to know your rights as a wage-earner and the right attitude to adopt to have a useful discussion with your boss, this practical guide will help you*

Je suis très fière d'avoir travaillé avec Jane Birkin = *I'm very proud to have worked with Jane Birkin*

Le printemps est là! je suis impatiente de découvrir mon corps et de profiter des beaux jours = *spring has arrived! I'm impatient to uncover my body and make the most of the fine days*

290 *de* linking a noun to a following infinitive

Some of the most common nouns involved are –

air (m) = *air, appearance,* ***autorisation*** (f) = *authorisation,* ***besoin*** (m) = *need,* ***capacité*** (f) = *ability,* ***chance*** (f) = *chance,* ***désir*** (m) = *desire,* ***droit*** (m) = *right,* ***envie*** (f) = *desire,* ***honte*** (f) = *shame,* ***impossibilité*** (f) = *impossibility,* ***incapacité*** (f) = *inability,* ***les moyens*** (mpl) = *the means,* ***nécessité*** (f) = *necessity,* ***obligation*** (f) = *obligation,* ***occasion*** (f) = *opportunity,* ***permission*** (f) = *permission,* ***peur*** (f) = *fear,* ***plaisir*** (m) = *pleasure,* ***rage*** (f) = *anger,* ***raison*** (f) = *reason, right,* ***risque*** (m) = *risk,* ***temps*** (m) = *time,* ***tort*** (m) = *wrong,* ***volonté*** (f) = *wish*

291 Examples of *de* linking a noun to a following infinitive

Avoir un trou sur ses dates de stage en entreprise ou hésiter sur ses qualifications fait plutôt mauvais genre. Au mieux vous aurez l'air de souffrir d'un Alzheimer précoce et au pire d'avoir bidonné votre CV = *having a gap in your dates for work experience or hesitating over your qualifications makes a rather bad impression. At best it will look as if you're suffering from the early onset of Alzheimer's, at worst as if you've cheated with your cv*

Tous mes patients éprouvent le besoin de se confier dès que je commence à manipuler leurs pieds = *all my patients feel the need to confide in me as soon as I start manipulating their feet*

Des mauvaises langues rapportent que les filles adeptes du gonflage des lèvres ont un désir, conscient ou inconscient, d'éveiller des envies chez le mâle = gossip-mongers say that girls who go for lip enhancement have the desire, conscious or subconscious, to arouse the male of the species

J'ai très envie de remonter sur scène, de refaire du cinéma = I'm very keen to return to the stage, to take up the cinema again

À ce moment-là, j'ai eu la sensation que le temps s'arrêtait, je n'avais pas les moyens de réagir = at that moment, I had the feeling that time stood still, I didn't have the means to react

Pour se défendre contre les prédateurs, portez un grand sac plastique. Pour l'honnête garçon, c'est la fille qui fait les courses et n'a pas peur d'aller lui chercher une bière quand il est fatigué = to protect yourself against predators, carry a large plastic bag. To the honest guy, it's the sign of a girl who does the shopping and isn't afraid to fetch him a beer when he's tired

Si vous n'ouvrez pas la porte, il n'ira pas plus loin, ou alors il fera preuve de violence, avec le risque de rameuter les flics = if you don't open the door, he won't go any further, or he may become violent, with the risk of alerting the cops

Ce rapport est menacé à cause de la volonté de l'Etat de voir les femmes se tourner de préférence vers un généraliste au lieu d'un spécialiste = this report is under threat because of the State's wish to see women preferably consult a GP rather than a specialist

292 *de* linking a verb to a following infinitive

The main verbs involved are –

s'abstenir = to abstain from, *accepter* = to accept, *accuser* = to accuse, *achever* = to complete, *s'affliger* = to be distressed, *(s')arrêter* = to stop, *attendre* = to wait, *s'aviser* = to realise, *blâmer* = to blame, *brûler* = to burn, *cesser* = to cease, *charger* = to make responsible, *choisir* = to choose, *comploter* = to plot, *consoler* = to console, *se contenter* = to be satisfied, *continuer* = to continue, *convaincre* = to convince, *craindre* = to fear, *décider* = to decide, *dédaigner* = to disdain, *demander* = to ask, *se dépêcher* = to hurry, *désespérer* = to despair, *détester* = to detest, *dire* = to say, *dispenser* = to dispense, *dissuader* = to dissuade, *douter* = to doubt, *s'efforcer* = to exert oneself, *s'empêcher* = to prevent oneself, *s'empresser* = to hurry, *enrager* = to be enraged, *entreprendre* = to undertake, *envier* = to envy, *envisager* = to envisage, *essayer* = to try, *s'étonner* = to be astonished, *éviter* = to avoid, *s'excuser* = to apologise, *bien faire* = to do well, *faire semblant* = to pretend, *feindre* = to feign, *(se) féliciter* = to congratulate, *finir* = to finish, *se flatter* = to flatter, *se garder* = to take care not, *gronder* = to scold, *se hâter* = to hurry, *hurler* = to howl, *implorer* = to beg, *s'indigner* = to be indignant, *s'inquiéter* = to worry, *interdire* = to forbid, *jurer* = to swear, *louer* = to praise, *manquer* = to fail, *en avoir marre* = to be fed up, *méditer* = to meditate, *se mêler* = to mix, *menacer* = to threaten, *mériter* = to deserve, *négliger* = to neglect, *s'occuper* = to be busy, *offrir* = to offer, *omettre* = to omit, *ordonner* = to order, *oublier* = to forget, *pardonner* = to forgive, *parler* = to speak, *permettre* = to allow, *persuader* = to persuade, *se piquer* = to like to make out, *plaindre* = to pity, *prendre garde* = to take care, *(se) presser* = to hurry, *prier* = to beg, *projeter* = to propose, *promettre* = to promise, *(se) proposer* = to propose, *recommander* = to recommend, *redouter* = to fear, *refuser* = to refuse,

regretter = *to regret*, ***se réjouir*** = *to rejoice*, ***remercier*** = *to thank*, ***se repentir*** = *to repent*, ***résoudre*** = *to resolve*, ***se retenir*** = *to restrain oneself*, ***rêver*** = *to dream*, ***risquer*** = *to risk*, ***rougir*** = *to blush*, ***simuler*** = *to simulate*, ***se soucier*** = *to worry*, ***soupçonner*** = *to suspect*, ***se souvenir*** = *to remember*, ***suffire*** = *to suffice*, ***suggérer*** = *to suggest*, ***supplier*** = *to beg*, ***supporter*** = *to tolerate*, ***tâcher*** = *to attempt*, ***téléphoner*** = *to telephone*, ***tenter*** = *to attempt*, ***se vanter*** = *to boast*, ***venir*** = *just* – see 143.

293 Examples of **de** linking a verb to a following infinitive

La première chose à faire, pour trouver son poids initial, est d'arrêter de boire des calories = *the first thing to do to recover your original weight is to stop drinking calories*

J'essayais de mettre tous les atouts de mon côté = *I tried to keep all the tricks up my sleeve*

Ne jamais ressentir de la haine est suspect – cela veut dire que l'on s'interdit d'éprouver un sentiment tout à fait normal = *never to feel hatred is suspect – that means that you forbid yourself experiencing a perfectly normal feeling*

Mon exemple peut permettre d'alerter des millions de gens = *my example can put millions of people on their guard*

Je refuse toujours de juger individuellement = *I refuse to judge individual cases*

C'est comme à la Bourse – plus on investit, plus on risque de perdre gros = *it's like the Stock Exchange – the more you invest, the more you risk losing big time*

À ce niveau il ne suffit pas de réaliser un bon match = *at this level it's not enough to pull off a good match*

Un de vos petits amis vous a déjà suggéré de changer quelque chose dans votre tête – le nez, le maquillage, la coiffure = *one of your boyfriends has already suggested changing something on your face – your nose, your make-up, your hairstyle*

294 **de** linking a verb to a noun

The major verbs involved are –

abuser = *to abuse*, ***s'accommoder*** = *to make the best*, ***s'accompagner*** = *to be accompanied*, ***accoucher*** = *to give birth*, ***s'agir*** = *to be a question* (***il s'agit de*** = *it's a question of*), ***s'aider*** = *to use*, ***s'alimenter*** = *to live on*, ***s'alourdir*** = *to increase*, ***s'apercevoir*** = *to notice*, ***(s')approcher*** = *to approach*, ***s'armer*** = *to arm oneself*, ***avoir besoin / envie / honte / peur*** = *to need / want / be ashamed / be afraid*, ***changer*** = *to change*, ***se charger*** = *to take responsibility*, ***convenir*** = *to admit, to agree*, ***se défier*** = *to distrust*, ***démissionner*** = *to resign*, ***dépendre*** = *to depend*, ***disposer*** = *to have at one's disposal*, ***se douter*** = *to suspect*, ***s'échapper*** = *to escape*, ***s'embellir*** = *to grow more attractive*, ***s'émerveiller*** = *to wonder*, ***s'emparer*** = *to seize*, ***s'ennuyer*** = *to be bored*, ***s'enrichir*** = *to get rich*, ***s'entourer*** = *to surround oneself*, ***s'envelopper*** = *to wrap oneself up*, ***s'évader*** = *to escape*, ***s'excuser*** = *to apologise*, ***s'indigner*** = *to be indignant*, ***s'inquiéter*** = *to worry*, ***s'inspirer*** = *to be inspired*, ***jouir*** = *to enjoy*, ***juger*** = *to judge*, ***manquer*** = *to lack*, ***se marrer*** = *to have a good laugh*, ***médire*** = *to malign*, ***se méfier*** = *to distrust*, ***se moquer*** = *to make fun*, ***s'occuper*** = *to be dealing with*, ***s'offenser*** = *to take offence*, ***s'orner*** = *to adorn oneself*, ***se parer*** = *to array oneself*, ***partir*** = *to start*, ***se passer*** = *to do without*, ***penser*** = *to think*, ***profiter*** = *to benefit*, ***répondre*** = *to be responsible*, ***rire*** = *to laugh*, ***se saisir*** = *to grab hold*, ***se servir*** = *to use*, *sortir* = to leave, *se souvenir* = to remember, *témoigner* = to bear witness, *triompher* = to triumph, *se tromper* = to be mistaken, *se vanter* = to boast, *vivre* = to live

295 Examples of *de* linking a verb to a noun

De fait, il ne s'agit pas d'une évolution brutale mais d'une accumulation de petites frustrations = in fact it's not a question of a painful evolution but of an accumulation of minor frustrations

Encore faut-il disposer d'outils pédagogiques efficaces = but you have to have effective pedagogical tools at your disposal

La vraie star intelligente épouse un industriel, elle sait que les acteurs sont des idiots – ne vous en riez pas! = the really intelligent star marries an industrialist, she knows that actors are idiots – don't laugh!

Beaucoup de scientifiques ont dû se marrer de cet article sur l'exercice des abdominaux = a lot of scientists must have had a good laugh at this article on exercising abdominal muscles

On peut jouir de la vie et du jour présent mais il faut aussi avoir de la chance = you can enjoy life and the present time but you also need luck

On peut juger de l'intérêt de ce sujet par la correspondance que nous avons reçue = you can judge the interest this subject has aroused by the mail we've received

En tant qu'écrivain c'est du drame que je m'occupe, du drame où les personnages principaux sont des femmes = as a writer, it's drama that interests me, drama in which the main characters are women

Grâce à ceci on peut profiter des indicateurs précoces de l'apparition de la fatigue = thanks to this we can benefit from the early indicators of the on-set of fatigue

Que pensez-vous de l'imagerie ultraviolente du Gangsta Rap? = what do you think of the ultraviolent imagery of Gangsta Rap?

Il vit de ses livres et de ses films sur le crime, qui rapportent bien plus d'argent aux honnêtes gens que le crime aux malfrats = he lives from his books and films on crime, which bring in much more money for honest guys than crime does for villains

296 Verbs with direct object and *de* with a second noun

The main verbs involved are –

absoudre = to absolve, *accabler* = to overwhelm, *accuser* = to accuse, *approcher* = to draw near, *arracher* = to snatch, *assurer* = to assure, *avertir* = to warn, *aviser* = to notify, *charger* = to entrust, *complimenter* = to compliment, *débarrasser* = to get rid of, *dégoûter* = to disgust, *délivrer* = to deliver, *détourner* = to divert, *dispenser* = to exempt, *écarter* = to move aside, *éloigner* = to move away, *enlever* = to take away, *excuser* = to excuse, *exempter* = to exempt, *féliciter* = to congratulate, *frapper* = to strike, *informer* = to inform, *libérer* = to free, *menacer* = to threaten, *ôter* = to remove, *persuader* = to persuade, *prévenir* = to warn, *remercier* = to thank, *traiter* = to call (somebody something)

297 Examples of verbs with direct object and *de* with a second noun

C'est une révolution dans ma vie et je n'excuserai jamais mes parents de leur manque de compréhension = *it's been a revolution in my life and I'll never forgive my parents for their lack of understanding*

J'ai la surprise de découvrir que je ne connais personne dont le nom de famille commence par F – je t'informe de cette nouvelle parce que ça devrait t'intriguer aussi = *I'm surprised to discover that I don't know anyone whose surname begins with F – I'm informing you of this piece of news because it ought to intrigue you as well*

Quand on croit en Dieu on a tendance à prier un Dieu mâle, ce qui est très bien, mais on ne doit pas oublier que Dieu est aussi une mère – quand on reconnaît ce concept, cela nous libère de beaucoup de complexes = *when you believe in God you tend to pray to a male God, which is good, but you mustn't forget that God is also a mother – when we acknowledge this concept it frees us from a lot of complexes*

Nous ne sommes pas faits pour être carnivores – j'essaie de persuader tous ceux que je rencontre de cette vérité fondamentale = *we're not made to be carnivores – I try to persuade all the people I meet of this fundamental truth*

Une nouvelle science inutile au progrès humain vient d'éclore – la nanologie, soit tout ce qui concerne l'univers du nain du jardin – il faut féliciter les Britanniques de Sudbury de cette addition au panthéon des -ologies = *a new science useless for human progress has just burst on the scene – gnomology, in other words everything relating to the universe of the garden gnome – we have to congratulate the inhabitants of Sudbury in Britain for this addition to the pantheon of -ologies*

Un mec gonflable a été inventé aux Etats-Unis – il se prête à l'investissement affectif mais ne vous accable pas d'exigences personnelles en échange = *an inflatable man has been invented in the USA – he is available for emotional attachment, but doesn't overwhelm you with personal demands in return*

Certaines pop stars entonnent une chanson lugubre, la voix se brise, la star cesse de chanter, baisse la tête et pleure – dans la salle c'est l'hystérie, mais ceci devient grotesque quand il se répète chaque soir – il faut prévenir le public de cette surenchère du marketing = *certain pop stars embark on a lugubrious song, their voice cracks, the star stops singing, lowers his or her head and weeps – the place goes mad, but this becomes grotesque when it's repeated every evening – the public should be warned about this piece of marketing extravagance*

298 Verbs involving *à* with a noun and *de* with an infinitive

For a sizeable group of verbs, it is important to remember that certain constructions in which they are involved necessitate the use of both *à* and *de* –
appartenir (impersonal usage) *il appartient* = *it is up to*, *arriver* (impersonal usage) *il arrive* = *it happens*, *commander* = *to order*, *conseiller* = *to advise*, *déconseiller* = *to advise against*, *défendre* = *to forbid*, *demander* = *to ask*, *dire* = *to say*, *imposer* = *to impose*, *interdire* = *to forbid*, *ordonner* = *to order*, *pardonner* = *to forgive*, *permettre* = *to allow*, *persuader* = *to persuade*, *prêter* = *to credit*, *reprocher* = *to reproach*, *savoir*

gré = *to be grateful*, **suggérer** = *to suggest*, **tarder** (impersonal usage) *il me tarde* = *I'm longing*, **en vouloir** = *to bear a grudge*

299 Examples of verbs involving *à* with a noun and *de* with an infinitive

Quand votre petit ami vient te chercher, est-ce qu'il arrive à ton père de se lancer dans un grand monologue sur la nécessité du respect d'un minimum de règles sociales pour que la vie soit plus supportable? = *when your boyfriend comes to take you out, does it happen that your dad launches into a great monologue on the necessity of respecting a minimum of social rules so that life is more bearable?*

On nous a conseillé de ne pas utiliser le terme « nain » dans notre article – mais de parler plutôt de « personne de petite taille » = *we were advised not to use the term 'dwarf' in our article, but rather to talk of 'people of small stature'*

La Carte 12–25 vous permet de bouger toujours plus loin = *the Young People's Card allows you to travel further and further*

Classiquement, on prête aux garçons d'appartenir au « sexe fort » et aux filles d'appartenir au « sexe faible » = *traditionally boys are credited with belonging to the 'stronger sex' and girls to the 'weaker sex'*

Je saurais gré à vos lecteurs de me fournir des renseignements sur la prévention de l'entorse du genou = *I'd be grateful to your readers for supplying me with information on how to prevent knee sprains*

300 Verbs with variable prepositional usage

Certain verbs may be followed by different prepositions depending upon the syntactic circumstances or register of the context or to indicate subtle nuances of meaning. Occasionally there seems to be no difference in the use of the different prepositions involved – in other words they are used in free variation.

301 Examples of verbs with variable prepositional usage

avoir droit / avoir le droit

avoir droit à = *to be entitled to* is linked to a noun by *à*

Il a droit à des sorties avec ses enfants le weekend = *he's entitled to weekend outings with his children*

avoir le droit de = *to have the right to* is linked to an infinitive by *de*

Il a le droit de sortir avec ses enfants le weekend = *he has the right to go out with his children every weekend*

commencer

Commencer is normally accompanied by *à* + infinitive, but *de* is used with a high register or to avoid a succession of /a/ sounds

Elle commença de rire = *she began to laugh* is preferred to *Elle commença à rire*

commencer, finir, terminer

Finir, terminer are used with **de** or **par** to convey different aspects of time –
finir, terminer + de = an action has just finished
finir, terminer + par = the action indicated by the infinitive occurs at the same time as the 'ending'.

Vous n'avez pas fini de vous disputer? = haven't you finished arguing?

Les grands établissements n'ont pas fini de faire des économies = *the big establishments haven't finished making economies*

Je voudrais finir / terminer par vous donner des chiffres = *I should like to end / conclude by giving you some figures*

En décembre dernier, les discussions à l'Assemblé nationale sur la loi de bioéthique ont fini par lever cette interdiction = *last December, discussions in the National Assembly on the bioethics law finished by lifting this ban*

Tu avances dans la vie et à travers les expériences tu finis par te trouver = *you advance in life and through your experiences you finish up by finding yourself*

The situation is the same with **commencer** except that **à** rather than **de** (see above) tends to be involved to indicate that an action has just begun –

Je voudrais commencer par vous donner des chiffres = *I should like to begin by giving you some figures*

An alternative to the **par** + infinitive construction with all three verbs is **en** + present participle –

Je voudrais commencer en vous donnant des chiffres = *I should like to begin by giving you some figures*

comparer

Comparer = *to compare* is normally followed by **à** + noun, but by **avec** in a low register situation –

Comparez la situation actuelle à / avec celle de nos aïeules qui avaient dû combattre pour défendre le droit de se colorer les lèvres sans être étiquetées filles de mauvaise vie = *compare the present situation with that of our grandmothers who had to fight for the right to paint their lips without being labelled tarts*

continuer

Continuer may be followed by **à** and **de** interchangeably –

Pour continuer à / de développer nos capacités génétiques, nous devons recevoir l'amour de l'autre = *in order to continue to develop our genetic capabilities, we have to receive another's love*

croire

Croire + en = *to believe in, to have faith in*

Je crois en Jésus-Christ, fils de Dieu = *I believe in Jesus Christ, Son of God*

Croire + à implies intellectual trust

Elle croit à la homéopathie = *she believes in homeopathy*

Croire + a direct object implies trust/confidence

Je la croyais = *I used to believe her*

demander
Demander + ***à*** + infinitive = *to ask*, when no indirect object is involved

Avec lui, je me sens en sécurité, je ne demande qu'à passer le reste de ma vie avec lui = *with him, I feel safe, all I ask is to spend the rest of my life with him*

Demander + ***de*** + infinitive = *to ask*, when an indirect object is specified

Une voiture s'arrête à ma hauteur, le conducteur me demande de lui indiquer le chemin d'un restaurant indien = *a car drew up beside me, the driver asked me to tell him the way to an Indian restaurant*

dire
Dire + ***de*** + infinitive = *to order*

Elle m'a convoquée pour me dire de partir le lendemain = *she summoned me to tell me to leave the next day*

Le bruit est devenu un véritable fléau citadin – on doit souvent dire à ses voisins de modérer le volume de leurs télévisions = *noise has become a real scourge in towns – you often have to tell your neighbours to turn down their televisions*

Dire + zero preposition + infinitive occurs when the subject for ***dire*** is the same as for the other infinitive –

Quoiqu'ils disent le faire, la majorité ne suit pas les règles préalables à l'instauration du traitement: un régime alimentaire contrôlé et l'arrêt du tabac = *although they say they do, the majority don't follow the rules which should precede the beginning of treatment: a controlled diet and an end to smoking*

échapper
Échapper + ***à*** = *to avoid*

Il a réussi à échapper à la prison = *he managed to avoid prison*

Normalement je m'endors en deux minutes, mais là j'ai mis une demi-heure – je n'ai pas pu échapper aux pensées négatives qui m'assaillaient = *normally I go to sleep in a couple of minutes, but then it took me half an hour – I couldn't avoid the negative thoughts that kept attacking me*

s'échapper de = *to escape from*
Il a réussi à s'échapper de ses kidnappeurs = *he managed to escape from his kidnappers*

Professionnel depuis 1987, il a été tout près d'abandonner son métier onze ans après ses débuts, de s'échapper des années d'angoisse et de stress = *a professional since 1987, he was very close to abandoning his job eleven years after beginning, to escape from the years of anguish and stress*

s'ennuyer

S'ennuyer = *to be bored, to get bored* may be followed by **à** and **de** + infinitive interchangeably –

On passe un tiers de sa vie au lit – alors, quand on choisit un partenaire, il ne faut pas s'ennuyer à / de prêter attention au comportement de celui-ci au lit = *we spend a third of our lives in bed – so, when you choose a partner, you mustn't get fed up with paying attention to his behaviour in bed*

S'ennuyer + **de** + noun = *to miss*

Elle commence à s'ennuyer de son petit ami = *she's beginning to miss her boyfriend*

Je change mes draps tous les trois ou quatre jours – je m'ennuie des draps hyperpropres = *I change my sheets every three or four days – I miss hyperclean sheets*

faire

Faire = *to do (with / to)* may be followed by **avec** and **de** + noun interchangeably –

Qu'est-ce qu'elle a fait avec / de ses cheveux? = *what has she done to / with her hair?*

Qu'est-ce que vous allez faire avec / de ce mec psychopathe? = *what are you going to do with this psychopath?*

faire = *to do (by)* may be followed by **de** and **par** interchangeably –

Il n'a pas le droit de le faire de / par lui-même = *he hasn't got the right to do it by himself*

finir *see* **commencer**

insister = *to insist* may be followed by **à** and **pour** + infinitive interchangeably –

Pour expliquer sa performance décevante, elle insiste à / pour dire que les conditions étaient trop difficiles = *to explain her disappointing performance, she insists on saying that the conditions were too difficult*

insister + **pour que** is used when a subordinate clause is involved –

Il m'a téléphoné pour insister pour que son ami soit réintégré dans l'équipe = *he telephoned me to insist that his mate was taken back into the team*

jouer

Jouer + **de** = *to play* used with musical instruments

Elle joue de la guitare acoustique = *she plays the acoustic guitar*

Jouer + **à** = *to play* used with sports

Nous jouons au tennis le mercredi soir = *we play tennis Wednesday evenings*

manquer

Manquer – this verb is particularly complicated to handle –

manquer = *to lack* can be used in two ways –

Si vous manquez de matériel pour réaliser
    les exercices de musculation
Si le matériel pour réaliser les exercices
    de musculation vous manque
= *if you lack the equipment to carry out muscle building exercises*

Avec un tel comportement vous n'allez pas
    manquer d'admiratrices
Avec un tel comportement les admiratrices
    ne vont pas vous manquer
= *with such behaviour you're not going to lack admirers*

manquer = *to miss* is followed by a direct object –

J'ai manqué un rendez-vous avec lui, je n'ai pas l'intention de manquer le **prochain** = *I missed one date with him, I don't intend missing the next one*

manquer = *almost* – **de** and zero preposition + infinitive are used interchangeably

Je t'observe à la dérobée, j'attends
que nos regards se croisent.
Enfin. Puis, je manque me dégonfler
Je t'observe à la dérobée,
j'attends que nos regards se croisent.
Enfin. Puis, je manque de me dégonfler
= *I watch you out of the corner of my eye, I wait for our eyes to meet. At last. Then I almost lose my nerve*

ne pas manquer + **de** + infinitive = *not to fail*

Ne manque pas de te brosser les dents le matin et le soir = *don't fail to brush your teeth morning and evening*

Si vous avalez de l'essence, ne manquez pas de prendre du lait ou un verre d'eau pour la diluer = *if you swallow petrol, don't fail to drink some milk or a glass of water to dilute it*

se mêler

Se mêler + **à** = *to mix* (physically) –

Beaucoup de gens sont très mal à l'aise quand il faut se mêler aux autres – c'est ce qui explique le boom des sites de rencontres sur Internet = *lots of people are very uncomfortable when they have to mix with others – that's what explains the popularity of Internet dating sites*

Se mêler + **de** = *to mix, to meddle* (implying intellectual involvement or interference) –

Tu ne devrais pas te mêler des affaires des autres = *you shouldn't stick your nose in other people's business*

s'occuper

S'occuper = *to be busy, to deal with* may be followed by **à** and **de** + infinitive interchangeably –

Trop souvent on s'occupe à / de masquer ses sentiments, parce qu'on veut éviter les échecs douloureux = *too often, we are busy hiding our feelings, because we want to avoid painful failures*

Il faut les caresser subtilement en s'occupant à / de s'attarder sur les bras ou les jambes= *you have to caress them subtly, taking care to linger over their arms and legs*

Être occupé – in the passive *à* + infinitive only is used
Si tu me téléphones quand je suis tout occupée à prendre un bain, tu peux laisser un message sur mon répondeur = *if you phone when I'm busy having a bath, you can leave a message on my answerphone*

J'étais occupé à boire une cannette de bière quand je l'ai vue, elle était si sexy! = *I was busy drinking a can of beer, when I saw her, she was so sexy!*

S'occuper / être occupé + noun – *de* only is used

Il faut s'occuper de la façon dont on s'habille pour attirer les filles = *you have to pay attention to the way you dress to attract the girls*

Je mangeais les hamburgers, les cheese-burgers, les frites, je n'étais pas du tout occupé des conséquences = *I used to eat hamburgers, cheeseburgers, chips, I wasn't at all concerned about the consequences*

penser
Penser + zero preposition = *to think, to intend*

Cela nous rappelle le temps où l'on donnait de l'huile de foie de morue aux enfants pensant contrecarrer leur retard de croissance = *that reminds me of the time when we gave cod liver oil to children thinking that we could counteract the fact that they were slow developers*

Penser + *à* = *to think of, about*

Après une dispute, vous vous réconciliez très facilement et vous n'y pensez plus = *after an argument, you make it up very easily and don't think about it any more*

Je pense à lui tout le temps, je l'aime parce que c'est lui qui descend la poubelle = *I think about him all the time, I love him because he's the one who puts the bin out*

Plus le blouson est délavé, plus vous devez lui accorder de l'élégance – pensez à le porter avec de belles chaussures = *the more faded your jacket is, the more you need to enhance its elegance – think about wearing it with a smart pair of shoes*

Penser + *de* = *to think about, to have an opinion on*

Qu'est-ce que tu penses de sa robe? = *what do you think of her dress?*

Selon les pays, on répond différemment au problème posé par l'hyperactivité des enfants. Dans la culture anglo-saxonne, on prescrit des médicaments. Dans les pays latin, on favorise l'approche psychothérapeutique. Qu'est-ce que vous pensez de cette différence d'approche d'ordre culturel? = *According to country, people react differently to the problem posed by hyperactivity amongst children. In Anglo-Saxon countries, medicines are prescribed. In Mediterranean countries, a psychotherapeutic approach is preferred. What is your opinion of this culture-based difference of approach?*

prendre

Prendre + à = *to take from* used with people –

J'ai pris la valise à la dame et l'a hissée dans le porte-bagages = *I took the case from the lady and heaved it onto the luggage rack*

Prendre + dans = *to take from* (= within)

Elle a pris sa chemise dans le tiroir = *she took her blouse from the drawer*

prendre + sur = *to take from* (= off)

Il ne peut monter que si tu as pris la lessive sur ton lit = *he can't come up till you've taken the washing off your bed*

répondre

Répondre + à = *to answer*

J'espère que tu pourras répondre à ma question = *I hope you'll be able to answer my question*

Répondre + de = *to be responsible*

Tout le monde doit répondre de ce qu'il a fait dans la vie = *everyone must be responsible for what they do in life*

J'ai une seule réflexion à faire à ton problème – tu seras condamnée à de telles histoires chaotiques si tu ne commences pas à répondre de tes actions = *I've got one simple comment to make on your problem – you'll be doomed to such chaotic episodes if you don't begin taking responsibility for your actions*

servir

Servir + à = *to be useful, to serve to*

Les documentaires télévisés servent à l'élargissement des esprits
Les documentaires télévisés servent à élargir les esprits
} = *television documentaries are useful for broadening the mind*

Sa formule aux micro-bulles et son agent anti-bactérien servent à combattre vos problèmes de peau = *its micro-bubble formula and antibacterial agent serve to combat your skin problems*

Servir + de = *to be used*

Organisez d'autres tentations – le shopping orgiaque peut servir d'alternative à la consommation de trop de sucreries = *organise other temptations – a shopping orgy can be used as an alternative to eating too many sweet things*

Chez les Indiens de Papouasie-Nouvelle-Guinée, les feuilles servent d'assiettes = *amongst the Papua New Guinea Indians, leaves are used as plates*

Se servir is always used with **de** –

Servez-vous de ce kit de rouges à lèvres pour obtenir une couleur bien à vous ou pour jouer la bouche bicolore, même tricolore = *use this lipstick kit to obtain your very own colour or to produce a two-colour or even three-colour mouth*

Je me sers d'internet pour m'informer sur les vols bon marché = *I use the Internet to get information on cheap flights*

tarder
Tarder + à = *to delay*

Ne tardez pas à dénicher un petit morceau de tissu capable d'arranger vos atouts = *don't delay getting hold of a little piece of tissue capable of displaying your best points to greatest effect*

Je suis folle amoureuse d'un mec et j'ai peur de trop tarder à le lui dire – mais comment? = *I'm madly in love with a guy and I'm afraid of leaving it too long before telling him – but how can I do it?*

Tarder + de = *to miss, to be keen to* – the impersonal form of the verb is used

Vous vouliez vivre en communauté, il vous tardait de faire la révolution, mais rien de tout cela ne s'est passé = *you wanted to live in a community, you were keen to take part in the revolution, but nothing of all that has come to pass*

Il me tarde de manger mes petits pots de crème au chocolat – si j'ai un peu de stress, c'est ma seule drogue = *I miss my little pots of chocolate cream – if I feel a bit stressed, it's the only drug I need*

tenir
Tenir + à = *to want to*

Je tiens à souligner que les Verts sont en train de s'améliorer = *I want to stress the fact that the Greens are in the process of improving*

Les nutritionnistes tiennent à nous dire que la betterave est riche en magnésium antistress et en vitamine B9 anti-anémique, deux micronutriments dont les carences affectent particulièrement les femmes = *nutritionists are keen to tell us that beetroot is rich in antistress magnesium and in anti-anaemia vitamin B9, two micronutrients whose lack particularly affects women*

Tenir + de = *to take after*

Mon fils tient de sa mère = *my son takes after his mother*

venir
Venir + zero preposition = *to come*

Méfiez-vous des poux – ils peuvent venir vous contaminer la tête sans que vous vous en rendiez compte = *beware of lice – they can come and infect your head without you realising it*

Venir + de = *just* – see 143.

Vous venez d'accumuler quelques petits kilos supplémentaires? – la meilleure façon de s'en débarrasser, c'est la marche = *if you've just put on a few extra kilos, the best way to get rid of them is walking*

Je venais de suivre un traitement contre la migraine quand je découvrais que cela m'avait fait prendre beaucoup de poids = *I had just followed a course to treat my migraines, when I discovered that it was making me put on weight*

Prepositional expressions

302 Prepositional expressions

Sometimes there is a one-to-one correlation between French and English prepositions, especially when those with fairly specific meanings are involved, but very often no such correlation exists, especially with those prepositions with a vague meaning. By providing a large number of examples for the most common prepositions and especially those with the vaguest meanings, it is hoped that the various values will emerge. What follows cannot be an exhaustive list of examples – the hope is that the flavour and typical uses of the prepositions will become clear.

303 *à*

À is equivalent to English *at*, *in*, *to*, *on* and sometimes zero preposition; it is used in relation to place, time, manner and measurement. It is extremely common.

304 *à* indicating place

À indicates position in and movement towards.

être à l'école = *to be at / in school*

aller à l'école = *to go to school*

être / aller à la faculté / à l'université = *to be at university / to go to university*

s'inscrire à la fac = *to register at university*

être / aller à l'église = *to be in / at church / to go to church*

être / aller à l'hôtel = *to be in the hotel / to go to the hotel*

être / aller au restaurant = *to be in the restaurant / to go to the restaurant*

être / aller au commissariat de police = *to be in the police station / to go to the police station*

être / aller au village = *to be in the village / to go to the village*

but *en ville** = *in town*

être / aller à Paris = *to be in Paris / to go to Paris*

au sud, au nord, à l'est, à l'ouest = *in / to the south, the north, the east, the west*

au nord de la France = *in / to northern France*

à la campagne = *in / to the country*

à la montagne = *in / to the mountains*

au jardin = *in / to the garden*

à la salle à manger = *in / to the dining room*

au pôle sud, au pôle nord = *at / to the south pole, at / to the north pole*

au plafond = *on the ceiling*

à la ferme* = *on / to the farm*

écrire au tableau blanc = *to write on the white board*

être à bicyclette / à pied = *to be on a bike / on foot*

être au téléphone / au portable = *to be on the telephone / on the mobile*

à la télévision = *on television*

à la radio = *on the radio*

au journal = *in the newspaper*

à la page numéro 2 = *on page number 2*

tomber aux genoux = *to fall on / to your knees*

frapper à la porte = *to knock on / at the door*

être à bord d'une voiture = *to be in a car*

au soleil = *in the sun*

à l'ombre = *in the shade*

tomber à l'eau = *to fall in the water*

tenir quelque chose à la main = *to hold something in your hand*

***être blessé au bras / genou**, etc* = *to be wounded in the arm / knee, etc*

porter quelque chose aux pieds = *to wear something on your feet*

travailler à la mine / aux chemins de fer* = *to work in the mine / on the railways*

tomber à terre** = *to fall to the ground* (from a height)

à l'intérieur = *inside, indoors*

à l'extérieur = *outside, outdoors*

à l'arrière = *in / at the back*

à l'envers = *back to front*

à la place de / au lieu de = *in place of / instead of*

* see 333, 390 **dans**

** see 374, 390 **par**

For **à** with names of countries, see 393.

305 à indicating time

à dix heures = at ten o'clock

à minuit / à midi = at midnight / at midday

à l'heure actuelle = at the present time

au début = at the beginning

à la fin = at the end

à la mi-temps = at half-time

au soir = in the evening

au printemps = in the spring

à l'automne = in the autumn

à notre époque = in our time

au 21e siècle = in the twenty-first century

à la mi-janvier = in mid-January

à la Saint-Sylvestre / à la Toussaint = (on) New Year's Eve / on All Saints' Day

à notre arrivée / à notre retour = on our arrival / on our return

arriver à temps = to arrive on time

la date à laquelle elle est partie = the date on which she left

à l'avance* = in advance

* see *de* and *par* 390.

306 à indicating manner

fabriqué à la main = hand-made

un à un = one by one

mot à mot = word for word

pas à pas = step by step

à pas lents / à pas de loup = slowly / stealthily

à reculons = backwards

à ce que j'ai entendu = from what I've heard

reconnaître quelqu'un à sa voix = to recognise someone from / by their voice

écrire au stylo / à l'encre = to write in pen / in ink

lire à la lumière d'une lampe = to read by the light of a lamp

être abattu à coups de pied / poing / couteau = to be kicked / punched / knifed to the ground *être au chômage* = *to be out of work*

le gouvernement au pouvoir = *the government in power*

une collection aux tons de sable et de terre = *a collection with tones of sand and earth*

un album aux accents romantiques = *an album with a romantic flavour*

à mon avis = *in my opinion*

à leur manière = *in their way*

à regret = *regretfully*

à la rigueur = *if need be*

au cas où = *in the case in which*

Au cas où les discussions seront bloquées = *in case discussion is foreclosed*

au secours! / au voleur! = *help! / thief!*

manger à l'indienne = *to eat squatting down*

à la française = *in the French style*

307 à to mark responsibility
à vous d'être positif = *it's up to you to be positive*

à vous de simplifier la tâche = *it's up to you to simplify the task*

c'est à lui de trouver une justification = *it's up to him to find a justification*

à moi le tour = *it's my turn*

308 à expressing measurement
à 21 ans = *at 21 (years old)*

elle a au moins 18 ans = *she's at least 18*

un billet à 10 euros = *a ten-euro note*

à une vitesse de 90 km à l'heure = *at 90 km per hour*

rouler à 120 km à l'heure = *to travel at 120 km an hour*

Paris se trouve à 20 km d'ici = *Paris is 20 km from here*

*il habite à au moins 5 km d'ici** = *he lives at at least 5 km from here*

ce produit est présent à forte concentration = *this product is present in a strong concentration*

* see *du moins* 390.

309 à expressing a compound phenomenon
Where English uses one noun adjectivally to qualify another, French often has recourse to a construction with *à*.

*un verre à bière / au vin** = *a beer / wine glass*

un pot à fleurs = *a flower pot*

un moulin à vent = *a windmill*

de la soupe à l'oignon = *onion soup*

une sauce au vin = *wine sauce*

une cuillère à soupe d'eau plate = *a soupspoon of still water*

une femme aux cheveux blonds = *a blonde*

un homme au nez tordu = *a man with a twisted nose*

une machine à traitement de texte = *a word-processor*

taper à la machine = *to type*

* see **de** 337.

310 à + infinitive
À l'écouter, vous diriez qu'il aime se donner en spectacle = *listening to him, you'd say he liked making a spectacle of himself*

À la voir, on n'aurait jamais cru qu'elle était riche = *looking at her, you'd never think she was well off*

311 à cause de = because of
À cause de la chaleur il a pris une douche froide = *because of the heat he took a cold shower*

312 à condition de = subject to
À condition de is only used with infinitives –

À condition de comprendre les dangers, vous pouvez profiter des joies du sexe en toutes circonstances = *subject to understanding the dangers, you can enjoy sex in each and every situation*

À condition d'afficher une endurance mentale à toute épreuve, il est possible de surmonter les douleurs rencontrées lors des marathons = *subject to possessing high-resistance mental endurance, it's possible to overcome the pain encountered during marathons*

313 à côté de = next to, in comparison with
Sa maison se trouve à côté de la mienne = *her house is next to mine*

A côté des icônes d'hier, celles d'aujourd'hui vendent plutôt le vice, le niais = *in comparison with the icons of yesteryear, today's purvey vice and stupidity*

314 afin de = in order to
Afin de is used only with infinitives –

Afin d'éviter des ennuis judiciaires, agissez la nuit – le clair de la lune assure la discrétion et accentue la tension = *in order to avoid problems with the law, act at night time – moonlight ensures discretion and increases tension*

Afin de profiter au maximum des asperges, il faut les choisir cassantes et de couleur franche = *in order to get the most out of asparagus, you have to choose them when they snap easily and are uniform in colour*

315 *à force de* = by virtue of

Je sais que c'est à force de tous vos efforts que vous avez réussi ce test = *I know that it was by virtue of all your efforts that you passed that test*

À force d'enchaîner les flirts d'un soir, vous risquez de vous noyer dans des aventures sans lendemain = *by virtue of a series of one-night stands, you run the risk of drowning yourself in a series of liaisons which lead nowhere*

316 *à moins de* = unless

À moins de is used only with an infinitive –

Une voiture c'est comme une femme, à moins de s'en servir, on se la fait piquer = *a car is like a woman, unless you use it someone will pinch it*

À moins d'être irréprochable, le brossage des dents manuel risque d'être trop superficiel = *unless it's absolutely thorough, cleaning your teeth by hand runs the danger of being too superficial*

317 *à partir de* = from

Je serai chez moi à partir de trois heures = *I'll be at home from three o'clock*

318 *après / d'après* = after / according to, from

Après alone is usually equivalent to English *after*; **d'après** = *according to, from*

après
après le début de l'émission = *after the programme begins / began*

J'arriverai après 21 heures = *I'll arrive after 9 o'clock*

Sélectionné génétiquement après fécondation in vitro = *genetically selected after in vitro fertilisation*

Après les études, le temps de l'emploi = *after your studies, it's time to get a job*

Note the difference between the French and English versions for the following examples

Après avoir fini mon yaourt nature = *having finished / after finishing my natural yoghurt*

Après lui avoir offert un bracelet en fibres naturelles = *having offered / after offering her a bracelet made of natural fibres*

Après s'être fait greffer un portable à l'oreille = *having had a mobile grafted onto his ear*

d'après
D'après ce qu'il a dit = *from what he said*

D'après moi, il ne faut jamais vous priver de dessert = *in my opinion you must never deprive yourself of a dessert*

D'après la télévision, il y aurait dix victimes = *according to the telly there were ten casualties*

319 à *travers* = through

Elle m'a appelé à travers ses larmes = *she shouted to me through her tears*

Je l'ai vue qui fumait à travers la porte = *I saw her smoking through the door*

Voyager à travers l'Europe / le temps = *to travel through Europe / time*

Sentir le froid à travers ses vêtements = *to feel the cold through your clothes*

320 *au bout de* = at the end of

Au bout de 6 km de marche, on commence à developper de nouvelles capacités respiratoires = *at the end of 6 kms walking, you begin to develop new respiratory capabilities*

Au bout de la cour tu trouveras des pots intéressants = *at the end of the yard you'll find some interesting pots*

au bout d'un an = *a year later*

Il est arrivé au bout de trente minutes = *he arrived half an hour later*

321 *au cours de* = during, in the course of

C'était au cours d'un rendez-vous avec un copain = *it was during a meeting with a mate*

Elle arrivera au cours de l'après-midi = *she'll arrive in the course of the afternoon*

322 *au-delà de* = beyond, apart from

Au-delà de l'originalité, ils n'offrent pas grand'chose = *beyond / apart from their originality, they don't have much to offer*

323 *au-dessous de* = underneath, beneath, below

Il y avait une station de métro au-dessous de leur hôtel = *there was an underground station beneath their hotel*

La température est au-dessous de 4 degrés = *the temperature is below 4 degrees*

Ce poste est au-dessous de ses capacités = *this job is beneath her ability*

au-dessous de la moyenne = *below average*

324 *au-dessus de* = over, above

Ce château féerique se trouve au-dessus d'une vallée pittoresque = *this fairy-tale castle stands above a picturesque valley*

Un chèque au-dessus de 1000 euros = *a cheque for over 1000 euros*

Vous pensez que c'est au-dessus de vos compétences de vous passer de sucre? = *you think it's beyond your ability to do without sugar?*

au-dessus de la moyenne = *above average*

325 *au lieu de* = instead of

Ce soir j'espère que tu porteras une jupe au lieu de ce jean affreux = *I hope you'll wear a skirt instead of those awful jeans this evening*

Il m'a apporté un Pepsi au lieu d'un Coke = *he brought me a Pepsi instead of a Coke*

326 *auprès de* = in relation to, in comparison with, among

Auprès des autres mascaras celui-ci est excellent = *in comparison with the other mascaras this one is outstanding*

Il s'est plaint auprès du directeur = *he complained to the headteacher*

Un sondage auprès de quatre mille personnes = *a survey among 4000 people*

327 *autour de* = around, round, about

Il a voyagé autour du monde = *he's travelled around the world*

Elle a organisé un colloque autour du thème du tatouage = *she organised a conference on the theme of tattooing*

328 *avant* = before (of time)

Tu dois rentrer avant onze heures = *you must be home before 11 o'clock*

Il se lève avant vous = *he gets up before you*

avant de + *infinitive*

Avant de vous engager, essayez de faire attention où vous mettez les pieds = *before committing yourself, try to be careful where you stick your feet*

Avant d'ajouter les framboises, faites dorer à la poêle 75 grammes d'amandes = *before adding the raspberries, lightly brown 75 grammes of almonds in a pan*

329 *avec* = with

Il est arrivé avec sa petite amie = *he turned up with his girlfriend*

C'est un vélo avec vingt vitesses = *it's a bike with twenty gears*

Un dépistage compatible avec un enfant nouveau-né = *screening compatible with a newly born infant*

Nous avons pris le dessert avec des cerises = *we went for the dessert with cherries*

Il est très gentil avec votre nouvel assistant = *he's very nice to your new assistant*

Une méthode qui ne marche qu'avec la complicité de tout le monde = *a method that only works with everyone's complicity / if everyone colludes*

330 *chez* = at the home of, among

Je serai chez moi à partir de trois heures = *I'll be at home from 3 o'clock*

La plupart des chutes ont lieu chez soi = *most falls occur in the home*

Il vous appelle chez vous le weekend pour régler quelques petits détails = *he calls you at home at the weekend to sort out a few minor details*

Cela peut provoquer de graves troubles du système nerveux chez le foetus = *that can cause major problems in the nervous system for the foetus*

331 *compris / y compris* = including

Y compris is used when the preposition precedes the noun, but *compris* alone when it follows, in which case it agrees with the gender and number of the noun (see 198) –

service compris / service non compris = *including service / excluding service*

TVA comprise / non comprise = *including VAT / excluding VAT*

Il y aura cinq épreuves sportives, y compris un saut à l'élastique et une demi-heure de kayak = *there'll be five sporting challenges, including a bungee jump and half an hour in a kayak*

Un demi-verre de Vanish suffit pour effacer toutes les taches, y compris les taches de vin et d'herbe – *half a glass of Vanish is enough to get rid of all stains, including wine and grass stains*

332 *contre* = against

Je n'ai rien contre les Anglais = *I haven't got anything against the English*

Il a changé deux mille livres contre des euros = *he changed two thousand pounds into euros*

Les tests contre placebo le prouvent = *tests with a placebo prove it*

Lutter contre la douleur = *to fight against pain*

333 *dans* = in, from, during
dans expressing position
dans l'espace = *in space*

dans l'air = *in the air*

dans la région parisienne = *in the Paris area*

dans la capitale = *in the capital*

dans l'aéroport = *in the airport* (buildings)

dans le parking = *in the carpark*

*travailler dans la mine** = *to work in a mine*

être dans la maison = *to be in the house* (not outside)

dans la campagne / le jardin = *in the country / the garden*

dans le train = *in the train*

dans l'eau = *in the water*

J'aime les vacances dans les Alpes = *I love holidays in the Alps*

La Butte Montmartre, c'est mon coin préféré dans Paris = *the Butte Montmartre is my favourite spot in Paris*

Il y a eu beaucoup de bruit dans la rue = *there was a lot of noise in the street*

Il est tombé dans l'eau = *he fell into the water*

La preuve dans ce numéro = *the proof is in this issue*

Dans l'intimité du fond de teint = *in the intimacy of foundation cream*

Du mercure dans le thon = *mercury in tuna*

Ma grand-mère préfère boire dans une tasse en porcelaine = *my grandmother prefers to drink out of a china cup*

Elle a pris son pull dans le tiroir = *she took her jumper out of the drawer*

* see 391 for discussion of different prepositions translating English *in*

dans expressing time
dans les années quatre-vingt-dix = *in the 1990s*

dans les prochains jours = *in the next few days*

J'arriverai dans vingt minutes* = *I'll be there in 20 minutes*

Je le ferai dans la semaine = *I'll do it during the week*

Je le ferai dans dix jours = *I'll do it in ten days' time*

* see 357 *en* below and also 391

334 *de*
De occurs with many different values and uses and, with *à*, is the most commonly encountered preposition in French. It is most frequently used to indicate some association or link of possession between two nouns. In many cases, the English version of a French phrase with *de* does not require a preposition. The following examples illustrate typical uses.

335 *de* indicating possession
L'équipe de foot de France = *the French football team*

Des cours de néerlandais et d'anglais = *courses in Dutch and English*

La cérémonie d'ouverture = *the opening ceremony*

Le meilleur athlète du pays = *the best athlete in the country*

Les meilleurs aliments de la gamme offerte aux enfants = *the best foods in the range for children*

Une place de parking vide = *an empty parking space*

La cause principale de mon anxiété = *the main cause of my anxiety*

C'est un style de vie qui me plaît = *it's a way of life that appeals to me*

J'interprète la petite amie d'un des potes du héros = *I play the girlfriend of one of the hero's mates*

Jacqueline Lens, responsable de la communication chez Références = *Jacqueline Lens, in charge of communication for 'Références'*

Vous avez des souvenirs de votre temps de serveuse? = *have you got some memories of your time as a waitress?*

Qu'est-ce qui vous dégoûte? – L'odeur et le goût du chou-fleur = *what turns you off? – The smell and taste of cauliflower*

Vous bénéficiez de nombreuses possibilités de promotion = *you benefit from numerous opportunities for promotion*

Vous trouverez sur notre site internet une description détaillée des profils que nous recherchons = *you'll find on our internet site a detailed description of the types of people we're looking for*

336 *de* expressing place, origin

Le train de / à destination de Paris = *the Paris train* (for Paris)

Le train de / venant de Paris = *the Paris train* (from Paris)

D'ici à Paris c'est cent kilomètres = *from here to Paris is 100 km*

Elle vient de Paris = *she comes from Paris*

L'Europe de l'Ouest = *Western Europe*

L'Afrique du Sud = *South Africa*

L'Amérique du Nord = *North America*

Le nord de l'Amérique = *north / northern America*

Je viens d'arriver de la Roumanie = *I've just got back from Romania*

Elle vient de l'autre côté de la ville = *she comes from the other side of town*

Un enfant de son mariage précédent = *a child from his previous marriage*

Il est né de parents immigrés du Pakistan = *he was born to parents who had immigrated from Pakistan*

Un disque qui passe de la plainte soul au murmure suggestif = *a record that goes from plaintive soul to suggestive murmurings*

À l'issue de l'opération = *at the end of the operation*

Au milieu de cette forêt de béton et d'acier = *in the midst of this forest of concrete and steel*

Pour se déplacer de bâtiment en bâtiment = *to move from building to building*

S'inspirant de la mythologie grecque = *taking his inspiration from Greek mythology*

Il convient de rester prudent si la proposition vient d'une société peu ou pas connue = *it's appropriate to be prudent if the offer comes from a firm that is little known or completely unknown*

337 **de** expressing the idea of containing, measurement

un verre de vin* = *a glass of wine* (not a *wine glass*)

un pot de fleurs = *a pot of flowers* (not a *flower pot*)

un pot de yaourt = *a pot of yoghurt*

une compote de pommes = *stewed apple*

une bouteille de bière = *a bottle of beer*

quatre blancs de poulet = *four chicken breasts*

un sachet de vanille sucré =*a sachet of sweetened vanilla*

une fusion de cèdre, de santal, de bois de rose = *a fusion of cedar, sandalwood and rosewood*

une cuillerée à café de jus de citron = *a teaspoon of lemon juice*

un sac de riz vaut mieux que les pommes de terre = *a bag of rice is better for you than potatoes*

250 grammes de fromage de chèvre = *250 g of goats' cheese*

une maison de poupées = *dolls' house*

l'ensemble de mes dessins = *the entire collection of my drawings*

un article de 200 mots = *an article 200 words long*

un quart d'heure = *quarter of an hour*

on a deux heures de retard = *we're two hours late*

avancer de deux jours = *to bring forward by two days*

réduire de cinq euros = *reduce by five euros*

battre quelqu'un de deux mètres / d'un dixième de seconde = *to beat someone by two metres / by a tenth of a second*

* see 309 **à**

338 **de** with expressions of quantity

J'ai envie d'explorer des voies nouvelles, de prendre beaucoup de risques = *I want to explore many new paths, to take lots of risks*

Son imagination délirante ne se tarit pas – il continue de mettre en scène un grand nombre de vedettes dans des décors kitsch = *his wild imagination doesn't dry up – he continues to present a large number of celebrities in kitsch surroundings*

Ecrivez un journal intime où vous vous inventerez plein d'histoires extraordinaires = *keep a diary in which you'll invent masses of amazing stories about yourself*

30 ans d'expérience – parce que la science des plantes ne s'improvise pas, Klorane met à profit 30 années d'expérience et de recherche pour vous faire bénéficier de leurs bienfaits = *30 years' experience – because plant science can't be* *improvised, Klorane takes advantage of 30 years' experience and research to help you profit from their beneficial effects*

10% de la population française gagnent plus de 1600 euros nets par mois = *10% of the French population earns more than 1600 euros net a month*

25% des femmes de plus de 35 déclarent vivre dans la solitude sexuelle, contre 15% des hommes = *25% of women over 35 declare that they live in sexual solitude, against 15% of men*

La majorité de ceux qui ont coché la bonne réponse ne savaient pas ce qu'ils faisaient = *the majority of those who ticked the right box didn't know what they were doing*

La plupart d'entre les femmes qui ont répondu au questionnaire ne s'imaginent pas avoir une relation sexuelle sans être amoureuses = *most of the women who answered the questionnaire don't conceive of having a sexual relationship without being in love*

Ce n'est pas un scoop, la moitié d'entre nous trompe notre fiancé = *it's no scoop – half of us deceive our fiancés*

La moitié de ceux qui ont des fantasmes n'osent pas en parler = *half the people with fantasies don't dare talk about them*

Note the use of either a singular or a plural verb with **moitié**; with other expressions of quantity, including **la plupart**, a plural verb is used; see 242–244.

339 **de** expressing function, material

un livre de grammaire = *a grammar book*

un cours de français = *a French course*

une salle de réunion = *a meeting room*

des protéines de soja et de blé = *proteins of soya and wheat*

un petit sac de sport = *a small sports bag*

ses lentilles de contact vertes = *her green contact lenses*

un pantalon en toile de coton = *cotton trousers*

des boucles d'oreilles en forme de fuchsia = *earrings in the shape of fuchsias*

un spécialiste d'informatique = *a computer expert*

340 **de** expressing time

d'heure en heure = *from one hour to the next*

de temps en temps = *from time to time*

du matin au soir = *from morning to evening*

de lundi à mercredi = *from Monday to Wednesday*

du temps des ancêtres = *at the time of our ancestors*

Je serai là de dix-huit heures à vingt heures = *I'll be there from six to eight*

Je n'ai rien fait de la journée = *I haven't done a thing all day*

Une boutique pour les enfants de trois mois à douze ans = *a shop for children from three months to twelve years*

Elle est enceinte de cinq mois = *she's five months pregnant*

341 **de** indicating cause
Elle mourait d'envie de le voir = *she was dying to see him*

Ce disque éveillera des envies de protection et d'affection = *this disc will arouse a desire to be protective and tender*

Il est mort de ses blessures / d'un cancer / d'une crise cardiaque = *he died from his wounds / cancer / a heart attack*

Elle pleurait de joie / de rage / de désespoir = *she wept with joy / anger / despair*

grelotter de froid = *to shiver with cold*

342 **de** expressing manner
d'une façon / manière amusante = *in an amusing way*

C'est un film d'un goût un peu douteux = *it's a film of dubious taste*

Il faut tirer de toutes ses forces = *you need to pull with all your might*

Il a répondu d'un geste obscène = *he replied with an obscene gesture*

Elle vit de haricots et lentilles = *she lives on beans and lentils*

frapper du pied = *to kick*

battre des mains = *to clap*

cligner des yeux = *to wink*

Il a poussé la porte de son pied = *he kicked the door open*

Il l'a cogné de sa tête = *he gave him a headbutt*

See 347.

de in passive voice
Être aimé de tout le monde = *to be loved by everyone*

Ce film a été suivi d'un autre beaucoup moins original = *the film was followed by a much less original one*

See 114, 376.

343 **de** introducing the attribute of a noun or pronoun
un bras de cassé = *a broken arm*

un seul ticket de valable = *only one valid ticket*

un livre d'emprunt = *a borrowed book*

un CD d'exception = *an exceptional CD*

quelque chose d'impressionnant = *something impressive*

J'ai encore une heure de libre = *I've still got one hour free*

Quelqu'un de dynamique a réussi à la faire sortir de soi = *some dynamic person succeeded in bringing her out of herself*

Personne d'intéressant n'était là = *no one interesting was there*

rien de nouveau = *nothing new*

Rien de si aimable qu'un homme séduisant, mais rien de plus odieux qu'un séducteur = *there's nothing more agreeable than a seductive man, but nothing more hateful than a seducer*

Ce parfum a quelque chose d'intemporel = *there's something timeless about this perfume*

Ce qu'il y a d'attirant chez elle, c'est sa naïveté = *what's attractive about her is her innocence*

Vous faites comme si de rien n'était = *you're acting as if nothing had happened*

ce qu'il y a d'intéressant = *the interesting thing is*

344 *de* introducing an infinitive

Elle se dit flattée d'être considérée comme l'une des sportives les plus sexy. Et d'ajouter: « Ma maman me répète tellement que je suis la plus jolie, que je vais finir par le croire » = *she says she's flattered to be considered one of the most sexy sporting stars. Then she adds, 'My mum tells me so often that I'm the prettiest that I'll finish up believing it'*

Pas de panique – les débuts des pères célibataires sont souvent difficiles, mais on prend vite le rythme, c'est le papa expérimenté qui le dit. Et d'ajouter qu'on adore entrer dans la peau d'un papa poule = *don't panic – it's often very difficult for a single dad to get started, but you get into the rhythm, it's an experienced dad who's telling you. I should also add that you can't beat getting into the skin of a daddy hen*

Tout est utile, assure le Dr Elisabeth Fresnel, directrice du Laboratoire de la voix. Et de poursuivre: Les Anglo-Saxons apprennent très tôt à parler en public = *everything has its uses, Dr Elisabeth Fresnel, director of the Voice Lab, assures us, and she continues: Anglo-Saxons learn to speak in public early on*

345 *de* forming expressions

Indicating age

un jeune homme de 20 ans = *a 20-year-old young man*

une fille âgée de 13 ans = *a 13-year-old girl*

Indicating a measurement

un mur haut de 2 mètres = *a wall two metres high*

une rivière large d'un demi kilomètre = *a river half a kilometre wide*

Elle a les jambes longues de 80 cm = *her legs are 80 cms long*

Set expressions

d'un air triste = *with a sad look*

Vous riez l'air de rien = *you're laughing as if nothing had happened*

De l'avis de mon professeur = *in my teacher's opinion*

Remercie-la de ma part = *thank her on my behalf*

Je le connais de vue / de réputation = *I know him by sight / by reputation*

d'un côté / de l'autre (côté) = *on the one hand / on the other*

de tout mon coeur = *with all my heart*

en cas de rébellion = *in case of a rebellion*

Au risque d'encaisser un refus = *at the risk of getting a refusal*

jamais de ma vie = *never in my life*

Tout au long de l'année les jeunes diplômés peuvent placer leur CV en ligne = *all year round newly qualified young people can put their cv on line*

Les résultats seront publiés au fur et à mesure de leur arrivée = *the results will be published as and when they arrive*

346 de crainte de / de peur de = for fear of

De crainte de / de peur de are only used with an infinitive –

De crainte de prendre des kilos, il a décidé de renoncer aux hamburgers et aux frites = *for fear of putting on weight, he decided to give up hamburgers and chips*

De peur d'effrayer votre partenaire peu expérimentée, vous devez dompter vos élans érotiques = *for fear of frightening your inexperienced partner, you must control your erotic impulses*

347 de façon à / de manière à = so as to

De façon à and **de manière à** are only used with an infinitive –

Je dois me forcer à être devant le public, de manière à apprendre le courage, la patience = *I have to force myself to appear before an audience, so as to learn courage and patience*

Une tunique kimono, très souple en viscose noire et rouge de façon à jouer en toute simplicité la carte de l'élégance = *a very soft kimono in black and red viscose so as to play very simply the elegance card*

348 depuis = since

With a date or point of time

depuis 1994 = *since 1994*

depuis le début = *since the beginning*

J'apprends le français depuis l'âge de onze ans = *I've been learning French since I was eleven*

Je vivais avec elle depuis juillet dernier = *I had been living with her since last July*

Elle luttait pour reconquérir ses droits depuis la fin de 2001 = *she had been fighting to reclaim her rights since the end of 2001*

Je ne l'ai pas vue depuis 2004 – *I haven't seen her since 2004*

depuis = *for* with length of time
depuis toujours = *for ever*

Il travaille là depuis douze ans = *he's been working there for twelve years*

Je vivais avec elle depuis longtemps = *I had been living with her for a long time*

Il est directeur artistique depuis cinq ans = *he's been artistic director for five years*

Je n'ai pas eu de leurs nouvelles depuis cinq ans = *I haven't had any news about them for five years*

See 140, 142.

349 **derrière** = behind
Le meilleur endroit pour le parfum, c'est derrière vos oreilles = *the best spot for perfume is behind your ears*

Serrez vos bras derrière votre dos tout en inspirant = *squeeze your arms behind your back while breathing in*

Quelquefois nous révélons ce que nous préférerions cacher derrière notre sourire = *sometimes we reveal what we would prefer to hide behind our smile*

Derrière cette histoire il y a des vérités qu'on ne peut pas éviter = *behind this story there are some truths you can't avoid*

350 **dès** = from
dès le début = *from the beginning / the outset*

dès maintenant = *from now on*

Dès le premier mouvement du foetus = *from the first movement of the foetus*

Dès les premières années de la vie = *from the earliest years of life*

Dès le moment où il l'a vue = *from the moment he saw her*

351 **devant** = in front of, before, faced with
mettre un pied devant l'autre = *to put one foot in front of the other*

Quand il n'est pas devant la télé, il se bat avec sa soeur = *when he's not in front of the telly, he's fighting his sister*

Je l'ai trouvé assis devant son ordinateur = *I found him sitting in front of his computer*

Je l'ai vue devant le bar à parler à mon rival = *I saw her at the bar talking to my rival*

Tous les hommes sont égaux devant la loi = *all men are equal before the law*

Le rôle des pleurs – manifester l'affliction éprouvée devant quelque situation pénible = *the role of tears – to demonstrate the distress experienced in the face of some painful situation*

Devant une personne qui se plaint d'être fatiguée le diagnostic de dépression est souvent évoqué = *faced with someone who complains about being tired, a diagnosis of depression is often mentioned*

Le bébé fait des grimaces devant les saveurs salées = *babies make faces when confronted with salty flavours*

Elle ne recule devant rien pour filer avec le mec = *she doesn't flinch one bit about making off with the guy*

Elle avait mis son pull devant derrière = *she had put her jumper on back to front*

352 **du côté de** = as for

Du côté des pellicules, pour les éradiquer, faites deux shampooings successifs = *as for dandruff, in order to eradicate it, shampoo your hair twice in succession*

Du côté des repas, il est important de retrouver le rythme des trois repas par jour = *as far as meals are concerned, it's important to get back to eating three meals a day*

The expression is sometimes shortened to just **côté** –

Côté gastronomie. . . . côté hygiène . . . = *from a gastronomic point of view . . . from a hygienic point of view . . .*

353 **du haut de** = from the top of

Il a calculé la possibilité d'un saut à l'élastique du haut de la falaise = *he calculated the possibility of a bungee jump from the top of the cliff*

Elle a récité le poème du haut du balcon = *she recited the poem from the balcony*

354 **durant** = for, during

Durant is virtually restricted to written French.

Durant des heures = *for hours*

Durant cette période de notre histoire = *during that period of our history*

En prendre deux le matin et à midi durant dix jours = *take two, morning and midday, for ten days*

Il m'a calomniée durant toute ma scolarité = *he bad-mouthed me throughout my time at school*

355 *en*

En is being used more and more frequently in contemporary French – in situations where in the past **dans** would have occurred. When its use contrasts with that of **dans**, it tends at times to have a more general, less specific value – this is because **dans** is usually accompanied by an article, whereas it is unusual for *en* so to be. As soon as some qualification of the noun occurs, *en* is replaced by *dans* + definite or indefinite article.

En le never occurs, *en la* very rarely, but *en l'*, as in the first example in the next section, is quite common. *En* is widely used in many fixed expressions.

356 *en* expressing position

en l'air = *in the air*

en région parisienne = *in the Paris area*

en métropole = *in the capital*

en banlieue = *in the suburbs*

en province = *in the provinces*

en montagne = *in the mountains*

en car = *in a coach, by coach*

en voiture = *in a car, by car*

en train = *in a train, by train*

en avion = *in a plane, by plane*

en bateau = *in a boat, by boat*

en ambulance = *in an ambulance, by ambulance*

en ville = *in town*

aller en ville = *to go to town*

en mer = *at sea*

en prison = *in prison*

en centre sportif = *in the sports centre*

en ligue des champions = *in the champions' league*

aller en classe = *to go to school*

être en sixième = *to be in year 5*

être en terminale = *to be in year 11*

être en faculté / en fac = *to be at university*

en librairie / en pharmacie = *in a bookshop, in bookshops / in a chemist's, in chemists'*

357 *en* expressing time

en hiver = *in winter*

en été = *in summer*

en automne* = *in autumn*

en janvier = *in January*

en juin = *in June*

en novembre = *in November*

en 2003 = *in 2003*

en l'an 2004 = *in the year 2004, in 2004*

mardi en quinze = *a fortnight on Tuesday*

demain en huit = *a week tomorrow*

en début de séance = *at the beginning of the session*

Je voudrais vivre autre chose en ce début du troisième millénaire = *I should like to live differently at the beginning of this third millennium*

en fin de journée = *at the end of the day*

en même temps = *at the same time*

en première / deuxième mi-temps = *in the first / second half* (of a match)

en retard = *late*

Il est en troisième année de thèse sur la liposuccion = *he's in the third year of his thesis on liposuction*

partir en weekend = *to go away for the weekend*

lancé en décembre dernier = *launched last December*

Dis adieu à la fatigue en deux temps trois mouvements = *say goodbye to tiredness in double quick time*

En trente ans nous avons grandi = *in 30 years we've got bigger*

En une semaine ce programme va vous réinvigorer* = *this programme will reinvigorate you in a week*

Je l'ai fait en trente minutes = *I did it in half an hour*

Il l'avait lu en une heure = *he'd read it in an hour*

En ce moment je la vois beaucoup = *I see her a lot at the moment*

* but ***au printemps*** = *in the spring*
** For the difference between ***dans*** and ***en*** in this context, see 390.

358 **en** with clothing, materials, containers
With clothing
en maillot de bain / en bikini = *in a bathing costume / in a bikini*

en tenue de soirée = *in evening dress*

en uniforme = *in uniform*

en jean = *in jeans*

une robe en coton = *a cotton dress*

une veste en cuir = *a leather jacket*

L'avocat plaide en robe noire = *a lawyer appears in court in a black robe*

Rien ne vaut un costume en lin = *nothing equals a linen suit*

en with materials and containers
une barrière en fer = *an iron gate*

un bol en bois = *a wooden bowl*

une statue en bronze = *a bronze statue*

un bracelet en or = *a gold bracelet*

des boucles d'oreille en argent = *silver earrings*

Il se présente en plaquette de vingt-huit jours = *it comes in a 28-day packet*

Un médecin conseillera un antiviral en crème ou en comprimés = *a doctor will prescribe an anti-viral cream or tablets*

Votre alimentation est trop riche en graisse et en sucre = *your diet is over-rich in fat and sugar*

359 *en* with names of languages and countries
en with languages
en français = *in French*

en espagnol = *in Spanish*

Traduis ça en roumain = *translate that into Romanian*

en with names of countries
   See 393.

360 *en* in fixed expressions
être en voyage = *to be on a trip*

en vacances = *on holiday*

en route = *en route*

en vente = *for sale*

en moyenne = *on average*

Nous avons gagné en moyenne 300 euros chacune = *each of us earned on average 300 euros*

en feu = *on fire*

rester en silence = *to stay quiet*

Votre père est remarquable – il souffre en silence d'un problème de prostate = *your father's incredible – he suffers in silence with a prostate problem*

être en deuil = *to be in mourning*

dormir en paix = *to sleep in peace*

être en danger = *to be in danger*

être en difficulté = *to be in difficulty*

mettre en valeur = *to highlight*

se mettre en marche = *to set out*

en matière de = *as far as . . . is concerned*

Elle conseille sur leurs droits en matière de contrats immobiliers = *she's an adviser on people's rights in the area of property contracts*

en l'occurrence = *in this case, in this instance*

en l'honneur de = *in honour of*

en présence de = *in the presence of*

en direct = *live* (broadcast)

Eurofoot 2004 – en direct de Lisbonne = *Euro 2004, live from Lisbon*

en jeu = *at stake*

en son nom = *in her name, in his name*

en revanche = *on the other hand*

en effet = *in fact* (supporting previous statement)

Rien ne sert de se retenir d'éternuer. En effet ce mécanisme de défense naturelle permet d'expulser hors du nez un corps étranger irritant = *there's no point holding back your sneezes. In fact this natural defence mechanism enables us to expel irritating foreign bodies from our nose*

en fait = *in fact* (contradicting previous statement)

en tant que = *as*

En tant qu'élève-fonctionnaire vous gagnerez 6 000 euros par mois = *as a trainee civil servant you'll earn 6,000 euros a month*

en promotion / en promo = *on special offer*

en solde = *in a sale*

Les articles achetés en solde doivent bénéficier des mêmes droits que les autres = *goods bought in a sale benefit from the same rights as any others*

gagner en mystère = *to grow in mystery*

avoir le vent en poupe = *to have the wind in your sails*

en cas de = *in case of*

en l'espèce = *in this instance*

Se déguiser en policier, c'est marrant = *disguising yourself as a policeman is a laugh*

agir en spécialiste = *to act as a specialist*

en plus = *in addition*

En plus des dix déjà existants = *in addition to the ten you've already got*

se mettre en colère = *to get angry*

en état de guerre = *in a state of war*

partir en tournée = *to go on tour* (eg of pop group)

en version originale / en VO = *in the original* (eg of film)

être en chômage = *to be out of work*

être en grève = *to be on strike*

en partie = *in part*

Votre succès dépend en partie du statut de votre directeur de thèse = *your success depends in part upon your thesis supervisor's status*

en réalité = *in reality, really*

En réalité, le choix dépend du résultat voulu = *in reality, what you choose depends upon the result you want*

un film en noir et blanc = *a black-and-white film*

parler en connaissance de cause = *to speak with full knowledge of the facts*

avec des teintes brillantes en contraste = *with brilliant contrasting tints*

des silhouettes en 3D = *silhouettes in 3D*

361 en-dehors de = outside, apart from
Je voulais la rencontrer en-dehors de la ville = *I wanted to meet her outside the town*

Je ne vois personne en-dehors de deux potes = *I don't see anyone apart from a couple of mates*

362 en dépit de = in spite of
En dépit de ce que je lui dis, ma femme réserve toujours une place dans notre lit pour son chien = *in spite of what I say to her, my wife still reserves a place in our bed for her dog*

En dépit de sa réticence, elle s'y habituera en douceur = *in spite of her reluctance, she'll gradually get used to it*

363 entre = between, among, through
entre nous = *between ourselves*

entre parenthèses / entre guillemets = *in brackets / in inverted commas*

entre le 25 et le 30 mai = *between the 25th and 30th May*

La route se faufile entre les petits villages = *the road winds its way through the tiny villages*

Un décalage entre les problèmes perçus par les parents et leurs enfants = *a gap between the problems perceived by parents and their children*

43% d'entre eux souhaitent être mieux informés sur le suicide = *43% of them want to be better informed on suicide*

L'enfance, une époque bénie entre toutes = *childhood, a time blessed amongst all others*

364 **envers** = towards

Je ne sens que de la reconnaissance envers elle = *I feel nothing but gratitude towards her*

Son attitude envers son travail est décevante = *her attitude towards her work is disappointing*

Si vous ressentez une attirance envers une de vos amies, c'est le moment de choisir votre camp = *if you feel yourself attracted towards one of your friends the same sex as you, that's the moment when you have to decide which side you're on*

365 **environ** = about

Un petit bijou de technologie qui coûte environ 150 000 euros = *a little peach of technology which costs about 150,000 euros*

À environ dix mètres, je ne vois plus rien sans mes lunettes = *at about ten metres I can't see a thing without my glasses*

366 **excepté** = except for, apart from

J'aime toutes les couleurs, excepté le bleu = *I like all the colours, except for blue*

Tout le monde sera là, excepté mon cousin = *everyone will be there apart from my cousin*

See 198.

367 **face à** = opposite, facing

face à l'hôpital = *opposite the hospital*

face aux caméras = *facing the cameras*

Face à l'augmentation des ventes de médicaments contre le cholestérol = *faced with the increasing sales of anti-cholesterol remedies*

Ils se disent désemparés face aux réponses reçues = *they say they're confused when confronted by the answers received*

368 **grâce à** = thanks to

Grâce à l'action de la vitamine C = *thanks to the action of vitamin C*

J'ai décroché mon bac grâce à mes lectures = *I got my A-levels thanks to all the reading I'd done*

369 **hors de** = out of
hors d'haleine = *out of breath*

J'étais hors de moi qu'il ait pu pensé ainsi = *I was beside myself that he could have such thoughts*

Tu seras hors de danger dans les toilettes = *you'll be out of danger in the loos*

370 **jusqu'à** = as far as, until
aller jusqu'à Biarritz = *to go as far as Biarritz*

jusqu'à présent = *up to the present moment*

jusqu'au 14 février = *until 14th February*

Restez vigilante jusqu'en septembre = *stay on your guard till September*

Vous ne percez jamais vos boutons, vous les laisser mûrir jusqu'à éclosion spontanée = *never squeeze spots – let them ripen until they form a head spontaneously*

J'irais jusqu'à dire qu'il ne faut pas réprimer vos éternuements sous peine de provoquer une nouvelle crise = *I'd go so far as to say that you shouldn't repress your sneezes – you might induce another attack*

Nous n'allons pas jusqu'à accepter cette décision ridicule = *we're not going so far as to accept that ridiculous decision*

371 **le long de** = along
Il traînait le long des couloirs avant d'entrer = *he wandered along the corridors before going in*

Promenade à vélo le long des quais de la Seine = *a bike ride along the banks of the Seine*

372 **lors de** = during, at the time of
Lors des dernières rencontres parlementaires = *at the time of / during the recent meetings of Parliament*

Lors d'un récent congrès = *at the time of / during a recent conference*

373 **malgré** = in spite of
Malgré les demandes croissantes des parents = *in spite of increasing demands from parents*

Malgré tout, il vaut mieux continuer = *in spite of everything, it's better to carry on*

374 **par** = through, by, per, on, in
par expressing position
voyager par chemin de fer / par le train = *to travel by rail / by train*

voyager par avion / par bateau = *to travel by plane / by boat*

par ici / par là = *this way / that way*

par-ci par-là = *hither and thither*

Vous regardez par la fenêtre les souris qui s'amusent = *through the window you watch the birds enjoying themselves*

Il dormait sur un matelas sans draps par terre = *he slept on a mattress without sheets on the floor*

par expressing time
par un temps pluvieux = *in rainy weather*

par le temps qui court = *as it* [the weather] *is*

par une journée d'hiver = *on a winter's day*

+ 20% par an = *+ 20% per year / + 20% a year*

En période d'extrême chaleur il faut boire 2,5 à 3 litres d'eau par jour = *in times of extreme heat, you should drink between 2.5 and 3 litres of water a day*

par expressing an agent, animate or inanimate – see 414 *de* and 390
Une efficacité prouvée par des dermatologues = *an effectiveness proved by dermatologists*

Commencez par un échauffement suffisant = *begin with sufficient warm-up exercises*

Un entraîneur a été mordu par un chien errant = *a trainer was bitten by a dog off the lead*

Il s'exprime par gestes = *he expresses himself through gestures*

On remplace le sucre par le fructose = *sugar may be replaced by fructose*

par in fixed expressions
par courrier = *by mail*

par écrit = *in writing*

par ordre alphabétique = *in alphabetical order*

par milliers = *in thousands, in their thousands*

par honte / par reconnaissance = *out of shame / out of gratitude*

par ignorance / par amour = *out of ignorance / out of love*

par exemple = *for example*

par contre = *on the other hand*

375 *par-dessous* = underneath
Pour y arriver il fallait passer par-dessous la haie = *to get there we had to climb under the hedge*

376 *par-dessus* = over

Il se plante derrière vous et regarde par-dessus votre épaule = *he plonks himself behind you and looks over your shoulder*

par-dessus le marché = *into the bargain*

377 *parmi* = among

Le village se trouve parmi les plus belles montagnes du monde = *the village is set amongst the most beautiful mountains in the world*

C'est une plainte exprimée surtout parmi les femmes = *it's a complaint commonly expressed among women*

Parmi les hommes l'idée de « mieux habillé » a changé = *among / for men the idea of 'best dressed' has changed*

378 *par suite de* = as a result of

Par suite de l'anxiété, vous tremblez comme une feuille à chaque fois que vous prononcez un discours devant une assemblée = *as a result of anxiety, you tremble like a leaf every time you give a speech at a meeting*

Par suite de sa délicatesse et générosité, vous jouissez de moments inoubliables ensemble = *because of her sensitivity and generosity you enjoy unforgettable moments together*

379 *pendant* = for, during

pendant la journée = *during the day*

Je l'ai attendue pendant une heure = *I waited for her for an hour*

On ne vous dit plus rien pendant des mois = *no one says anything else to you for months*

Pendant les années 70 je portais un pull col V en mohair rouge = *during the 70s I used to wear a V-neck pullover in red mohair*

See 390.

380 *pour* = for

pour expressing time

Elle n'était là que pour quelques jours = *she was only there for a few days*

pour la troisième année consécutive = *for the third consecutive year*

Pour cet été l'association recherche des étudiants en médecine = *for this summer the association is seeking medical students*

Pour l'avenir immédiat elle n'a aucun projet professionnel = *for the immediate future she hasn't got any professional plans*

See 390.

pour in other contexts

C'est le minimum à faire pour ceux qu'on appelle les nouveaux pauvres = *it's the least that can be done for those we call the new poor*

Petits soins pour zones sensibles = *delicate care for delicate areas*

Une bonne nouvelle pour tous les parents concernés = *good news for all concerned parents*

Avec symptôme de désintérêt pour son travail et sa vie = *with the symptom of lack of interest in his work and life*

Pour son nouveau film il veut une jeune fille susceptible d'incarner un idéal de pureté = *for his latest film he wants a girl who is capable of embodying an ideal of purity*

Bouger pour une saine fatigue = *keep moving for good, healthy tiredness*

Eau de toilette pour homme = *eau de toilette for men*

Elle se prend / se passe pour une star = *she considers herself / passes herself off as a star*

Pour vous faciliter la vie, voici notre sélection d'articles sympas = *in order to simplify your life, here's our selection of great items*

Les ados peuvent utiliser le service « Fil santé jeunes » pour poser les questions qui les tracassent = *youngsters can use the Help Line to ask the questions that worry them*

381 **près de** = close to, near
L'essentiel de mon travail consistait à me tenir près de lui = *the essential part of my work involved me staying close to him*

J'aime garder mes choses près de moi = *I like keeping my things close to me*

Près du magasin il y a toujours des mecs qui chahutent = *near the shop there are always some guys messing about*

382 **quant à** = as for
quant à moi = *as for me*

Quant aux pères, même si on n'en a pas, on a une image de père = *as for fathers, even if you haven't got one, you've got an image of them*

383 **sans** = without
Je suis sans regrets = *I'm without regret, I have no regrets*

Je traîne de salle en salle sans but précis = *I mope from room to room without any precise aim*

Une moto sans silencieux = *a motorbike without a silencer*

De l'énergie sans les kilos = *energy without putting on weight*

sans fin = *endless, ad infinitum*

les sans domicile fixe = *the homeless*

les sans-papiers = *illegal immigrants*

Ils peuvent poser des questions personnelles sans révéler leur identité = *they can ask personal questions without revealing their identity*

Vous pouvez faire votre shopping sans quitter la maison = *you can do your shopping without leaving the house*

384 **sauf** = except for, apart from
Tous les premiers jeudis du mois à partir de 21 h sauf janvier = *all the first Thursdays of the month from 9pm except for January*

Si un mec vous plaît, dites-lui tout – sauf la vérité = *if a guy appeals to you, tell him everything – apart from the truth*

385 **selon** = according to
Selon un sondage réalisé par ce magazine = *according to a poll undertaken by this magazine*

Selon cette étude, un bâton de rouge à lèvres exerce un pouvoir de séduction incroyable sur les hommes = *according to this study, a lipstick exerts an unbelievable power of seduction on men*

386 **sous** = underneath, beneath
Sous ma chemise j'aime porter un bustier en jean = *underneath my blouse I like wearing a denim bustier*

Sous cette plainte courante = *beneath this frequent complaint*

Le couteau sous la gorge = *with a knife under / at his throat*

Voir la vie sous un angle convenable = *to see life from an appropriate angle*

J'ai sous la main tout ce dont j'ai besoin pendant la journée = *I've got everything I need during the day to hand*

Son homosexualité, est-ce que on peut continuer de la passer sous silence? = *can we keep on keeping quiet about his homosexuality?*

sous la pluie = *in the rain*

sous la présidence de = *under the presidency of*

sous peu = *shortly*

sous un jour favorable = *in a favourable light*

sous tous les rapports = *in all respects*

387 **suivant** = following
Suivant la discussion, j'ai dit que j'étais gay = *following the discussion I said I was gay*

Suivant une enquête sur la nutrition des teenagers = *following an investigation into the eating habits of teenagers*

388 **sur** = on, over, about
Passez le jet sur tout le corps = *direct the jet all over your body*

Le pistolet sur la tempe = *with a pistol to his temple*

Le point sur ces interventions = *the latest on these speeches*

On vous dit tout sur la meilleure façon de marcher = *we tell you everything about the best way to walk*

Un test clinique sur 28 femmes = *a clinical test on 28 women*

Un Français sur quatre souffrira d'hémorroïdes, un sur dix s'en plaint régulièrement = *one French person out of four will suffer from piles, one out of ten will complain about it regularly*

Pourquoi cette sensation de « chape de plomb » sur nos épaules? = *why do we have this sensation of a 'leaden cloak' on our shoulders?*

Un programme bâti sur mesure = *a programme made to measure*

Sur des milliers de gens je n'ai eu que quelques très grosses mauvaises surprises = *out of thousands of people I've only had a few unpleasant surprises*

sur le parking = *in the (open-air) car park*

sur la mer = *at sea*

sur le stade = *in the stadium*

sur le ring = *in the boxing ring*

marcher sur la route / le trottoir = *to walk on the road / the pavement*

donner sur la rue = *to look onto the street* (of a building)

sur scène / sur la scène = *on stage*

la clef est sur la porte = *the key is in the door*

grimper sur le toit = *to climb onto the roof*

être sur un vélo = *to be on a bike*

revenir sur ses pas = *to retrace your steps*

un livre sur la mode = *a book on fashion*

naviguer sur Internet = *to surf the net*

sur Internet = *on the Internet*

sur un ton satisfait / content = *in a satisfied / content tone of voice*

389 **vers** = to, towards, about

Poussez les bras et les jambes vers l'arrière = *push your arms and legs towards the back*

Il s'est tourné vers les autres = *he turned to the others*

Nos discussions se sont orientées vers le sexe = *our discussion turned towards sex*

vers 15 heures = *about three o'clock*

vers le début du mois = *towards the beginning of the month*

390 Slight shifts in meaning brought out by varying the prepositions

Accurate handling of prepositions is a very delicate and complicated matter and one that puts the seal on competent use of the language. There are one or two patterns of alternation between prepositions that allow shades of meaning to be conveyed in a subtle way. There are also occasions, often fixed expressions, where a particular noun attracts one preposition rather than another

à / dans

à cet endroit = *in this place*

dans ce lieu = *in this place*

à / dans / en

When translating English *in*, a distinction may be drawn between the physical and the abstract values of the preposition: ***dans*** implies the former, ie a more specific, more concrete or physical value and ***à*** the latter, ie a more vague, less well-defined value –

Les parents sont entrés dans l'école pour voir le prof de leur fils = *the parents went into the school to see their son's teacher*

Il est entré à l'école en 1998 = *he began his school career in 1998*

Dans mon jardin il y a une grande variété de plantes = *in my garden there's a wide variety of plants*

J'aime travailler au jardin pour profiter de l'air frais = *I like working in the garden to benefit from the fresh air*

The same applies to the following examples –

être à Paris / être dans Paris = *to be in Paris*

J'ai toujours aimé être à Paris = *I've always liked being in Paris*

Trouver une station d'essence dans Paris est de plus en plus difficile = *finding a petrol station in Paris is getting more and more difficult*

être à la campagne / dans la campagne = *to be in the country*

être aux champs / dans les champs = *to be in the fields*

être au salon / dans le salon = *to be in the drawing room*

être à la cuisine / dans la cuisine = *to be in the kitchen*

être à l'ombre / dans l'ombre = *to be in the shade*

tomber à l'eau / dans l'eau = *to fall in the water*

However, ***à la ferme*** = *on the farm*, whereas ***dans la ferme*** = *in the farmhouse*.
  In in relation to names of countries, departments, etc, is dealt with in 393.
  In / on in relation to streets is often represented by a zero preposition in French –

Visitez son studio rue Guénégaud = *visit her studio in the rue Guénégaud*

Son nouveau restaurant se trouve place de l'Église = *his new restaurant is situated on the Place de l'Église*

In / by with modes of transport may be translated by ***dans, en*** or ***par***, with occasional slight differences of interpretation –

voyager dans / par le bus, dans / par le train = *to travel by bus, train*

voyager en ambulance, en auto, en avion, en bateau, en hélicoptère, en vélo, en moto, en voiture = *to travel by ambulance, car, plane, boat, helicopter, bike, motorbike, car*

voyager par bateau = *to travel by boat*

voyager dans un taxi, dans une ambulance = *to travel in a taxi, an ambulance*

As with the ***à / dans*** contrast above, the use of ***dans*** underlines the physical position of the traveller.

dans l'avion = *in the plane* (stressing the position of who or what is doing the travelling)

en avion = *by air* (stressing the method of transport)

par avion = *by airmail*

When it is desired to qualify the noun, ***dans*** or ***par***, not ***en***, must be used –

Je suis arrivé dans la voiture de mon mec = *I arrived in my boyfriend's car*

Je suis arrivé par le train de quinze heures = *I arrived by the three o'clock train*

à / de

With verbs denoting moving/snatching, ***à*** is used to refer to people, ***de*** to things –

Elle l'a arraché à son amie = *she snatched it from her friend*

Il l'a enlevé / ôté de la table = *he took it from / off the table*

When linking two nouns, ***à*** denotes that the nouns form a single unit and stresses the function of the object, whereas ***de*** denotes a looser connection, stressing what is contained in the object.

un pot à moutarde = *a mustard pot*

un verre à vin = *a wine glass*

un pot de moutarde = *a pot of mustard*

un verre de vin = *a glass of wine*

The first two items could be empty, whereas the second two must contain some mustard or wine.

à sa manière = *in his / her way*

d'une certaine manière = *in a certain way*

au moins = *at least* (of numbers)

Il y a au moins dix coffrets de portables parmi lesquels choisir = *there are at least ten mobile holders to choose from*

du moins = *at least, the bottom line*

Les chanteuses à grosse voix prennent dix rides à chaque concert – du moins c'est ce qu'on prétend = *female singers with big voices develop ten wrinkles per concert – at least that's what's claimed*

(*jouer* +) *à / de*
With ***jouer***, ***à*** is used with names of sports and ***de*** with musical instruments

jouer au tennis, au foot, au golf = *to play tennis, football, golf*

jouer d'un instrument de musique, du piano, de la guitare, de la batterie = *to play a musical instrument, the piano, the guitar, the drums*

See 301.

à / en
être au village = *to be in the village*

être en ville = *to be in town*

à la mi-temps = *at half-time*

en première / deuxième mi-temps = *during the first / second half*

à / par
When translating English *to* (in *to the ground*), use of ***à*** implies from a height, and use of ***par*** from a standing position –

Il était dans l'arbre et est tombé à terre après s'être penché trop en avant = *he was up the tree and fell to the ground because he'd leant out too far*

Il faut se jeter par terre pour éviter la fusillade de l'ennemi = *you have to throw yourself to the ground to avoid the shots coming from the enemy*

à / sur
With reference to radio and TV, the former is used generally, the second more specifically (ie to a specific station or channel) –

Il y a très peu d'émissions intéressantes à la télé = *there aren't many interesting programmes on the telly*

Sur Canal Plus il y a un grand nombre de films américains = *on Canal Plus there are lots of American films*

dans / en
When used with reference to time, ***dans*** is used to indicate that the action will be accomplished after the period of time specified by ***dans*** has elapsed; ***en*** indicates the period of time during which the action will be accomplished –

Je lui ai dit que je le ferais dans dix minutes = *I told him I'd do it in ten minutes* (begin to do it in ten minutes)

Je lui ai dit que je le ferais en dix minutes – *I told him I'd do it in ten minutes*
[it would take ten minutes to complete it]

dans / sur

The difference between (***stationner***) ***dans le parking*** and ***sur le parking*** is that the first refers to a multi-storey carpark and the latter to an open-air one; in the case of (***être***) ***dans le stade*** and (***être***) ***sur le stade***, the former refers to the spectators, the latter to the competitors/players.

dans le square = *in the square* (a small public square with a garden)

sur la place = *in the square* (a large public square)

dans l'aéroport = *at the airport* (in the airport buildings)

sur l'aéroport = *at the airport* (on the runway)

être assis dans un fauteuil = *to be sitting in an armchair*

être assis sur une chaise, un banc, un siège = *to be sitting on a chair, a bench, a seat*

dans l'allée, dans l'avenue, dans la rue = *on the path, in the avenue, in the street*

sur le boulevard, sur la chaussée, sur le chemin, sur la route, sur le trottoir = *on the boulevard, on the road* (not the pavement), *on the track, on the road, on the pavement*

de / en

When used with materials, ***de*** implies a vaguer connection than ***en***, which emphasises the material from which the object is made –

un pantalon en coton – un pantalon de coton = *cotton trousers*

de / par

When introducing the agent in the passive voice or in a similar construction (ie *I was chased **by** a mugger*), ***de*** is used when the agent is relatively passive or a state is described, ***par*** when the agent is more dynamic.

Pour avoir un buste branché, la gorge doit être enduite d'un produit luisant = *to have a really trendy bust, your neck needs to be covered with something shiny*

Servez aussitôt accompagné d'une salade de pousses d'épinard = *serve it straightaway accompanied by a salad of spinach sprouts*

Un avertissement – il est attiré par les jeunes, il te jettera rapidement pour une cadette = *a word of warning – he's attracted by young women, he'll soon throw you over for a younger version*

Pour vous aider à mincir sans vous priver trop, votre boisson habituelle doit être remplacée par un thé infusion = *to help you slim without depriving yourself too much, your usual drink must be replaced by an infusion*

However, at times these two prepositions seem to have exactly the same value and are used in identical contexts.

pendant / pour

When these prepositions are used to express a certain period of time, **pendant** normally refers to time that is past and **pour** to time to come, as the examples given under each preposition above show. However, **pendant** may also be used with reference to time to come when the event is being stressed, for example in the case of medical directions –

Une ampoule chaque matin pendant une semaine = *one capsule each morning for a week*

plus de, moins de / plus que, moins que

Plus de, moins de are used to express quantity, and normally precede a numeral, whereas **plus que, moins que** are used to express a comparison and are not necessarily followed by a numeral –

Le sac à dos ne doit pas être plus large que le dos de l'enfant et ne doit pas peser plus de 500 g pour les plus jeunes et pas plus d'un kg pour les adolescents = *the rucksack must not be wider than the child's back and must not weigh more than 500 grammes for the youngest and not more than one kg for teenagers*

Bonne nouvelle, les adultes qui goûtent sont proportionnellement plus minces que ceux qui ne goûtent pas! = *good news – adults who indulge are proportionately slimmer than those who don't!*

Pour plus d'informations, contactez notre site internet = *for more information, contact our website*

391 Prepositional alternation

In other cases, it is possible to use different prepositions before a noun without altering the sense.

remplir avec / remplir de = *to fill with*

à l' / d' / par avance = *in advance*

au début de l'après-midi / en début de l'après-midi = *early in the afternoon*

à la fin de la réunion / en fin de la réunion = *at the end of the meeting*

à l'automne / en automne = *in autumn*

dans la / en région parisienne = *in the Paris area*

dans le secret / en secret = *in secret*

dans / en l'air (note the use of an article with **en** here) = *in the air*

aux / sous les Tropiques, l'équateur = *in the Tropics, at the Equator*

à la / en faculté = *at university*

dans / sous une tente = *in a tent*

tomber dans / entre les mains de quelqu'un = *to fall into the hands of someone*

dans la semaine / en semaine = *during the week*

d'un ton sérieux / sur un ton sérieux = *in a serious tone*

de toutes façons / en tout cas = *at any rate*

en mer / sur la mer = *at sea*

échanger une chemise pour / contre une autre = *to exchange one shirt for another*

être à / en chômage = *to be out of work*

aller dans / sur la lune = *to go to the moon*

392 The interlocking of French and English prepositions

The following chart lists English prepositions and prepositional expressions and shows the French equivalents –

about	***auprès de, environ, vers***
above	***au-dessus de***
according to	***d'après, selon***
after	***après***
against	***contre***
along	***le long de***
among	***chez, entre, parmi***
apart from	***au-delà de, en-dehors de, excepté, sauf***
around	***auprès de***
as a result of	***par suite de***
as far as	***jusqu'à***
as for	***du côté de, quant à***
at	***à, en, sous, sur***
at the end of	***au bout de***
at the home of	***chez***
at the time of	***lors de***
because of	***à cause de***
before	***avant, devant***
behind	***derrière***
below	***au-dessous de***
beneath	***sous***
beside	***hors de***
between	***entre***
beyond	***au-delà de, au-dessus de***
by	***à, de, en, par***
by virtue of	***à force de***
close to	***près de***
during	***au cours de, dans, durant, lors de, pendant***
except for	***excepté, sauf***
faced with	***devant***
facing	***face à***
following	***suivant***
for	***à, chez, depuis, durant, en, par, pendant, pour***
for fear of	***de crainte de, de peur de***
from	***à, à partir de, d'après, dans, de, dès, sous***
from the top of	***du haut de***
in	***à, chez, dans, de, en, entre, par, sous, sur***

(cont.)

including	*(y) compris*
in comparison with	*à côté de*
in front of	*devant*
in order to	*afin de*
instead of	*au lieu de*
in spite of	*en dépit de, malgré*
in the course of	*au cours de*
into	*dans*
near	*près de*
next to	*à côté de*
of	*de, entre*
on	*à, de, en, par, sur*
opposite	*face à*
out of	*dans, hors de, par, sur*
outside	*en-dehors de*
over	*au-dessus de, par-dessus de, sur*
per	*par*
round	*auprès de*
since	*depuis*
so as to	*de façon à, de manière à*
subject to	*à condition de*
than	*de*
thanks to	*grâce à*
through	*à travers, entre, par*
till	*jusqu'à*
to	*à, en, vers*
towards	*envers, vers*
under	*au-dessous de, sous*
underneath	*au-dessous de, par-dessous de, sous*
unless	*à moins de*
until	*jusqu'à*
up to	*à*
with	*à, avec, de*
without	*sans*
zero	*à, de, en, par, sans*

393 Prepositions with place names

in

1 With names of countries

With masculine names of countries beginning with a consonant – ***au***

in Europe

au Danemark = *in Denmark,* ***au Luxembourg*** = *in Luxemburg,* ***aux Pays Bas*** = *in the Netherlands,* ***au Pays de Galles*** = *in Wales,* ***au Portugal*** = *in Portugal,* ***au Royaume-Uni*** = *in the United Kingdom*

in Africa

au Bénin = *in Benin,* ***au Botswana*** = *in Botswana,* ***au Burkina Faso*** = *in Burkina Faso,* ***au Burundi*** = *in Burundi,* ***au Cameroun*** = *in Cameroon,* ***au Gabon*** = *in Gabon,* *au Ghana* = *in Ghana*, *au Kenya* = *in Kenya*, *au Libéria* = *in Liberia*, *au Malawi* = *in Malawi*, *au Mali* = *in Mali*, *au Maroc* = *in Morocco*, *au Mozambique* = *in Mozambique*, *au Niger* = *in Niger*, *au Nigéria* = *in Nigeria*, *au Ruanda* = *in Rwanda*, *au Sénégal* = *in Senegal*, *au Soudan* = *in Sudan*, *au Tchad* = *in Chad*, *au Togo* = *in Togo*, *au Zimbabwe* = *in Zimbabwe*

in Asia

au Bangladesh = *in Bangladesh*, *au Cambodge* = *in Cambodia*, *au Japon* = *in Japan*, *au Laos* = *in Laos*, *au Népal* = *in Nepal*, *au Pakistan* = *in Pakistan*, *au Tibet* = *in Tibet*, *au Vietnam* = *in Vietnam*

in the Middle East

au Liban = *in Lebanon*, *au Yémen* = *in Yemen*

in the Americas

au Brésil = *in Brazil*, *au Canada* = *in Canada*, *au Chili* = *in Chile*, *au Costa Rica* = *in Costa Rica*, *aux États-Unis* = *in the United States*, *au Guatémala* = *in Guatemala*, *au Honduras* = *in Honduras*, *au Mexique* = *in Mexico*, *au Panama* = *in Panama*, *au Paraguay* = *in Paraguay*, *au Salvador* = *in San Salvador*, *au Vénézuéla* = *in Venezuela*

With masculine names beginning with a vowel – *en*

en Équateur = *in Ecuador*, *en Irak* = *in Iraq*, *en Iran* = *in Iran*, *en Israël* = *in Israel*

With feminine names – *en*

in Europe

en Albanie = *in Albania*, *en Allemagne* = *in Germany*, *en Angleterre* = *in England*, *en Autriche* = *in Austria*, *en Belgique* = *in Belgium*, *en Biélorusse* = *in Belorus*, *en Bosnie* = *in Bosnia*, *en Bulgarie* = *in Bulgaria*, *en Croatie* = *in Croatia*, *en Écosse* = *in Scotland*, *en Espagne* = *in Spain*, *en Estonie* = *in Estonia*, *en Finlande* = *in Finland*, *en France* = *in France*, *en Grande Bretagne* = *in Great Britain*, *en Grèce* = *in Greece*, *en Hollande* = *in Holland*, *en Irlande du Nord / du Sud* = *in Northern / Southern Ireland*, *en Italie* = *in Italy*, *en Lettonie* = *in Latvia*, *en Lithuanie* = *in Lithuania*, *en Norvège* = *in Norway*, *en Pologne* = *in Poland*, *en République tchèque* = *in the Czech Republic*, *en Roumanie* = *in Romania*, *en Russie* = *in Russia*, *en Serbie* = *in Serbia*, *en Slovaquie* = *in Slovakia*, *en Slovénie* = *in Slovenia*, *en Suède* = *in Sweden*, *en Suisse* = *in Switzerland*, *en Turquie* = *in Turkey*, *en Ukraine* = *in Ukraine*

in Africa

en Afrique du Sud = *in South Africa*, *en Algérie* = *in Algeria*, *en Angola* = *in Angola*, *en Éthiopie* = *in Ethiopia*, *en Guinée* = *in Guinea*, *en Libye* = *in Libya*, *en Mauritanie* = *in Mauritania*, *en Namibie* = *in Namibia*, *en Ouganda* = *in Uganda*, *en République centrafricaine* = *in the Central African Republic*, *en Sierra Léone* = *in Sierra Leone*, *en Somalie* = *in Somalia*, *en Tanzanie* = *in Tanzania*, *en Tunisie* = *in Tunisia*, *en Zambie* = *in Zambia*

in Asia and Australasia

en Afghanistan = *in Afghanistan*, *en Australie* = *in Australia*, *en Birmanie* = *in Burma*, *en Chine* = *in China*, *en Corée du Nord / du Sud* = *in North / South Korea*, *en*

Inde = *in India*, **en Indonésie** = *in Indonesia*, **en Malaisie** = *in Malaysia*, **en Nouvelle Calédonie** = *in New Caledonia*, **en Nouvelle Zélande** = *in New Zealand*, **en Thaïlande** = *in Thailand*

in the Middle East

en Arabie Séoudite = *in Saudi Arabia*, **en Égypte** = *in Egypt*, **en Jordanie** = *in Jordan*, **en Syrie** = *in Syria*

in the Americas

en Argentina = *in Argentina*, **en Bolivie** = *in Bolivia*, **en Colombie** = *in Colombia*, **en Guyane** = *in Guyana*, **en République dominicaine** = *in the Dominican Republic*, **en Uruguay** = *in Uruguay*

If the name of the country is qualified, **en** is replaced by **dans** and the definite article. This applies to both masculine and feminine names of countries –

dans la Roumanie de l'ère post-Ceausescu = *in post-Ceausescu Romania*

dans le Japon contemporain = *in contemporary Japan*

2 With names of islands and island states
Usage is more variable –

à

à Chypre = *in Cyprus*, **à Cuba** = *in Cuba*, **à Madagascar** = *in Madagascar*, **à Majorque** = *in Majorca*, **à Malte** = *in Malta*, **à (l'île) Maurice** = *in Mauritius*, **à Singapour** = *in Singapore*, **à Sri Lanka** = *in Sri Lanka*

à la

à la Dominique = *in Dominica*, **à la Jamaïque** = *in Jamaica*, **à la Réunion** = *in Réunion*

aux

aux Antilles = *in the West Indies*, **aux Bahamas** = *in the Bahamas*, **aux Baléares** = *in the Balearic Islands*, **aux Malouines** = *in the Falklands*, **aux Philippines** = *in the Philippines*

en

en Corse = *in Corsica*, **en Sardaigne** = *in Sardinia*, **en Sicile** = *in Sicily*
à or **en**

à / en Haïti = *in Haiti*
à la or **en**

à la / en Guadeloupe = *in Guadeloupe*, **à la / en Martinique** = *in Martinique*

3 With names of French regions and departments
With masculine names

dans

dans le Centre = *in the Centre*, **dans le Poitou** = *in the Poitou*, **dans le Rhône** = *in the Rhône* but **en Anjou** = *in Anjou*, **en Limousin** = *in the Limousin*

dans le Berry = *in the Berry*, **dans le Gard** = *in the Gard*, **dans le Jura** = *in the Jura*

With feminine singular names –

en

en Bretagne = *in Brittany*, **en Corrèze** = *in the Corrèze*, **en Normandie** = *in Normandy*, **en Provence** = *in Provence*, **en Saône et Loire** = *in Saône et Loire*, **en Vendée** = *in the Vendée*

dans la

dans la Charente = *in the Charente*, **dans la Haute-Garonne** = *in the Haute-Garonne*, **dans la Marne** = *in the Marne*

With feminine plural names

dans les Alpes Maritimes = *in the Alpes-Maritimes*, **dans les Hautes-Pyrénées** = *in the Hautes-Pyrénées*, **dans les Landes** = *in the Landes*

4 With names of British counties
dans

dans le Nottinghamshire, **dans le Suffolk**, **dans le Yorkshire**

exception **aux Cournouailles** = *in Cornwall*

5 With names of American states
dans

dans la Louisiane, dans le Texas, dans l'Utah

6 With names of towns preceded by the definite article
au Havre = *in le Havre*, **au Mans** = *in le Mans*, **au Touquet** = *in le Touquet*

à la Rochelle = *in la Rochelle*

from
With names of countries
With masculine names beginning with a consonant –

du

venir du Danemark, venir du Bénin, venir du Bangladesh

With masculine names beginning with a vowel –

d'

venir d'Irak, venir d'Iran, venir d'Israël

with feminine names –

de

venir d'Albanie, venir d'Afrique du Sud, venir d'Afghanistan

Exercises

1 **Les prépositions qui relient**
  Réécrivez les phrases suivantes en ajoutant dans le blanc, si c'est
  nécessaire, la préposition qui convient –

  a *J'aimerais . . . avoir des conseils pour m'aider . . . éradiquer ce*
    problème.
  b *Parfois un enfant hausse le ton parce qu'on ne le laisse pas*
    suffisamment . . . s'exprimer.
  c *Agée de 22 ans, je suis atteinte . . . une maladie du système nerveux.*
  d *J'aimerais que quelqu'un me dise les effets secondaires . . .*
    craindre.
  e *Cela arrive, mais il s'agit . . . cas très rares.*
  f *Lorsque je dois . . . faire un gros saut dans le vélo acrobatique, je*
    cherche d'abord . . . maîtriser le stress dans ma tête – cela m'aide . . .
    le passer.
  g *Il a beau . . . être la plus grande star française – il fait toujours de très*
    gros efforts pour plaire . . . ses admiratrices.
  h *Les voleurs et politiciens ripoux ont toujours bénéficié . . . une*
    certaine considération de la part du public.
  i *C'est une mode qui plaît . . . jeunes filles comme . . . femmes plus*
    âgées.
  j *Comment est-ce que vous pouvez . . . aider votre enfant . . . vaincre le*
    bégaiement – reformuler les mots après lui de façon correcte, sans lui
    demander . . . les répéter. Vous devez vous amuser . . . faire ensemble
    des bruits avec la bouche.
  k *Il ne manque jamais . . . raconter ses conquêtes.*
  l *Ces lentilles sont faciles . . . poser et . . . enlever.*
  m *On se promet . . . reprendre une activité physique, histoire . . . garder*
    la forme, . . . s'aérer et . . . s'occuper . . . soi.
  n *Pour séduire, une femme peut . . . passer beaucoup de temps . . .*
    s'apprêter.
  o *J'éprouve un besoin terrible . . . dormir après le déjeuner.*
  p *On m'expliquait que je ne risquais pas . . . devenir stérile.*
  q *Les bénéfices des lavages du nez ne sont plus . . . démontrer.*
  r *Est-ce qu'il a tendance . . . augmenter le son de la télévision?*
  s *Cette réaction permet . . . ceux qui sont dotés . . . une peau*
    délicate . . . résister . . . la brûlure du soleil.
  t *Leur usage convient très bien . . . jeunes filles, car ils s'adaptent . . .*
    leur style de vie.
  u *J'ai impression que les coussins ont besoin . . . être secoués et*
    tapotés, et je ne me prive pas . . . le faire.
  v *Je ne m'adonne . . . ce vice compulsif avec n'importe quoi – j'ai une*
    préférence pour les tickets de cinéma!
  w *Si vous avez avalé seulement une quantité infime d'essence, du lait ou*
    un verre d'eau suffira . . . le diluer.
  x *Tu devrais éviter . . . prendre l'avion si vous avez un rhume.*

y *Vous en sortez plutôt bien, compte tenu . . . vos petites mauvaises habitudes.*

z *Finalement, mes parents se sont débarrassés . . . moi.*

2 **Les prépositions qui forment les locutions prépositives**
Réécrivez les phrases suivantes en ajoutant la préposition qui convient.
Quelquefois plus d'une préposition conviendrait.

a *La natation peut se pratiquer . . . allure modérée, . . . douleur ni essouflement même si l'on reprend . . . une période . . . inactivité.*

b *J'ai pris trois comprimés . . . jour, une prise . . . sang . . . semaine au début et puis une . . . mois . . . la suite.*

c *Nous avons dominé . . . la majeure partie du match, . . . le terrain . . . Milan.*

d *Vous avez le choix . . . deux formules. La première assure votre enfant seulement lorsque l'accident survient . . . les activités organisées . . . l'établissement ou . . . le chemin . . . l'école. Elle est obligatoire . . . les voyages organisés.*

e *. . . leur second bébé, nombre de femmes ne retrouvent pas leur ventre « d'avant », . . . la gym.*

f *. . . la salle de fitness et d'autres clubs, les propositions ne manquent pas. On choisit . . . ses besoins.*

g *Les salariés ont droit . . . quatre jours . . . congé lorsqu'ils se marient, trois jours . . . la naissance ou l'adoption . . . un enfant, un . . . le mariage . . . un enfant, deux jours . . . le décès du conjoint et un jour . . . le décès du père ou de la mère.*

h *Je considère que je vis à peu près normalement, . . . les contraintes dues au traitement.*

i *. . . une situation comme celle-ci, une partie des soins vous sera remboursée.*

j *. . . l'esprit, il voyage lui aussi . . . votre randonnée – on part . . . tension, mais on rentre apaisé, serein.*

k *. . . les tout-petits, les produits alcoolisés sont . . . proscrire. Une même quantité de produit appliquée . . . un bébé aboutit . . . des concentrations . . . cinq fois supérieures . . . son faible poids.*

l *Le chignon existe . . . la nuit des temps.*

m *Elle portait une veste . . . jean surpiqué . . . dentelle . . . un jupon . . . coton.*

n *Il est conseillé d'agir précocement . . . l'âge . . . 3 ans.*

o *Une directive européenne applicable . . . France . . . le début de l'année a renforcé les normes . . . qualité de l'eau.*

p *. . . la douleur postopératoire, elle varie . . . 2 et 4 . . . une échelle de 10.*

q *J'aime passer . . . le miroir . . . la salle de bains.*

r *C'est . . . pantalon . . . coton noir et . . . tee-shirt qu'elle est arrivée.*

s *L'opération . . . anesthésie générale dure . . . deux heures.*

t *Les coiffeurs s'y résignent . . . bonheur.*

u *Les Parisiens, . . . deux buts spectaculaires ont battu Porto.*

v *. . . un contrôle sanguin, j'ai découvert que je souffrais . . . une anomalie physique.*

w *Il figure . . . les meilleurs super-légers mais il fait figure d'inconnu . . . France.*

x *La compétence . . . le plaisir, le talent . . . la joie ne servent à rien.*

y *Souvent . . . l'acheteur compulsif, l'achat se fait . . . la honte et . . . une grande solitude.*

z *76% des hommes se tournent . . . leur partenaire pour chercher soutien . . . une situation difficile.*

Chapter 9 *Adverbs and adverbial expressions*

394 The role of adverbs
The role of an adverb is to modify the meaning of a word, a phrase or a sentence.

Characteristic of adverbs
Adverbs are invariable in form (but see 480 for **tout** as adverb of degree).

Types of adverbs
adverbs of manner
adverbs of time
adverbs of place
adverbs of degree
adverbs of affirmation and negation
interrogative adverbs
adverbs as connectors

395 Formation of adverbs
Only a small sample of examples is given below.

1 By adding –ment to the masculine form of the adjective –
This category includes those adjectives which do not distinguish masculine from feminine gender and those ending in **–é, –i, –u** (see 3 below) or **–û –**

absolu + ment = absolument = *absolutely*

aisé + ment = aisément = *easily*

ambigu + ment = ambigument = *ambiguously*

atroce + ment = atrocement = *atrociously*

deuxième + ment = deuxièmement = *secondly*

dû + ment = dûment = *duly*

gauche + ment = gauchement = *awkwardly*

modeste + ment = modestement = *modestly*

poli + ment = poliment = *politely*

vrai + ment = vraiment = *truly*

2 By adding –ment to the feminine form of the adjective

actif > *active* + *ment* = *activement* = *actively*

dernier > *dernière* + *ment* = *dernièrement* = *lastly*

fou > *folle* + *ment* = *follement* = *madly*

grossier > *grossière* + *ment* = *grossièrement* = *coarsely*

léger > *légère* = *légèrement* = *lightly*

premier > *première* = *premièrement* = *firstly*

public > *publique* = *publiquement* = *publicly*

tel > *telle* + *ment* = *tellement* = *so*

total > *totale* + *ment* = *totalement* = *totally*

exception – *gentil* > *gentiment* = *kindly*

3 A small number of adjectives in –u form their adverb in –ûment

assidu > *assidûment* = *assiduously*

continu > *continûment* = *continuously*

cru > *crûment* = *crudely*

4 Adjectives ending in –ant or –ent form their adverb in –amment or –emment

abondant > *abondamment* = *abundantly*

brillant > *brillamment* = *brilliantly*

constant > *constamment* = *constantly*

fréquent > *fréquemment* = *frequently*

négligent > *négligemment* = *negligently*

prudent > *prudemment* = *prudently*

violent > *violemment* = *violently*

exception – *lent* > *lentement* = *slowly*

Notamment = *notably*, **précipitamment** = *precipitously* have no corresponding adjectives – see 7 below.

5 Adverbs derived from past participles used as adjectives

aveugler > *aveuglé* + *ment* = *aveuglément* = *blindly*

forcer > *forcé* + *ment* = *forcément* = *necessarily*

préciser > *précisé* + *ment* = *précisément* = *precisely*

6 Other adjectives forming their adverbs in –ément

conforme > *conformément* = *in accordance with*

énorme > *énormément* = *enormously*

intense > *intensément* = *intensely*

obscur > *obscurément* = *obscurely*

profond > *profondément* = *profoundly*

7 Adverbs with no corresponding adjective

brièvement = *briefly*

grièvement = *seriously*

See also 4 above.

8 Adjectives used as adverbs without any change of form

bas = *low*, as in *parler bas* = *to speak quietly*

bon = *good*, as in *sentir bon* = *to smell good*, *tenir bon* = *to hold firm*

chaud = *hot*, as in *servir chaud* = *to serve hot*

cher = *dear*, as in *coûter cher* = *to cost dear*

   chèrement = *dearly* (but not involving money) –

   une indépendance chèrement acquise = *an independence acquired at great cost*
(politically, emotionally, intellectually, etc)

clair = *clear*, as in *voir clair* = *to see clearly*

court = *short*, as in *s'arrêter court* = *to stop abruptly*, *s'habiller court* = *to dress in
short skirts*

droit = *straight*, as in *aller tout droit* = *to go straight ahead*

dur = *hard*, as in *travailler dur* = *to work hard*

ferme = *firm*, as in *tenir ferme* = *to hold fast*

fort = *loudly, strong*, as in *crier fort* = *to shout loudly*, *sentir fort* = *to smell strong*

frais = *cool*, as in *servir frais* = *to serve cool*

gros = *a lot*, as in *perdre / risquer gros* = *to lose/risk a lot*

haut = *aloud, high*, as in *lire haut* = *to read aloud*, *parler haut* = *to speak loudly*,

   viser haut = *to aim high*

juste = *accurately*, as in *deviner juste* = *to guess accurately*

lourd = *heavily*, as in *peser lourd* = *to weigh heavily*

mauvais = *bad*, as in *sentir mauvais* = *to smell bad*

net = *plainly, point blank*, as in *parler net* = *to speak plainly*, *refuser net* = *to refuse point
blank*

9 *Using* **d'une manière, d'une façon, d'un air**

Most of the adverbs illustrated above derive from relatively short adjectives; to avoid a rather clumsy, multi-syllabic adverb, the expressions ***d'une manière*** + adjective or ***d'une façon*** + adjective may be used –

d'une façon indescriptible = *in an indescribable fashion*

d'une façon ridicule = *in a ridiculous way*

d'une manière extraordinaire = *in an extraordinary way*

d'une manière fantaisiste = *in an eccentric manner*

   D'un air + adjective may be used in a similar way –

d'un air soupçonneux = *in a suspicious way*

d'un air surpris = *in a surprised way*

10 *Adverbial phrases*

   In the section on prepositional expressions a large number of adverbial phrases were illustrated. Here are some very common ones –

au maximum = *to the utmost*

à la fois = *at the same time*

à l'heure = *on time*

à part = *separately*

à peu près = *almost*

à qui mieux mieux = *outdoing the other*

au fur et à mesure = *as you go along*

à côté = *beside*

côte à côte = *side by side*

de bonne heure = *early*

de plus belle = *with renewed vigour*

de temps en temps / de temps à l'autre = *from time to time*

d'habitude = *usually*

du même coup = *by the same token*

en arrière = *behind*

en avance = *early*

en avant = *in front*

en bas = *down(stairs)*

en dehors = *outside*

en général = *in general*

en haut = *up(stairs)*

en particulier = *especially*

en retard = *late*

en vain = *in vain*

et ainsi de suite = *and so on*

mot à mot = *word by word*

n'importe où = *anywhere*

n'importe quand = *at any time* – see 245, 246

par ailleurs = *in addition*

par contre = *on the other hand*

par hasard = *by chance*

sans cesse = *constantly*

tout à coup = *suddenly*

tout à fait = *quite*

tout à l'heure = *in a moment, a moment ago*

tout de suite = *immediately*

tout d'un coup = *suddenly*

396 Meaning of adverbs

As with most words, some adverbs have more than one meaning and may belong to more than one of the types of adverbs listed below –

ainsi = *in the same way* is both a connector and an adverb of manner.
alors = *then* is an adverb of time and a connector
aussi = *so* as a connector, = *also* as an adverb of degree

397 Position of adverbs

Adverbs are placed in different positions according to the part of speech being modified –

1 With a verb

With simple tenses the adverb normally follows the verb –

Le calcium est surtout présent dans le lait = *calcium is especially present in milk*

Elle égalisa rapidement = *she equalised quickly*

L'huile d'olive peut aussi aider à ramollir les écailles = *olive oil can also help soften scaly skin*

Sa nouvelle vie lui convient parfaitement = *her new life suits her perfectly*

With compound tenses the adverb is normally placed between the auxiliary and the past participle –

La gestion électronique des documents a peu à peu remplacé le document papier = *electronic management of documents has gradually replaced paper documents*

Les pellicules sont parfois accompagnées de démangeaisons et surviennent généralement en périodes de stress = *dandruff is at times accompanied by itching and generally occurs at times of stress*

Elle avait bien attaqué le match en dominant largement Sprem au premier set = *she had attacked the match well by easily dominating Sprem in the first set*

J'ai quand même réussi à constituer une équipe de quatre personnes = *all the same I've managed to get together a team of four people*

2 With an adjective, the adverb normally precedes the adjective
Il est absolument indispensable de maîtriser la langue française = *it's absolutely indispensable to master French*

Ce traitement de la peau nécessite une utilisation de produits de soins parfaitement adaptés à votre sensibilité = *this skin treatment requires use of care products that are perfectly adapted to the sensitivity of your skin*

Même pour des questions très compliquées, on peut trouver des réponses très simples = *even for very complicated questions you can find very simple answers*

3 With an adverb, the adverb normally precedes the adverb
Séchez très doucement vos cheveux = *dry your hair very gently*

Bien bizarrement, tous les gens oublient quelque chose chez toi = *very strangely, everyone forgets something in your house*

Il ne monte jamais plus sur les tables de l'amphi pour affirmer qu'il existe = *he never climbs on the lecture room tables any more in order to prove he exists*

The principles set out illustrate the normal practice as far as the positioning of adverbs is concerned. However, if the adverb is being highlighted or is accompanied by another adverb it may follow the adjective –

Etre prof dans une école maternelle est épuisant nerveusement et physiquement = *being a nursery school teacher is tiring both nervously and physically*

Certain adverbs tend to be more mobile than others, especially those of time, those that are relatively long, and those consisting of prepositional expressions.

Time

Demain on étudiera toutes les familles d'aliments et leurs propriétés nutritionnelles = *tomorrow we'll study all categories of foodstuffs and their nutritional properties*

Hier nous avons laissé la voiture pour suivre un chemin abrupt = *yesterday we left the car to follow a steep track*

Les autres invités vont pratiquer VTT, escalade et ski d'hiver demain = *the other guests are going to do some mountain biking, climbing and skiing tomorrow*

Une page dans l'histoire du club a été tournée hier = *a page in the history of the club was turned yesterday*

Long adverbs and adverbial expressions
On peut se tromper mutuellement et, de la même manière, on peut se quitter = *you can cheat on each other mutually and, in the same way, you can split up*

When a number of adverbs occur in the same sentence, they are usually organised according to length, the shortest closest to the verb, the longest furthest away – but again considerations of rhythm, logic, emphasis and style may decide otherwise –

L'agence nous propose de fournir de quoi vivre nos aventures [1] ***sans anxiété,*** [2] ***en parfaite sécurité*** = *the agency proposes supplying us with the wherewithal to live out our adventures without anxiety and in complete safety*

[1] ***Sur le parvis de l'Hôtel de Ville,*** [2] ***dans la nuit de samedi à dimanche, il a parlé du jeu*** = *on the square outside the Town Hall, on Saturday–Sunday night, he spoke about the game*

Il fonctionnera [1] ***avec sa propre personnalité,*** [2] ***avec sa capacité à écouter les autres*** = *he'll carry on with his own personality and his ability to listen to others*

398 Adverbs of manner
These adverbs describe the way in which something is done and are extremely numerous.

They answer questions introduced by ***comment***, such as –

Comment l'a-t-il fait ? = *how did he do it?*

A number of the most common adverbs of manner are short words, that do not end in ***–ment*** –

ainsi = *thus*

bien = *well*

debout = *standing*

ensemble = *together*

exprès = *deliberately*

mal = *badly*

mieux = *better*

pis = *worse*

plutôt = *rather*

vite = *quickly*

volontiers = *willingly*

Many others do end in ***–ment*** –

attentivement = *attentively*

brusquement = *abruptly*

cyniquement = *cynically*

doucement = *gently*

efficacement = *efficiently*

fermement = *firmly*

gaiement = *gaily*

heureusement = *happily*

intelligemment = *intelligently*

joliment = *prettily*

librement = *freely*

mollement = *idly*

nonchalamment = *nonchalantly*

ouvertement = *openly*

précipitamment = *precipitously*

richement = *richly*

solidement = *solidly*

tranquillement = *quietly*

unanimement = *unanimously*

vaillamment *courageously*

There is virtually an infinite number of adverbial phrases of manner, including those mentioned in the section on formation of adverbs and discussed under prepositional expressions –

à dessein = *on purpose*

à grande vitesse = *at top speed*

à la fois = *at the same time*

à tort = *wrongly*

avec enthousiasme = *enthusiastically*

de tout son coeur = *whole-heartedly*

en connaissance de cause = *with full knowledge of the facts*

en n'hésitant pas = *by not hesitating*

en utilisant toutes ses forces = *by using all his strength*

par erreur = *in error*

sans attendre = *without waiting*

tout droit = *straight ahead*

together with similes introduced by **comme** = *like*

dormir comme un loir / une souche = *to sleep like a log*

être malade comme un chien = *to be as sick as a dog*

être soûl comme une grive / un Polonais = *to be as drunk as a lord*

rire comme un bossu = *to laugh like a drain*

399 Examples of adverbs of manner

Ceux qui ne savent pas s'habiller à la mode ne demandent pas mieux que d'être conseillés = *those who don't know how to dress fashionably can't do better than ask for advice*

Lors d'un divorce, le juge doit méticuleusement veiller aux intérêts de chacun des époux = *during a divorce, the judge must meticulously pay attention to the interests of each spouse*

Nouez la ficelle solidement = *tie a tight knot in the string*

'Philtre d'amour' est un vaporisateur que l'on glisse facilement dans son sac = *'Philtre d'amour' is a spray that you can easily slip into your bag*

Si la soupe vous paraît trop épaisse, rallonge-la idéalement avec un reste de bouillon = *if the soup seems too thick, thin it ideally with some of the left-over stock*

Les doutes elle les chasse avec un revers de la main = *she brushes away doubts with the back of her hand*

L'auteur décrit sans empathie la mécanique ravageuse d'une manipulation mentale qui paralyse la victime = *the author describes without empathy the destructive mechanism of mental manipulation which paralyses the victim*

Cette version oscille allègrement entre les genres: chansons, cirque, comédie = *this version oscillates merrily between various genres – song, circus, comedy*

Maintenez chaque tube en place en tordant soigneusement le fil de fer au dos du tableau = *hold each tube in place by carefully twisting the wire at the back of the picture*

Réparez votre capital jeunesse en atténuant visiblement rides et ridules grâce à un extrait de ginkgo = *restore your youthfulness by visibly reducing wrinkles and fine lines with an extract of ginkgo*

Il montre à la fois l'étendue de son talent comme acteur comique et son expérience comme producteur de films = *he demonstrates at one and the same time the extent of his skill as a comic actor and his experience as a film director*

Elle s'est présentée comme une sacrifiée, docile comme un phoque, résignée comme une actrice qui ne trouve pas de rôles = *she came across like someone being sacrificed, docile like a seal and resigned like an actress who can't find a part*

400 Adverbs of place

Adverbs of place indicate where an event takes place and answer the question–

Où est-ce que cela a eu / aura lieu ? = *where did / will that happen?*

Typical adverbs and adverbial expressions are –

à dix kilomètres = *10 kilometres away*

à droite / à gauche = *on the right / on the left*

ailleurs = *elsewhere*

à Paris = *in Paris*

au-dedans = *on the inside*

au-dehors = *on the outside*

au-dessous = *below*

au-dessus = *above*

au loin = *in the distance*

autour = *around*

chez moi = *at home*

ci-dessous = *below*

ci-dessus = *above, aforementioned*

dedans = *inside*

dehors = *outside*

derrière = *behind*

dessous = *underneath*

en bas = *down below*

en dessous = *underneath* (indicating static position)

en haut = *up above*

ici = *here*

là = *there*

loin = *far away*

par-dessous = *underneath* (indicating movement)

partout = *everywhere*

près = *nearby*

Expressions introduced by *dans* –

dans la chambre = *in the bedroom*

Expressions introduced by ***près de*** –

près de la résidence universitaire = *near the hall of residence*

Note –

ailleurs = *elsewhere*, but ***d'ailleurs*** = *moreover* (unless it is being used to mean *from elsewhere*) and is a connector.

401 Examples of adverbs of place

Je veux passer toute ma vie ici avec toi = *I want to spend all my life here with you*

Le dernier concours s'est déroulé à Anvers hier = *the last competition took place in Antwerp yesterday*

Là, ces douze pays seront groupés dans trois groupes = *there, these twelve countries will be divided into three groups*

Il faut que je me relance, que j'aille partout pour trouver ce qu'il me manque = *I've got to get myself going again, I've got to go everywhere to find what's missing in my life*

Servez avec des croûtons aillés dessus = *serve with garlic croutons on top*

Des tiroirs ont été placés dessous pour éviter ce fameux désordre des salles de bains = *drawers have been placed underneath to avoid that notorious untidiness of bathrooms*

Dans les intervalles, glissez des plantes vivaces = *in the spaces slip in some hardy plants*

402 Adverbs of time

These adverbs indicate the time at or during which an event takes place and answer the question –

Quand est-ce que cela est arrivé / arrivera ? = *when did / will that happen?*

Typical adverbs and adverbial expressions are –

actuellement = *at present*

alors = *then, at that time*

après = *afterwards*

   après la naissance de mon bébé = *after my baby's birth*

à présent = *at present*

aujourd'hui = *today*

auparavant = *beforehand*

au printemps = *in the spring*

aussitôt = *immediately*

autrefois = *in the past*

bientôt = *soon*

d'abord = *first of all*

déjà = *already*

demain = *tomorrow*

demain matin = *tomorrow morning*

depuis = *since then*

dès lors = *from then on*

désormais = *from now on*

en ce moment = *at the moment*

encore = *still, again*

en février = *in February*

enfin = *finally*

en hiver = *in winter*

en retard = *late*

ensuite = *afterwards*

fréquemment = *frequently*

hier = *yesterday*

immédiatement = *immediately*

jamais = *ever*

longtemps = *a long time*

maintenant = *now*

mercredi soir = *Wednesday evening*

parfois = *at times*

précédemment = *previously*

prochainement = *soon*

quelquefois = *sometimes*

récemment = *recently*

six semaines plus tard = *six weeks later*

soudain = *suddenly*

souvent = *often*

sur-le-champ = *straightaway*

tard = *late*

tôt = *early*

toujours = *always, still*

tout à coup = *suddenly*

tout à l'heure = *soon, a moment ago*

tout de suite = *immediately*

and the ordinal numbers – ***premièrement, deuxièmement,*** etc.

403 Comments on certain adverbs of time

Encore and ***toujours*** cover similar semantic domains as well as distinct ones –

encore = *still*
J'ai encore ton débardeur = *I've still got your top*

Une transmission de la maladie de la vache folle aux humains est encore possible = *the transmission of mad cow disease to humans is still possible*

encore = *again*
Je lui ai encore demandé de me prêter le cd = *I asked him again to lend me the CD*

Elle s'est encore vexée quand j'ai fumé à la maison = *she got angry again when I smoked in the house*

encore + noun / adverb = *still more, even* (with a comparative)
Je prendrai encore du vin, s'il vous plaît = *I'll have some more wine please*

Le silence apporte encore du poids à vos propos = *silence adds still more weight to what you say*

C'est encore mieux si vous le faites comme ça = *it's even better if you do it like that*

toujours = *still*
Elle est toujours là = *she's still there*

Si tout se passe bien, à 90 ans, vos os seront toujours en bon état = *if everything goes well, your bones will still be in good condition when you're 90*

toujours = *always*
Je vais toujours à l'étranger pour mes vacances = *I always go abroad for my holidays*

Une voix de crooner rocailleuse mais toujours émouvante = *a crooner's voice, gravelly but always moving*

For word order with ***toujours,*** see 210.

Tard and ***en retard*** = *late*, but with different connotations – ***tard*** bears no negative meaning –

J'aime me lever très tard le samedi = *I like getting up very late on a Saturday*

Je rentrais tard de la boîte quand deux mecs qui traînaient dans la rue se sont approchés de moi = *I was coming home late from the nightclub when two guys who were hanging about in the street approached me*

Only ***en retard*** carries the connotation of being behind time –

Il m'a dit que si je continuais d'arriver en retard il me virerait = *he told me that if I kept on arriving late he'd fire me*

Je devenais de plus en plus anxieuse parce que le train était déjà en retard d'une demi-heure = *I was becoming more and more anxious because the train was already half an hour late*

404 Examples of adverbs of time

Ce sera alors au juge d'évaluer les conséquences = *then it will be up to the judge to assess the consequences*

Cette capacité à tenir son service sera la clef de son match aujourd'hui = *this ability to hold his service* [in tennis] *will be the key to his match today*

Mes parents sont divorcés depuis six ans = *my parents have been divorced for six years*

Désormais, j'apprécie qu'on ne me trouve plus moche = *from now on I'm very pleased that no one finds me ugly any more*

Quinze minutes d'entraînements musculaires et cardio-vasculaires [1] ***le matin permet de maigrir et de gagner en énergie*** [2] ***pour toute la journée*** = *fifteen minutes of muscular and cardio-vascular exercises in the morning help you lose weight and gain energy for the whole day*

Les deux hommes ne s'étaient pas parlé depuis samedi midi = *the two men hadn't spoken since midday Saturday*

Depuis la loi Madelin, ces cotisations sont déductibles des revenus = *since the 'loi Madelin' these subscriptions are deductible against your income*

Maintenant je suis dans tous les journaux = *now I'm in all the papers*

J'ai toujours aimé les cochons = *I've always liked pigs*

405 Adverbs of degree

Adverbs of degree indicate the intensity with which an action expressed by the verb is undertaken, or the intensity with which a quality expressed by an adjective or adverb is perceived. Adverbs of degree answer questions introduced by ***combien?*** = *how much?* Typical adverbs are –

absolument = *absolutely*

à peine = *hardly*

à peu près = *almost*

assez = *enough*

au moins = *at least*

aussi = *also*

autant = *as much*

beaucoup = *much, a lot*

bien = *really*

complètement = *completely*

de loin = *by far*

démesurément = *disproportionately*

encore = *still, again*

énormément = *enormously*

entièrement = *entirely*

immensément = *enormously*

juste = *just*

même = *even*

moins = *less*

particulièrement = *particularly*

peu = *little*

plus = *more*

plutôt = *rather*

presque = *almost*

si = *so*

tant = *so much*

tellement = *so, so much*

terriblement = *terribly*

totalement = *totally*

tout(e) = *quite, completely*

tout à fait = *completely*

très = *very*

trop = *too, too much*

un peu = *a little, a little bit*

vraiment = *really, truly*

406 Comments on certain adverbs of degree

Assez and **trop** – when followed by an infinitive, the preposition **pour** is used to introduce it –

Il a assez de talent artistique pour s'attirer le respect des autres en faisant des caricatures des profs = *he has enough artistic talent to attract the others' respect by drawing caricatures of the teachers*

Ces chaussures sont trop serrées pour marcher confortablement = *these shoes are too tight to walk comfortably in*

Presque never elides the final *–e* before a vowel (except in the compound ***une presqu'île*** = *peninsula*)

Tout – when used as an adverb, ***tout*** varies for number and gender before feminine adjectives beginning with a consonant, and varies optionally if a feminine adjective beginning with a vowel or non-aspirate ***h*** is involved, but not in other circumstances (that is not in masculine plural) –

Le message doit être tout simple = *the message must be quite simple*

Les hommes tout seuls attendent celles qui s'imposeront à eux = *men who are completely alone wait for women who will impose themselves on them*

Chérie, tu es tout / toute irrésistible = *darling, you're quite irresistible*

Entre, la maison est toute vide = *come in, the house is quite empty*

Elles ont une beauté toute froide = *they've got a really cold beauty*

407 Examples of adverbs of degree

Merci de me répondre – je suis assez pressée = *thank you for answering, I'm in quite a hurry*

Si l'on épouse quelqu'un qu'on n'aime pas assez, cela tourne vite au calvaire = *if you marry someone you don't love enough, it will soon become a nightmare*

Les bijoutiers vous accordent leur savoir-faire aussi longtemps que vous gardez votre bijou = *the jewellers will give you their expert advice for as long as you keep the item of jewellery*

Nous avons un très bon indice de satisfaction = *we have a very good record of satisfaction*

Il sont rémunérés entre 75% et 100% du SMIC, soit un peu plus que ce que prévoit la législation = *they are paid at a rate between 75% and 100% of the minimum wage, in other words a little bit more than is laid down by legislation*

Il joue un patron de salle de gym totalement mégalo = *he plays the completely megalomaniac owner of a gym*

On est juste amoureux – où en est le mal? = *we're just in love – what's wrong with that?*

Il a bénéficié de quarante-huit heures de repos presque complet = *he profited from forty-eight hours of almost complete rest*

Un peu moins nombreux que les organisateurs ne l'espéraient = *a little less well-attended than the organisers were hoping for*

Etre gênée par l'attitude de son petit ami en public, est-ce donc l'aimer un peu moins? = *being embarrassed by the attitude of your boyfriend in public, does it mean you love him a little less?*

Les fans lui apportèrent une dose supplémentaire d'énergie bien nécessaire pour passer le prochain obstacle = *the fans gave him an extra dose of energy, very necessary to overcome the next obstacle*

Je me sens vraiment respectée = *I feel really respected*

408 assez, autant, beaucoup, bien, tant, tellement, trop

These adverbs of degree can also function as quantifiers modifying nouns –

Elle a reçu assez de conseils pour savoir comment se comporter dans cette situation = *she's had enough advice to know how to act in such a situation*

Je ne savais pas que cela coûterait autant d'argent que cela = *I didn't know that that would cost as much money as that*

Pour obtenir un effet graphique, il faut beaucoup de fleurs de couleurs différentes = *in order to obtain a graphic effect, you need a lot of flowers of different colours*

Bien des chemins les plus escarpés demandent une durée d'au moins cinq heures = *many of the steepest tracks require at least five hours*

Après tant de recherches, on peut enfin conclure qu'une femme avec un long nez et un gros visage doit opter pour les cheveux longs ou au carré = *after so much research, we can conclude that a woman with a long nose and fat face should go for long or square-cut hair*

Nous avons eu tellement de problèmes que nous avons décidé de nous séparer = *we've had so many problems that we've decided to split up*

Tout le monde est d'accord, nous importons trop de produits et n'en exportons pas assez = *everyone agrees – we import too many products and don't export enough*

409 Comparative and superlative forms of adverbs

The comparative forms of most adverbs in French are created by placing *plus, moins* or *aussi* before the adverb; the superlative by placing *le plus* or *le moins* before the adverb –

Le psychiatre va plus loin = *the psychiatrist goes further*

Pour éviter les pieds empestants, changez vos chaussettes plus régulièrement = *to avoid stinking feet, change your socks more regularly*

Il le dit d'autant plus facilement qu'il faisait partie de ceux qui avaient refusé de tirer = *it was all the easier for him to say it because he was among those who refused to shoot*

Elle a décidé d'agir au plus vite = *she decided to act as quickly as possible*

Ce remède bloque moins ponctuellement les manifestations corporelles gênantes = *this treatment blocks embarrassing physical manifestations less selectively*

Il y a beaucoup d'autres chanteurs assez âgés qui continuent, mais ils chantent moins bien = *there are lots of other fairly old singers who carry on, but they sing less well*

S'ils étaient aussi lâchement liés aux causes honorables que lui, ils n'auraient pas accompli grand'chose = *if they were as loosely linked to noble causes as him, they wouldn't have achieved very much*

However, a very small number of adverbs of degree have special comparative and superlative forms –

beaucoup = *much*
Plus = *more*; ***le plus*** = *the most*

Ne mangez que des trucs bons, on brûle plus quand on diversifie les mets = *only eat good-quality stuff, you burn up more when you vary what you eat*

Ne sautez aucun repas – on stocke deux fois plus le repas suivant = *don't skip meals – you stock up twice as much at the next meal*

For the comparison of adjectives, see 257.

English *the more . . . the more . . .* is conveyed by ***plus . . . plus*** in French (see 201); as far as word order is concerned with adjectives, in French ***plus*** precedes the verb and the adjective follows it

Une étude a montré que plus la main est située bas sur la fourchette, plus la personne est grosse = *a study has shown that the lower you hold your fork, the fatter you are*

Plus vous êtes angoissé, plus vous tremblez, et plus vous tremblez, plus vous angoissez à l'idée que l'on s'en aperçoive = *the more anxious you are, the more you tremble, and the more you tremble, the more anxious you become that people are noticing*

Plus j'avançais, plus je réalisais que c'était moi et non les autres qu'il fallait comprendre = *the older I got, the more I realised it was myself and not others that I had to understand*

bien = *well*
Mieux = *better*; ***le mieux*** = *best*

Vous êtes arrivé à vous connaître ? – Mieux qu'avant = *you've managed to get to know yourself? – Better than before*

La digestion commence en mâchant – alors, mâchez et vous digérerez mieux = *digestion begins with chewing – so, chew and you'll digest your food better*

Ce n'est pas votre cas! – Tant mieux! = *that's not your style! – So much the better*

Sur quels vols mange-t-on le mieux ? = *on what flights do you eat best?*

Elle a dansé le* mieux de la salle = *she danced the best in the room*

* *le* not ***la*** (agreeing with ***elle***), because ***mieux*** is an adverb and not an adjective.
   Moins bien = *less well*, ***le moins bien*** = *least well*, ***aussi bien*** = *as well* are formed normally – but ***plus bien*** is not possible.

mal = *badly*
has a double set of comparative and superlative forms –
   plus mal / pis = *worse*; ***le plus mal / le pis*** = *the worst*

The forms with **mal** are the normal forms –

Il a joué plus mal que d'habitude = *he played worse than usual*

Cela va de plus en plus mal maintenant – elle ne me parle même pas = *things are going from bad to worse now – she doesn't even speak to me*

Il a organisé son horaire le plus mal du monde – il est complètement épuisé = *he's organised his timetable in the worst possible way – he's completely worn out*

Il s'est défendu le plus mal des candidats = *he performed the least well of the candidates*

Pis is limited to a small number of fixed expressions –

Elle ne te prête pas attention – tant pis pour toi! = *she doesn't pay any attention to you – hard luck on you!*

Tout va de mal en pis = *everything's going from bad to worse*

Si vous ne faites rien, la situation va aller de mal en pis – *if you don't do something, things will go from bad to worse*

peu = *little*
Moins = *less*; **le moins** = *the least*

Tricot, poterie ou peinture, peu importe l'activité, ça fait un bien fou = *knitting, pottery or painting, it doesn't matter which activity, it does you a tremendous amount of good*

On rit moins qu'on aurait pensé devant cette comédie peu réussie = *we laughed less than you would have thought at this not very successful comedy*

Elle a peu d'imagination = *she's got little imagination*

Si vous avez moins d'un kilo à perdre, oubliez les régimes, amusez-vous = *if you've got less than a kilo to lose, forget diets, enjoy yourself*

Le corps supporte de moins en moins bien d'être privé de nourriture = *our bodies cope less and less well with being deprived of food*

Je l'aime le moins du tout = *I like it the least of all*

410 Adverbs of affirmation, negation and doubt

Typical adverbs are –

bien entendu = *of course*

bien sûr = *of course*

certainement = *certainly*

certes = *certainly*

évidemment = *obviously*

non = *no*

oui = *yes*

peut-être = *perhaps*

probablement = *probably*

sans aucun doute = *without a doubt*

sans doute = *probably*

si = *yes*

vraisemblablement = *probably*

oui and *si*

Oui is used to say *yes* to affirmative yes/no questions, whereas **si** is used to say *yes* to negative yes/no questions, contradicting the expected answer –

Tu l'as fait? – Oui = *have you done it? – Yes*
Tu ne l'as pas fait ? – Si = *you haven't done it? – Yes (I have)*

  Oui = *so* in the following type of expressions –

J'espère que oui = *I hope so*

  non = *no, not* – see 428.

J'apprends à dire non = *I'm learning to say no*

J'espère que non = *I hope not*

Evidemment que non = *obviously not*

  The strength of the reply may be reinforced by adding

mais –

mais oui / mais si = *definitely*

mais non = *definitely not*

Note that **merci** can be used = *no thank you* –

Tu veux des sels de bain pour ton anniversaire ? – Merci = *would you like some bath-salts for your birthday? – No thank you*

411 Examples of adverbs of affirmation, negation and doubt

Une assurance « tous risques » couvre bien sûr les frais médicaux = *comprehensive insurance certainly covers medical expenses*

Mon amie m'a dit que le chocolat est probablement la cause de mon acné = *my friend has told me that chocolate is probably the cause of my acne*

Sans aucun doute une botte noire, pointue et fine, ça titille l'inconscient masculine = *beyond a doubt a black, pointed, slender boot titillates the masculine subconscious*

Si vous ne faites rien, la situation va vraisemblablement empirer = *if you don't do anything, the situation will probably get worse*

***Ne serait-ce pas une façon de me manipuler ? – Un peu, sans doute** = wouldn't that be a way of manipulating me? – A little, probably*

***Votre poids varie, mais vous ne changez pas de régime alimentaire – ceci pourrait bien entendu être un symptôme de la rétention d'eau** = your weight varies but you haven't changed your eating habits – this might of course be a symptom of water retention*

412 Interrogative adverbs

The interrogative adverbs are –

combien? = *how much, how many?*

comment? = *how?*

où? = *where?*

pourquoi? = *why?*

quand? = *when?*

These are discussed in 479.

413 Adverbs as connectors

The role of a connector is to indicate the connection between what is being said and what was said before. Connectors are not integrated into the clause but express some evaluation or comment on the speaker's/writer's part.

Typical connectors are –

ainsi = *in the same way*

alors = *so*

au contraire = *on the contrary*

au / du moins = *at least*

aussi = *thus*

autrement dit = *in other words*

cependant = *yet*

c'est-à-dire = *in other words*

d'ailleurs = *besides*

de toute façon / manière = *anyway*

en conséquence = *consequently*

en effet = *in effect*

en fait = *in fact*

en général = *in general*

en revanche = *on the other hand*

en somme = *briefly, in a nutshell*

évidemment = *obviously*

heureusement = *fortunately*

malheureusement = *unfortunately*

néanmoins = *nevertheless*

or = *now*

par conséquent = *consequently*

par contre = *on the other hand*

plutôt = *rather*

pourtant = *however*

puis = *then*

quand même = *even so*

seulement = *only*

soit = *so be it*

toutefois = *nevertheless*

and expressions like ***d'une part . . . de l'autre part*** = *on the one hand . . . on the other*, ***d'un côté . . . de l'autre côté*** = *on the one hand . . . on the other*; and words like ***bizarrement*** = *strangely*, ***franchement*** = *frankly*, ***naturellement*** = *naturally*, which are also adverbs of manner but as conjuncts convey some assessment of what is being said.

au / du moins = *at least*; ***au moins*** is also used as an adverb of degree

puis = *then*, both as an adverb of time and a connector.

414 Examples of connectors
Alors, j'ai opté pour le français = *so I opted for French*

En revanche, tu n'as aucune raison de culpabiliser = *on the other hand, you've got no reason to feel guilty*

Même si l'on ne peut complètement contrôler sa vie, on peut au moins en donner l'impression = *even if you can't control your life, you can at least give the impression you do*

De l'autre côté ce n'est peut-être pas la meilleure solution = *on the other hand, it's perhaps not the best solution*

De toute manière, tu me connais – si je peux aider = *in any case, you know me, if I can help*

Or, oui, je pense que c'est bien de se poser cette question = *well, yes, I think it's a good idea to ask yourself that question*

Et [1] *puis,* [2] *globalement, il est plus agréable de recevoir un bouquet de fleurs qu'une paire de baffes* = *and then, on the whole, it's more pleasant to get a bouquet of flowers than a box round the ears*

Exercises

Traduisez en français les passages qui suivent en anglais –

a *Loneliness isn't a medical defect or a stroke of fate, but a necessary phase, from which you often emerge more aware, more sensitive and more human.*

b *I think that the reason why I became a writer is to a large extent linked to my father and my feelings towards him.*

c *Fast-food culture has completely changed our eating habits and, even more seriously, the amounts we consume.*

d *We live in a very competitive society in which you construct your own self-esteem by constantly comparing yourself to others.*

e *The symptoms of the crisis in the Catholic church in France are so well known that it's scarcely necessary to list them: in half a century regular church-going has collapsed, it's been divided by four and is stagnating around 10%; the number of priests being ordained every year is nowadays a tenth of what it was in the '50s, and Catholic charities are no more than the shadow of what they used to be.*

f *At the present time, no one is in a position to know if Lille will equal Saint-Étienne and Marseille by pulling off a fourth consecutive national title, nor what its fate will be in the Champions' League.*

g *Allow it to cook for 15 mins. on a low heat, then add the stock and cream, allow to cook for a further 15 mins. on a medium heat. Remove the thyme and mix everything together with the remainder of the cream. Add a little stock if it is too thick.*

h *Frequently used to relieve stress, essential oils can also be used, according to their properties, to soothe your skin or fight against wrinkles.*

i *Apply black or very dark brown eyeliner in a classical style on your upper eyelid, going from the centre and extending the line beyond the outer corner of your eye. Once the make-up is completely dry, you apply a slightly shorter identical line of eyeliner to the edge of your lower lashes.*

j *Patches are good at performing conjuring tricks. They are applied locally, like a cream, but they act on the whole of the body, like a pill. The trick consists in enclosing the active ingredient under a small piece of adhesive material, which allows it to spread through the skin in order to connect with the blood supply.*

k *On a wall purée of broccoli is spread like a coating, at the foot of the wall there are two cones of carrots. With time the wall and the cones will*

*assume colours that will change under the effect of decomposition –
that's contemporary art for you!*

1 *Traditionally, it is accepted that boys belong to the 'stronger sex' and
girls to the 'weaker sex'. This distinction may reflect a difference in
terms of muscles. But when you consider existence as a whole, the
reverse is clearly true. Generally speaking, women resist illness better;
they eat more healthily; they're more cautious when driving and kill
each other less spontaneously. As a consequence, they live longer.*

Chapter 10 *Negation*

415 Negation + verb
To negate a verb, the negative particle *ne* is used:

alone (but very rarely) –
Si ce n'est de garder cette bonne habitude d'avoir toujours une bouteille
d'eau à portée de main = *unless it is to keep this good habit of always having a bottle of water to hand*

in conjunction with another item which may be
a negative particle –
Monogamie ne rime pas avec monotonie = *monogamy and monotony are not the same thing*

a pronoun –
Personne ne veut provoquer un oedème des cordes vocales et une laryngite
chronique – ne fumez donc pas – *no one wants to cause oedema of the vocal cords and chronic laryngitis – so don't smoke*

a determiner –
D'autres objets ne doivent en aucun cas être introduits dans la bouche de
l'enfant = *under no circumstances must other objects be placed in the child's mouth*

an adverb –
Un tiers des couples français ne font plus l'amour = *a third of French couples no longer make love*

All these items require *ne* when negating a verb – except in informal French when the *ne* is often dropped – see 431. However, when they are used without a verb, they still retain their negative values; in other words, *personne* = *no one* (but *une personne* = *a person*), *aucun* = *no, none*, *jamais* = *never* (but in certain circumstances, it can also = *ever*).

416 *ne* + negative particle – *ne . . . pas* = *not*
The negative particle most commonly used – in fact in the vast majority of cases – is *pas*. *Point* also exists but is rarely found in contemporary French usage.

Word order
Ne precedes the verb and any unstressed object pronouns or *y, en* that also precede it.

The particle follows the finite verb in simple tenses and the auxiliary verb in compound tenses. It can however be separated from the verb by certain adverbs – see below.

ne . . . pas + *finite verb in simple tenses*
L'important n'est pas d'être meilleur que les autres mais d'être au mieux de soi-même = *the important thing is not to be better than others but to be at your best*

Je crois fermement que le succès n'arrive pas par accident = *I sincerely believe that success does not come by accident*

Les assurances les plus chères ne sont pas toujours les meilleures = *the most expensive insurance is not always the best*

La mauvaise réputation des crèmes à base de cortisone n'est pas justifiée si on prend les précautions nécessaires = *the bad reputation of creams with a cortisone base is not justified if you take the necessary precautions*

ne . . . pas + *auxiliary verb in compound tenses*
Malgré un service capricieux, la tenniswoman française ne s'est pas mise en danger face à sa rivale russe = *despite a capricious serve, the French tennis player didn't cause herself any serious problems against her Russian opponent*

L'équipe tchèque ne lui a pas laissé le temps de se construire = *the Czech team didn't give him the time to get his game together*

Le Ministre de la Justice n'a pas caché son inquiétude face à la situation dans les prisons = *the Minister of Justice did not hide his anxiety over the situation in the prisons*

Ils n'ont pas pu riposter aux tirs de canon venant des rebelles = *they couldn't return the cannon fire coming from the rebels*

Je n'aurais pas cru que préserver sa santé dentaire est si difficile = *I wouldn't have thought that preserving your dental health is so difficult*

ne + *unstressed pronouns*
Je ne me sens pas menacé maintenant = *I don't feel that I'm threatened now*

C'est de ceux qui ne l'ont pas connu que vient l'hommage le plus émouvant = *it's from those who didn't know him that the most touching homage has come*

C'est déjà bien beau que le moral ne m'ait pas laissée plus tôt = *it's already very nice that my morale didn't abandon me earlier*

Ne te laisse pas abattre, prends ce mal en patience = *don't let yourself get depressed, be patient with this problem*

Si je voulais un pain de chocolat et qu'il n'y en avait pas, ça créait un mouvement de panique = *if I wanted a bar of chocolate and there weren't any, that created a feeling of panic*

ne . . . pas *with imperative*
Antibiotiques – ne les mélangez pas au lait de biberon = *don't mix antibiotics in the baby's bottle*

Ne vous courbez pas sur votre assiette, tenez-vous droite = *don't bend over your plate, sit up straight*

N'hésitez pas à vous faire plaisir, vous n'en serez que plus irrésistible = *don't hesitate to give yourself some pleasure, you'll only look the more irresistible*

ne . . . pas + *inverted interrogative* – see 472.
Ne . . . pas surround the verb and pronoun –

N'avez-vous pas envie de lui dire d'aller se faire voir? = *don't you want to tell him to take a running jump?*

N'accepterez-vous pas de conformer aux règles, de respecter les interdits? = *won't you agree to conforming to the rules, to respecting the taboos?*

Ce besoin d'accumuler les conquêtes, ne révèlerait-il pas une peur de la solitude ou de l'engagement? = *doesn't this need to collect conquests reveal a fear of loneliness or of commitment?*

ne pas *precedes an infinitive* –
and also any pronouns that precede the infinitive –

Le musée n'est pas encore né et pourrait ne pas voir le jour = *the museum isn't yet born and might not see the light of day*

On lui reproche de ne pas tenir compte du facteur humain dans sa quête de la rigueur scientifique = *they reproach him for not taking account of the human factor in his quest for scientific rigour*

Il est important de ne pas servir vos repas dans de grandes assiettes blanches, mais dans de petites assiettes colorées = *it's important not to serve your meals on big white plates but on small coloured ones*

Il vous faut des compléments alimentaires – indispensables pour ne pas être crevée de fatigue = *you need some food complements – indispensable so as not to be exhausted with fatigue*

Il est conseillé de ne pas s'attarder, achetez maintenant = *it's advisable not to delay, buy now*

Pourquoi ne pas lui proposer une escapade dans les dunes? = *why not suggest a romp in the dunes to her?*

ne . . . pas *surround the auxiliary with a past infinitive* –
Je m'en voulais de n'avoir pas su préserver notre bonheur = *I was angry with myself for not being able to preserve our happiness*

ne . . . pas *surround the present participle* –
En n'oubliant pas de l'amener avec toi = *not forgetting to bring her with you*

Pour calmer votre stress, faites des promenades, mais en ne mangeant pas en route = *to calm your stress, go for walks, but without eating at the same time*

Le rôle du comique – produire de la critique sociale mais en ne déversant pas trop son fiel = *the comic's role – to produce social criticism, but not venting his spleen excessively*

Vous faites un affront à vos lecteurs en ne respectant pas la voix du peuple = *you insult your readers by not respecting the voice of the people*

pas *separated from the verb by an adverb*
The adverbs in question tend to consist of a single word only; but ***quand même*** = *even so,* ***sans doute*** = *probably* are also used in this way –

Le champion n'était peut-être pas dans un grand jour si l'on en croit ses mimiques significatives = *perhaps the champ wasn't on top form if you believe his significant gestures*

Votre bébé a horreur du bruit – ne soyez donc pas étonnée de le voir crier si votre radio hurle = *your baby can't stand noise – so don't be surprised if you see him screaming if your radio is blasting away*

Il ne doit surtout pas se réveiller avec une gueule de bois = *above all he mustn't wake up with a hangover*

Le président du club n'est même pas sûr de rester en place = *the president of the club is not even sure of keeping his job*

La société n'est cependant pas composée uniquement de professeurs et d'ouvriers = *society is, however, not composed entirely of teachers and workers*

Vous n'allez quand même pas vous lancer dans une autre aventure = *even so you're not going to launch yourself into another adventure*

Le fait de tomber amoureux n'est sans doute pas un pur hasard = *the fact of falling in love is not a pure accident*

ne . . . pas + *indefinite article* (***un, une, du, de la, de l', des***) + *direct object* –
the indefinite article is contracted to ***de*** (see 260) –
Les pâtes ne manquent pas d'atouts nutritionnels = *pasta is not without nutritional benefits*

L'angoisse est considérablement exacerbée s'ils n'ont pas de recours médical = *their anxiety is considerably increased if they haven't got medical help*

L'anesthésiste est là pour s'assurer que le patient n'a pas de nausées = *the anaesthetist is there to assure himself that the patient is not nauseous*

J'ai remarqué qu'il n'y avait pas d'immigrés dans les cortèges = *I noticed that there weren't any immigrants among the marchers*

Ça ne me pose pas de problème d'attendre = *it's no problem for me to wait*

Il n'y a pas de mal à se faire du bien = *there's no harm in doing yourself some good*

This situation is to be distinguished from the following –
ne . . . pas + ***de*** combined with the definite article, producing ***du, de l', de la, des*** –

Mais ne servez-vous pas encore du sirop que vous avez mis de côté = *but don't use the syrup that you've put to one side yet*

Il ne se contente pas du shampooing quotidien – il utilise en plus le gel pour cheveux, et la cire à cheveux = *he's not satisfied with his daily shampoo – he also uses hair gel and wax*

ne . . . pas + **de** combined with the indefinite article, producing **pas un, pas une** –

Si elle n'a pas une bonne dose d'humour, oubliez = *if she hasn't got a reasonable dose of good humour, forget it*

417 *ne* alone

The use of **ne** without **pas** is limited to a small number of circumstances, with certain verbs and expressions –

With **cesser**
Les choses n'ont cessé d'empirer = *things have kept on getting worse*

Je ne cessais de me demander comment on avait pu en arriver là = *I kept on asking myself how things could have got to such a state*

With **n'avoir de cesse** = *to persist until*
Cette fois, c'est décidé, vous sortez les grands moyens – le love-coach – il n'aura de cesse de vous caser avec votre idéal = *this time it's for sure, you bring out the big guns – a love-coach – he won't give up till he's fixed you up with your perfect partner*

Elle a été initiée à un nouveau monde qui n'aura de cesse de libérer son esprit = *she has been initiated into a new world which will continually liberate her mind*

With **pouvoir**
Je ne peux m'empêcher d'être nerveuse lorsque mon mari doit prendre l'avion pour ses déplacements professionnels = *I can't help being nervous when my husband takes the plane when he's travelling professionally*

La culpabilité de ne pouvoir être à la hauteur de cette image sociale de la sexualité = *guilt at not being able to maintain this social image of sexuality*

L'on ne peut prétendre en permanence que les préceptes républicains sont bafoués chaque fois qu'on lance une réforme = *you can't keep on claiming that every time a reform is launched republican principles are flouted*

With **si ce n'est** = *but for, unless*
Si ce n'est de garder cette bonne habitude d'avoir toujours une bouteille d'eau à portée de main = *unless it is to keep this good habit of always having a bottle of water to hand*

With **je ne sais quoi** = *goodness knows what*
J'en ai marre de ces féministes agressives qui veulent que leurs mecs fassent le ménage, la vaisselle, le repassage et je ne sais quoi encore = *I'm fed up with those aggressive feminists who want their fellers to do the housework, the washing up, the ironing and goodness knows what else*

With **n'importe qui** = *anyone*, **n'importe quoi** = *anything* – see 245
N'importe qui accepterait pour lui faire plaisir = *anyone would accept to please her*

Vous feriez n'importe quoi pour éviter une situation pénible = *you'd do anything to avoid a painful situation*

With some archaic formulae
Qu'à cela ne tienne! = *never mind!*

There is also the case of 'expletive' ***ne*** – used, optionally, in certain types of clause. Unlike the previous cases, this ***ne*** has no negative value. Its use here is often but not always associated with high-register French –

After ***avant que*** = *before*
On ne pouvait pas l'empêcher de voir ses copains, on le harcelait avant qu'il ne parte = *you couldn't stop him seeing his mates, you tackled him about it before he left*

After expressions of prevention
En fait ça évitera qu'il ne se sente obligé de se rendre à la fac ce soir = *in fact that will save him from going back to the uni. this evening*

After ***sans que*** = *without*
C'est le cas des employés qui suivent leur entreprise sans que leur conjoint ne puisse partir avec eux = *it's the case of workers who follow their firm around without their spouse being able to go with them*

Si vous êtes mal dans votre peau, vous ne serez pas perçu positivement, sans que la personne ne puisse réellement en expliquer la cause = *if you're not comfortable with yourself, you won't be perceived positively, without the person being really able to explain the reason why*

418 ne . . . personne = no one, not anyone
As subject
Personne ne doit perdre la face = *no one must lose face*

La société actuelle souhaite nous aligner tous sur le même modèle – personne n'ose ne pas paraître jeune, beau, productif = *contemporary society wants to make us all conform to the same model – no one dares not appear young, good-looking, productive*

La combine fonctionne – mais personne n'est dupe = *the scams work – but no one is taken in*

Personne ne devrait manquer une telle possibilité = *no one should miss such a chance*

Personne ne voulait de moi = *no one wanted me*

As object
With compound tenses the pronoun follows the past participle (instead of preceding it, as with most of the other negators) –

Je n'ai personne à qui me confier = *I haven't got anyone to confide in*

Je n'ai reconnu personne dans la salle – *I didn't recognise anyone in the room*

Je vous écris parce que je ne trouve personne avec qui je peux partager ma passion des cravates et petits boutons fantaisie = *I'm writing to you because I can't find anyone with whom I can share my passion for ties and small novelty buttons*

As indirect object

Ne parlez à personne comme ça, pas de réflexion, ni de prise de tête = *don't speak to anyone like that, without thinking, without arguing*

Ne faites confiance à personne et gardez votre langue dans votre poche = *don't trust anyone and keep your tongue buttoned up*

L'idée n'arriverait à personne d'utiliser de tels comprimés sans l'autorisation de son médecin = *the idea wouldn't occur to anyone to use those pills without their doctor's authorisation*

After a preposition

J'ai découvert que je ne peux compter sur personne sauf mon amie = *I've discovered that I can't count on anyone except my girlfriend*

Les poignées d'amour ne flattent l'image de personne = *love handles don't flatter anyone's image*

Les divorcés qui sont restés des années sans personne = *divorcees who go for years without anybody*

Without a verb

Avec qui es-tu sortie hier soir? – Personne = *who did you go out with last night? – No one*

Qui est responsable des fiches de paie des travailleurs intérimaires? – Réponse habituelle – personne = *who is responsible for temporary workers' pay slips? – Usual answer – nobody*

419 *ne . . . rien* = *nothing, not anything*

As subject

Rien n'est prouvé, mais vous pouvez essayer = *nothing is proved, but you can try*

Rien ne doit vous empêcher de régler vos histoires de coeur = *nothing must prevent you from sorting out your romantic attachments*

Rien n'est plus dangereux pour la santé que le cholestérol de basse densité = *nothing is worse for our health than low-density cholesterol*

Rien n'y fait – tout le monde est toujours fâché = *nothing can be done about it – everyone is still cross*

As object

Ces positions n'ont rien de très confortable = *these positions aren't at all comfortable*

Si vous ne faites rien la situation va empirer = *if you don't do something the situation is going to get worse*

Il ne faut rien effacer, tout se rappeler, pour mieux rebondir = *you mustn't leave out anything, remember everything, to bounce back more effectively*

Les hauts fonctionnaires n'ont rien sacrifié de leurs privilèges = *the top civil servants have not sacrificed any part of their privileges*

Before an infinitive
Vous êtes un peu maladroite, mais c'est toujours mieux que de ne rien faire = *you're a bit clumsy, but it's always better than doing nothing*

After a preposition
Il ne faut toucher à rien = *you mustn't touch anything*

Elle ne se souvient de rien de cette nuit-là = *she can't remember anything about that night*

Je ne sortirais avec lui pour rien au monde = *I wouldn't go out with him for anything in the world*

Je n'échangerais pas ça pour rien au monde = *I wouldn't change that for anything in the world*

rien de + adjective = *nothing* + adjective
The adjective is invariable; the expressions may be used with a verb, in which case **ne** is required before the verb, **rien** precedes the participle when the verb is compound and the adjectival part follows it, or **rien de** may be used without a verb, in which case it retains its full negative value –

with simple tense
Je crois qu'il n'y a rien de pire qu'une fille qui fait l'étalage de ses conquêtes comme pourrait le faire un mec = *I think there's nothing worse than a girl who displays her conquests, like a guy would do*

with compound tense
Je n'y ai rien appris de nouveau = *I didn't learn anything new there*

Il n'y avait rien eu d'extravagant à la « Disco Infernale » = *there hadn't been anything that out of the ordinary at the 'Disco Infernale'*

*without **ne, rien** still preserves its negative value*
Rien de plus triste que des petits déjeuners qui se suivent et se ressemblent = *there's nothing sadder than breakfasts one after the other all the same*

Rien de tel qu'une bonne fête paillarde pour échapper au stress = *there's nothing like a good old wild knees-up to avoid stress*

Rien de pire que les pâtes trop cuites = *there's nothing worse than over-cooked pasta*

With sans = *without anything*
Monaco se trouve bredouille, sans rien = *Monaco ends up empty-handed, without a thing*

rien que without negative = *only, just*
Voilà pourquoi elle peut s'octroyer de temps à autre des moments rien que pour elle = *here's why she can allow herself from time to time some moments just for herself*

Rien que de penser à tout ce que ma copine va endurer, je me dis que j'ai la chance d'être solo = *simply thinking about what my friend is going to go through, I tell myself I'm lucky to be on my own*

rien as noun = *the slightest thing* and functions as a normal noun

Il ne suffit pas de réaliser un bon match, tout se joue sur des petits détails, des petites erreurs, des riens = *it's not enough to play a good match, everything turns on small details, minor errors, the slightest thing*

Les repas prêts en un rien de temps, vous vous en souvenez? = *meals ready in the blink of an eye – do you remember them?*

420 **ne ... aucun** = no, none

As adjective

Je ne plaisais à aucune fille = *I didn't appeal to any girl*

Je n'ai aucun lien de sang avec ce monsieur-là = *I've no blood tie with that man*

Dans aucune démocratie du monde, on ne trouve pareille situation = *in no democracy in the world do you find a similar situation*

Aucune planète ne vous nuit ce mois-ci = *no planet will harm you this month*

Elle n'a aucune trace écrite de son travail = *she's not got any written proof of her job*

Without a verb

Quel homme résisterait à une jolie femme? – Aucun = *what man could resist a pretty woman? – None*

Vous êtes tombée sur un mec en boîte, mais vous apprenez qu'il est marié – votre réponse? – Aucun problème, suis pas jalouse = *you come across a bloke in a club, but you find out he's married – your reaction? – No prob, I'm not jealous*

Aucun is not used as an adjective in the plural – its role there is assumed by the partitive article **de** or **sans** – see 260, 383.

As pronoun

Aucun de mes amis ne comprend pourquoi je préfère vivre en solo = *none of my friends understands why I prefer to live alone*

Aucune de ses victimes n'a osé décrire leur calvaire personnel = *none of his victims dared describe their personal suffering*

421 **ne ... nul** = no, no one

Ne ... nul is not very common in contemporary French – it survives particularly in the expression **nulle part** = *nowhere* and occasionally as a pronoun and also as an independent adjective.

As adjective

Partout et jamais nulle part = *everywhere and never nowhere*

As pronoun

Pieds malodorants, pellicules, mauvaise haleine, nul n'est épargné = *smelly feet, dandruff, bad breath, no one is spared*

= nil, useless

Son taux de croissance n'est pas nul = *its growth rate is not unimportant*

La Norvège a gagné nuls points = *Norway got no points*

422 ne . . . guère = hardly, scarcely

Il n'eut guère de peine à montrer qu'il aurait pu aussi partir dans le Tour avec le maillot jaune = *he scarcely had difficulty showing that he could have set off in the Tour* [cycle race] *wearing the yellow jersey*

La région, où dominent les grosses cheminées pleines de fumées industrielles, n'amuse guère = *the region, where enormous chimneys spout industrial fumes, is hardly attractive*

423 ne . . . jamais = never

As with **ne . . . pas**, an indefinite article dependent on **jamais** is contracted to **de** – see 416.

After the verb

Du fait que la France n'a jamais connu de gouvernement libéral, la gauche n'a pas eu à bouger vers le centre = *since France has never had a liberal government, the left has never had to move towards the centre*

Elle tombe amoureuse une fois par mois, mais à son grand désespoir, le coup de foudre n'est jamais réciproque = *she falls in love once a month, but, to her great despair, the crush is never reciprocated*

Ce grand champion, Raymond Poulidor, n'a jamais porté le maillot jaune = *this great champion, Raymond Poulidor, never wore the yellow jersey*

Before the verb

Unlike English, French does not invert the verb when **jamais** precedes it –

Jamais les Portugais ne donnent l'impression d'être dépassés = *never do the Portuguese give the impression of being outdone*

With infinitive

Au coup de sifflet final, on le voit balancer le ballon dans le ciel en espérant ne jamais le voir réapparaître = *at the final whistle, you could see him boot the ball into the sky hoping never to see it reappear*

Les jeunes vieux d'aujourd'hui cherchent à rajeunir et surtout à ne jamais faire leur âge = *today's young oldies try to look young and especially not to act their age*

With infinitive as imperative

Ne jamais donner une réponse immédiate si l'on sent que le « petit service » que l'on vous demande va se transformer en gros calvaire = *never reply straightaway if you feel the 'small service' they're asking you is going to change into a real ordeal*

Without **ne** = *never*

On peut s'habiller en bleu, jamais en rouge = *you can wear blue, never red*

On y va pour draguer les filles, jamais pour écouter la musique = *you go there to chat up girls, never to listen to the music*

Le conseil de mes amies – jamais le premier soir = *my friends' advice – never the first night*

After *sans, jamais* = *ever*

Il y retourne dix minutes plus tard sans jamais trouver la fille qu'il voulait draguer = *he goes back ten minutes later without ever being able to find the girl he wanted to chat up*

Elle enchaîne les relations sans jamais parvenir à construire une histoire durable = *she goes from one relationship to another without ever managing to construct one that lasts*

Vous attendez qu'il vous appelle, sans jamais oser l'appeler = *you wait for him to call you, without ever daring to call him*

424 **ne . . . plus** = no longer, not any more

Je ne sais plus comment me coiffer = *I no longer know how to do my hair*

Il a compris que la France ne pouvait plus refuser la réforme = *he understood that France could no longer refuse reforms*

N'ayez plus peur de l'anesthésie = *don't be afraid of anaesthetics any more*

Après 70 ans, il faudra veiller à boire suffisamment, car les mécanismes de la soif ne fonctionnent plus comme avant = *after 70 years of age, you have to be careful to drink enough, because the mechanisms controlling your thirst no longer work as they used to*

Il faudra réformer le système de santé dont les coûts ne sont plus contrôlés = *it will be necessary to reform the health system whose costs are no longer under control*

With infinitive

Les craintes du bébé peuvent être dues à des angoisses de toute sorte, celle de ne plus vous voir dans son champ de vision = *the baby's fears may be due to all sorts of anxieties, such as no longer having you in its field of vision*

Il lui suffisait de garder son calme et ne plus chercher l'as mais de mettre sa première balle en jeu = *all he had to do was to keep calm and no longer go for the ace but get his first ball in*

Ne plus se réveiller – là réside la source d'angoisse principale des patients devant l'anesthésie = *not to wake up again – that's the principal source of anxiety for patients when faced with going under an anaesthetic*

Je me disais qu'elle finirait par ne plus y penser = *I told myself she'd end up not thinking about it any more*

Depuis que vous avez trouvé le créneau qui vous convient au mieux vous devriez ne plus en sortir = *since you've found the slot that suits you best, you shouldn't abandon it ever again*

In the expression ***n'en plus pouvoir*** = *not to be able to bear*
Elle n'en peut plus de sa solitude = *she can't bear being alone any more*

425 *ne . . . que* = only

In French the ***que*** of this combination immediately precedes the element it qualifies –
unlike English where the position of *only* is less strictly applied. ***Ne . . . que*** can be used
to exclude clauses as well as items which do not involve a verb –

10 kilos de trop – ça ne se perd que sous contrôle médical = *10 kilos overweight –
that can only be lost under medical supervision*

Pour moi, une femme qui fume dans la rue ne peut être que vulgaire = *to me,
a woman who smokes in the street can only be common*

Ce n'est qu'un geste anodin, mais vous êtes sûr de le désorienter = *it's only a
harmless gesture, but you're sure to put him off his stroke*

Le reste, ce ne sont que quelques images volées ci et là = *as for the rest, it's just a
few images stolen here and there*

Cette soupe légère ne contient que 25 calories aux 100 millilitres = *this light
soup only contains 25 calories per 100 millilitres*

Je viens de prendre conscience que je n'ai que 20 ans = *I've just realised that I'm
only 20 years old*

  Ne . . . que is often used with a verb to = *the only thing, all*

Peut-être vivez-vous avec un volcan qui ne demande qu'à se réveiller =
perhaps you're living with a volcano and all she wants is to burst into life

Elle n'a qu'à se laisser aller et savourer = *all she has to do is let herself go and enjoy*

Pour se protéger des moustiques, on n'a qu'à s'asperger de citronnelle = *to
protect yourself from mosquitoes, all you have to do is sprinkle yourself with citronella*

ne . . . que + pas = *not just, not only*
On n'y va pas que pour rencontrer le mec dont on a toujours rêvé = *you don't
just go there to meet the guy of your dreams*

On ne partage pas que des souvenirs = *you don't only share memories*

Dans sa bande d'amis, il n'y avait pas que des mecs bien = *in his gang of mates,
there were not only good guys*

***Mais le pire c'est qu'il n'y a pas que les proches qui tirent partie de votre
gentillesse*** = *but the worst thing is it isn't just your own relatives that exploit your kindness*

426 *ne . . . (pas) . . . ni . . . ni* = neither . . . nor, not . . . or, not . . . either . . . or

Ne . . . ni . . . ni can be used with any part of speech – from adjectives to clauses (see
452).

  If ***ne . . . pas*** (or equivalent) is used – and this is the most frequent combination – ***ni***
does not occur before the first of the set of items –

Le résultat n'est pas dénué de charme, ni parfois d'émotion = *the result is not without charm or at times emotion*

Le rapport vite fait n'est pas moins respectable qu'un rapport long, ni moins utile dans la vie quotidienne d'un couple = *a relationship that is quickly made is no less respectable than a long one, nor less useful in a couple's everyday life*

Je n'ai pas croisé ses yeux bleus le lendemain ni les jours suivants = *I didn't come across his blue eyes the next day or the following days*

With *ne . . . plus*
Avec tous les nouveaux règlements, à quoi ça rime d'être gardien, si on ne peut plus se servir de ses mains, ni de ses pieds, ni de rien? = *with all the new regulations, what's the point of being a goalie, if you can't use your hands, your feet or anything any more?*

With *ne . . . aucun*
Cela va faire bientôt un an que je n'ai aucune vie sentimentale ni sexuelle = *it's soon going to be a year since I had any emotional or sexual attachment*

If no negative particle is used (ie, no *pas*), then *ni* precedes every item of the set –

Ce n'est ni l'endroit ni le moment = *it's neither the right place nor the right moment*

Je portais des talons hauts et il ne fallait ni que je perde l'équilibre ni que je dévie de la cible = *I was wearing high heels and it was necessary for me not to lose my balance or deviate from the target*

Parfois on n'est ni homo, ni hétéro, mais les deux = *sometimes you're neither homosexual nor heterosexual, but both*

ni . . . ni without a verb
S'agit-il d'une mode ou d'un phénomène de société? – Ni l'un, ni l'autre = *is it a matter of fashion or a social phenomenon? – Neither one nor the other*

Ni coincée, ni dévergondée, vous avez une perception assez réaliste des mecs = *neither stuck in your ways nor outrageous in your behaviour, you've got a fairly realistic perception of men*

427 *pas* alone = *not*
Pas is used alone to negate a word or a phrase that does not contain a verb.

Remplacez la bouffe par des mots, mais pas par des clopes = *replace your food with words, but not with fags*

La vie pas toujours facile des solos = *the not-always-easy life of those who live alone*

La France épouse la logique des loisirs et pas celle du travail. Pourquoi pas, d'ailleurs? = *France is wedded to the demands of leisure but not of work. Whyever not?*

Nous avons celle qui est la plus décente, mais pas la moins sexy = *we've got the girl who's the most decent, but not the least sexy*

Ça marche? – Pas du tout = *OK? – Not at all*

Pourquoi pas organiser un voyage? = *why not organise a trip?*

J'étais venue pour m'amuser, pas pour me lamenter = *I'd come to enjoy myself not to moan*

Je l'utilise ou pas? = *shall I use it or not?*

Je n'ai jamais su s'il plaisantait ou pas = *I never knew whether he was joking or not*

With indefinite articles, ***pas de*** (instead of ***du, de la, des,*** etc) is used, as with ***ne . . . pas*** above (see 416) –

Pas d'alcool, bien sûr = *no alcohol, that's for sure*

Pas de linge sale à ramasser au quatre coins de la maison = *no dirty clothes to pick up from the four corners of the house*

428 **non** = no, not

Apart from in its role as a negative reply, ***non*** functions in much the same way as ***pas***, but is found less frequently.

non = *no* in negative answer
Non, solo ne veut pas dire que vous êtes disponible pour toutes les corvées = *no, being alone does not mean you're available for each and every nasty job*

Les gens ont tellement peur de dire non = *people are so scared to say no*

Que non emphasises negation of negative answer –

Vous avez peur qu'on aille vous aimer moins après. Évidemment que non! = *you're afraid that they're going to like you less afterwards. Of course not!*

non = *not*
Quand nous nous voyons, c'est que nous le voulons vraiment, et non par obligation = *when we see each other, it's because we really want to, and not out of obligation*

Non soignée, une angine bactérienne peut entraîner des complications graves = *if bacterial angina is not treated, it can cause serious complications*

In English *not only* introducing a clause is followed by inversion; the French equivalent, ***non seulement***, is not –

Non seulement ce débardeur à brassière intégrée met notre silhouette en valeur, mais en plus il soutient notre fragile poitrine = *not only does this crop top with integrated bra show off our silhouette but in addition it supports our fragile bust*

For ***non que . . .*** , see 148.

429 . . . **pas non plus** = neither, ... not . . . either, nor
Les tensions ne lui réussissent pas non plus = *tension doesn't do him any good either*

Le bon moment de suivre un régime – quand vous êtes hyper motivée – pas en état de stress, pas en période de révisions, pas non plus en période de fêtes (tentations) = *the best moment to go on a diet is when you're highly motivated – not in a state of stress, not revising, nor when you're celebrating (temptations)*

Si ce rallye n'est pas interdit, il n'est pas autorisé non plus = *even if this rally hasn't been banned, it hasn't been authorised either*

430 Multiple negators

Frequently more than one negator is used in a sentence. The rule for the order of multiple negators following a finite verb is –

ne jamais plus rien	past participle	***personne que***
guère	infinitive	

Vous n'invitez jamais personne ou des gens que vous n'aimez pas = *you never invite anyone round or people you don't like*

Les trucs qui moisissent dans le frigo n'appartiennent jamais à personne = *the bits and bobs that are going mouldy in the fridge never belong to anyone*

Je ne peux plus rien faire des quelques cheveux qui me restent = *I can't any longer do a thing with the few hairs I've still got*

Rien ne va plus dans ma vie = *nothing is going right in my life any more*

Elle ne veut plus rien faire = *she doesn't want to do anything any more*

C'était fini. Il n'y avait plus de finale, plus de rencontre, plus rien = *it was all over. There wasn't going to be a final, no more matches, nothing whatsoever*

Un bébé ne pleure jamais pour rien = *a baby never cries for nothing*

Ce qui me fait le plus de mal, c'est savoir que personne ne m'a jamais aimée en dehors de ma famille et que je n'ai jamais aimé personne = *what hurts the most is to know that no one has loved me outside my family and that I've never loved anyone*

However, if the negators precede the verb, the order ***plus jamais*** is also found –

Je jure que plus jamais il ne m'accompagnera dans les magasins = *I swear that never again will he go shopping with me*

431 Omission of *ne*

In modern informal French, the omission of ***ne*** is very common –

Viens pas te plaindre si on dîne tard = *don't start complaining if your dinner is late*

T'avais qu'à y penser avant de le lui dire = *you should have thought about it before telling her*

On parlait du boulot – ah! – j'avais pas compris = *they were speaking about work – ah! – I hadn't understood*

C'était pas le moment = *it wasn't the right time*

Fontainebleau, c'est pas un peu ennuyeux comme ville? = *isn't Fontainebleau a bit boring as a town?*

Une mère, on en a qu'une, des mecs, y en a pleins = *you only have one mother, but there are stacks of guys*

Tu te fais engueuler parce que c'est rien comparé à la faim dans le monde
= *you have your head bitten off because it's nothing compared to the hunger in the world*

Exercises

**Traduisez en français la section en anglais des phrases suivantes.
Souvent il y a plus d'une solution.**

a *J'ai consulté plusieurs médecins, mais* no treatment gives me any relief.

b Allegedly *78% des Français* do not understand *que les enseignants boycottent les examens.*

c *Nous passons nos soirées* just talking.

d Families no longer hesitate *à insulter les enseignants.*

e Nothing prevents you *de commencer la randonnée devant chez vous, en toute saison.*

f I can no longer move my body nor speak nor even breathe.

g *La douleur* only set in *plusieurs semaines plus tard.*

h *Faut-il se priver de boeuf? – Ah! non, car, tout d'abord* meat has never been so safe from a health point of view *et surtout parce que* beef isn't as fat as all that.

i No passer-by can suspect *que l'un des plus grands sex symbols du cinéma se cache derrière ces verres fumés.*

j Neither does anyone know what he intends.

k You can't, *lorsqu'on est attaché à la cause palestinienne, s'empêcher de reprendre timidement espoir.*

l *Je vis dans un centre antidouleurs qui me prescrit de la morphine, mais* I no longer have any hope. I can't work any longer.

m My problems keep on increasing.

n There's nothing simpler *pour protéger sa santé.*

o In less time than you need to say it, *la peau épaissit.*

p *Signez une reconnaissance de dette, ainsi* no one will be able to accuse you *d'exploiter la situation.*

q *Dans la plupart des familles du temps de notre arrière-grand-mère,* they only got washed on Sundays.

r *Si au second rendez-vous,* I don't give you a kiss, *alors cela signifie que* I never will.

s *Aujourd'hui on sait que* there is no perfect health *sans une bonne hygiène.*

t *Il y a une ligne blanche que* the French don't want to cross.

u She never kisses on the mouth nor does she spend the night *avec sa proie.*

v *C'est le tabou* that should not be transgressed.

w *Fréquemment la question* isn't even hinted at.

x *Il faut éviter de se moquer de lui,* not ask him to speak *moins vite.*

y *Il est plus tard que* you think.

z He's never so comfortable *que lorsqu'il renoue avec ses racines provinciales.*

aa There's scarcely any doubt that it's a case of suicide.

bb I never realised.

cc *Pour ceux qui* have neither drawn up a will nor made a gift, *le Code civil s'occupe de tout.*

dd *Les dispositions prises par testament* are never definitive: *elles peuvent être changées à tout moment.*

ee This mega-star can't buy his bread *tranquillement,* nor his cigarettes.

ff *Il a réussi et* no longer has anything much *à prouver.*

gg *Sa tenue de foot, déchirée, crottée,* couldn't last any longer.

hh *Ce type de relation sexuelle* doesn't involve any consequence or any commitment.

ii *Ces artisans* don't need any tricks or structures *pour accomplir leurs buts.*

jj No one will be able to say *qu'elle ne soit pas attentive aux autres.*

kk Don't say: *« J'arrête de manger n'importe comment ». Il faut éviter* a situation of all or nothing.

ll *Unless the president* intervenes, *la situation continuera à empirer.*

Chapter 11 *Numerals*

432 Cardinal numbers and ordinal numbers
Cardinal numbers denote quantity

un, deux, trois, quatre

Ordinal numbers denote a position in a sequence

premier, deuxième, troisième, quatrième

433 Cardinal numbers
0–10
zéro, un, deux, trois, quatre, cinq, six, sept, huit, neuf, dix

zéro = *zero, nil, nought, love*

Le numéro de téléphone est 02 38 46 89 89 (zéro deux trente-huit . . .) = *the telephone number is 02 38 46 89 89 (zero two, thirty-eight . . .)*

Elle enseigne les enfants de zéro à quatre ans = *she teaches kids from nought to six years old*

Le prof était furieux – nous avons tous eu zéro dans la dictée = *the teacher was furious – we all got nought in the dictation*

La France a battu le Danemark trois buts à zéro = *France beat Denmark 3 nil*

Elle a remporté le premier set 6–0 (six–zéro) = *she won the first set 6 love*

un (m)*, une* (f)
These numerals vary for gender according to the noun they qualify –

J'ai un frère et une soeur = *I've got one brother and one sister*

Il est une heure = *it's one o'clock*

Je n'ai qu'un vrai ami = *I've only got one real friend*

Masculine *un* is also used in the following contexts –

C'est à la page un = *it's on page one*

Elle est le numéro un de l'opposition = *she's the number one of the opposition*

Il portait le numéro un = *he was wearing the number one shirt*

Feminine *une* is also used in the following context –

à la une = *on the front page*

Both numerals also act as pronouns –

Le site est un des majeurs du marché = *the site is one of the major players in the market*

Prenez une des tranches de pain de mie et passez-la sous le gril du four = *take one of the slices of bread and put it under the grill*

The plural *uns* occurs in such contexts as –

Il y a trois uns dans cent onze = *there are three ones in one hundred and eleven*

11–20
onze, douze, treize, quatorze, quinze, seize, dix-sept, dix-huit, dix-neuf, vingt

21–30
vingt et un, vingt-deux, vingt-trois, vingt-quatre, vingt-cinq, vingt-six, vingt-sept, vingt-huit, vingt-neuf, trente

No hyphens are used with cardinal numbers in *et un*, but they are used with the others.

Vingt et un becomes *vingt et une* before a feminine noun. This applies to all the cardinal numbers in –*un* –

Vingt et une années se sont écoulées depuis notre premier rendez-vous = *twenty-one years have passed since our first rendez-vous*

31–40
trente et un, trente-deux, trente-trois, trente-quatre, trente-cinq, trente-six, trente-sept, trente-huit, trente-neuf, quarante

41–50
quarante et un, quarante-deux, quarante-trois, quarante-quatre, quarante-cinq, quarante-six, quarante-sept, quarante-huit, quarante-neuf, cinquante

51–60
cinquante et un, cinquante-deux, cinquante-trois, cinquante-quatre, cinquante-cinq, cinquante-six, cinquante-sept, cinquante-huit, cinquante-neuf, soixante

61–70
soixante et un, soixante-deux, soixante-trois, soixante-quatre, soixante-cinq, soixante-six, soixante-sept, soixante-huit, soixante-neuf, soixante-dix

In a number of French-speaking countries outside France, eg Belgium, Switzerland, Canada, **soixante-dix** is replaced by **septante**.

71–80
soixante et onze, soixante-douze, soixante-treize, soixante-quatorze, soixante-quinze, soixante-seize, soixante-dix-sept, soixante-dix-huit, soixante-dix-neuf, quatre-vingts

327

In those countries where **soixante-dix** is replaced by **septante, soixante et onze** is replaced by **septante et un, soixante-douze** by **septante-deux,** etc.

81–90

quatre-vingt-un, quatre-vingt-deux, quatre-vingt-trois, quatre-vingt-quatre, quatre-vingt-cinq, quatre-vingt-six, quatre-vingt-sept, quatre-vingt-huit, quatre-vingt-neuf, quatre-vingt-dix

Quatre-vingts = *80* loses its **–s** when it is combined with another number, eg **quatre-vingt-deux**; in other words, it is only in **quatre-vingts** = *80* that the final **–s** appears. **Quatre-vingts** = *80* also loses its **–s** when it is used as a page or paragraph number – **au paragraphe quatre-vingt**.

Huitante is used alongside **quatre-vingts** in Switzerland.

In those countries where **soixante-dix** is replaced by **septante, quatre-vingt-dix** is replaced by **nonante**.

91–100

quatre-vingt-onze, quatre-vingt-douze, quatre-vingt-treize, quatre-vingt-quatorze, quatre-vingt-quinze, quatre-vingt-seize, quatre-vingt-dix-sept, quatre-vingt-dix-huit, quatre-vingt-dix-neuf, cent

Quatre-vingt-onze is replaced by **nonante et un, quatre-vingt-douze** by **nonante-deux** in Belgium, Switzerland and Canada.

Cent = *a hundred, one hundred* (in other words, there is no word for *a, one*) –

J'ai envoyé cent une invitations = *I sent out a hundred and one invitations*

101–110

cent un, cent deux, cent trois, cent quatre, cent cinq, cent six, cent sept, cent huit, cent neuf, cent dix

111, 112, etc

cent onze, cent douze, etc

121, 122, etc

cent vingt et un, cent vingt-deux, etc

200–210

deux cents, deux cent un, deux cent deux, deux cent trois, deux cent quatre, deux cent cinq, deux cent six, deux cent sept, deux cent huit, deux cent neuf, deux cent dix

Usage with **cent** is similar to that with **quatre-vingts** – **cents** preserves its final **–s** when it is used to indicate round hundreds – **deux cents, trois cents**, etc. However, when it is qualified by another number, the **–s** is dropped – **deux cent un, trois cent deux**.

1,000 – 1,999

1 000 = mille, 1 001 = mille un, 1 010 = mille dix, 1 011 = mille onze, 1 100 = mille cent, 1 101 = mille cent un

Mille = *a thousand, one thousand* (in other words, there is no word for *a, one*) –

mille animaux = *a thousand animals*

Numbers between **1 100** and **1 999** may be expressed in two ways – **1 100** is either **onze cents** or **mille cent, 1567** is either **quinze cent soixante-sept** or **mille cinq cent soixante-sept**

2,000 . . .
2 000 = **deux mille, 3 000** = **trois mille**

Usage with **mille** is different from that with **cent** – it never takes an **–s** whatever the circumstances.

Where in English a comma is used to separate the figures representing thousands from those representing hundreds – *1,111* – in French simply a space is used – **1 111**. The same applies to figures involving millions – *1,111,111* in English, **1 111 111** in French.

Usage with dates – the above does not apply to dates – **2005** (not **2 005**). In neither French nor English are commas used to separate thousands from the hundreds – **2005** = *2005*. If a date is written out in French (which is extremely rare, see below), the spelling **mil** is preferred to **mille** –

en l'an deux mil cinq = *in 2005*

1 000 000 = **un million, 1 000 001** = **un million un, 1 111 111** = **un million cent onze mille cent onze**

Since **million** is a noun, when used in the singular it is preceded by **un**. The same applies to **milliard** and **billion** below.

2 000 000 = **deux millions, 2 345 678** = **deux millions trois cent quarante-cinq mille six cent soixante dix-huit**

Another consequence of the fact that **million** is a noun is that it always has an **–s** in the plural. In addition when used with another noun it functions as a noun expressing quantity and is followed by **de**. Again the same applies to **milliard** and **billion** below.

13 millions de Français possédaient un lecteur DVD en 2003 = *13 million people in France owned a DVD player in 2003*

However, if the figure is not a round million, no **de** is required –

La population de la ville est de deux millions cinq cent mille personnes = *the population of the town is 2,500,000 persons*

1 000 000 000 = **un milliard** = *a thousand million, a billion* (American English)
1 000 000 000 000 = **un billion** = *a billion* (British English)

434 Use of **et** and hyphens with cardinal numerals
et
Used in **21, 31, 41, 51, 61, 71**

hyphens
Used for **17, 18, 19, 22–29, 32–39** up to **79**, then **80–99**

no hyphen *or* et

cent, mille, million are not connected to any other numeral –

cent vingt-deux, deux mille trois cent quarante-cinq

435 Pronunciation matters

Cinq is always pronounced /sɛ̃k/ except before **cent**, when it is pronounced /sɛ̃/.

Six is pronounced in a number of ways according to its verbal context –

/sis/ at the end of a sense group –

> **J'en ai six** = *I've got six*

/siz/ before a word beginning with a vowel or non-aspirate **h** –

> **six heures** = *six o'clock*, **six ombres à paupières** = *six eye-shadows*

/si/ before a word beginning with a consonant –

> **six débardeurs** = *six tops*

Huit is pronounced differently according to its verbal context –

/ɥit/ at the end of a sense group and before a word beginning with a vowel or non-aspirate **h** –

> **J'en ai huit** = *I've got eight*, **huit amis** = *eight friends*

/ɥi/ before a word beginning with a consonant –

> **huit couleurs** = *eight colours*

Neuf is always pronounced /nœf/ except before **heures** and **ans**, when it is pronounced /nœv/

Dix – as for **six**

Vingt is pronounced /vɛ̃/ before a word beginning with a consonant and at the end of a sense group –

> **J'en ai vingt** = *I've got twenty*, **vingt magazines** = *twenty magazines*

/vɛ̃t/ before a word beginning with a vowel and in the numerals **21–29** inclusive –**Vingt-deux amies sont arrivées** = *twenty-two friends turned up*

Cent is pronounced /sã/ before a word beginning with a consonant and at the end of a sense group –

> **Cent mannequins ont défilé devant le public** = *a hundred models paraded before the audience*

/sãt/ in **cent un, cent huit, cent onze** and before a word beginning with a vowel –

> **Cent arbres ont été plantés au bord de la rivière** = *a hundred trees have been planted by the river*

436 When to use figures to express cardinal numbers

Figures are used

in dates –

> ***l'an 2000, le 29 janvier 1950***

in prices –

> ***L'armoire coûte 449 euros*** *= the cupboard costs 449 euros*

in weights and measures –

> ***Vous pesez 56 kilos pour 1,70 mètre*** *= you weigh 56 kilos for 1 metre 70*

in mathematical formulae –

> ***29 + 45 = 74 = 29 plus 45 égale 74***
>
> ***3 + 4 = 7 = 3 et 4 font 7***
>
> ***45 – 29 = 16 = 45 moins 29 égale 16***
>
> ***45 × 3 = 135 = 45 multiplié par 3 égale 135***
>
> ***45 ÷ 3 = 15 = 45 divisé par 3 égale 15***

> ***Votre indice de masse corporelle est égal à 56 divisé par 1,70 × 1,70 = 19,37 soit votre nombre de kilos par mètre carré de surface corporelle =*** *your body mass index equals 56 divided by 1.7 times 1.7 = 19.37, in other words your weight in kilos per square metre of body surface*

in percentages –

La prépondérance féminine est particulièrement marquée en matière de divorce par faute, soit 75% *= the preponderance of women is particularly noticeable in the matter of divorce by admission of guilt, namely 75%*

in addresses and telephone numbers –

33 avenue Georges-Bernanos, 75005 Paris

Renseignements: 0810600243 read as ***zéro huit – dix – soixante – zéro deux – quarante-trois*** *= for information . . .*

437 Approximate numbers

The pattern is to add **–aine** to the 'ten' concerned –
une dizaine *= about 10*

une quinzaine *= about 15*, also *a fortnight*

une vingtaine *= about 20*

une trentaine *= about 30*

une centaine *= about 100*

des centaines de photos *= hundreds of photos*

But **un millier** *= about a thousand*

des milliers de photos *= thousands of photos*

Environ can also be used to express approximate numbers –

Elle a environ 40 ans = *she's about 40*

But ***une douzaine*** = *a dozen, 12*

438 Fractions and decimals
Fractions
un demi = *a half* –
cinq et demi = *five and a half*

but ***la moitié*** = *half* when a mathematical fraction is not involved –

Ajouter la moitié des pâtes aux dés de mozzarella et les tomates = *add half the pasta to the cubes of mozzarella and the tomatoes*

When *half* is part of a compound expression, ***demi*** is used before the noun and remains invariable for number and gender –

un demi-verre de vin = *half a glass of wine*, ***une demi-heure*** = *half an hour*, ***une demi-douzaine*** = *half a dozen*

Il a deux demi-soeurs = *he's got two half-sisters*

When ***demi*** occurs after a noun, it varies for gender –

Il est cinq heures et demie = *it's half past five*

Il mesure déjà un mètre et demi = *he's already a metre and a half tall*

The adverbs ***à demi*** and ***à moitié*** = *half* are interchangeable –

Est-ce que tu dirais que ton verre est à moitié vide ou à moitié plein? = *Would you say your glass was half-full or half-empty?*

Laisse la porte à demi ouverte s'il te plaît = *leave the door half-open please*

The prefix ***mi-*** is also used in certain expressions –

La première mi-temps du match était fascinante = *the first half of the match was fascinating*

L'arrêt d'autobus se trouve à mi-chemin entre ma maison et le lycée = *the bus stop is half-way between my house and the school*

un tiers = *a third*

but as an ordinal numeral, ***le troisième*** = *third*

un quart = *a quarter*

un cinquième = *a fifth*

un sixième = *a sixth*

un septième = *a seventh*

un huitième = *an eighth*

un neuvième = *a ninth*

un dixième = *a tenth*, etc

When the fraction is above one, the following construction, using the definite article rather than no article as in English, is used –

Les deux tiers des lecteurs préfèrent les articles sur les rapports sexuels = *two thirds of the readership prefer articles on sexual relationships*

Les trois quarts des parents ont contacté le site interministériel de protection des mineurs sur Internet = *three quarters of parents have contacted the interministerial site for the protection of minors on the Internet*

un et demi = *one and a half*
deux et trois quarts = *two and three quarters*

Decimals
French uses a comma where English uses a decimal point and treats the numbers after the comma as one complete number, not as separate units –

2,5 = deux virgule cinq = *2.5*

0,54 = zéro virgule cinquante-quatre = *0.54*

6,268 = six virgule deux cent soixante-huit = *6.268*

439 Ordinal numbers
1st–10th
premier (m), **première** (f) = *first*

deuxième, second = *second*

troisième = *third*

quatrième = *fourth*

cinquième = *fifth*

sixième = *sixth*

septième = *seventh*

huitième = *eighth*

neuvième = *ninth*

dixième = *tenth*

11th–20th
onzième = *eleventh*

douzième = *twelfth*

treizième = *thirteenth*

quatorzième = *fourteenth*

quinzième = *fifteenth*

seizième = *sixteenth*

dix-septième = *seventeenth*

dix-huitième = *eighteenth*

dix-neuvième = *nineteenth*

vingtième = *twentieth*

21st, 22nd, 30th, 31st, 32nd, 70th, 71st, 80th, 81st, 90th, 91st, 100th, 101st, 200th, 1,000th, 2,000th, 1,000,000th

vingt et unième = *twenty-first*

vingt-deuxième = *twenty-second*

trentième = *thirtieth*

trente et unième = *thirty-first*

trente-deuxième = *thirty-second*

soixante-dixième = *seventieth*, ***septantième*** in Belgium, Switzerland, Canada

soixante-onzième = *seventy-first*, ***septante et unième***

quatre-vingtième = *eightieth*, ***huitantième*** *in Switzerland*

quatre-vingt-unième = *eighty-first*

quatre-vingt-dixième = *ninetieth*, ***nonantième*** in Belgium, Switzerland, Canada

quatre-vingt-onzième = *ninety-first*, ***nonante et unième***

centième = *hundredth*

cent et unième = *hundred and first*

deux-centième = *two hundredth*

millième = *thousandth*

deux millième = *two thousandth*

millionième = *millionth*

Vous êtes la deuxième personne à me poser cette question = *you're the second person to ask me that question*

Le premier et le centième bébés à naître le premier janvier recevront un cadeau de l'hôpital = *the first and the hundredth baby to be born on January 1st will receive a present from the hospital*

440 Telling the time

All times are introduced by ***il est*** = *it is*. The 24-hour clock is used for public purposes but not always for more personal use. It is obligatory to use ***heures*** (except when it is ***midi*** or ***minuit***) when giving the time.

Hours
Quelle heure est-il? = *what's the time?*

Il est une heure = *it's one o'clock*

Il est midi / minuit = *it's midday / midnight*

Il est quatre heures / seize heures = *it's four o'clock / four pm*

Quarter past and quarter to the hour
Il est deux heures et quart = *it's quarter past two*

Il est quatre heures moins le quart = *it's quarter to four*

Il est huit heures quinze = *it's eight fifteen*

Half past the hour
Il est cinq heures et demie = *it's half past five*

Il est midi / minuit et demi = *it's half past midday / midnight*

Il est neuf heures trente = *it's nine thirty*

Other times
Il est sept heures cinq = *it's five past seven*

Il est onze heures moins vingt = *it's twenty to eleven*

12-hour clock versus 24-hour clock
The 12-hour clock specifies the time of day – **du matin / de l'après-midi / du soir** and uses times with **moins / et** –

Il est quatre heures moins dix de l'après-midi = *it's ten to four in the afternoon/pm*

Il est dix heures et demie du soir = *it's half past ten in the evening*

The 24-hour clock does not use **moins / et** nor does it specify the time of day; on the other hand, it specifies the minutes after the hour –

Il est seize heures dix = *it's ten past four pm*

Il est vingt-deux heures trente = *it's ten thirty pm, half past ten*

Il est vingt-trois heures cinquante-cinq = *it's five to midnight*

Precisely
Il est six heures précises / justes = *it's exactly six o'clock*

Il est six heures sonnantes / pile = *it's dead on six o'clock*

Approximately
Il est vers neuf heures / vers les neuf heures = *it's about nine o'clock*

À environ dix heures, je t'appellerai = *at about ten o'clock, I'll give you a call*

441 Dates

The date is always preceded by **le**, which is not contracted before numbers beginning with a vowel or non-aspirate **h**. Apart from **le premier**, cardinal numbers are used with dates. Names of months and days always begin with a lower-case letter.

Months

Quelle est la date aujourd'hui / On est le combien aujourd'hui? = *what's the date today / what's today's date?*

le premier juin = *1st June*

le deux juillet = *2nd July*

le huit août = *8th August*

le onze septembre = *11th September*

le trente et un octobre = *31st October*

Years

2005 = deux mil / mille cinq

When giving a year including a hundred, it is necessary to say **cent** –

1950 = mille / mil neuf cent cinquante / dix-neuf cent cinquante

L'an is used to refer to specific years, **les années** to decades –

l'an 2000

les années soixante = *the sixties* (numbers are invariable)

Days

Referring to a specific day, no article is used –

Le match retour aura lieu samedi prochain = *the return match will take place next Saturday*

Lundi, je laverai les serviettes de toilette et mon peignoir de bain = *I'll wash my bathroom towels and my bathrobe on Monday*

With a date, a definite article is required –

Le match retour aura lieu le samedi 23 octobre / samedi le 23 octobre = *the return match will take place on Saturday 23rd October*

Elle est née mardi le 8 novembre = *she was born on Tuesday 8th November*

Otherwise use of the definite article indicates an habitual occurrence –

Ils s'entraînent le lundi soir et le mercredi après-midi = *they train on Monday evenings and Wednesday afternoons*

Le dimanche le culte a lieu à 10 heures et demie = on Sundays, the service is at half past ten

Periods of the day / the year

The definite article is used to indicate an habitual occurrence –

Je trouve difficile de me lever le matin = I find it hard to get up in the morning

Elle fait la lessive le matin et le repassage l'après-midi = she does the washing in the morning and the ironing in the afternoon

L'été / en été, il faut ouvrir les fenêtres pour laisser entrer l'air frais = in summer you have to open your windows to let the fresh air in

Le printemps / au printemps j'aime ne plus porter les lourds vêtements de l'hiver = in the spring I like not having to wear heavy winter clothes any more

442 Miscellaneous matters
Cardinal numbers

Used with titles, except for *first*; English uses ordinal numbers consistently –

François I = François Premier = Francis 1st

Louis XV = Louis Quinze = Louis 15th

Page and chapter numbers

à la page 36 = on page 36

au chapitre quatre = in chapter 4

Word order – cardinal number + ordinal number or adjective in French but ordinal or adjective + cardinal in English

Les cinq premiers mois tout s'est bien passé = everything went well during the first five months

Pendant les six dernières semaines j'ai porté ma queue-de-cheval très haut = for the last six weeks I've worn my pony-tail very high

Ordinal numbers

Used with districts of Paris

le seizième arrondissement / le seizième = the 16th arrondissement

To express the number of times an action is repeated, *fois* = time(s) is used –

Pour la troisième fois, je te conseille de ne pas porter les talons de plus de sept centimètres = for the third time, I advise you not to wear heels more than seven centimetres high

Pour la énième fois, tais-toi! = for the nth time, shut up!

Je te l'ai dit cinq fois = I've told you five times

Exercises

Écrivez en mots les chiffres qui ne sont pas en italique dans les phrases suivantes –

a *Le nombre de bêtes malades est passé, en France, de 274 en 2001 à* 137 *en 2003 pour un cheptel de* 11 *millions de têtes.*

b 4, 58 *millions – c'est, en Inde, le nombre de personnes infectées par le virus du sida.*

c *Tous les Français peuvent maintenant consulter les fiches biographiques de plus de* 1 325 000 *soldats morts pour la France pendant la guerre de '14–18.*

d *Entre* 229 000 *et* 269 000 *Français sont victimes chaque année d'une infection alimentaire.*

e *Guy Lux,* 83 *ans, et Georges Coulonges,* 80 *ans, sont morts cette semaine.*

f *Plus de* 100 000 *baladeurs devraient se vendre cette année, soit une hausse de* 250% *en un an.*

Chapter 12 *Sentences and clauses*

443 Sentences
Sentences in writing
Sentences are very visible in writing – they begin with a capital letter and end with a full stop, question mark or exclamation mark – and what comes next is usually another sentence beginning with another capital letter and so on. When we write, we automatically construct what we want to say out of sentences – sentences are the building blocks of connected language, and we use punctuation marks of various types to show where sentences begin and end and how they hang together internally.

Sentences in speech
However, in speech, things are different. When we speak we are not so aware of forming sentences – our speech seems to flow naturally, we do not think in terms of full stops and commas, and we have little consciousness of passing from one sentence to another. However, if we transcribe our speech into writing, and if we analyse what we say, we would soon discover that the most convenient way of dividing it up is into sentences. So, in order to discuss speech and how it is constructed, we need to have recourse to the concept of the sentence and to realise that sentences underlie the way we express ourselves in speech as well as in writing. There are of course differences between the two modes of expression, and these will be pointed out in what follows.

Therefore, we can say that sentences constitute the normal unit into which what we want to write or say is divided for communication.

The normal structure of a sentence
Normally, sentences consist of one or more clauses.

Sentences consisting of a single clause –

Dans ce dossier vous allez entendre beaucoup de choses rassurantes = *in this report, you're going to hear a lot of reassuring things*

Je suis très content pour les joueurs = *I am very happy for the players*

Sentences consisting of two clauses –

Mon dermatologue m'a avertie: l'acné mal traité peut laisser des cicatrices = *my dermatologist has told me – badly treated acne can leave scars*

On me trouve nulle, mais on ne peut pas me taxer de tricher = *you may think me useless, but you can't accuse me of cheating*

Si votre bébé a soif, donnez-lui un biberon = *if your baby is thirsty, give him a bottle*

Sentences consisting of three clauses –

Lorsque quelqu'un bat mon record du monde, c'est encore plus excitant car je fais tout pour le récupérer = *when someone breaks my world record, it's even more exciting, because I do my utmost to get it back*

Lavez les pommes, pelez-les ou non selon les goûts et coupez-les en lamelles = *wash the apples, peel them or not according to taste and cut them into slices*

Sentence consisting of four clauses –

Les études scientifiques montrent incontestablement que les oestrogènes limitent la perte osseuse, mais la masse osseuse diminue à nouveau dès qu'on arrête de les prendre = *scientific studies demonstrate incontrovertibly that oestrogen limits bone loss, but bone mass diminishes again as soon as you stop taking it*

Sentence consisting of five clauses –

Il parle très fort, il rit aux éclats, drague tout ce qui bouge, se mêle des conversations des autres = *he speaks at the top of his voice, guffaws with laughter, chats up anything that moves and interrupts other people's conversations*

However, some sentences may consist of a single word or phrase, units smaller than a clause. Grammatically speaking, **Salut!** is as much a sentence as any of the above examples – see 444, 446, 453.

444 Sentence types

There are four types of sentence:

Declarative sentences which make statements –

Ma femme réserve toujours une place dans son lit pour son chien = *my wife always reserves a place in her bed for her dog*

Dans les stations-service, on voit des affichettes interdisant les mobiles = *in petrol stations you can see notices forbidding the use of mobile phones* (**interdisant** is not a finite verb according to the definition given below; it is a present participle and as such does not exhibit person, tense or mood)

Interrogative sentences which ask questions –

Que conseillez-vous? = *what do you advise?*

Ne serait-ce pas une façon de me manipuler? = *would it not be a way of manipulating me?*

Quelle est la différence entre le « bon » et le « mauvais » cholestérol? = *what's the difference between 'good' and 'bad' cholesterol?*

Imperative sentences which give orders –

Ne transformez pas tout en négatif! = *don't be negative about everything!*

N'hésitez pas à peindre, une petite entrée par exemple, de la même couleur du sol au plafond = *don't hesitate to do some decorating, a little entrance hall, for example, the same colour from floor to ceiling*

Apportez une touche de gaieté dans votre cuisine avec cet accroche-torchon en bois peint! = *introduce a touch of light-heartedness into your kitchen with this painted wood duster-holder*

Dansons sous la pluie = *let's dance in the rain*

Exclamative sentences which convey exclamations –

Qu'elle est belle, cette fille! = *how beautiful that girl is!*

Salaud! = *blighter!*

Sentence structure

445 Sentence structure

There are two sentence types –

Minor sentences and major sentences

446 Minor sentences

1 In speech, sentences are often left unfinished, or the speaker may find it satisfactory to express him- or herself with a single word or phrase. In this way, the speaker avoids using major sentences or main clauses – but the required sense is conveyed successfully. It is not essential to speak in sentences to make oneself fully understood.

2 In written French, in journalistic French in particular, articles, reports and interviews are often punctuated in idiosyncratic ways; in this way prominence may be given to certain elements of what is being written. And if the writer is trying to imitate speech, he or she will use similar techniques to those described above.

Minor sentences are sentences which do not contain a main clause. In other words, they may consist of –

1 a subordinate clause –

Pour être star aussi jeune, il faut qu'il y ait eu un coach parental derrière. Parce que c'est souvent le désir du parent qui pousse l'enfant
      subordinate clause
= *to be a star so young, there has to have been a parent coach behind her. Because it's often the parent's desire which pushes the child*

À en croire les enfants le goûter est un de leurs repas préférés. Encouragez-les à goûter. Des petits plats qui plaisent à nos enfants
      subordinate clause
= *If we are to believe our children, a snack is one of their favourite meals. Encourage them. Small dishes that our children like*

2 a phrase

À vos marques! = *on your marks!*

Le monde à l'envers? Non, pas tout à fait = *the world back to front? No, not quite*

Un choc! C'est le souvenir que je garde du premier baiser échangé avec mon copain actuel = *a shock! That's the memory I've got of the first kiss I exchanged with my current boyfriend*

Simplement hors norme = *simply out of the ordinary* (advertisement)

3 a single word

Chouette! = *great!*

Bon! = *fine!*

Comment? = *what?*

447 Major sentences

Major sentences are sentences that contain at least one main clause.

Major sentences fall into four sentence types:

1 Simple sentences

These consist of a single main clause

Chacun doit suivre la religion de son coeur = *everyone must follow the religion of their heart*

Boire ou séduire, il faut choisir = *you have to choose whether to drink or seduce*

2 Compound sentences

These consist of at least two main clauses linked by a coordinating conjunction.

Je m'intéresse à d'autres choses qu'au tennis, comme à la mode, mais mon sport
main clause 1   main clause 2
reste ma seule occupation professionnelle = *I'm interested in other things besides tennis, such as fashion, but my sport remains my only professional occupation*

3 Complex sentences

These consist of one main clause and one or more subordinate clauses –

S'il résiste,   *pratiquez l'hypnose* = *if he resists, use hypnosis*
subordinate clause   main clause

4 Compound-complex sentences

These consist of at least two main clauses and at least one subordinate clause

Je travaille comme une folle depuis que j'ai cinq ans et
main clause 1   subordinate clause 1   main clause 2a

si on parle d'un conte de fées à mon sujet, je ne le vis que cette année =
subordinate clause 2   main clause 2b

I've worked like someone possessed since I was five and if someone mentions a fairytale about me, I've only been living it this year

448 Simple sentences

The single main clause may be declarative, interrogative, imperative or exclamative –

Declarative

L'emploi de mannequins ramasseuses de balles est taxé de sexisme par la secrétaire d'État espagnole à l'égalité des sexes = *the use of models as ball girls is criticised as sexism by the Spanish Secretary of State for sexual equality*

À 18 ans, seule une personne sur cinq a encore toutes ses dents en bon état = *at 18 only one person in five has still got all their teeth in good condition*

Interrogative

Comment puis-je faire pour affiner mes hanches et mes jambes? = *what can I do to slim down my hips and legs?*

Pourquoi les surfeurs ont-ils les yeux bleus? = *why have surfers got blue eyes?*

Imperative

Pour un maquillage facile, focalisez-vous sur les yeux, les pommettes et les lèvres = *to make yourself up easily, concentrate on your eyes, cheeks and lips*

Pondérez vos réactions = *weigh your reactions carefully*

Exclamative

C'est bon à la cantine scolaire! = *it's good in the school canteen!*

Tout ça, c'était pour rire! = *that was just for a joke!*

Qu'à cela ne tienne! = *never mind!*

449 Compound sentences

A compound sentence consists of two or more main clauses, which may or may not be linked by coordinating conjunctions. Compound sentences are more often than not declarative, but may also be imperative, less often interrogative or exclamative.

Compound sentence consisting of two main clauses –

À 40 ans, le même régime ne nous fait pas perdre un gramme et
clause 1   clause 2
s'apparente à un vrai calvaire = *at 40, the same diet doesn't make us lose a gramme and is just like torture*

Compound sentence consisting of more than two main clauses –

Sur scène, je semble être très sûre de moi, mais dans la vraie vie, je suis hyper-timide,
clause 1   clause 2
je ne trouve rien à dire, je deviens nerveuse, j'ai des noeuds au ventre
clause 3   clause 4   clause 5
= *on stage, I seem to be very sure of myself, but in real life, I'm hyper-shy, I can't find anything to say, I become nervous, my stomach is all knotted up*

Compound sentence consisting of three main clauses without coordinating conjunctions –

Je ne me plains pas du tout, je ne désespère pas non plus, ce n'est pas un état négatif = *I don't complain at all, I don't despair either, it's not a negative condition*

450 Complex sentences

A complex sentence consists of a main clause and at least one subordinate clause. Complex sentences are more often than not declarative, less often imperative, interrogative or exclamative.

The subordinate clause can precede, follow or be embedded in the main clause.

Main clause + subordinate clause

À 20 ans, on peut se permettre d'essayer un régime fantaisiste, qui nous fait tout
main clause   subordinate clause
de suite retrouver une taille de guêpe = *at 20 you can allow yourself to experiment with a fanciful diet, which gives you back your wasp-like waist straightaway*

Freud appelle « transfert » le mouvement par lequel le patient revit un fragment
main clause   subordinate clause
de son passé = *Freud calls 'transfer' the movement by which the patient relives a fragment of his past*

Subordinate clause + main clause –

Si vous m'avez bien compris, j'ai dû m'exprimer mal
subordinate clause   main clause
= *if you understood me easily, I must have expressed myself badly*

Quoi qu'il arrive, gardez la tête froide = *whatever happens, keep cool*
subordinate clause   main clause

Main clause + embedded subordinate clause –

Un jour, une jolie Suédoise, avec qui je sortais, m'a redonné confiance =
main clause a   subordinate clause   main clause b
one day, a pretty Swedish girl I was going out with gave me back my confidence

Le mari et les beaux-parents, qui ont aidé leur fils à battre et à étrangler leur
main clause a   subordinate clause
belle-fille, ont été inculpés de tentative de meurtre = *the husband and parents-in-law, who*
          main clause b
helped their son to beat and strangle their daughter-in-law, have been charged with attempted murder

In addition, a second or subsequent subordinate clause can depend upon an earlier subordinate clause –

Pour chasser nos kilos intelligemment, il n'existe pas une solution mais
main clause

plusieurs, parce qu'on ne maigrit pas de la même façon quand on est étudiante
          subordinate clause 1   subordinate clause 2
ou mère de famille de trois ados = *in order to rid ourselves of our extra pounds in an intelligent way, there is no single solution but several, because we don't slim in the same way when we're students or the mother of three teenagers*

À moins que votre linge soit vraiment très sale, ne lavez pas vos beaux T-shirts
subordinate clause 1   main clause
blancs à une température supérieure à 40 degrés, surtout s'ils sont en fibres
                                                                              subordinate clause 2
naturelles, à moins que vous n'ayez décidé* de vous fabriquer un T-shirt à la
              subordinate clause 3
mode métrosexuel**, très moulant = *unless your linen is really very dirty, don't wash your lovely white T-shirts at a temperature over 40 degrees, especially if they're natural fibre, unless you've decided to make yourself a fashionable metrosexual T-shirt, very body-hugging*

*Note that the use of expletive ***ne*** is optional with ***à moins que*** – not present in the first case, it is inserted in the second – see 417.
** ***un métrosexuel*** = *a heterosexual man very concerned about his personal appearance and hygiene*

451 Compound-complex sentences

As their name implies, these sentences combine the clause combinations associated with a compound and a complex sentence. Compound-complex sentences are usually declarative. The permutations are considerable.
Main clause + subordinate clause + main clause

Des millions d'êtres humains rêvent d'une vie éternelle, et s'il pleut le dimanche après-midi, ils ne savent pas quoi faire = *millions of human beings dream of eternal life, and if it rains Sunday afternoon, they don't know what to do*

Subordinate clause + main clause + subordinate clause + main clause

Quand nous sommes jeunes, nous dépensons notre santé pour faire fortune; et quand nous sommes vieux, nous dépensons notre fortune pour nous refaire une santé = *when we're young, we expend our health to build a fortune; and when we're old, we spend a fortune to rebuild our health*

Main clause + subordinate clause + main clause + subordinate clause + subordinate clause + main clause

La femme épouse l'homme en espérant qu'il va changer, et il ne change pas, alors que l'homme épouse la femme en espérant qu'elle ne changera pas, et elle change = *a woman marries a man hoping that he'll change, and he doesn't, whereas a man marries a woman hoping that she won't change, and she does*

452 Coordinating conjunctions

The coordinating conjunctions in French are – ***car, et, mais, ni, ou***. Coordinating conjunctions link clauses and elements of clauses at the same syntactic level, whereas subordinating conjunctions show a dependence of what follows on what precedes. In other words, coordinating conjunctions link subject with subject, object with object, adjective with adjective, adverb with adverb, clause with clause, whereas subordinating conjunctions link a subordinate clause with a clause of higher level in the sentence.

car = *for, because*

The conjunction **car** is usually translated as *for* in English, but, since *for* sounds very pedantic in English, in the examples of its use below it is translated by *because* –

linking elements –

La vision à distance des filles est plus réduite que celle des garçons car plus petites en moyenne de 10 cm que les garçons = *girls' long distance sight is more reduced than that of boys, because they're smaller than boys by 10 cm on average*

linking clauses –

Dans ce métier, vous vous sentez seule, car vous êtes souvent à l'hôtel = *in this job, you feel lonely, because you're often in an hotel*

Je ne dirai pas que c'est moi qui ai lancé la mode du nombril à l'air, car je ne veux pas qu'on en parle dans les journaux = *I'm not saying I was the one who started the trend of the exposed navel, because I don't want it spoken about in the papers*

Je l'aurais conseillé de faire de la marche à pied, car la pratique de randonnée contribue à densifier les os = *I would have advised him to do some walking, because walking helps make our bones denser*

et = *and*

linking elements of a clause –

Voici un pantalon à porter avec un pull noir et une doudoune sans manche = *here's a pair of trousers to wear with a black pullover and sleeveless body-warmer*

Il leur parlait de la pluie, de leur famille et de la vie chère = *he would talk to them about the rain, their families and the high cost of living*

Le nez a trois fonctions: filtrer l'air, le réchauffer et l'humidifier = *your nose has three functions – filtering the air, heating it up and humidifying it*

linking clauses –

Après, nous nous sommes repliés en défense et nous n'avons jamais pu ressortir = *afterwards we fell back into defence and we were never able to come forward again*

Pour moi, Matthieu est un frère et je ne peux vraiment pas lui en vouloir de m'avoir fait souffrir ce soir = *to me, Matthew is a brother and I can't really bear him a grudge for making me suffer that evening*

mais = *but*

linking elements –

Charlotte Gainsbourg, fragile mais radieuse = *CG, vulnerable but radiant*

Les quinze différences entre hommes et femmes – égaux mais pas identiques = *the fifteen differences between men and women – equal but not the same*

linking clauses –

Ah! ces sacrées émotions, elles nous font honte parfois, mais imaginez le monde sans elles = *ah! those blessed emotions, they make us ashamed at times, but imagine a world without them*

Cette maladie est peu connue, mais toucherait 2 à 5% de la population = *this condition is not well known, but reputedly affects between 2 and 5% of the population*

Il est épuisé, je crois, mais cet album est parfait d'un bout à l'autre = *it's no longer available, I think, but this album is perfect from start to finish*

ni = nor, or (see 426)
linking elements –
Elle n'a pas perdu pour autant son temps ni son argent = *for all that she didn't waste her time or her money*

Si vous vous maîtrisiez parfaitement, vous ne seriez pas la même femme ni la même actrice? = *if you were in complete control of yourself, do you think you wouldn't be the same woman or the same actress?*

linking clauses –
Le plaisir vient dans sa vie par instants – je ne les décide pas, ni je ne les programme pas* = *pleasure comes into your life in moments – I don't decide them nor do I programme them*

* Note that, unlike English, there is no inversion after *ni* in French.

ou = or
linking elements –
Internet, les associations d'anciens élèves ou tout simplement l'annuaire, tous les moyens sont bons pour renouer avec son passé = *the Internet, old boy and old girl associations or quite simply the telephone directory are all useful ways of linking up with your past*

Ces femmes ont accueilli des enfants venus du Vietnam, du Mali ou d'Haïti = *these women have welcomed into their homes children from Vietnam, Mali or Haiti*

Rien n'est jamais tout blanc ou tout noir = *nothing is ever completely black or white*

linking clauses –
Même si les gens étaient rassurants ou essayaient de me rassurer, je n'étais pas rassurée = *even if people were reassuring or tried to reassure me, I wasn't reassured*

Ces symptômes s'effacent spontanément ou peuvent rester invalidants pendant plus de dix ans = *these symptoms disappear spontaneously or can remain disabling for over ten years*

Clauses

453 Clauses
Definition of a clause
A clause consists of a single word or sequence of words which must contain a finite verb or verbal expression. A finite verb is a verb which shows a person, a tense and a

mood – see 1. A clause contains only one finite verb – consequently, there is one finite verb per clause, and there are as many clauses as there are finite verbs.

Clauses consisting of a single word (verb) – these very often involve commands –

Essayez! = *try!*

Arrêtez! = *stop!*

Clauses consisting of a sequence of words (verb or verbal expression) –

Asseyez-vous! = *sit down!*

Cet homme veut vous faire maigrir = *this man wants to make you lose weight*

Parce qu'il respecte les codes vestimentaires les plus classiques = *because he respects the most classic dress codes*

454 Clause types

Clauses fall into two categories – ***main clauses*** and ***subordinate clauses***.

Main clauses

A main clause can act as a simple sentence (see below) – a main clause is not introduced by a subordinating conjunction (see below), as subordinate clauses are –

Les caprices du destin sont le sel de la vie (main clause 1; also = simple sentence). ***Sans cela, les types brillants ratisseraient les meilleurs boulots et les plus belles femmes*** (main clause 2; also = simple sentence) = *the whims of destiny are the salt of life. Without them, smart guys would scoop up the best jobs and the best-looking women*

L'intelligence est un mythe (main clause 1); ***la compétence est réelle*** (main clause 2; also = compound sentence) = *intelligence is a myth; competence is real*

Subordinate clauses

A subordinate clause is dependent upon a subordinating conjunction which may be part of a main clause or of another subordinate clause –

Je me suis mise à me moquer d'un collègue (main clause), ***que je trouvais trop naze*** (subordinate clause) = *I began to make fun of a colleague whom I found absolutely useless*

Même si ce n'est pas très élégant (subordinate clause 1), ***j'ai cette manie*** (main clause) ***qui m'oblige à faire toujours le même geste avant de me coucher*** (subordinate clause 2) = *even if it isn't very elegant, I've got this habit that makes me always do the same thing before going to bed*

Quand une femme en est à vous dire (subordinate clause 1) ***pourquoi elle vous aime*** (subordinate clause 2), ***c'est*** (main clause) ***qu'elle commence à se le demander*** (subordinate clause 3) = *when a woman reaches the point when she tells you why she loves you, it's because she's beginning to wonder about it*

If there is more than one subordinate clause in a sentence, each clause is introduced by a subordinating conjunction, and not, as often in English, a conjunction before the first clause only –

Faites des enfants, parce qu'être maman rallonge l'espérance de vie et parce que les femmes ayant eu trois enfants ont un risque de décès de 10% inférieur aux autres = *have children, because being a mother increases life expectancy and (because) women who have had three children have a 10% lower chance of dying than others*

See comments on **quand** 465 and **si** 458.

455 Types of subordinate clauses
The following types of subordinate clauses will be examined – causal clauses, concessive clauses, conditional clauses, consecutive clauses, final clauses, manner clauses, noun clauses, time clauses, relative clauses.

456 Causal clauses
Causal clauses express the cause of something and are introduced by **comme** = *as*, **parce que** = *because*, **puisque** = *since*; less common conjunctive expressions are **étant donné que** = *given that*, **vu que** = *seeing that*.

In clauses introduced by these expressions, the verb is always in the indicative mood.

comme = *as*
Comme il s'agit de l'acte sexuel, il faut se rendre compte que le baiser réussi passe d'abord par l'échange = *as it's a question of having sex, you have to realise that a successful kiss involves an exchange*

parce que = *because*
On ne peut pas se nourrir de la même façon à 20 et à la cinquantaine – tout simplement parce que notre métabolisme ralentit = *we can't eat in the same way at 20 as we can in our fifties – for the simple reason that our metabolism slows down*

Il ne faut pas se priver de boeuf, parce qu'il n'est pas si gras que ça = *you don't have to deny yourself beef, because it's not as fat as all that*

Les études montrent qu'on trouve plus de cancers chez les gros carnivores, parce qu'ils laissent moins de place aux légumes verts = *studies show that cancer is more prevalent among big meat-eaters, because they leave less room for green vegetables*

puisque = *since*
Puisque le Français va officiellement amorcer sa saison internationale ce soir, elle espérait être là à saluer son héros = *because the Frenchman is going to open his international season officially this evening, she was hoping to be there to greet her hero*

Peu de gens considèrent la voix comme quelque chose d'important, puisqu'ils n'imaginent pas ce qu'on peut faire avec = *few people consider the voice as something important, since they can't imagine what you can do with it*

étant donné que = *given that*
Étant donné qu'ils ralentissent le vieillissement, forcez sur les fruits et légumes = *given that they slow down the ageing process, go overboard on fruit and veg*

vu que = *seeing that*

Quelle est la pire drague que vous avez subie? – Vu que je n'ai dû me faire draguer que deux fois dans ma vie, il n'y en a jamais eu de pire! = *what was the worst pick-up you've undergone? – Seeing that I've only been picked up a couple of times in my life, there hasn't ever been a worst one!*

Vu que je sortais d'une école catholique, j'étais innocente – je ne l'ai même pas embrassé = *seeing that I came from a good Catholic school, I was innocent – I didn't even kiss him*

457 Concessive clauses

Concessive subordinate clauses are introduced by a number of subordinating conjunctions which = *although* **– quoique, bien que, encore que, malgré que** and a number of other expressions equivalent to English words ending in *–ever* (eg *however, whoever, whatever*): **qui que** = *whoever*, **quoi que** = *whatever* (pronoun), **quel . . . que** = *whatever* (adjective), **où que** = *wherever*, etc; see 148, 153.

All these concessive conjunctions, pronouns and adjectives introduce clauses in which the verb is always in the subjunctive mood.

bien que = *although*
Bien que vous ayez décidé de vous entretenir en faisant du sport, vous n'arrivez pas à trouver cette forme éblouissante que vous cherchiez = *although you decided to keep fit by doing some sport, you haven't managed to find that dazzling physique you were looking for*

Bien qu'elle sache que j'ai des sous, ma copine n'en profite pas = *although she knows I've got money, my girlfriend doesn't take advantage of it*

encore que = *although*
Encore que vous ayez des soucis juridiques et des contrariétés en tout genre, vous aurez un formidable soutien relationnel = *although you've got all sorts of troubles with the law and upsets, you'll have tremendous support*

malgré que = *although*
Malgré que l'horizon soit obscurci pour l'instant, il faut régler vos affaires de coeur et tirer les choses au clair = *although the horizon is dark at the moment, you must put your love life in order and sort it out thoroughly*

quel . . . que = *whatever*, ***où que*** = *wherever*, etc
Il faut pouvoir vous sentir bien avec lui, quelles que soient les circonstances = *you have to be able to feel at ease with him whatever the circumstances*

Il faut garder à l'esprit que, où qu'il soit, votre partenaire reste toujours votre partenaire = *you need to remember that, wherever he is, your partner is always your partner*

D'aussi loin que mon avis puisse importer, j'ai déjà dit que l'important n'est pas le commentaire mais l'acte = *as far as my opinion may carry any weight, I've already said that the important thing is not talking about it but doing it*

quoi qui / que = *whatever*
Gardez la tête froide, quoi qu'il arrive = *keep cool, whatever happens*

For other examples of these constructions, see 153.

quoique = *although*
Quoique 82% des hommes affirment mettre volontiers la table ou la débarrasser, est-ce que vous ne trouvez pas un léger décalage avec la réalité? = *although 82% of men state that they are happy to set or clear the table, don't you find a slight gap with reality?*

Note the difference, only visible in written French, between **quoique** = *although* and **quoi que** = *whatever* –

Quoique tu puisses me répondre, je ne te parlerai plus = *although you may write back to me, I'll not talk to you again*

Quoi que tu puisses me répondre, je pense toujours à toi = *whatever you may say in reply to me, I am always thinking of you*

458 Conditional clauses

Conditional clauses suggest an hypothesis and are introduced mainly by **si** = *if*, but also by **à condition que** = *on the condition that, provided that*, **à moins que** = *unless*, **au cas où** = *if*, **dans la mesure où** = *in so far as*, **dans le cas où** = *if*, **pour peu que** = *if*, **pourvu que** = *provided that*, **que . . . ou** = *whether . . . or*, **supposé que** = *supposing that*.

In clauses introduced by conjunctions ending in **que**, the verb is in the subjunctive mood. In clauses introduced by **si** and expressions ending in **où**, the verb is in the indicative mood.

à condition que = *on the condition that, provided that*
Le sexe peut améliorer avec les années, à condition que l'on fasse preuve d'imagination et de ténacité = *sex can improve over the years provided that you show imagination and tenacity*

Ça change de routine et c'est très excitant, à condition que cela ne devienne pas la norme = *that changes your routine and it's very exciting, provided that it doesn't become the norm*

à moins que = *unless*
Ça va, à moins que votre préférence ne* soit la musique classique = *that's OK, unless your preference is for classical music*

* Note that an expletive **ne** may be used in subordinate clauses introduced by **à moins que** – see 417.

au cas où = *in case*
Choisissez un loueur qui disposent d'agences partout en Europe, au cas où vous en auriez besoin = *choose a hire company with agencies throughout Europe in case you need one*

dans la mesure où = *in so far as*
Dans la mesure où vous voulez mettre vos boutons de manchette en valeur, relevez légèrement vos manchettes de costume = *in so far as you want to show off your cuff links, pull the cuffs on your suit back slightly*

pour peu que = *if*
Pour peu que la nature vous ait donné un organe en bonne et due forme, votre voix peut faire des étincelles = *if nature has given you a first-class organ, your voice can make sparks fly*

pourvu que = *provided that*
J'aime les parfums raffinés et discrets, pourvu qu'on ne s'en serve pas avec excès = *I like refined, discreet perfumes, provided they're not used excessively*

que . . . ou = *whether . . . or*
Que la chute de vos cheveux soit d'origine hormonale ou héréditaire, ce nouveau sérum en réactivera la croissance = *whether your hair loss is hormonal or hereditary in origin, this new serum will reactivate its growth*

Que votre problème soit lié à une incompréhension sexuelle ou à un énorme malentendu, seule une discussion peut éclaircir la situation = *whether your problem is linked to a sexual misunderstanding or to a serious lack of general understanding, only a discussion can shed light on the situation*

si = *if*
Si l'on n'y fait pas attention, on prend 500 grammes chaque année = *if you're not careful, you can put on 500 grammes every year*

Leur mauvaise réputation n'est pas justifiée si on prend les précautions nécessaires = *their bad reputation isn't justified if you take the necessary precautions*

Si vous laissez voir votre torse viril et poilu, vous passerez pour un individu franchement ringard = *if you reveal your virile, hairy chest, you'll be taken for someone really behind the times*

Pratiquer dans un club reconnu par une fédération vous couvre seulement si vous blessez quelqu'un = *playing in a club recognised by a federation covers you only if you hurt somebody*

Although ***si*** normally = *if*, it is sometimes to be translated by *even if, whereas* –

Si cette confiture ne contient pas de sucre classique, elle n'est en revanche pas allégée en calories = *even if this jam doesn't contain orthodox sugar, it isn't, for all that, light in calories*

Si la schizophrénie ne peut pas être guérie, ses symptômes peuvent être atténués = *even if schizophrenia can't be cured, its symptoms can be reduced*

Si les végétaux crus apportent des vitamines, ils se comportent comme de véritables petites râpes pour le côlon = *even if raw vegetables give us vitamins, they act like little graters on our colons*

Si 71% d'entre nous affirment se doucher tous les jours, les 3,8% qui ne prennent ni douche ni bain doivent, eux, être adeptes de la toilette de chat = *whereas 71% of us contend that we take a shower every day, the 3.8% who take neither a shower nor a bath must use the cat's routine*

When two or more conditional clauses are dependent upon the same main clause, the second and subsequent clauses may be introduced by *que* rather than *si* –

Si je voulais un pain de chocolat et qu'il n'y en avait pas, ça créait un moment de panique = *if I wanted a bar of chocolate and there weren't any, that created a moment's panic*

Si j'ai un mauvais jour et que je me retrouve sur une scène devant des milliers de personnes, j'oublie tout = *if I'm having a bad day and I'm on stage in front of thousands of people, I forget everything*

But *si* can also be used in these circumstances, here for the sake of rhetorical symmetry –

Si je savais comment me servir d'émotions enfouies, si je savais comment les canaliser, ça me rassurerait = *if I knew how to use buried emotions, if I knew how to channel them, that would reassure me*

As far as tense usage with *si* is concerned, it should be noted that the future, future perfect, conditional and conditional perfect are never used in the *si* clause – the other tenses are regularly used.

For *si* = *if, whether* introducing indirect questions, see 482.

supposé que = *supposing that*
Supposé que vous ayez gagné six points dans notre enquête, cela suggère que certaines zones d'incertitude persistent dans votre esprit = *supposing you've notched up six points in our investigation, that suggests that certain areas of uncertainty persist in your mind*

Supposé que vous aimiez que vos actions soient beaucoup plus rentables, essayez de faire preuve de patience = *supposing you'd like your stocks and shares to be more profitable, try to be patient*

459 Consecutive clauses

Consecutive subordinate clauses mark the consequence of something and are introduced by the following expressions, all of which = *so that* – *de sorte que, si bien que, de telle façon que, de telle manière que, de telle sorte que, à tel point que, si . . . que, tant . . . que, tel . . . que, tellement . . . que; d'autant (plus) que* = *all the more because*

The verb of the subordinate clause is always in the indicative mood.

d'autant (plus) que = *all the more because*
La salle de bains devient un endroit de lutte dans 23% des ménages, d'autant plus que 41% des Français aiment se prélasser dans leur bain une fois par semaine = *the bathroom is becoming a warground in 23% of households, all the more because 41% of the French like to relax in their bath once a week*

Vous grignotez entre les repas, d'autant que vous avez des sautes d'humeur et c'est votre façon de les gérer = *you nibble between meals, all the more because you have mood swings and it's your way of managing them*

si . . . que = *so that*
Les campagnes antitabac ont eu un si grand succès en Grande-Bretagne que le gouvernement propose de taxer la « malbouffe » = *anti-smoking campaigns have been so successful in Great Britain that the government proposes taxing unhealthy foods*

tant . . . que = *so many . . . that*
Il y a tant de raisons pour lesquelles une première rencontre peut tourner court qu'il serait dommage de ne pas tenter la seconde fois = *there are so many reasons why a first meeting may come to a sudden halt that it would be a shame not to try again*

tel . . . que = *so . . . that*
Votre frustration est telle que, parfois, vous brusquez les choses pour obtenir la satisfaction = *you get so frustrated that sometimes you rush things so as to get satisfaction*

à tel point que = *to such an extent that*
Areva a dû restructurer ses entreprises à tel point que la compagnie a fermé dix usines en France = *Areva has had to restructure its enterprises to such an extent that it has closed ten factories in France*

tellement . . . que = *so much . . . that*
J'ai été tellement blessée par des gens que je prenais pour des amis qu'aujourd'hui je suis méfiante = *I've been hurt so much by people I thought were friends that nowadays I'm suspicious*

Elle a été tellement mise en avant à un moment où se construit sa personnalité, que ça ne lui permet pas d'évoluer d'une manière harmonieuse = *she has been so exposed at a time when her personality was being formed that it doesn't allow her to develop in a consistent way*

Note the word order in the following example, where **tellement** has a causal and consequential value –

Je me suis abonnée l'année dernière tellement votre magazine me plaît = *I subscribed last year because your magazine appealed to me so much*

460 Final clauses
Final clauses express the reason why something is done and are introduced by such expressions as **afin que, pour que, de sorte que**, all of which = *in order that, so that*.

In clauses introduced by final conjunctions, the verb is always in the subjunctive mood – see 148.

afin que = *in order that, so that*
Laissez l'entre-côte se reposer une minute à l'air afin que les fibres se détendent = *allow the steak to rest for one minute to let its texture settle*

pour que = *in order that, so that*
***Il suffit qu'une étincelle se produise à cet instant précis, pour qu'une
catastrophe arrive*** = *all it needs is for a spark to be produced at that precise moment in order for
a catastrophe to happen*

***Il n'en fallait pas plus pour que les médias demandent l'interdiction de la
vente du boeuf*** = *that was all it took for the media to demand a ban on the sale of beef*

de sorte que = *so that*
***Un homme qui se parfume à longueur de journée, ça fait sourire – est-ce
qu'il s'y adonne de sorte que nous le remarquions?*** = *a man who puts on perfume
all day long makes me smile – does he do it so that we notice him?*

Note that when ***de sorte que*** is followed by the indicative it indicates a consequence –
see 459 – and when it is followed by the subjunctive it indicates a purpose.

461 Manner clauses
Manner clauses indicate how something is done and are introduced by such expressions
as ***ainsi que*** = *as*, ***aussi . . . que*** = *as*, ***comme*** = *how, as*, ***de même que*** = *same as*.
The verb occurs in the indicative mood.

ainsi que = *as*
***La compétition des femmes va donc cruellement manquer de saveur, ainsi
que les reporters l'avaient prévu*** = *so the women's competition is going to suffer from a
cruel lack of flavour, just as the commentators had predicted*

aussi . . . que = *as*
***Là, l'atmosphère est aussi légère que les pelotes de laine éparpillées sur la
table*** = *there the atmosphere is as light as the balls of wool scattered over the table*

comme = *how, as*
Une femme qui peut s'habiller comme elle veut se sent plus libre = *a woman
who can dress how she wants feels freer*

Ils me traitaient comme si j'étais un dieu vivant = *they treated me as if I was a
living god*

***Les crooners américains murmurent dans leur micro comme s'ils
faisaient l'amour à une femme*** = *American crooners whisper into their mikes, as if they're
making love to a woman*

de même que = *same as*
***Deux ans de cours de théâtre ont, dit-elle, transformé sa vie, de même
qu'ils lui ont appris à ne plus craindre le regard des autres*** = *two years at theatre
school have, she says, transformed her life, in the same way as they have taught her not to be afraid of the
way other people look at her any longer*

462 Noun clauses
Noun clauses are introduced by ***que*** and follow verbs of speech, verbs of emotion, of
comprehension, of knowledge. Whether or not ***que*** is followed by the indicative or

subjunctive mood depends upon the type of verb governing it. For those verbs which are followed by the subjunctive, see 149, 150.

que + indicative mood –
Quand elle m'appelle par mon nom de famille, je sais que j'ai dû faire une connerie = *when she calls me by my last name, I know I've done something really stupid*

J'ai l'impression que chaque partie de mon corps réagit = *I get the impression that every part of my body reacts*

Elle m'a répondu qu'elle avait rêvé que j'étais mort = *she told me she'd dreamt I was dead*

Elle m'a dit que je lui manquais = *she told me she missed me*

que + **subjunctive mood**
On ne peut pas dire que l'arrivée du joueur portugais ait beaucoup apporté au club = *you can't say that the arrival of the Portuguese player benefited the club very much*

Il semble qu'il y ait dans ces cursus une vraie dérive = *it seems that in these programmes there is a tendency to depart from the point*

Je suis content pour Pedro qu'il ait marqué contre Porto = *I'm pleased that Pedro scored against Porto*

Il arrive que le choix de la mort soit un hymne à la vie = *it happens that choosing death is an anthem to life*

463 Highlighting with *c'est*

Highlighting is the process that allows an element in a clause to be given more prominence than normal. One way of achieving highlighting an element is to introduce it with ***c'est . . . qui /que***. ***C'est . . . qui*** is used when the highlighted element is the subject of the clause; ***ce sont*** if the subject is plural; ***c'est . . . que*** when it is another part of speech. See also 223.

c'est . . . qui
C'est le mauvais brossage des dents qui cause la mauvaise haleine = *it's bad tooth-brushing that causes bad breath*

Tahiti, c'est l'endroit qui offre des plages magnifiques = *Tahiti's the place that offers magnificent beaches*

Ce sont leurs deux plus petits enfants qu'ils ont amenés avec eux = *it's their two youngest children that they've brought with them*

c'est . . . que
C'est avec Dominique qu'on va commencer ce rapport = *it's with Dominique that we're going to begin this report*

C'est la première fois qu'on va exposer les photos de Claude Berri = *it's the first time that Claude Berri's photos will be on show*

Il semble que ce soit à partir de Toulouse que le virus s'est infiltré en France = *it seems that it's from Toulouse that the virus has been introduced into France*

464 Relative clauses

Relative clauses provide more information about their antecedents and are introduced by such pronouns as –

qui = *who, which, that* (subject)

que = *whom, which, that* (object)

dont = *whose, of whom, of which*

de qui = *whose, of whom*

duquel / de laquelle / desquels / desquelles = *of which*

preposition + *qui* /*lequel*, etc = preposition + *whom*

preposition + *lequel*, etc = preposition + *which*

où =*in which, where*

In these cases the antecedent is a specific noun – compare *ce qui, ce que, ce dont* below.

qui = *who* (subject)
Une femme qui peut s'habiller comme elle veut se sent plus libre = *a woman who can dress as she wants feels freer*

L'autre aspect intéressant concerne les débutants, ceux qui signent leur premier contrat professionnel = *the other interesting aspect involves beginners, those who are signing their first contract as professionals*

Les spécialistes conseillent aux femmes qui tentent d'avoir un enfant de ne pas dépasser un apport en protéines de 20% = *specialists advise women who are trying to have a child not to exceed a protein intake of 20%*

Note that the person of the verb matches the person indicated by *qui* –

C'est moi qui l'ai fait = *it was me who did it / I was the one who did it*

C'est toi qui l'as fait = *you're the one who did it*

que = *whom* (object)
Côté positif du métrosexuel – vous vivez avec un homme qui sent bon que vous aimez respirer dans le cou = *the positive side of the metrosexual – you live with a man who smells good and whose neck you like sniffing*

Il pense à sa femme, à son fils de deux ans qu'il ne reverra peut-être plus = *he thought about his wife, his two-year-old son whom he might never see again*

Les troupes qu'il commandait avaient traqué les agents ennemis dans les cavernes et les tunnels = *the troops he commanded had tracked down the enemy agents in the caves and tunnels*

Preposition + *qui*
En dehors de ceux pour qui la voix est un outil professionnel, peu de gens considèrent la voix comme quelque chose d'important = *apart from those for whom the voice is a professional tool, few people consider it as something important*

Un strip-tease a un effet direct sur les hommes, pour qui le visuel est la première source de stimulation = *strip-tease has a direct effect on men, for whom the visual is the principal source of sensations*

qui = *which* (subject)
Les maladies de la rétine, qui entraînent la cécité, frappent de 30 000 à 40 000 personnes en France = *diseases of the retina, which cause blindness, affect between 30,000 and 40,000 people in France*

Le forfait hospitalier à la charge des patients, qui couvre le coût du repas et de l'hébergement, passe à 14 euros = *the hospital levy charged to patients, which covers board and lodging, is going up to 14 euros*

Utilisez cette plaque en fonte qui est équipée de stries qui laisseront sur vos pièces de viande les mêmes marques qu'une grille de barbécue = *use this griddle with grooves which will leave the same marks on your pieces of meat as a barbecue grill*

que = *which, that* (object)
Heureusement, on peut avoir un maillot de bain que l'on n'hésitera pas à montrer = *fortunately you can have a swimsuit you won't hesitate to wear in public*

Comptez 800 euros les dix séances, une somme que l'on peut régler en deux ou trois fois = *you have to reckon on 800 euros for ten sessions, a sum which you can settle in two or three payments*

Caché parmi les projecteurs de mon père, j'ai même vu tourner des films que je n'aurais pas eu le droit de voir en salle = *hidden among my dad's projectors, I even saw films being made that I wouldn't be allowed to see in a cinema*

dont = *whose, of whom*
Because ***dont*** is the product of the preposition ***de*** + pronoun, it is sometimes translated as *with which, from which*, etc. Word order with ***dont*** needs to be noted –

with reference to people –
Une aide sera accordée à ceux dont les revenus ne dépassent pas 650 euros par mois = *help will be given to those whose income doesn't exceed 650 euros a month*

with reference to things –
Nous avons fait appel à la Croix Rouge dont nous trouvions initialement les tarifs trop élevés = *we appealed to the Red Cross whose charges we initially found too high*

Votre corps dégage des signaux dont ces insectes raffollent = *your body gives off signals which these insects are crazy about*

C'est lié à la façon dont nous nous en servons = *it's linked to the way we use it*

Il faut choisir le contrat dont les cotisations s'ajustent le mieux à votre profil = *you must choose the contract whose payments best suit your status*

L'ensemble correspondait à ce dont je rêvais – j'avais retrouvé la poitrine de mes 20 ans = *the whole thing matched up to what I was dreaming of – I had rediscovered the bust I had when I was 20*

où = *in which, where*
La salle de bains est devenu un lieu où les membres de la famille aiment à se retrouver = *the bathroom has become a place where family members like to meet*

Preposition + *lequel, laquelle, lesquels, lesquelles*
Attention au délai de carence: c'est le temps pendant lequel vous payez l'assurance sans bénéficier des garanties = *beware of the waiting period – that's the time during which you pay for the insurance without benefiting from the warranty*

Sa voix est capable de vibrations auxquelles les groupies ne restent pas insensibles = *his voice is capable of vibrations to which the groupies are not insensitive*

Un match au cours duquel il a montré une capacité inédite à foudroyer l'adversaire = *a match during which he demonstrated a totally new ability to overwhelm his opponent*

Il y a tant de raisons pour lesquelles* une première rencontre peut tourner court = *there are so many reasons why a first meeting may come to a sudden halt*

C'est la raison pour laquelle* je suis persuadé que l'activité sportive est excellente pour tout le monde = *it's the reason why I'm convinced that sport is excellent for everybody*

*Note *la raison pour laquelle* (rather than *la raison pourquoi*) = *the reason why*

ce qui, ce que, ce dont, de quoi
These do not refer to a single antecedent but to the idea expressed in the previous clause –

ce qui = *which*
45% des femmes françaises prennent la pilule, ce qui en fait les premières utilisatrices en Europe = *45% of French women take the pill, which makes them the leading users in Europe*

Les vacances sont idéales pour refuser les contraintes – ce qui veut dire être un peu plus égoïste = *holidays are ideal for rejecting constraint – which means you can be a little more self-centred*

Ces cotisations sont déductibles des revenus, ce qui permet de payer moins d'impôts = *these payments are deductible from your income, which allows you to pay less tax*

Je ne sais pas ce qui est beau, mais je sais ce que j'aime = *I don't know what is beautiful, but I know what I like*

ce que = *what*
J'ai dû me battre pour faire ce que j'avais envie de faire = *I had to fight to do what I wanted to do*

La géométrie variable de notre ventre est liée à ce qu'on mange, à ce que l'on boit = *the variable geometry of our stomach is linked to what we eat, to what we drink*

On ne peut pas être complètement surpris par ce qu'on trouve sur soi = *you can't be completely surprised by what you find in yourself*

Nantes s'est élevé à un niveau de jeu inhabituel par rapport à ce qu'il a montré jusque-là = *Nantes has risen to a level of play which is unusual in comparison with what they have demonstrated until now*

ce dont = *which*
Se raser une fois par semaine et se balader en tongs et en short toute la journée est un bonheur vraiment évident – ce dont on ne devrait pas se priver! = *shaving once a week and walking about in flip-flops and shorts all day long is a really obvious pleasure – which no-one should deprive themselves of!*

de quoi = *the wherewithal, food for thought*
C'est dans ce groupe de rats que les chercheurs ont observé les tumeurs les moins développées. De quoi nous inciter à privilégier les aliments remarqués pour leurs vertus anticancer = *it's among this group of rats that researchers have noticed the least developed tumours – this should inspire us to give top priority to food noted for its anticancer qualities*

Voilà de quoi vous convaincre qu'en matière de sexualité, la fatalité n'a pas sa place = *this should be enough to convince you that in matters of sex, fate has no place*

465 Time clauses

Time clauses indicate when something occurs.

The following conjunctions indicate that the action expressed by the main verb has happened before the action expressed by the verb in the subordinate clause –
    avant que = *before*, *jusqu'à ce que* = *until*.
The mood of the verb in the subordinate clause in these cases is the subjunctive –

avant que = *before*
Avant que les contacts ne* se durcissent, Thierry obligeait le gardien à repousser des poings = *before the game really hotted up, Thierry forced the keeper to punch the ball away*

Il avait été invisible sauf lorsqu'il fut crédité du seul carton jaune du soir avant que Mourinho ne* se décide à le sortir quelques minutes plus tard = *he'd been invisible except when he was awarded the only yellow card of the evening before Mourinho* [the manager] *decided to take him off a few minutes later*

*Note the use of an expletive *ne* with *avant que* – see 417.

jusqu'à ce que = *until*
Jusqu'à ce qu'il boive, il se conduit parfaitement, mais après . . . = *until he has a drink, he behaves admirably, but afterwards . . .*

Jusqu'à ce qu'on atteigne la quarantaine, il n'est pas nécessaire de surveiller autant ce qu'on mange = *until you get to forty, it's not necessary to watch what you eat so much*

With *jusqu'au moment où, jusqu'au temps où* = *until*, the mood of the verb in the subordinate clause is the indicative (*où* is never followed by the subjunctive) –

Une femme sur deux prend entre 4 et 6 kilos jusqu'au moment où elle est ménopausée = *one woman out of two puts on between 4 and 6 kilos until she is menopausal*

Je me sentais un peu en dehors des choses, jusqu'au temps où j'ai eu des enfants = *I felt a little left out of things, until I had children*

Quand = *when* and *lorsque* = *when* indicate that the action expressed by the main verb either occurs after or at the same time as that indicated by the verb in the subordinate clause. The mood of the verb in the subordinate clause in these cases is the indicative.

quand = *when*
Une majorité de couples avouent que c'est surtout quand ils se sentent bien avec l'autre qu'ils ont envie du sexe = *a majority of couples admit that it's especially when they feel good with each other that they want sex*

Quand je proteste, elle dit que si on avait un enfant, elle n'aurait pas pris de chien = *when I protest, she says that if we had a child, she wouldn't have got a dog*

Dis-lui que tu aimerais voir son visage quand tu l'embrasses = *tell her you'd like to see her face when you kiss her*

lorsque = *when*
Ce massage épaissit l'épiderme, lorsque celui-ci est distendu par une naissance = *this massage thickens your skin, when it's distended as a result of giving birth*

Lorsque le corps subit un effort, il secrète de l'adrénaline = *when the body makes an effort, it secretes adrenalin*

Lorsque l'entre-côte est à votre convenance, ne la servez pas tout de suite = *when the steak is how you like it, don't serve it straightaway*

When two or more time clauses are dependent upon the same main clause, the second and subsequent clauses may be introduced by *que* rather than *lorsque* or *quand* (compare usage with *si* – see 458) –

Quand vous n'avez pas assez mangé et que vous êtes stressée, vous vous offrez une barre de chocolat ou un gâteau = *when you haven't eaten enough and you're stressed, you indulge yourself with a bar of chocolate or a cake*

The following conjunctions indicate that the action expressed by the main verb happens at the same time as the action expressed by the verb in the subordinate clause – *alors que* = *while, whereas*, *comme* = *as*, *où* = *when*, *pendant que* = *while*, *tandis que* = *whereas, while*, *en même temps que* = *at the same time as*, *tant que* = *as long as*. The mood of the verb in the subordinate clause in these cases is the indicative.

alors que = *while, whereas*
Alors que les sénateurs avaient décidé de maintenir les distributeurs automatiques de boissons sucrées dans les établissements scolaires, une commission a recommandé qu'ils soient bannis = *whereas the Senate had decided to retain sweet-drink vending machines in schools, a committee has recommended that they be banned*

J'ai l'impression que mon corps gonfle, alors que je ne change pas de régime alimentaire = *I've got the impression that my body is swelling up, whereas I haven't changed my eating habits*

comme = *as*
Comme l'hiver avance, la mortalité infantile va presque tripler = *as winter advances, infant mortality is almost going to increase threefold*

où = *when*
Normally **où** is a relative pronoun = *where*, but when combined with a noun of time, it = *when* –

Il revient sur les années noires, où l'on découvre un homme à l'opposé de l'image que l'on s'est faite de lui = *he goes back over the dark years, when you discover a man opposite to the image you had formed of him*

Passée la période de flamme où chacun est sur le qui-vive en matière de séduction = *once the time of passion is over when everyone is on the alert as far as seduction is concerned*

pendant que = *while*
Pendant que vous coupez les fruits secs, plongez les escalopes de dinde dans une casserole d'eau bouillante = *while you're chopping up the dry fruit, immerse the turkey escalopes in a saucepan of boiling water*

Mon collocataire a fait une soirée dans notre appartement pendant que j'étais en boîte avec mes potes = *my flatmate had a party in our flat while I was in the club with my mates*

tandis que = *whereas, while*
Le froid pousse les gens à se replier sur eux-mêmes, tandis que sous la chaleur ils ouvrent leur corps et leur esprit = *cold makes people turn in upon themselves, whereas when it's hot, they open up their bodies and minds*

Laissez-la vous parler tandis que vous êtes assis sur la marche = *let her speak to you while you're sitting on the step*

tant que = *as long as*
Tant que vous avez de l'imagination, toutes les combinaisons sont possibles = *for as long as you've got imagination, all combinations are open to you*

The following conjunctions indicate that the action expressed by the main verb happens after the action expressed by the verb in the subordinate clause –

après que = *after*, ***aussitôt que*** = *as soon as*, ***depuis que*** = *since*, ***dès que*** = *as soon as.*

The mood of the verb in the subordinate clause in these cases is the indicative –

après que = *after*
Après que le premier changement fut imposé* par la blessure de Rothen, Porto décida de modifier la structure de son équipe = *after the first change was imposed by Rothen's injury, Porto decided to modify the structure of its team*

*Note the use of the past anterior when the verb in the main clause is past historic – see 133.
Note too that in the case of ***après que***, the subjunctive is sometimes used – see 157.

Trois semaines après qu'elle m'ait quitté, j'ai trouvé une autre petite amie = *three weeks after she left me, I found another girlfriend*

Même après qu'il ait effectué le tournant, il n'a pas regardé derrière lui = *even after he had gone round the corner, he didn't look behind him*

aussitôt que = *as soon as*
Aussitôt que j'ai compris en quoi mes comportements influaient sur les événements, j'ai su que ça ne pourrait qu'aller au mieux = *as soon as I understood that my behaviour influenced events, I realised that things could only get better*

depuis que = *since*
Depuis que je travaille à Paris, ma peau devient très grasse = *since I've been working in Paris, my skin has become very greasy*

Depuis que vous avez trouvé le créneau qui vous convient le mieux, vous n'en sortez plus = *since you've found the slot that suits you best, you stick to it*

dès que = *as soon as*
Dès que je m'approche de ma femme pour l'aider, elle se fâche = *as soon as I go to help my wife, she gets angry*

Les moustiques, c'est le cauchemar de l'été, dès que le soleil se couche = *mosquitoes are a nightmare in summer, as soon as the sun sets*

466 Declarative clauses
The following elements may appear in a declarative clause –
    compulsory – a verb
    optional but verging on the compulsory – a subject; the subject does not appear if it is
the same as in an immediately preceding clause at the same level –

Je pratique la moto, fume depuis l'âge de 14 ans et ne refuse pas un verre d'alcool = *I ride a motorbike, have smoked since I was 14 and don't say no to a drink*

Peu grasse, cette partie du saumon fond sous la langue et laisse un parfum de mer délicatement iodé = *containing little fat, this section of salmon melts under your tongue and leaves a flavour of the sea with a delicate hint of iodine*

    optional – an object, direct and/or indirect
    optional – a complement of the subject and/or the object

optional – one or more adverbs and/or adverbial expressions; the only limit to the number of adverbs and/or adverbial expressions which may occur in a declarative clause is the listener's or reader's ability to absorb them.

Entre-temps, passez les tranches de pain de mie sous le gril du four
adverb 1   verb   direct object   adverb 2
= *in the meantime place the slices of bread under the grill*

Lassées de la sangria et du Bordeaux de leurs ancestrales destinations migratoires,
complement of the subject
plus de 14 000 grues cendrées ont choisi, cet hiver, de se mettre . . . au
subject   verb a   adverb 1   verb b
champagne sur le lac du Der-Chantecoq = *fed up with the sangria and Bordeaux*
adverb 2
wine of their migratory destinations from time immemorial, over 14,000 common cranes have chosen, this winter, to sample champagne on the Lake of Der-Chantecoq

Each of the combinations is illustrated in more detail below.

467 Word order in declarative clauses

In what follows a small number of examples are given to illustrate the main word orders that occur in declarative clauses. Sometimes elements not given in the rubric also occur in the examples: the purpose of the examples is to show the principal word orders.

Subject + verb

Normally the subject precedes the verb –

J'arrive = *I'm coming*

Les mains tremblent = *your hands are trembling*

Notre équipe a perdu = *our team lost*

Subject + verb + complement of subject

The complement of the subject is a noun or adjective which relates to the subject and is usually separated from it by a verb such as ***devenir*** = *to become*, ***être*** = *to be*, ***paraître*** = *to appear*, ***sembler*** = *to seem*

La peur est une réponse saine à une situation de danger = *fear is a healthy response to a dangerous situation*

Vous devenez sage = *you're getting wise*

Mis à l'écart, il a décidé de se défendre = *having been put on the sidelines, he decided to fight back*

Subject + verb + direct object

Normally the object follows the verb, unless it is a pronoun, in which case it precedes the verb – see 210 –

Elle portait une jupe en velours = *she wore a velvet skirt*

Le concombre contient des molécules apaisantes = *cucumbers contain calming molecules*

La somnolence entraîne des périodes de micro-sommeil = *drowsiness makes you sleep for very short periods*

Les Français ont apporté un début de réponse = *the French have produced the beginnings of a reply*

Le foyer DVD moyen en France achète 12 DVD par an = *the average DVD-owning household in France buys 12 DVDs a year*

Subject + verb + prepositional object
Les pêcheurs locaux spéculent sur d'éventuelles fuites radioactives = *the local fishermen speculate on possible radioactive leaks*

Il a beaucoup de talent et le football a besoin de joueurs comme lui = *he's got a lot of talent and football needs players like him*

Complement of subject + subject + verb
Simple, le fer lisse ou sculpte les mèches pour une coiffure sophistiquée = *easy to use, the tongs smooth or shape your hair for a sophisticated hair-style*

Passionnés ou novices, tout le monde y trouve son compte grâce à une programmation d'excellente qualité = *whether they're enthusiasts or novices, everyone will find something that interests them thanks to excellent-quality programming*

Griffes facétieuses et moustaches philosophes, le Chat, héros de BD, exporte sa douce fantaisie à Bordeaux = *with its facetious claws and philosophical whiskers, the Cat, now a cartoon hero, brings its gentle fantasy to Bordeaux*

Subject + verb + direct object + indirect object
On a accordé le prix du Forum d'Ermua au ministre de la justice = *the Forum d'Ermua prize has been awarded to the Minister of Justice*

C'est le sondage secret qui met du baume au coeur du Premier ministre = *it's the secret poll which soothes the Prime Minister's heart*

Les accords de Dayton ont mis un terme au conflit le plus meurtrier que l'Europe ait connu depuis 1945 = *the Dayton agreements brought to a close the most bloody conflict in Europe since 1945*

Subject + verb + adverbial expression
Il s'est rarement trouvé en position de conclure = *he rarely found himself in a position to finish off*

Votre grand-mère profitait de la chicorée au petit déjeuner = *your grandmother used to have the pleasure of chicory for her breakfast*

Adverbial expression + subject + verb (+ direct object)
À Paris, personne ne le soutient = *in Paris, no one supports him*

Mercredi 3 décembre, un peu plus d'un million d'exemplaires de « Harry Potter et l'ordre du Phénix » envahiront la France = *on Wednesday 3 December, just over a million copies of 'Harry Potter and the order of the Phoenix' will invade France*

Techniquement, il a été le moins à l'aise des défenseurs = *technically, he was the least comfortable of the defenders*

Multiple adverbial expressions
Dégustez les mirabelles 1 *nature*, 2 *en clafoutis*, 3 *sur une tarte ou* 4 *au fond d'un crumble* = *enjoy greengages raw, in a clafoutis, in a tart or in a crumble*

1 *Bref, vous marchez* 2 *d'un bon pas* 3 *vers le précipice* = *in short, you're walking steadily towards the precipice*

1 *À la 63e minute*, 2 *sur un ballon de la droite de Poborsky, il s'infiltra* 3 *plein axe* = *in the 63rd minute, on a ball from Poborsky's right foot, he manouvered himself into the centre*

468 Inversion in declarative clauses
Normally, as demonstrated above, 467, the subject precedes the verb in declarative clauses.

However, occasionally, inversion of the subject and verb takes place –

In main clauses after certain adverbs –
À peine sont les nuits plus longues qu'on a envie de se lover dans des draps hypergrands = *scarcely have the nights become longer than you want to curl up in ultra-big sheets*

À peine avez-vous posé l'ongle sur laquelle vous avez mis ce produit sur vos lèvres, que vous avez envie de rendre = *scarcely have you put the nail on which you've put this product on your lips, than you want to throw up*

Encore faut-il savoir en profiter = *you still have to know how to benefit from it*

Peut-être suis-je trop pudique pour cela = *perhaps I'm too modest for that*

Peut-être ne devrais-je pas le dire = *perhaps I shouldn't say so*

Peut-être le désir de l'homme est-il quelque chose qui vous rassure mais aussi qui vous fait peur = *perhaps a man's desire for you is something that reassures you but frightens you at the same time*

In main clauses introduced by an adjective complement of the subject –
Peu nombreux sont les socialistes qui prennent sa défense = *the socialists who come to his defence are very few in number*

Dans les parkings nombreuses sont les femmes qui cherchent leur voiture sous l'oeil narquois de leur compagnon = *in car parks many women try to find their cars under the mocking eye of their companion*

In main clauses in sentence-initial position, with verbs such as rester = to remain, venir = to come

L'entraîneur a annoncé qu'il va quitter Paris. Reste à savoir si le conseil d'administration acceptera sa décision sans lutter pour le garder = the trainer has announced that he's going to leave Paris. It remains to be seen whether the board of directors will accept his decision without fighting to keep him

On stocke plus facilement les graisses au fil du temps. Vient ensuite la période de préménopause = we stock up fat more easily as time goes by. Then arrives the premenopause

On rencontrait ensuite ces pays qui décidaient de s'abstenir sans autre forme de procès. Venaient enfin la France, la Russie qui ajoutaient à leur abstention une « guerrilla » diplomatique = then there were those countries who decided to abstain without any other form of involvement. Finally there were France and Russia who added a diplomatic 'skirmish' to their abstention

In relative subordinate clauses

On ferme le livre ravi par la tournure que prend cette aventure = we shut the book, delighted by the turn the adventure took

Comment faire avancer les réformes économiques que prône le président quand la moitié de l'Assemblée résiste? = how can they make progress with the economic reforms that the President is advocating when half of the National Assembly is resisting?

La Société des Amis du musée national d'Art moderne que préside François Trèves fête son centenaire = the Society of Friends of the National Museum of Modern Art of which François Trèves is the president is celebrating its centenary

Le président a beaucoup consulté sur les interrogations que soulèvent les valeurs qui fondent la société française = the President consulted widely on the questions raised by the values that undergird French society

To achieve stylistic effect –

reserving the subject to a prominent position at the end of a sentence in a noun clause – see 462.

C'est des livres que vient le salut = it's from books that salvation comes

En attendant mieux, l'Élysée souhaite que soient au moins remaniés certains cabinets ministériels = while waiting for something better to turn up, the Élysée (the President's official residence) is wanting certain ministerial cabinets to be reshuffled

Les analyses diront si le navire, ainsi que l'affirment les Américains, est demeuré étanche = analyses will tell if the ship, as the Americans insist, remained watertight

La loi sera précédée de médiations pour que soient respectés « les équilibres qui rassemblent » = the law will be preceded by mediation in order that the 'balances that unite' are respected

469 Highlighting

Highlighting is the process whereby an element in a clause or sentence is moved from its conventional position to a different position – usually at the beginning or at the end of the clause – in order to focus attention upon it. Highlighting may also be achieved by introducing the element that the speaker wishes to focus on by ***c'est . . . qui / que*** – see 223, 463.

If the element highlighted is a noun, it is repeated in the form of a pronoun before the verb:

normal word order –

Je ne vois pas ces peurs comme négatives = *I don't see these fears as negative*

direct object in initial position with repetition as pronoun –

Ces peurs, je ne les vois pas comme négatives

direct object in final position with repetition as pronoun –

Je ne les vois pas comme négatives, ces peurs

subject repeated as stressed pronoun in initial position –

Moi, je ne vois pas ces peurs comme négatives

Nous, on ne se plaindra pas du premier roman cocasse d'un auteur de 22 ans = *we're not going to complain about the first amusing novel of a 22-year-old author*

subject repeated as stressed pronoun in final position –

Je ne vois pas ces peurs comme négatives, moi

subject introduced by ***c'est . . . qui*** –

C'est moi qui ne vois pas ces peurs comme négatives = *I'm the one who doesn't see these fears as negative*

Ce n'est pas moi qui vois ces peurs comme négatives = *I'm not the one who sees these fears as negative*

C'est l'époque où l'homme politique ignore que le petit écran est aussi parlant = *it was the time when politicians didn't realise that the small screen can also talk*

Highlighting can also be achieved by delaying the mention of the subject (or other element) – see 467.

Mais, avec le temps, vers ses 70 ans, est né un autre Resnais, léger, facétieux = *but, with time, as he approached his 70th year, another Resnais was born, light-hearted, facetious*

Interrogative sentences

470 Interrogative sentences

There are two types of interrogative sentences –

1 questions inviting a *oui – non* / *yes – no* answer –

Est-ce que c'est vrai qu'un bruit fort gêne davantage qu'un bruit faible? = *is it right that a loud noise does more harm than a soft noise?*

Vous avez faim? = *are you hungry?*

À part l'odeur de certains hommes, y a-t-il des odeurs qui vous dégoûtent? = *apart from the smell of certain men, are there any smells that turn you off completely?*

2 questions inviting more information, introduced by a question word –

Quelle est votre plage préférée? = *which is your favourite beach?*

Qu'est-ce qui vous répugne chez une femme? = *what puts you off in a woman?*

Pourquoi le rideau de douche se colle-t-elle au corps? = *why does a shower curtain stick to your body?*

oui – non questions

471 *oui – non* questions

Oui–non – *yes–no* questions are 'closed' questions in the sense that there can only be a yes- or a no-answer. No question word requiring a more discursive answer is present – see below. Question 1 can only be answered by *oui* or *non* (unless it's *je ne sais pas*!), whereas question 2 expects a longer, detailed answer –

1 *Ces sites, est-ce qu'ils servent à quelque chose?* = *are these sites any use?*
2 *Ces sites, à quoi servent-ils?* = *what's the use of these sites?*

These questions fall into a number of categories.

472 *oui – non* questions – 1: those involving inversion of the subject and the verb

The following situations occur:

When the subject is a noun, it is placed in first position followed by the verb and an unstressed subject pronoun referring back to the subject –

Ces produits sont-ils sans danger? = *are these products safe?*

Les Parisiens, ont-ils vraiment battu les champions d'Europe? = *did Paris-Saint-Germain really beat the European champions?*

La perruque, est-elle bonne pour remplacer les boucles qui ne bougent plus? = *is a wig any good for replacing curls that no longer move?*

When the subject is an unstressed pronoun, it is placed after the verb –

Savez-vous qu'un couple sur trois ne fait plus l'amour? = *did you know that one couple out of three no longer makes love?*

Ne regardez-vous pas quelquefois le mur en pensant à autre chose? = *don't you sometimes look at the wall thinking about something else?*

Faut-il se priver de boeuf? = *should we give up eating beef?*

A ton âge, est-ce bien raisonnable de se remettre au disco? = *at your age is it a good idea to go back disco dancing?*

When the inverted pronoun begins with a vowel – *il* or ***elle, ils*** or ***elles*** – it is always preceded by a /t/ in pronunciation. If one of the plural pronouns is involved, it is the final ***t*** of the verb ending that is sounded –

Osent-ils aborder ces sujets avec leurs parents? = *do they dare bring up these subjects with their parents?*

Sont-ils satisfaits des réponses que vous donnez? = *are they satisfied with the answers you give?*

Vos livres ne risquent-ils pas de confirmer les préjugés que les gens ont sur les gays? = *don't your books run the risk of confirming the prejudices people have about gays?*

If one of the singular pronouns is involved, the /t/ comes either from the verb ending itself –

Est-il sage de ne laver votre linge que quand il ne vous reste plus rien de propre? = *is it sensible only to wash your clothes when you've nothing clean left?*

Est-il possible d'être doux et puissant à la fois? = *is it possible to be strong and gentle at one and the same time?*

or, if the verb does not end in ***t***, a ***t*** is inserted between the verb ending and the pronoun –

Y a-t-il un principe de base? = *is there a basic principle?*

Y a-t-il des risques que nous nous fassions arrêter par la police? = *is there the danger that we might get ourselves arrested by the police?*

A-t-il osé refuser de vous épouser après tout ça? = *did he dare refuse to marry you after all that?*

A-t-elle toujours décidé de porter ce chemisier en pois? = *has she still decided to wear that spotted blouse?*

Existe-t-il une question caractéristique? = *is there a typical question?*

But you also find –

J'aimerais beaucoup me faire tatouer – mais existe-il une contre-indication pour certains endroits du corps? = *I'd love to be tattooed – but are there certain parts of the body that are counter-indicated?*

As far as the first person singular pronoun, ***je***, is concerned, it is frequently inverted with modal verbs and ***être***, but not with non-modal ones –

Serai-je dans le coup si je colore mes lèvres et mes ongles d'un bel orange vif? = *will I be really with it if I colour my lips and nails bright orange?*

Puis-je annoncer ce que je veux faire? = *may I announce what I want to do?*

Dois-je reprendre une activité physique pour développer encore ma masse musculaire? = *have I got to resume some physical activity to develop my muscle mass more?*

The use of *n'est-ce pas*

N'est-ce pas is the French tag question that can be attached to any statement to turn it into a question – it is the equivalent of English *can't I, do you, don't you*, etc –

L'affaire est dans le sac, n'est-ce pas? = *it's in the bag, isn't it?*

Elle peut deviner vos pensées, n'est-ce pas? = *she can guess your thoughts, can't she?*

Vous avez besoin d'une voiture pour le weekend, n'est-ce pas? = *you need a car for the weekend, don't you?*

Il ne faut pas trop en mettre, n'est-ce pas? = *you mustn't put too much on, must you?*

Sometimes questions using inversion of subject and verb offer an alternative rather than a *oui – non* /*yes – no* answer –

Faut-il faire sa couleur avant ou après la permanente? = *should I add the hair colour before or after the perm?*

Faut-il ou non rentrer le rabat de la poche de mon blazer? = *should I turn the flap of my blazer pocket in or not?*

473 *oui – non* questions – 2: those involving *est-ce que* + direct order of the subject and verb

Est-ce que la douleur a disparu deux heures après la prise? = *did the pain disappear two hours after taking the pill?*

Est-ce que vous avez eu des expériences pénibles dans votre adolescence? = *have you had unpleasant experiences during your teenage years?*

Est-ce que vous n'écartez pas les jambes lorsqu'il fait chaud? = *don't you sit with your legs apart when it's hot?*

Vous gagnez dix fois moins que lui. Est-ce que vous estimez que vous êtes dix fois moins bon que Roger Federer? = *you earn ten times less than him. Do you consider that you're ten times worse than Roger Federer?*

Vous cultivez votre image d'homme marié et de père de famille. Est-ce que ça suffit à refroidir les admiratrices ou est-ce qu'on vous drague malgré tout? = *you cultivate your image as a married man, with children. Is that enough to cool the ardour of your female admirers or do they go after you in spite of everything?*

474 *oui – non* questions – 3: those involving intonation only

The rising intonation associated with the other types of interrogative sentences can be used with the direct order to indicate that a question is being asked and that a statement is not intended. This is extremely common in spoken French –

La fumée ne vous dérange pas? = *is the smoke disturbing you?*

C'est passionnant? = *is it exciting?*

Vous n'avez jamais eu peur de sombrer dans la dépression? = *have you ever been afraid of becoming depressed?*

Vous avez des problèmes avec vos voisins? = *do you have problems with your neighbours?*

Votre femme vous laisse de l'argent de poche chaque mois? = *does your wife give you some pocket money every month?*

Vous avez des souvenirs sexy de votre expérience de serveuse? = *have you got some sexy memories of your experience as a waitress?*

In the following examples, highlighting is used as well as intonation –

La plage, vous y allez souvent? = *do you often go to the beach?*

Votre permis, vous l'avez eu du premier coup? = *did you get your licence at the first attempt?*

Et votre fils, il conduit, lui? = *and does your son drive?*

In the following example, the question is conveyed through a very polite formula –

Si Madame veut bien goûter? = *would Madam care to taste it?*

475 Elliptical *oui – non* questions

In speech it is common for the question to be elliptical – that is to say, for there to be no verb and for the person being addressed to supply missing details from the context in which the question is uttered –

Pas mal, non? = *not bad, eh?*

Une marque brune sur la tempe ou le dos de la main? = *you've got a brown spot on your temple or the back of your hand?*

Connaissez-vous ses limites ? Et les vôtres? = *do you know her limits? And your own?*

Bourgogne ou Bordeaux ? = *Burgundy or Bordeaux ?*

Celui-ci? = *this one?*

Questions introduced by question words

476 Questions introduced by question words

This type of question is sometimes known as a k-question, because most of the question words in French include a /k/ sound in their pronunciation – in addition to those beginning with /k/ – the ***qui, que, quel, quand*** series, plus ***combien, comment*** – there is also ***pourquoi*** where the /k/ sound occurs mid-word. The exception to this principle is ***où***.

The position of k-words and the structure of interrogative sentences containing a k-word are extremely flexible. Similar possibilities to those with ***oui – non*** questions – and more – are available here. In the following examples, it is important to note the position of the subject in relation to the verb and the k-word –

if the subject is a pronoun, it will either be inverted as in 1 below or occur in the direct order as in the case of 2 and 3 below;

if it is a noun rather than a pronoun, it can precede or follow the k-word and be echoed by a subject pronoun, which then is used as above.

However, this does not apply to **que** = *what* (object), in which case the subject follows the verb – see below – nor to the **quel** series – see 477, 478.

1 Placing the k-word first and inverting the subject and verb

Depuis quand n'avez-vous pas pleuré au cinéma? = *since when didn't you cry at the pictures?*

Quelle est votre plage préférée dans le monde? = *which is your favourite beach in the world?*

If a noun rather than a pronoun is the subject, the noun precedes or follows the k-word and a subject pronoun echoing the noun is used in the inverted position –

Comment la monotonie s'installe-t-elle dans un couple?
La monotonie, comment s'installe-t-elle dans un couple?
= *how does boredom set in in a couple?*

Pourquoi le téléphone s'avère-t-il un moyen idéal pour les confidences? = *why does the telephone turn out to be the ideal way of passing on secrets?*

2 Placing the k-word first and using **est-ce que** after it with direct word order

Qu'est-ce que vous trouvez sensuel chez elle? = *what do you find sexy in her?*

Comment est-ce que je peux faire pour avoir des rapports normaux? = *how can I work it so that I can have normal relationships?*

3 Using rising intonation

Vous avez combien de points sur votre permis ? = *how many points have you got on your licence?*

Ça veut dire quoi « sans savon »? = *what does 'soap-free' mean?*

4 Elliptical questions with a k-word

Quoi de neuf pour vos dents? – *what's new for your teeth?*

It should be noted that the order of unstressed pronouns and the use of **ne . . . pas** is not affected by the inversion of the subject and verb.

477 Question words – pronouns
qui = *who* (subject), and = *who(m)* (object)
subject
Qui en prend la décision? = *who takes the decision for it?*

Qui vous a dit cela? = *who told you that?*

Qui sont les hommes les plus sexy pour vous? = *who are the sexiest men in your book?*

Qui se met entre vous au lit – votre mère, votre patron, votre ex? = *who puts themselves between you in bed – your mother, your boss or your ex?*

object
Qui avez-vous chargé de trouver une propriété convenable? = *who have you delegated to find a suitable property?*

Qui voulez-vous inviter à dîner ce soir? = *who do you want to invite to dinner this evening?*

Qui = *who(m)* after a preposition; as explained above, inversion occurs if a subject pronoun is used; if a noun rather than a pronoun is the subject, the noun can follow or precede the k-word – in the latter case, a subject pronoun echoing the noun is used in the inverted order –

À qui dois-je m'adresser pour des renseignements? = *who should I refer to for information?*

Avec qui partez-vous en vacances cet été? = *who are you going on holiday with this summer?*

À qui appartient ce brûle-parfum?
Ce brûle-parfum, à qui appartient-il? } = *who does that oil-burner belong to?*

De qui vient ce message?
Ce message, de qui vient-il? } = *who is this message from?*

qu'est-ce qui = *what* (subject)
Qu'est-ce qui me pousse à écrire dans la presse des choses concernant ma personne? = *what pushes me to write things about myself in the press?*

Qu'est-ce qui vous dégoûte le plus? = *what turns you off the most?*

Qu'est-ce qui vous a séduite dans le rôle de Judith? = *what was there in the part of Judith that seduced you?*

que = *what* (object)
followed by inversion of the subject and the verb, whether pronoun or noun –

Que me conseillez-vous? = *what do you advise me to do?*

Que reste-t-il de votre vie de sportif? = *what's left of your life as a sportsman?*

Qu'y a-t-il de vous dans ce personnage? = *what is there of you in this character?*

Aujourd'hui tout se passe bien. Mais qu'en sera-t-il demain? = *today everything's all right. But what will it be like tomorrow?*

Que couvre l'assurance scolaire? = *what does school insurance cover?*

Délinquants sexuels – que peut faire la médecine? = *sex offenders – what can medicine do?*

qu'est-ce que = *what* (object)

followed by the direct order, subject preceding the verb; if a noun rather than a pronoun is the subject, the noun precedes the k-word and a subject pronoun echoing the noun is used in the direct order –

Qu'est-ce que tu attends pour lui dire que tu l'aimes? = *what are you waiting for to tell her you love her?*

Qu'est-ce qu'on risque en l'admettant? = *what do you risk by coming clean?*

Les voisins, qu'est-ce qu'ils vont dire? = *what are the neighbours going to say?*

Votre passeport, qu'est-ce que vous avez fait avec? = *what have you done with your passport?*

quoi = *what*

quoi is the stressed form of ***que*** and is used when separated from its normal position immediately next to the verb (or separated from it by an unstressed pronoun) or when preceded by a preposition –

Quoi de plus féminin qu'un joli décolleté avec une peau lisse et sans défaut? = *what can be more feminine than a pretty low neck-line with a smooth, clear skin?*

La vérité, c'est quoi? = *what is truth?*

Pour toi, le moyen de lutter contre la homophobie, ce serait quoi? = *what in your opinion would be the way to fight against homophobia?*

Après avoir fait l'amour, mon partenaire est pris d'une série d'éternuements – cette réaction, à quoi est-elle due? = *after making love, my partner has a sneezing fit – what is this reaction due to?*

En quoi consiste au juste le traitement? = *what's the treatment like exactly?*

combien = *how many*

Combien de couples sont-ils concernés par les difficultés sexuelles? = *how many couples experience sexual problems?*

Combien de temps est-ce que ça prend? = *how long does that take?*

Combien de fois dois-je te dire que je ne veux pas sortir avec toi? = *how many times do I have to tell you I don't want to go out with you?*

Thierry Henry, combien de buts a-t-il marqués cette saison? = *how many goals has Thierry Henry scored this season?*

Vous voulez perdre combien? = *how much weight do you want to lose?*

lequel *series*

The ***lequel*** series of interrogative pronouns invites the hearer to choose between a specified group of objects or items, unlike the ***quel*** series – see below – which offers a completely open choice. Like the ***quel*** series, the ***lequel*** series agrees in number and gender with the noun it qualifies. Note that this series consists of pronouns and not adjectives; consequently the pronoun is followed by **de** when it is linked to a noun –

Lequel de ces pulls préfères-tu? = *which of these pullovers do you prefer?*

Laquelle des stars de tennis féminines va gagner à Roland-Garros cet été = *which female tennis star is going to win Roland-Garros this summer?*

Le magasin a une grande gamme de déodorants – lequel dois-je prendre? = *the shop's got a large range of deodorants – which one should I take?*

478 Question words – adjectives

The **quel** series of adjectives agrees in number and gender with the noun it qualifies.

Quel type de matériel devrait-on choisir pour transformer son salon en stade olympique? = *what sort of equipment should you choose to convert your living room into an Olympic stadium?*

Quels produits me conseillez-vous pour m'assécher? = *what sorts of products do you advise to dry me out?*

Quelle est la différence entre le « bon » et le « mauvais » cholestérol? = *what is the difference between 'good' and 'bad' cholesterol?*

Quelle est votre relation avec vos parents? = *what's your relationship with your parents like?*

Quelle agence choisir? = *what agency should we choose?*

From the following two examples, the difference between **quel** and **qui** can be deduced –

1 ***Qui est l'animatrice télé la plus sexy?*** = *who is the sexiest TV presenter?*

2 ***Quelle est l'animatrice télé la plus sexy?*** = *which one is the sexiest TV presenter?*

For question 1 the choice is completely free; for question 2 a list follows the question from which the reader is invited to select his/her preference.

479 Question words – adverbs

comment = *how* – often used with an infinitive –

Comment puis-je faire comprendre à ma femme que je voudrais l'aider dans la cuisine? = *how can I make my wife understand that I'd like to help her in the kitchen?*

Comment définiriez-vous la misère sexuelle? = *how would you define sexual misery?*

Comment y arriver? = *how can we manage that?*

Comment venir à bout de la maladie de Verneuil qui me fait souffrir d'infections cutanées répétées? = *how can I overcome Verneuil's disease which keeps making me have one skin infection after another?*

Comment lui faire comprendre que je voudrais moi aussi participer? = *how can I make her understand that I'd like to join in as well?*

Comment faire renaître le désir dans notre couple et traiter les difficultés de mon ami? = *how can we rekindle some passion in our relationship and treat my boyfriend's problems?*

où = *where*
Où êtes-vous allé en vacances l'année dernière? = *where did you go on holiday last year?*

Où en êtes-vous avec la santé de vos dents? = *where have you got to with your dental health?*

Où peut-on trouver du fluor? = *where can you find fluoride?*

D'où est-ce que ça vient que tout le monde veut faire l'amour dans un avion? = *where has the idea come from that everyone wants to make love in a plane?*

pourquoi
Pourquoi les femmes entrent-elles toujours dans les détails quand elles nous racontent leur journée et ne savent pas, comme nous, aller à l'essentiel? = *why do women always go into great detail when they tell us how their day has been and not cut to the chase like us?*

Pourquoi faut-il éviter les bains trop chauds? = *why should you avoid over-hot baths?*

Pourquoi a-t-elle sans arrêt le vertige? = *why is she always dizzy?*

Pourquoi tout ça? = *what's all that about?*

Pourquoi ne pas profiter de tous les horaires pour le faire? = *why not take advantage of all hours of the day and night to do it?*

quand
Quand faut-il inspirer et expirer en musculation? = *when do you have to breathe in and breathe out when you're doing your muscle-building exercises?*

Quand avez-vous senti que vous êtes devenu un homme? = *when did you feel that you'd become a man?*

Quand avez-vous découvert que votre meilleure amie vous trompait? = *when did you find out that your best friend was cheating on you?*

480 Elliptical questions without a question word but suggesting one

Occasionally elliptical questions without a k-word seem to indicate that one is implied.

Aujourd'hui tout roule avec votre partenaire. Et demain? = *today everything is running smoothly with your partner – but what about tomorrow?*

Cette maladie toucherait 2 à 5% de la population. Les symptômes? Insomnies, migraines et douleurs musculaires = *this illness reputedly affects between 2 and 5% of the population. What are its symptoms? Insomnia, migraines and muscular pains*

481 Indirect questions

Indirect questions result from the reporting in indirect speech of direct questions.

1 ***Oui – non*** questions become noun clauses introduced by ***si*** = *if, whether* in indirect speech. Tense changes take place as required.

direct question –

Est-ce que vous êtes couvert contre les risques majeurs sans payer cher des garanties inutiles? = *are you covered against major risks without paying a lot of money for useless guarantees?*

indirect question –

Faites ce test pour savoir si vous êtes bien couvert contre les risques majeurs sans payer cher des garanties inutiles = *take this test to know if you are well covered against major risks without paying a lot of money for useless guarantees*

direct question –

Est-ce qu'elle ne traîne pas quelque part? = *is she hanging about somewhere?*

indirect question –

J'ai fait le tour de tous les magasins pour voir si elle ne traînait pas quelque part = *I've been round all the shops to find out if she was hanging about somewhere*

Elle voulait savoir s'il fallait contrôler le temps que son fils passe à l'ordinateur = *she wanted to know if she should control the amount of time her son spent on the computer*

2 K-word questions become noun clauses introduced by the k-word or, in the case of the interrogative pronouns ***qu'est-ce qui*** = *what* (subject) and ***que*** = *what* (object), by ***ce qui*** and ***ce que*** –

direct question –

Quels points communs est-ce qu'on peut trouver entre l'homme à notre bras et notre sac à main ou nos escarpins? = *what points can we find in common between the man on our arm and our handbag or shoes?*

indirect question –

L'homme à notre bras est tout pour nous sauf un accessoire, et on ne voit vraiment pas quels points communs lui trouver avec notre sac à main ou nos escarpins = *the man on our arm is everything to us except an accessory, and we can't really see what points we can find in common between him and our handbag or shoes*

direct question –

Demain, de quoi sera-t-il fait? = *what will tomorrow be like?*

indirect question –

On ne sait pas de quoi demain sera fait = *we don't know what tomorrow will be like*

direct question –

Qu'est-ce qui pourrait vous procurer un plaisir comparable? = *what could give you a comparable amount of pleasure?*

indirect question –

Demandez-vous ce qui pourrait vous procurer un plaisir comparable = *ask yourself what could give you a comparable amount of pleasure.*

Il a demandé à son médecin comment il pouvait se débarrasser de cette habitude gênante = *he asked his doctor how he could get rid of this embarrassing habit*

Cette anecdote démontre bien à quel point notre organisme peut avoir des caprices aux conséquences dramatiques = *this anecdote illustrates well to what extent our body may have whims that may have dramatic consequences*

Lorsqu'on lui demande quelle ville elle préfère, elle répond sans hésiter: « Londres, parce que j'ai gagné Wimbledon » = *when she's asked which town she prefers, she replies without hesitating: 'London, because I won Wimbledon'*

Il m'a dit qu'il sortait avec une de ses copines ce soir, mais je ne sais pas laquelle = *he told me he was going out with one of his girlfriends this evening, but I don't know which one*

Des millions d'êtres humains rêvent d'une vie éternelle, et s'il pleut le dimanche après-midi, ils ne savent pas quoi faire = *millions of human beings dream of eternal life, and if it rains Sunday afternoon, they don't know what to do*

Ma copine ne me dit jamais qu'elle m'aime, sauf un jour dans une brasserie – je ne sais pas ce qui lui a pris ce jour-là = *my girlfriend never says she loves me, except one day, in a bar – I don't know what possessed her that day*

In the following example there are two indirect questions, one **oui – non** and the other introduced by a k-word –

direct question 1 *Est-ce que vous savez . . .?*
direct question 2 *Qu'est-ce qu'une Française dépense sur ses produits de beauté?*

Il m'a demandé si je savais ce que, en moyenne, chaque Française dépense par an pour ses produits de beauté = *he asked me if I knew what on average every French woman spends per year on beauty products*

In the following example there is an indirect question within a direct question –

Est-ce que les scientifiques arriveront jamais à découvrir comment on peut contrôler les pellicules, les pets, les rots? = *will scientists ever succeed in discovering how we can control dandruff, farting and belching?*

482 Rhetorical questions

Rhetorical questions sit on the borderline between interrogatives and exclamatives – see 483. They ask questions to which no answer is required – usually because the person asking the question already knows it! – and express an emotion typically expressed by an exclamative.

In the following example, the person asking the questions knows how many tests s/he has had – it's the number of tests that provokes the question/exclamation –

Combien d'examens médicaux ai-je passé pour découvrir que j'étais en parfaite santé! = *how many medical tests have I had to find out I was in perfect health!*

Qu'est-ce que j'ai dû supporter pour parvenir à cette étape de ma carrière! = *what haven't I had to put up with to reach this stage in my career!*

Exclamative sentences

483 Exclamative sentences

Exclamative sentences express surprise, anger, disgust, amusement and other strong emotions. Five types of construction are available:

1 With ***comme*** or ***que***. In exclamative sentences formed this way, ***comme*** or ***que*** is simply placed at the head of the sentence followed by the direct order –

   Que ma femme est belle! = *how beautiful my wife is!*

   Qu'il est difficile d'accepter que l'intelligence est un mythe et que c'est la compétence qui est réelle = *how difficult it is to accept that intelligence is a myth and that it's ability that's real*

   Comme je trouve ennuyeux de faire de la gym! = *how boring I find it to go to the gym!*

   Comme il est important de garder son sang-froid! = *how important it is to preserve your self-control!*

   Qu'est-ce que may be used like ***comme*** and ***que*** in informal French –

   Qu'est-ce qu'il est fou! = *how daft he is!*

   Qu'est-ce qu'il est bon de prendre une douche pour se déstresser! = *how good it is to have a shower to relieve your stress!*

2 With ***quel*** qualifying a noun, agreeing in number and gender; ***quel*** + singular noun normally = *what a* in English (but see the last example) –

   Quel dommage! = *what a shame!*

   Quel pantalon affreux! = *what a ghastly pair of trousers!*

   Quelles dents blanches! = *what white teeth!*

   Quelle ironie! = *what irony!*

3 With ***que de*** + noun; ***que de*** = *what a lot of*

   Que de monde! = *what a lot of people!*

   Que de magasins sensationnels! = *what a lot of fantastic shops!*

4 With **que** + subjunctive – this construction has close affinities with the imperative, where it is treated in more detail – see 122.

> ***Il me manquait une chose – un but, et quand j'ai marqué mon premier but pour le club, le président est venu me dire – Que ce soit le premier d'une longue série!*** = *one thing was missing – a goal, and when I scored my first goal for the club, the chairman came to see me and said – May it be the first in a long line!*

> ***Bref, qu'on prenne le temps de bien faire les choses*** = *in short, please take time to do things well*

5 With exclamative intonation – our speech is often dotted with exclamations consisting of single words or short phrases –

> ***Désastre! – les poils sur le mollet*** = *disaster! – hairy calves*

> ***Horreur! – les pieds qui empestent*** = *it's the pits! – pongy feet*

> ***Atomique Ivanisovic!*** = *Ivanisovic the rocket!*

> ***Merde!*** = *blast and damnation!*

> ***Fini! Enfin!*** = *finished! At last!*

Punctuation

484 Punctuation

For most punctuation marks – full stop, comma, question mark, exclamation mark, hyphen/dash, semi-colon, suspension marks – the rules of use are much the same in French as in English.

Differences occur to a greater or less extent as far as capital letters, the colon and comma and inverted commas are concerned.

1 Capital letters

Adjectives denoting nationality and names of languages begin with a lower-case letter in French but not in English –

un footballeur espagnol = *a Spanish footballer*

le public anglais = *the English public*

un plat provençal = *a Provençal dish*

une vedette américaine = *an American star*

le français = *the French (language)*

le danois = *the Danish (language)*

However, nouns denoting a person of a certain nationality begin with a capital letter –

une Française = *a French woman*

un Espagnol = *a Spaniard*

Names of countries – those consisting of more than one word usually have a capital letter for each significant word –

les Pays-Bas = *the Netherlands*

les États-Unis = *the United States*

la Corée du Nord / du Sud = *North / South Korea*

Professional names and official titles – here the French practice is not to use capital letters – although usage is not always consistent. In the case of names of ministers, the name of the actual ministry is presented with a capital letter.

le président = *the President*

la reine d'Angleterre = *the queen of England*

le ministre de l'Education = *the Minister of Education*

la ministre de la Justice = *the Minister of Justice*

le professeur de français = *the Professor of French*

But **le Premier ministre** = *the Prime Minister* is normally accompanied by a capital letter – but examples also occur where it is not!

Book titles – whereas the English custom is to capitalise each significant word in the name or title, in French it is usually only the very first word that is capitalised, or if the first word is a determiner, the first significant word as well –

Les Bouts de bois de Dieu (*Ousmane Sembène*)

La Révolte des anges (*Enzo Cormann*)

Mémoires d'une sale gosse (*Cédric Erard*)

However, sometimes only the first word is capitalised –

À la recherche du temps perdu (*Marcel Proust*)

Names of French organisations – it is usually only the first significant word that is capitalised in French – but here again there may be variation –

l'Institut français d'opinion publique

la Société nationale des chemins de fer français

le Conseil supérieur de la magistrature

le Parti socialiste

l'Union pour la démocratie française

Names of international organisations – here each significant word is given a capital letter, especially if the name is not translated into French –

le Foreign Office

la Malta Maritime Authority

l'Organisation des Nations Unies (but *l'Onu* when the initial letters are treated as an acronym)

2 Colons and commas

Observation would seem to indicate that these punctuation marks are more frequently used in French than in English. The comma, for example, is regularly used to separate an initial adverb or adverbial expression from the following part of speech, whereas this is not always the case in English –

Cette année, nous avons dû convoquer d'urgence nos vendangeurs le 28 août = *this year we had to summon our grape-pickers urgently on 28 August*

Professionnellement, une belle opportunité peut faire naître des projets plus ambitieux = *professionally a golden opportunity may lead on to more ambitious projects*

Quant à l'amélioration de la qualité de la vie, aucune étude scientifique n'est disponible = *as far as improvement in the quality of life is concerned, no scientific study is available*

The colon is especially common in journalism to highlight what precedes it and to lend a dramatic tone to a passage and/or to explain what precedes it. Often in English a dash is used instead.

C'est l'heure de la collation: jus de fruits et biscuit = *lunchtime – fruit juice and a biscuit*

Objectif: une silhouette de rêve! = *the object – the silhouette of your dreams!*

Les marques ne lancent pas ces promesses au hasard: elles sont validées par des recherches = *the manufacturers don't throw these promises around at random – they're validated by research*

Personnes âgées: gare aux chutes = *warning to elderly folk – be careful not to fall*

Preuve indiscutable selon eux: les appuis médiatiques = *indisputable proof they say – support from the media*

3 Inverted commas

The French convention concerning the use of inverted commas is very different from the English one. Inverted commas – *les guillemets* – tend to be less common and less systematically used in French than in English.

Quotations included in text are enclosed in *guillemets* –

« Il n'y a pas de place pour les hommes d'une trentaine d'années » = 'there's no room for thirtysomething men'

« Je repars la tête haute » = 'I'm leaving with my head held high'

This particularly applies to quotations and also to short passages of speech. In the case of extended dialogue, the usage is more variable, with dashes being used to indicate change of speaker rather than a new set of **guillemets**. The entire dialogue is enclosed in **guillemets**, but within them dashes are used for each speaker –

« Comment expliquez-vous la nette domination du Stade de France au cours de la finale?

– On a pris le dessus sur Perpignan dans tous les secteurs du jeu. On a eu une telle maîtrise du jeu que le spectacle a été gâché.
– Avez-vous des souvenirs particuliers de la saison?
– Le plus grand plaisir est la victoire contre Toulouse à Toulouse.
– Envisagez-vous de revenir en France un jour?
– Pour l'instant, il n'est pas question que je me relance dans le rugby. Mais je me sens à moitié français et mon rêve c'est de revenir travailler en France. » =

'How do you account for the clear domination of the Stade de France in the final?'
'We got the upper hand over Perpignan in all aspects of the game. We had such control of the play that it spoilt the spectacle.'
'Have you got any special memories of the season?'
'The greatest pleasure was the win over Toulouse at Toulouse.'
'Do you think you might come back to France one day?'
'At the moment, there's no question of taking up rugby again. But I feel half French and it's my dream to come back and work in France.'

Exercises

1 **Reliez ces phrases en une seule, en les réorganisant et en utilisant une ou plus d'une conjonction de subordination – souvent il y aura plusieurs solutions –**
Exemple:
Ce système de surveillance électronique, fixé au poignet, est de la taille d'une montre de plongée. Il est relié par ondes magnétiques à la prison.
Ce système de surveillance électronique, fixé au poignet, qui est de la taille d'une montre de plongée, est relié par ondes magnétiques à la prison.
a **Votre physionomie vous pose des problèmes? Aidez la nature en adoptant judicieusement nos produits de beauté.**
b **J'ai quitté mon mari. Mes amis ne comprenaient pas. Pour eux nous formions un couple idéal.**
c **Il y a des différences entre la sexualité masculine et la sexualité féminine. L'homme fait l'amour à l'extérieur de son corps. La femme le fait à l'intérieur.**
d **Avec mon mari, j'avais l'amour et la stabilité. De l'autre, je découvrais la passion.**
e **Ça m'est égal que ce soit des meubles ou des fringues. Je me balade sur tous les sites Internet à la recherche de la meilleure affaire.**

f *Cet homme ne veut rien laisser échapper de lui-même et ne tutoie pas.
Ses amis ont ignoré son remariage célébré à Paris.* Est-ce qu'il mène
une deuxième vie tortueuse et noire?

g *Je ne crois pas à une grande manipulation de la droite.* Cela
n'empêche pas des initiatives individuelles et quelques coups tordus
via les flics et les magistrats.

h *En un siècle la France s'est réchauffée de 0,9 degrés C.* Ceci est
davantage dû à un relèvement des températures minimales qu'à celui
des températures maximales.

2 **La mise en relief**

Réécrivez les phrases suivantes en utilisant *c'est . . . que / qui* pour
mettre en relief la section qui n'est pas en italique.

Exemple:

Le bourgogne possède un bouquet subtil qui exhale des parfums de
chèvrefeuille et des senteurs de tilleul.

Ce sont des parfums de chèvrefeuille et des senteurs de tilleul
qu'exhale le bouquet subtil que possède le bourgogne.

a *Les 4 000 pilotes ont dit oui par référendum* à un accord salarial pour
les deux prochaines années.

b *L'ancien député maire a été condamné* à un an de prison et à la
privation pour deux ans de ses droits civiques et civils.

c *La plupart des femmes séparées ont souvent une bonne raison de ne
pas fléchir:* leurs enfants.

d *Tout peut arriver* à condition d'être un peu attentive à ce qui se passe
autour de vous.

e *Vous devez vous exposer au soleil avec modération, mais jamais
entre 11 et 14 heures, toujours progressivement, et mettre une
crème.*

f *Le seul vice qui m'inquiète vraiment est* ma paresse.

g *La situation ne pourra se normaliser avant* deux ans au moins.

3 **Utilisez une autre stratégie pour mettre en relief les sections qui ne
sont pas en italique dans les phrases suivantes –**

a *J'ai aussi rencontré* des filles idiotes, *mais je ne vais pas donner de
noms.*

b *Rien n'est pire que* la drague en meute.

c *Va-t-on un jour légaliser* l'euthanasie *en France?*

d *J'attire* les lions *en diffusant par haut-parleur un enregistrement d'une
bagarre autour d'une proie.*

4 **Réécrivez les propositions interrogatives suivantes en remplissant le
blanc du mot interrogatif qui convient le mieux –**

a *C'est bientôt les soldes. . . . sont mes droits?*

b *. . . les femmes n'aiment-elles pas qu'on lise des magazines de
charme?*

c *J'ai un surplus de peau détendue et disgracieuse. . . . puis-je m'en
débarrasser?*

d *Dois-je utiliser un produit avant-rasage ou raser directement à même
la peau? . . . en pensez-vous?*

e *Un beau-père peut-il prendre la place d'un vrai père absent? . . .*
  attitude doit-il adopter?
f *. . . sont vos chances de trouver un mec dans l'année?*
g *Alors, les gars, . . . vous ferait plaisir?*
h *. . . a marqué le dernier but?*
i *. . . y a-t-il de vous dans les personnages que vous jouez?*
j *. . . est-ce que vous allez nous rendre visite?*

Key to exercises

Chapter 1

1 Formation des verbes
indicatif
le présent

cours, crains, cueille, dois, écris, suis, lis, sais, viens, veux

allez, avez, commencez, finissez, mangez, partez, pouvez, prenez, voyez, valez

l'imparfait

avais, étais, faisais, finissais, mangeais, perdais, recevais, riais, valais, vendais,

allaient, commençaient, conduisaient, couraient, devaient, jetaient, portaient, recevaient, savaient, voulaient

le futur

achètera, ira, boira, courra, sera, pourra, saura, viendra, verra, voudra

irons, commencerons, devrons, enverrons, jetterons, mènerons, mourrons, partirons, tiendrons, vendrons

le passé simple

alla, but, crut, cueillit, fut, porta, finit, put, sut, voulut

eûtes, conduisîtes, courûtes, dûtes, écrivîtes, fîtes, lûtes, menâtes, mîtes, vécûtes

subjonctif
le présent

ait, dise, soit, fasse, finisse, jette, porte, sache, vaille, veuille

alliez, buviez, deviez, soyez, fassiez, mangiez, mettiez, puissiez, vendiez, vouliez

l'imparfait

allât, eût, bût, commençât, fût, fît, finît, menât, sût, voulût

achetassions, courussions, dussions, fussions, fissions, partissions, portassions, pussions, vendissions, voulussions

2 Les auxiliaires
aller – être, arriver – être, s'asseoir – être, dire – avoir, falloir – avoir, mourir – être, naître – être, porter – avoir, pouvoir – avoir, recevoir – avoir, venir – être

3 Les verbes pronominaux

il s'assied – vous vous asseyez, il se lave – vous vous lavez, il se lève – vous vous levez, il se plaint – vous vous plaignez, il se souvient – vous vous souvenez

elle s'en est allée – vous vous en êtes allés, elle s'est assise – vous vous êtes assis, elle s'est bercée – vous vous êtes bercés, elle s'est lavée – vous vous êtes lavés, elle s'est levée – vous vous êtes levés, elle s'est méfiée – vous vous êtes méfiés, elle s'est plainte – vous vous êtes plaints, elle s'est portée – vous vous êtes portés, elle s'est rappelé – vous vous êtes rappelé, elle s'est souvenue – vous vous êtes souvenus

4 Réécrivez les passages suivants en transposant les verbes actifs en leur équivalent passif –

   a *Le tableau électronique interactif peut être utilisé comme un tableau normal – la craie est remplacée par le stylet. Des infos prises directement sur internet peuvent également y être projetées; sur internet cartes, photos, graphiques peuvent être trouvés; les cours peuvent être illustrés facilement.*

   b *Vous ne pouvez être satisfait(e) que par une solution associant robustesse et maîtrise totale de votre consommation.*

   c *Vous êtes accompagné(e/s/es) par ce conseiller à chaque étape de votre projet.*

   d *La clémentine confite sera trouvée chez les confiseurs.*

Chapter 2

1 Les impératifs – réécrivez les passages suivants en donnant les formes de l'impératif qui conviennent –

   a *N'oubliez pas de fermer le récipient avant de mouliner son contenu.*

   b *Le look gothique est à la page. Sachez toutefois qu'il faut en user avec modération.*

   c *Avec un blouson en cuir, risquez les grosses ceintures cloutées ou à boucle en argent.*

   d *Vous avez des problèmes de pellicules et pas de shampooing adéquat? Prenez deux aspirines effervescentes, dissolvez-les dans un verre d'eau et frottez le cuir chevelu avec la préparation obtenue.*

   e *Allongé sur le dos, la main droite derrière la tête, étendez votre jambe droite à la verticale et fléchissez celle de gauche, le pied au sol. En expirant, approchez votre main gauche de votre cheville droite. Faites cinq séries de 15 répétitions.*

   f *Evitez de poser la question brutalement.*

   g *Concentrez-vous, calmez votre coeur: le stress se calme à son tour et disparaît.*

   h *Saisonnez de sel, poivre et quatre-épices. Mélangez. Incorporez les morceaux de foie gras. Couvrez. Faites cuire 1h 30 au bain-marie dans le four. Laisser refroidir. Réservez 48h au réfrigérateur.*

2 Réécrivez le texte suivant en style indirect, en changeant les temps du verbe, les pronoms, etc

Planète Foot a demandé à Thierry quels sentiments lui avaient traversé l'esprit lorsque l'arbitre avait donné le coup de sifflet final de la dernière journée du championnat anglais. Thierry Henry a répondu en disant que terminer un championnat invaincu était vraiment formidable. Mais, sur le coup, il ne s'en était pas rendu compte. Il a dit qu'il savait que l'arbitre avait sifflé, mais son équipe était champions depuis presque un mois et, cinq jours après, il savait que l'équipe jouerait le Brésil au Stade de France. Il n'avait pas réellement eu le temps d'en profiter. Il a avoué qu'il ne l'appréciait pas vraiment et qu'il fallait passer à autre chose.

3 Subjonctif ou indicatif? Réécrivez les phrases suivantes en donnant la forme du verbe qui convient –

 a *Il faut bien que votre chéri se détende de temps en temps.*

 b *Je veux t'embrasser avant qu'on (ne) soit de retour à Calais.*

 c *La première fois que je l'ai vu, c'était en classe de seconde.*

 d *Je veux qu'elle s'en sorte vite.*

 e *C'est le cinquième de ce type qu'elle connaît.*

 f *Pour que le sommeil soit réellement réparateur, mettez votre esprit et votre corps en veille.*

 g *Utilisez plusieurs cotons en vous démaquillant jusqu'à ce que vous ayez enlevé toute trace de votre maquillage.*

 h *Dans certaines séries les filles n'hésitent pas à se bagarrer, que ce soient les forces du mal ou les vampires.*

 i *Il faut pondérer deux critères majeurs: la proportion de blessures enregistrées par sport en fonction du nombre des pratiquants et la gravité de celles-ci, quel que soit le niveau de pratique.*

 j *En cas de surchauffe, un dispositif de coupure thermique évite que le robot (ne) parte en fumée.*

 k *Dommage que tu ne sois pas là.*

 l *Si votre chapeau est vert clair avec des détails graphiques, la fille que vous draguez pensera que vous avez de l'humour.*

 m *La seule chose qu'il sache de son père c'est qu'il a probablement étudié ici.*

 n *Garçons et filles ont des relations homosexuelles à cet âge sans que ce soit définitif.*

4 Réécrivez les phrases suivantes en donnant la forme du verbe modal qui convient –

 a *Ils comprennent vite que pour réussir ils doivent fabriquer leurs propres produits.*

 b *La compagnie n'aurait pas pu réussir ses campagnes de publicité, sans ses produits phares.*

 c *Quel pourrait être l'objet d'une nouvelle loi?*

 d *Il devait / a dû éviter d'insulter ses collègues.*

 e *Paris et Berlin ne voulaient pas / n'ont pas voulu édulcorer un projet qui donne à chaque État membre un nombre de voix plus en rapport avec son poids démographique.*

 f *Le handball français peut bien compter 220 000 licenciés dans tous les coins du territoire.*

g *Si ce traitement ne suffit pas, le dermatologue pourra vous prescrire des médicaments adaptés.*

h *Pour un soutien de poitrine optimal, deux mesures doivent être prises en compte, celle du tour de buste (le chiffre) et celle des bonnets (la lettre).*

i *Des en-cas aux desserts les plus fins, le robot de cuisine sait tout faire.*

j *Si l'insolation est grave, elle peut nécessiter une hospitalisation, et la victime devra être à jeun.*

k *Il est seul à pouvoir atteindre sa cible de façon sélective.*

l *Si je l'avais rencontrée, j'aurais pu l'aimer, mais pas m'entendre avec elle.*

m *On se rassure comme on peut.*

n *En Coupe d'Europe on ne doit pas céder l'avantage à l'adversaire.*

o *On ne devrait pas accepter cet éloge funèbre de la presse – l'avenir appartient à la télévision digitale: la presse écrite est finie.*

Chapter 3

Réécrivez les passages suivants en donnant les formes du verbe qui conviennent –

a *Naissance de la haine dans le couple*

> *« Je dépérissais en son absence. Je me vidais de mon sens. Il supportait mal. En fait, je voulais être lui. Mais il a changé les règles du jeu; l'intranquillité me rendait haineuse. »*

> *« Elle m'entraînait dans cette intensité et s'était lassée. J'avais la haine» reconnaît Franck, « Je me sentais manipulé et perdu. »*

> *« Si j'avais 20 ans, je le quitterais avec un plan de reconquête; mais à mon âge, je sais que le temps passé sera perdu pour son désir. Je pourrais me flinguer parce que tout sera joué et que je suis lasse. »*

b *Mon patron et moi*

> *Ce lundi-là, je causais à Pénélope près de la machine à café. Mon patron est passé devant nous et m'a lancé, sans même nous regarder: « Je peux te voir, s'il te plaît? », le «s'il te plaît » qui finit un ton au-dessus du « Je peux te voir . . . », un « s'il te plaît » qui veut dire: « Si ça te plaît pas, c'est pareil. » J'ai jeté mon gobelet et j'ai obéi docile comme un chien. Je sentais dans mon dos le regard de Pénélope plantée devant le distributeur d'expressos. C'est en suivant le patron dans le couloir que j'ai su ce que j'avais à faire. J'ai dit: « Hervé! », avec le « vé » de Hervé un ton au-dessus. Il s'est retourné et je lui ai sauté à la gorge en plantant mes incisives dans son cou trop gras. Il est mort en gigotant comme un ver, dans le sang qu'il avait toujours eu tiède.*

c *Le Land Rover*

> *Si par essence toutes les automobiles sont conçues pour le voyage, certaines en sont devenues des icônes. C'est le cas du Land Rover dont la simple apparition évoque la jungle la plus profonde, les sables du désert.*

Le « land » est une légende vivante. Il a été créé en 1947 et à l'origine fut construit avec une carrosserie aluminium qui avait été récupérée sur les carlingues des avions de chasse. Depuis ce temps-là, il a poursuivi sa carrière sans que rien ne semble pouvoir l'arrêter. Quoi qu'en disent certains, cette automobile reste un extraordinaire moyen de transport.

d *J'aime le mec qu'il ne faut pas*

Tu ne convoiteras point. « Les filles sont jalouses et envieuses même entre elles » plaisante Victor Gérard. Elles veulent toujours ce qu'ont leurs copines. Même leur mec. Alors quand Anne, votre meilleure amie, vous a annoncé toute fière qu'enfin elle avait mis ses mains sur Matthieu . . . Hier encore, vous ne l'aviez même pas remarqué, mais aujourd'hui il a tout de suite beaucoup plus d'intérêt. Avec le temps, les regards se font de plus en plus appuyés entre vous et lui. Il faut se rendre à l'évidence: vous craquez pour ce beau brun!

e *J'ai guéri de mon hépatite C*

Le virus a disparu, mais il fallait toutefois continuer les injections hebdomadaires d'interféron. Je m'étais renseignée via Internet. Je savais que l'interféron est une substance naturelle produite par les cellules chargées de défendre l'organisme. Cela me rassurait lors des injections, que je faisais moi-même. Je me sentais de plus en plus fatiguée mais je me suis accrochée. L'enthousiasme de mon hépatologue me portait. Mais j'ai décidé de chercher de l'aide ailleurs et je me suis fait prescrire des séances de kinésithérapie, qui m'ont réconfortée. J'ai aussi fait appel à un acupuncteur dans l'idée de mieux faire circuler les énergies – cela m'a aidée à soulager mes douleurs musculaires.

Chapter 5

1 Réécrivez les passages suivants en remplissant les blancs avec l'article qui convient –

a *Nous offrons une opportunité unique de contribuer à la croissance d'une société de renommée internationale active dans le monde artistique. Une ambiance de travail jeune et informelle dans une petite équipe soudée.*

b *L'avènement des programmes d'échange interuniversitaires de type Erasmus ou l'extension des stages professionnels à l'étranger ont également motivé le secteur jusqu'ici assez traditionnel et relativement coûteux, des échanges internationaux des jeunes.*

c *Un billet d'avion de dernière minute à un prix défiant toute concurrence? Voilà qui est tentant, mais peut-être dangereux si la précipitation nous fait oublier les précautions à prendre. Chaque année des milliers de gens s'envolent pour des pays où sévit le paludisme, mais plus d'un tiers entre eux ne sont pas correctement protégés contre cette maladie.*

d *Compositeur phare de la musique vocale italienne baroque, Alessandro Scarlatti s'est illustré aussi bien dans l'opéra que dans le genre religieux de l'oratorio. La musique y explose à tout moment d'une joie lumineuse, toujours originale, mêlant magnifiquement les voix à une écriture instrumentale scintillante.*

e *La vigne rouge et l'algue marine améliorent la fermeté et l'élasticité de la peau, tandis que l'huile essentielle de lavande accélère la pénétration des composants et active la micro-circulation. On a gardé le meilleur pour la fin: la texture est un régal. Parfaitement invisible, elle est moelleuse, fondante et onctueuse. Elle disparaît en un clin d'oeil dans l'épiderme sans laisser de trace et file au coeur des cellules.*

f *Si quelqu'un, vous, moi ou n'importe qui, veut tester la sûreté des aéroports, il le fera sans angoisse s'il sait qu'à tout moment il peut dire: « Stop, ceci est un jeu! » En revanche, l'attitude de vrais terroristes réellement désireux de commettre un attentat les trahira et permettra aux personnels de sûreté de les identifier.*

g *Pour faire parler un cadavre d'abeille dont la mort brutale, en compagnie de 22 millions de ses congénères, vient de plonger les campagnes françaises dans une polémique violente sur l'utilisation de deux pesticides, il suffit de pratiquer une autopsie.*

h *Le bac en poche ou les examens de fac réussis, une nouvelle épreuve attend les étudiants: la chasse au logement. C'est le marché qui fixe les règles et surtout les prix. Or, les petites surfaces, cibles naturelles des étudiants, sont celles dont le renchérissement est le plus important.*

i *Tout le monde peut avoir une maison, quatre murs, un toit. Mais une propriété, une demeure – Bien entendu, une propriété, à la base, n'est rien d'autre qu'une maison. Mais c'est, dans l'imaginaire immobilier, bien autre chose: de l'ancien, du grand, du noble, du beau, du prestige. « Je vous invite à ma propriété » ça a tout de même une toute autre allure que « on se fait un barbecue à la maison ».*

j *Je trouve que le maquillage me révèle plus qu'il ne me cache. C'est donc une façon de m'exhiber. Je me suis beaucoup inspiré du maître de cérémonies du film Cabaret. C'est à la fois le transformiste et le vampire, le monsieur Loyal, mais quelqu'un de festif. J'aime bien ce balancement entre le bien, c'est-à-dire la fête, et le mal. J'aime bien l'ambiguïté, y compris sexuelle.*

k *Votre point faible: le manque de persévérance. Vous ne prenez pas de décision, ou alors pas de façon durable: vous êtes incapable d'effort, pas plus motivée par le succès que par l'échec. Il n'y a que la nouveauté, l'idée du plaisir pour vous stimuler.*

l *Un beau jour, devant le miroir, on se prend à relever le coin de ses yeux, à tirer sur ses pommettes, et l'on se dit qu'on aurait l'air moins fatiguée, plus gaie comme ça. On oublie, et puis on apprend qu'une telle a eu un lifting mais que « ça se voit », alors que pour telle autre « on ne voit rien ». On lit les magazines, on examine les « avant / après », on note des noms. On ne sait jamais.*

2 Réécrivez les passages suivants en donnant les formes des adjectifs et participes passés qui conviennent –

a *Il a beau jouer le super ministre, animé par de géniales et nouvelles idées, ce sont les vieilles recettes libérales qu'il nous assène.*

b *Ce printemps aussi incertain que venteux n'aura pas facilité la tâche des jardiniers. Mais il faut maintenant sortir certaines plantes de là où elles ont été remisées pendant la mauvaise saison. Si ces plantes ont été laissées intactes, juste débarrassées de leurs feuilles gâchées, elles poussent déjà, elles aussi vilaines comme tout, blanches comme des endives ou vert pâle, plus proches du tilleul que de l'épinard.*

c *Une dernière condition, à première vue surprenante, est nécessaire à la réussite d'une e-formation: l'accompagnement d'un formateur bien réel. Avec des taux d'abandon assez élevés cette présence peut s'avérer essentielle. Même à l'heure de la formation à distance, rien ne remplacera une présence humaine.*

d *On trouve dans la collection des sweaters rehaussés d'une lettre ou d'un chiffre, des pantalons militaires amples ou des joggings combinés à des tops athlétiques et des maillots de corps ou des vestes zippées, mariées à une minijupe.*

e *Les designers belges commencent à se tailler une solide réputation sur la scène internationale. Originales, bien pensées, voire carrément visionnaires, leurs créations séduisent un public de plus en plus large.*

f *Ils sont trois sur leur île parisienne. La mère qui se bat contre un cancer. Cette lutte est la raison de vivre de sa fille. Puis il y a un jeune homme affable, qui a su se rendre indispensable en rendant légers les moments insupportables de la maladie.*

g *Les cassis utilisés pour cette crème de cassis sont les noirs de Bourgogne, cueillis dans la Côte-d'Or. Cette crème est d'une rare authenticité. Ses parfums frais, son fruité onctueux, sa bouche ample et généreuse et ses arômes pleins en font une liqueur d'exception.*

h *Vous souffrez des symptômes d'un état proche de l'effondrement: l'horrible sensation d'être lourde et flasque, engourdie et tendue à la fois, contractée au niveau des vertèbres, de la nuque jusqu'aux reins. Il est temps de remettre un peu d'huile dans les rouages!*

i *À l'occasion du nouvel an, un de mes potes avait organisé une grosse fiesta chez lui. Il y avait de l'alcool à gogo, du foie gras à en veux-tu en voilà, et des filles splendides aux quatre coins de la maison. Bref, tout était parfait. Le seul problème: c'était moi! A minuit moins cinq, j'ai eu une crise d'angoisse et je suis allé m'enfermer dans les chiottes. Je ne voulais pas me plier à ce rituel ridicule d'embrassades.*

j *«Je suis déçue, dit Sandrine Casar, car je me sentais bien en jambes, mais j'étais trop isolée face aux Brioches, qui avaient un comportement bizarre. Je n'ai pas compris leur façon de courir, leurs choix tactiques, et je ne suis pas la seule. Elles-mêmes donnaient parfois l'impression de ne pas comprendre ce qu'elles faisaient. Dans de telles circonstances, elles ont dû être très satisfaites du résultat.»*

k *On trouvera une grande baie, très belle, bordée par une réserve naturelle, baptisée le parc national de Los Halises, que l'on visite en bateau, découvrant oiseaux multicolores, perroquets et tortues dans une végétation de mangroves tropicale.*

Chapter 6

1 Réécrivez les passages suivants en changeant tout ce qui a rapport aux pronoms personnels comme il vous est indiqué –

tu > *vous*

a *Ce qui s'est passé pour votre amie aurait pu arriver n'importe quand. Vous n'avez pas contraint votre amie, vous l'avez simplement encouragée. Vous pouvez être fière d'être à ses côtés et de la soutenir.*

b *Cette année, vous organisez le réveillon du jour de l'an chez vous et vous avez envie de profiter de la fête sans passer votre temps à faire des aller-retours entre la table et la cuisine. Alors, adoptez la formule buffet. Vous pourrez ainsi préparer vos plats à l'avance et la soirée sera détendue pour vous.*

vous > *tu*

c *Te voici à présent dans un climat de grande sensibilité, et ta vie relationnelle et intime sera la plus touchée. Ton rythme de vie risque d'être bouleversé après une rencontre, et certains contacts pourraient jouer un rôle important dans l'aboutissement de tes projets. D'heureuses perspectives s'offrent à toi.*

d *Tu vas te dépenser sans compter, en relevant de nombreux défis. Tes démarches sont menées avec une détermination qu'on ne te connaît pas, et tu prends des décisions importantes en ce qui concerne tes parents ou tes amis. Tu orientes ainsi ta vie sociale et affective conformément à tes aspirations.*

je > *elle* et puis *je* > *il*

e *Elle a l'impression que son identité a été remise en question. Elle n'arrive plus à faire de projets, sa vie est comme suspendue. C'est terrible car elle n'est pas de nature dépressive, elle aime la vie, elle a un compagnon formidable, elle est très attachée à ses animaux. Elle se sent terriblement seule face à ce problème.*

   Il a l'impression que son identité a été remise en question. Il n'arrive plus à faire de projets, sa vie est comme suspendue. C'est terrible car il n'est pas de nature dépressive, il aime la vie, il a un compagnon formidable, il est très attaché à ses animaux. Il se sent terriblement seul face à ce problème.

vous > *elle*

f *Elle a eu la main un peu lourde sur la pince à épiler. Résultat, ses sourcils sont beaucoup trop fins, son regard n'est plus aussi envoûtant et son visage a perdu en caractère. En attendant que les poils repoussent, elle doit se mettre à ses pinceaux. Pour redessiner et étoffer tout ça, elle doit utiliser un crayon. Elle doit choisir toujours une teinte proche de la couleur de ses cheveux, pas trop sombre, pour ne pas durcir son regard.*

je > *il*

g *Il gagne très bien sa vie, alors c'est normal qu'il paye des impôts et que ça profite aux autres. Et plus tard à ses enfants. Il aurait pu partir à l'étranger comme beaucoup de sportifs, mais il a toujours dit que s'il avait décidé de payer des impôts en France, c'est parce que sa famille et lui ont une qualité de vie qu'il ne trouverait pas ailleurs.*

elles > nous

h *Il ne voulait pas savoir ce que nous avons fait, où nous étions ni de quoi nous avions parlé.*

2 Réécrivez les passages suivants en remplaçant **on** par d'autres pronoms ou en utilisant d'autres stratégies de remplacement –

a *Un teint qui atteint la perfection? Toutes les femmes en rêvent.*

b *Pourquoi ne pas faire les corvées avec une copine: vous vous sentez moins seule et vous vous en amusez. Tout de suite vous êtes moins tendue.*

c *À peine êtes-vous de retour des vacances que vous avez déjà l'impression d'avoir perdu le bénéfice qu'elles avaient apporté ou pire de n'être jamais parti/partie.*

d *Pour cet examen, le spécialiste voit apparaître l'image du squelette sur l'écran. Sur le tableau de l'écran il repère différentes courbes de couleur. Ainsi il peut analyser différentes parties du squelette qu'il sait plus fragiles que d'autres.*

Or *vous voyez*, etc.

e *Pour une femme, se sentir belle et séduisante lorsqu'elle est ronde, c'est la mission de Taillisime qui propose des modèles jusqu'au 58. Adieu la lingerie tristoune et vieillotte quand vous avez la chance d'avoir un décolleté généreux!*

3 Réécrivez les passages suivants en remplissant les blancs du pronom qui convient – pronom démonstratif, possessif, personnel ou relatif. Notez que quelquefois il y a plus d'un blanc à remplir –

a *Il faut connaître ses émotions, pour mieux en tenir compte.*

b *Le bon cadeau est un autre langage que l'inconscient perçoit comme positif, et qui peut amener celle qui reçoit à tomber amoureuse.*

c *Elle porte un gros carton sur lequel est collée une longue plume rose.*

d *Dans le film, il s'agit de deux jeunes filles, comme le titre l'indique.*

e *Quelquefois ceux qui se trompent sur nos goûts y trouvent un intérêt.*

f *La fatigue est la manifestation d'un blocage qui empêche l'énergie de circuler. Bonne nouvelle, celle-ci ne demande qu'à être débloquée.*

g *Listez une dizaine de petites joies. Chaque jour piochez dans la liste pour vous en offrir trois.*

h *Mes désirs évoluent avec le temps, je les laisse venir. J'y crois à fond et j'imagine des plans pour les réaliser.*

i *Tu connais Amélie – quand on a des fesses comme les siennes, on évite le cuir rouge!*

j *On attendait avec une infinie curiosité le livre où il allait raconter une autre de ses passions: l'Afrique.*

k *Même sans les muscles, tu peux y arriver.*

l *Rien ne vous empêche de prendre une vraie collation quelques heures après le réveil: celle-ci vous évitera le coup de barre de fin de matinée.*

m *Il me dit « Inutile de me faire un cadeau, t'avoir à mes côtés est déjà le plus beau des présents imaginables. » Je ne sais jamais quoi lui offrir.*

n *Les gentils font partie de cette catégorie-là, celle qui n'utilisera jamais vos faiblesses pour en tirer profit, celle qui ne vous enviera jamais votre magnifique petit copain ou vos succès.*

o *Il faut choisir une tonalité qui se superpose le plus exactement possible à la vôtre.*

p *Il est issu d'une famille de petits entrepreneurs de bâtiments. Lui-même a exercé toutes sortes de petits boulots.*

q *J'ai commencé à travailler sur des églises et des discothèques gonflables, qu'on m'a demandés de créer.*

r *2,92 milliards d'euros, c'est la somme dépensée en un an par les Britanniques pour l'achat de cocaïne, dont la consommation a augmenté de plus de 200% ces trois dernières années.*

s *Le président a été consulté sur la réforme du Sénat que souhaitent bon nombre des sénateurs.*

t *La victoire de la jeune Belge n'a rien à voir avec le style des Américaines. Là où celles-ci affichent des parents envahissants et peu sympathiques, Justine évoque la figure émouvante d'une mère disparue alors qu'elle avait 13 ans.*

u *C'est un accessoire que les femmes achètent pour le plaisir – le leur mais aussi celui de leur partenaire.*

v *Pensez à vous lancer dans un programme d'activités physiques. Préférez celles de plein air.*

w *On va m'offrir des cadeaux. Ça, j'y avais déjà pensé, mais c'est bon de se le répéter.*

x *Ce sont des personnes avec qui j'avais sympathisées dans mon ancien travail qui m'ont signalé un poste à prendre.*

y *Toute perte est irréparable. Et le monde dans lequel l'enfant aurait dû vivre n'est plus le même monde.*

z *J'ai vu Béatrice au « Bon Marché »: une vendeuse m'a dit qu'elle lui a vendu un string.*

aa *Son père se heurte à ce qui aurait pu être, à ce qui aurait dû être, à ce qui n'est pas et ne sera jamais.*

bb *Cette situation peut témoigner d'un problème au niveau des relations personnelles. Celles-ci peuvent être difficiles ou inexistantes.*

cc *Elle a dû démonter la douche en bois construite sur son toit, dont la présence gênait le voisinage.*

dd *Quant aux cadeaux, le tien – je te le donnerai plus tard, quand on sera en tête à tête.*

ee *25 raisons d'aimer Noël auxquelles vous n'auriez pas pensé.*

Chapter 7

1 Réécrivez les passages suivants en ajoutant les articles qui conviennent –

a *Pour savoir si on a des jambes de rêve, repérez dans la glace un creux entre les cuisses, un autre au-dessus du genou et le dernier au niveau* des chevilles. S'il en manque un ou deux, il faut déclencher le plan Orsec!

b *Chez l'homme le cerveau est responsable de toutes les facultés cognitives et du contrôle des émotions et des instincts. Toutes les informations provenant du monde extérieur y sont reçues et traitées, les comportements organisés, les raisonnements élaborés et les actions décidées. Sa fonction essentielle est de nous permettre d'apporter des réponses originales aux problèmes posés par notre environnement. C'est avec lui que nous sommes capables de faire des choix, bons ou mauvais.*

c *Après les vêtements jetables, maintenant les frasques mangeables. L'idée arrive du royaume des pommes chips. Une styliste anglaise a préparé la première robe à frites, avec chapeau assorti. C'est d'un goût exquis!*

d *Les mirabelles – elles doivent être dorées avec des taches de rousseur, et exhaler un parfum léger. Leur peau, souple sous le doigt, est recouverte d'une fine pellicule qui les protège du dessèchement.*

e *Lorsqu'une crise se produit ou un scandale est dévoilé, la première réaction de nombreux personnages publics de nos jours est de jaillir en un torrent de remords.*

f *La nouvelle Peugeot 407 intègre des produits innovants qui répondent aux exigences de sécurité, confort et environnement. En particulier le nouveau système d'essuie-glace qui permet d'optimiser la surface et la qualité de l'essuyage.*

g *Quatorze patients hospitalisés au CHU ont trouvé la mort au terme de pratiques d'euthanasie directe ou indirecte. Telle est la conclusion d'une expertise médicale citée dans la presse régionale.*

h *Le gouvernement espagnol a décidé de rapporter d'au moins un an l'entrée en vigueur, prévue pour le 25 mai, d'une loi visant à ouvrir le transport ferroviaire à la concurrence. Cette loi avait été condamnée par plusieurs régions autonomes du pays et par les cheminots des chemins de fer espagnols.*

i *La nuit, pendant qu'une bonne partie de la population ronfle tranquillement, un demi-million d'auditeurs, de tous les âges et tous les milieux sociaux, restent collés à leur poste de radio.*

j *Les rosiers sont de plus en plus souvent proposés en pot. Tentant, mais est-ce bien raisonnable? Non, s'il s'agit de rosiers malingres mis en pot au dernier moment ou encore de rosiers produits industriellement dans la tourbe pure. Mais s'il s'agit de rosiers mis en pot depuis l'hiver, dans des conteneurs profonds remplis d'un terreau contenant de l'argile, pas d'hésitation.*

k *Votre point faible: un manque de persévérance. Vous ne prenez pas de décision, ou alors pas de façon durable; vous êtes incapable d'effort, pas plus motivée par le succès que par l'échec. Il n'y a que la nouveauté, l'idée du plaisir pour vous stimuler.*

l *La bonne alimentation – des sucres lents (pâtes, pommes de terre) qui apportent de l'énergie tout au long de la dure journée, et non des sucres rapides – pâtisseries, bonbons – qui donnent un coup de fouet*

immédiat, mais induisent un coup de pompe dans les heures qui
suivent.

m *Yacco propose une nouvelle gamme de 14 lubrifiants moteurs.
Conduite urbaine, trajet autoroutier, compétition: tous les besoins sont
pris en compte par ces huiles qui répondent aux nouvelles exigences –
réduction des émissions polluantes, réduction de la consommation de
carburant, espacement des vidanges, lutte contre l'usure, etc.*

n *Si l'on se réfère au langage des couleurs, le jaune stimule la mémoire
et l'attention, le bleu calme les esprits, le vert apporte l'équilibre et le
rouge stimule les sens.*

2 Réécrivez les passages suivants en ajoutant le déterminant possessif ou l'article qui
convient –

a *Pompe avec levé de jambe. En position de pompe classique, les mains
sont dans l'alignement des épaules, mais un peu plus espacées que la
largeur de ces dernières. Descendez le corps en fléchissant les bras et
en levant une jambe aussi haut que possible sans plier le genou.
Quand le torse est près du sol, gardez la pose quelques secondes, puis
tendez les bras pour revenir à la position de départ. Changez de jambe.*

c *Mon corps est couvert de taches blanches – j'ai des taches blanches
sur le corps, le visage, les cheveux, et mes poils sont également
affectés. Je suis obsédée par mon corps et surtout mon visage.*

b *Pour utiliser le flexi-ball, un gros ballon en plastique souple, posez le
ventre sur le flexi-ball, les mains au sol, bras tendus. Les jambes sont
jointes et tendues. En faisant pression avec les hanches, levez les
jambes le plus haut possible. Gardez la position 5 secondes.*

3 Réécrivez les passages suivants en ajoutant le déterminant démonstratif qui convient

a *Ce mois-ci, on examine la machine à laver le linge.*

b *Il s'agit de faire plaisir à toute la famille. Celui-ci se nourrirait
exclusivement de pâtes et de riz, cet autre rechigne face à une assiette
de courgettes, et ce dernier ne tolère pas les légumes.*

c *Une circulaire ministérielle précisait que le poids d'un cartable
d'écolier ne devrait pas excéder de 10% celui de l'enfant. Cette norme
n'est toujours pas respectée.*

d *Disposez de l'herbe tondue en l'éparpillant autour des légumes. En 15
jours, ce paillis disparaît.*

e *Sans l'aide de cette crème, j'aurais certainement mis plus de temps à
me débarrasser de tous ces kilos.*

f *Seul point commun entre ces enfants psychiquement atteints: ces
cocktails hormonaux pris par les mères! D'où l'idée d'un lien possible
entre ces psychoses et l'empreinte hormonale au stade foetal.*

4 Réécrivez les passages suivants en ajoutant le déterminant possessif qui convient –

a *Les huiles diffèrent par leur teneur en vitamine E, leur résistance à la
chaleur et, bien sûr, leur goût.*

b *Il est urgent que nous redonnions à nos enfants le goût de l'eau.*

c *Dire que Golovin joua à son meilleur niveau serait exagéré.*

d *Entre ces deux compétitions, j'aurai le temps de changer mes patins et
de corriger mes programmes.*

e *Comment qualifieriez-vous votre sexualité actuelle?*

f *L'apparence est fondamentale pour une femme qui veut réussir dans notre société. Je suis donc très attentive à maintenir mon image sur mon lieu de travail.*

g *On tient à te féliciter de ton bon sens et tes réponses toujours percutantes.*

h *Ce qui peut être intéressant pour nous, c'est qu'il apporte plus de profondeur à notre jeu.*

Chapter 8

1 Les prépositions qui relient

Réécrivez les phrases suivantes en ajoutant dans le blanc, si c'est nécessaire, la préposition qui convient –

a *J'aimerais avoir des conseils pour m'aider à éradiquer ce problème.*

b *Parfois un enfant hausse le ton parce qu'on ne le laisse pas suffisamment s'exprimer.*

c *Agée de 22 ans, je suis atteinte d'une maladie du système nerveux.*

d *J'aimerais que quelqu'un me dise les effets secondaires à craindre.*

e *Cela arrive, mais il s'agit de cas très rares.*

f *Lorsque je dois faire un gros saut dans le vélo acrobatique, je cherche d'abord à maîtriser le stress dans ma tête – cela m'aide à le passer.*

g *Il a beau être la plus grande star française – il fait toujours de très gros efforts pour plaire à ses admiratrices.*

h *Les voleurs et politiciens ripoux ont toujours bénéficié d'une certaine considération de la part du public.*

i *C'est une mode qui plaît aux jeunes filles comme aux femmes plus âgées.*

j *Comment est-ce que vous pouvez aider votre enfant à vaincre le bégaiement – reformuler les mots après lui de façon correcte, sans lui demander de les répéter. Vous devez vous amuser à faire ensemble des bruits avec la bouche.*

k *Il ne manque jamais de raconter ses conquêtes.*

l *Ces lentilles sont faciles à poser et à enlever.*

m *On se promet de reprendre une activité physique, histoire de garder la forme, de s'aérer et de s'occuper de soi.*

n *Pour séduire, une femme peut passer beaucoup de temps à s'apprêter.*

o *J'éprouve un besoin terrible de dormir après le déjeuner.*

p *On m'expliquait que je ne risquais pas de devenir stérile.*

q *Les bénéfices des lavages du nez ne sont plus à démontrer.*

r *Est-ce qu'il a tendance à augmenter le son de la télévision?*

s *Cette réaction permet à ceux qui sont dotés d'une peau délicate de résister à la brûlure du soleil.*

t *Leur usage convient très bien aux jeunes filles, car ils s'adaptent à leur style de vie.*

u *J'ai impression que les coussins ont besoin d'être secoués et tapotés, et je ne me prive pas de le faire.*

v *Je ne m'adonne à ce vice compulsif avec n'importe quoi – j'ai une préférence pour les tickets de cinéma!*

w *Si vous avez avalé seulement une quantité infime d'essence, du lait ou un verre d'eau suffira à le diluer.*

x *Tu devrais éviter de prendre l'avion si vous avez un rhume.*

y *Vous en sortez plutôt bien, compte tenu de vos petites mauvaises habitudes.*

z *Finalement, mes parents se sont débarrassés de moi.*

2 Les prépositions qui forment les locutions prépositives

Réécrivez les phrases suivantes en ajoutant la préposition qui convient –

a *La natation peut se pratiquer à allure modérée, sans douleur ni essouflement même si l'on reprend après une période d'inactivité.*

b *J'ai pris trois comprimés par jour, une prise de sang par semaine au début et puis une par mois par la suite.*

c *Nous avons dominé pendant la majeure partie du match, sur le terrain de Milan.*

d *Vous avez le choix entre deux formules. La première assure votre enfant seulement lorsque l'accident survient pendant les activités organisées par l'établissement ou sur le chemin de l'école. Elle est obligatoire pour les voyages organisés.*

e *Après leur second bébé, nombre de femmes ne retrouvent pas leur ventre « d'avant », malgré la gym.*

f *Entre la salle de fitness et d'autres clubs, les propositions ne manquent pas. On choisit selon ses besoins.*

g *Les salariés ont droit à quatre jours de congé lorsqu'ils se marient, trois jours pour la naissance ou l'adoption d'un enfant, un pour le mariage d'un enfant, deux jours pour le décès du conjoint et un jour pour le décès du père ou de la mère.*

h *Je considère que je vis à peu près normalement, en dépit des contraintes dues au traitement.*

i *Dans une situation comme celle-ci, une partie des soins vous sera remboursée.*

j *Quant à l'esprit, il voyage lui aussi pendant votre randonnée – on part sous tension, mais on rentre apaisé, serein.*

k *Chez les tout-petits, les produits alcoolisés sont à proscrire. Une même quantité de produit appliquée chez un bébé aboutit à des concentrations jusqu'à cinq fois supérieures en raison de son faible poids.*

l *Le chignon existe depuis la nuit des temps.*

m *Elle portait une veste en jean surpiqué de dentelle sur un jupon en coton.*

n *Il est conseillé d'agir précocement à partir de l'âge de 3 ans.*

o *Une directive européenne applicable en France depuis le début de l'année a renforcé les normes de qualité de l'eau.*

p *Quant à la douleur postopératoire, elle varie entre 2 et 4 sur une échelle de 10.*

q *J'aime passer devant le miroir de la salle de bains.*

r *C'est en pantalon de coton noir et en tee-shirt qu'elle est arrivée.*

s *L'opération sous anesthésie générale dure environ deux heures.*

t *Les coiffeurs s'y résignent avec bonheur..*

u *Les Parisiens, grâce à deux buts spectaculaires ont battu Porto.*

v *Lors d'un contrôle sanguin, j'ai découvert que je souffrais d'une anomalie physique.*

w *Il figure parmi les meilleurs super-légers mais il fait figure d'inconnu en France.*

x *La compétence sans le plaisir, le talent sans la joie ne servent à rien.*

y *Souvent pour l'acheteur compulsif, l'achat se fait dans la honte et dans une grande solitude.*

z *76% des hommes se tournent vers leur partenaire pour chercher soutien dans une situation difficile.*

Chapter 9

Traduisez en français les passages qui suivent en anglais –

a *La solitude n'est pas une tare ou une fatalité, mais un passage obligé, dont on sort souvent plus conscient, plus sensible, plus humain.*

b *Je pense que la raison pour laquelle je suis devenu écrivain est en grande partie liée à mon père, à mes sentiments envers lui.*

c *La culture du fast-food a totalement changé notre façon de nous nourrir et, plus grave encore, les quantités avalées.*

d *On vit dans une société très compétitive où l'on bâtit sa propre estime de soi en se comparant sans cesse aux autres.*

e *Les symptômes de la crise catholique en France sont si bien connus qu'il est à peine besoin de les aligner: en un demi-siècle, la pratique régulière s'est effondrée, se divisant par quatre pour stagner autour du 10%; le nombre de prêtres ordonnés chaque année est aujourd'hui le dixième de ce qu'il était dans les années 50; les mouvements d'action catholiques ne sont plus que l'ombre d'eux-mêmes.*

f *A l'heure actuelle, personne n'est en mesure de savoir si Lille égalera Saint-Etienne et Marseille en décrochant un quatrième titre national consécutif, ni quel sera son destin en Ligue des champions.*

g *Laissez cuire 15 min. à feu doux, puis versez le bouillon et la crème, laissez cuire encore 15 min. à feu moyen. Retirez le thym et mixez le tout avec la crème restante. Ajoutez un peu de bouillon si c'est trop épais.*

h *Souvent utilisées pour chasser le stress, les huiles essentielles peuvent aussi être employées, selon leurs vertus, pour apaiser l'épiderme ou lutter contre les rides.*

i *L'eye-liner, noir ou brun très foncé, est travaillé de manière classique sur la paupière supérieure, en partant du centre pour étirer le trait au-delà du coin externe de l'oeil. Une fois que le maquillage est parfaitement sec, on effectue un tracé d'eye-liner identique, légèrement plus court, à la lisière des cils du bas.*

j *Les patchs réalisent un vrai tour de passe-passe! On les applique localement, comme une crème, mais ils agissent sur l'ensemble de l'organisme, comme un comprimé. L'astuce consiste à enfermer le*

*produit actif sous un petit adhésif, qui lui permet de diffuser à travers
la peau afin de rejoindre la circulation sanguine.*

k *Sur un mur de la purée de brocolis étalée tel un enduit. Au pied du mur
deux cônes de carottes. Avec le temps, le mur et les cônes adopteront
des couleurs changeantes sous l'effet de la décomposition – ça c'est l'art
contemporain!*

l *Classiquement, on prête aux garçons d'appartenir au « sexe fort » et
aux filles au « sexe faible ». Cette distinction reflète peut-être une réalité
musculaire. Mais lorsqu'on s'intéresse à la globalité de l'existence,
c'est évidemment l'inverse. Dans l'ensemble, les femmes résistent
mieux aux maladies. Elles mangent plus sainement. Elle sont plus
prudentes en voiture et s'entretuent moins spontanément. En
conséquence de quoi, elles vivent plus longtemps.*

Chapter 10

Traduisez en français la section en anglais des phrases suivantes.

a *J'ai consulté plusieurs médecins, mais aucun traitement ne me soulage.*

b *78% des Français ne comprendraient pas que les enseignants
boycottent les examens.*

c *Nous passons nos soirées à ne faire que parler.*

d *Les familles n'hésitent plus à insulter les enseignants.*

e *Rien ne vous empêche de commencer la randonnée devant chez vous, en
toute saison.*

f *Je ne peux plus bouger mon corps, ni parler, ni même respirer.*

g *La douleur ne s'est réveillée que plusieurs semaines plus tard.*

h *Faut-il se priver de boeuf? – Ah! non, car, tout d'abord la viande n'a
jamais été aussi sanitairement correct et surtout parce que le boeuf
n'est pas si gras que ça.*

i *Aucun passant ne peut soupçonner que l'un des plus grands sex
symbols du cinéma se cache derrière ces verres fumés.*

j *Personne ne connaît non plus ses intentions.*

k *On ne peut, lorsqu'on est attaché à la cause palestinienne, s'empêcher
de reprendre timidement espoir.*

l *Je vis dans un centre antidouleurs qui me prescrit de la morphine,
mais je n'ai plus d'espoir. Je ne peux plus travailler.*

m *Mes problèmes ne cessent de monter.*

n *Il n'y a rien de plus simple pour protéger sa santé.*

o *En moins de temps qu'il n'en faut pour le dire, la peau épaissit.*

p *Signez une reconnaissance de dette, ainsi personne ne pourra vous
accuser d'exploiter la situation.*

q *Dans la plupart des familles du temps de notre arrière-grand-mère, on
ne se lavait que le dimanche.*

r *Si au second rendez-vous, je ne t'embrasse pas, alors cela signifie que je
ne le ferai jamais.*

s *Aujourd'hui on sait qu'il n'y a pas de parfaite santé sans une bonne
hygiène.*

t *Il y a une ligne blanche que les Français ne veulent pas franchir.*

u *Elle n'embrasse jamais sur la bouche ni ne passe la nuit avec sa proie.*

v *C'est le tabou à ne pas transgresser.*

w *Fréquemment la question n'est même pas évoquée.*

x *Il faut éviter de se moquer de lui, ne pas lui demander de parler moins vite.*

y *Il est plus tard que vous ne pensez.*

z *Il n'est jamais aussi à l'aise que lorsqu'il renoue avec ses racines provinciales.*

aa *Le suicide ne semble guère faire de doute.*

bb *Je ne m'en suis jamais rendu compte.*

cc *Pour ceux qui n'ont ni rédigé de testament ni procédé à une donation, le Code civil s'occupe de tout.*

dd *Les dispositions prises par testament ne sont jamais définitives: elles peuvent être changées à tout moment.*

ee *Cette mega-star ne peut pas aller acheter son pain tranquillement, ni ses cigarettes.*

ff *Il a réussi et n'a plus grand'chose à prouver.*

gg *Sa tenue de foot, déchirée, crottée, n'en pouvait plus.*

hh *Ce type de relation sexuelle n'implique aucune conséquence, aucun engagement.*

ii *Ces artisans n'ont nul besoin d'artifice ni de structure pour accomplir leurs buts.*

jj *Personne ne pourra dire qu'elle ne soit pas attentive aux autres.*

kk *Ne dites pas: « J'arrête de manger n'importe comment ». Il faut éviter le tout ou rien.*

ll *À moins que le president n'intervienne, la situation continuera à empirer.*

Chapter 11

Écrivez en mots les chiffres qui ne sont pas en italique dans les phrases suivantes –

a *Le nombre de bêtes malades est passé, en France, de deux cent soixante-quatorze en 2001 à cent trente-sept en 2003 pour un cheptel de 11 millions de têtes.*

b *Quatre virgule cinquante-huit millions – c'est, en Inde, le nombre de personnes infectées par le virus du sida.*

c *Tous les Français peuvent maintenant consulter les fiches biographiques de plus d'un million trois cent vingt-cinq mille soldats morts pour la France pendant la guerre de '14–18.*

d *Entre deux cent vingt-neuf mille et deux cent soixante-neuf mille Français sont victimes chaque année d'une infection alimentaire.*

e *Guy Lux, quatre-vingt-trois ans, et Georges Coulonges, quatre-vingts ans, sont morts cette semaine.*

f *Plus de cent mille baladeurs devraient se vendre cette année, soit une hausse de deux cent cinquante pour cent en un an.*

Chapter 12

1 Reliez ces phrases en une seule, en les réorganisant et en utilisant une conjonction de subordination –

  a *Si votre physionomie vous pose des problèmes, aidez la nature en adoptant judicieusement nos produits de beauté.*

  b *Mes amis ne comprenaient pas pourquoi j'ai quitté mon mari, parce que, pour eux, nous formions un couple idéal.*

  c *Ce qui différencie la sexualité masculine et la sexualité féminine, c'est que l'homme fait l'amour à l'extérieur de son corps, alors que la femme le fait à l'intérieur.*

  d *Avec mon mari, j'avais l'amour et la stabilité, tandis que de l'autre, je découvrais la passion.*

  e *Que ce soit des meubles ou des fringues, je me balade sur tous les sites Internet à la recherche de la meilleure affaire.*

  f *Cet homme qui ne veut rien laisser échapper de lui-même et qui ne tutoie pas, dont ses amis ont ignoré son remariage célébré à Paris, est-ce qu'il mène une deuxième vie tortueuse et noire?*

  g *Je ne crois pas à une grande manipulation de la droite, ce qui n'empêche pas des initiatives individuelles et quelques coups tordus via les flics et les magistrats.*

  h *Si en un siècle la France s'est réchauffée de 0,9 degrés C, c'est davantage dû à un relèvement des températures minimales qu'à celui des températures maximales.*

2 La mise en relief

  Réécrivez les phrases suivantes en utilisant *c'est . . . que / qui* pour mettre en relief la section qui n'est pas en italique.

  a *C'est à un accord salarial pour les deux prochaines années que les 4 000 pilotes ont dit oui par référendum.*

  b *C'est à un an de prison et à la privation pour deux ans de ses droits civiques et civils que l'ancien député maire a été condamné.*

  c *C'est à cause de leurs enfants que la plupart des femmes séparées ont souvent une bonne raison de ne pas fléchir.*

  d *C'est à condition d'être un peu attentive à ce qui se passe autour de vous que tout peut arriver.*

  e *C'est entre 11 et 14 heures que vous ne devez jamais vous exposer au soleil, autrement il faut le faire avec modération, toujours progressivement, et il faut mettre une crème.*

  f *C'est ma paresse qui est le seul vice qui m'inquiète vraiment.*

  g *Ce sera deux ans au moins avant que la situation ne se normalise.*

3 Utilisez une autre stratégie pour mettre en relief les sections qui ne sont pas en italique dans les phrases suivantes –

  a *Je les ai aussi rencontrées, des filles idiotes, mais je ne vais pas donner de noms.*

  b *La drague en meute, rien n'est pire que ça.*

  c *L'euthanasie, va-t-on un jour la légaliser en France?*

  d *Les lions, je les attire en diffusant par haut-parleur un enregistrement d'une bagarre autour d'une proie.*

4 Les propositions interrogatives

Réécrivez les propositions interrogatives suivantes en remplissant le blanc du mot interrogatif qui convient le mieux –

a *C'est bientôt les soldes. Quels sont mes droits?*

b *Pourquoi les femmes n'aiment-elles pas qu'on lise des magazines de charme?*

c *J'ai un surplus de peau détendue et disgracieuse. Comment puis-je m'en débarrasser?*

d *Dois-je utiliser un produit avant-rasage ou raser directement à même la peau? Qu'en pensez-vous?*

e *Un beau-père peut-il prendre la place d'un vrai père absent? Quelle attitude doit-il adopter?*

f *Quelles sont vos chances de trouver un mec dans l'année?*

g *Alors, les gars, qu'est-ce qui vous ferait plaisir?*

h *Qui a marqué le dernier but?*

i *Qu'y a-t-il de vous dans les personnages que vous jouez?*

j *Quand est-ce que vous allez nous rendre visite?*

Bibliography

For standard French grammar –

Batchelor, R. and Offord, M., *Using French: a Guide to Contemporary French Usage*. 3rd edition. Cambridge: Cambridge University Press, 2000.

Colin, J.-P., *Difficultés du français*. Paris: Le Robert, 1993.

Grevisse, M., *Le Bon usage: grammaire française*. 13th edition by A. Goosse. Paris and Louvain la Neuve: Duculot, 1993.

Hawkins, R. and Towell, R., *French Grammar and Usage*. 2nd edition. London: Arnold, 2001.

Judge, A. and Healey, F., *A Reference Grammar of Modern French*. London: Arnold, 1983.

L'Huillier, M., *Advanced French Grammar*. Cambridge: Cambridge University Press, 1999.

Nott, D., *French Grammar Explained*. London: Hodder and Stoughton, 1993.

Price, G., *A Comprehensive French Grammar*. 5th edition. Oxford: Blackwell, 2003.

For low register French grammar –

Ball, R., *Colloquial French Grammar: a Practical Guide*. Oxford: Blackwell, 2000.

Index